The Truth We Owe Each Other

With regards,
Olav Fykse Tveit

THE TRUTH WE OWE EACH OTHER

Mutual Accountability
in the Ecumenical Movement

Olav Fykse Tveit

THE TRUTH WE OWE EACH OTHER
Mutual Accountability in the Ecumenical Movement
Olav Fykse Tveit

Copyright © 2016 WCC Publications. All rights reserved. Except for brief quotations in notices or reviews, no part of this book may be reproduced in any manner without prior written permission from the publisher. Write: publications@wcc-coe.org.

WCC Publications is the book publishing programme of the World Council of Churches. Founded in 1948, the WCC promotes Christian unity in faith, witness and service for a just and peaceful world. A global fellowship, the WCC brings together 345 Protestant, Orthodox, Anglican and other churches representing more than 550 million Christians in 110 countries and works cooperatively with the Roman Catholic Church.

Opinions expressed in WCC Publications are those of the authors.

Scripture quotations are from the New Revised Standard Version Bible, © copyright 1989 by the Division of Christian Education of the National Council of the Churches of Christ in the USA. Used by permission.

Cover and book design and typesetting: Michelle Cook / 4 Seasons Book Design
Cover image courtesy of Dreamstime
ISBN: 978-2-8254-1681-5

World Council of Churches
150 route de Ferney, P.O. Box 2100
1211 Geneva 2, Switzerland
http://publications.oikoumene.org

CONTENTS

Prologue   vii

Chapter 1. Introduction   1
   The Scene, Perspective, and Focus of This Study   1
   The Material and the Method of This Study   14
   The Thesis   19
   Mutual Accountability: Toward a Preliminary Definition   20
   Summary   25

Chapter 2. Ecumenical Attitudes and Premises for Ecumenical Ecclesiology: From Amsterdam (1948) to Montreal (1963)   27
   The Significance of Attitudes in the Premises
      for the World Council of Churches   27
   The Ecumenical Attitude of "The Fully Committed Fellowship":
      The Statement on Unity (New Delhi 1961)   42
   The Significance of Ecumenical Attitudes in the Preparations
      and Reports from Montreal (1963)   45
   Summary: Ecumenical Attitudes as Premises in the Pioneer Phase
      of the WCC   74

Chapter 3. Mutual Accountability and Conciliar Fellowship: From Montreal (1963) to Canberra (1991)   77
   A Universal Council, Conciliarity, and Conciliar Fellowship   77
   Authoritative Teaching in Mutually Accountable Relations   101
   Giving Account of Hope—in Accountability to Other Churches   118
   The Convergence of the Document *Baptism, Eucharist and
      Ministry* (BEM): A Result of a Mutually Accountable Process   144
   Toward a Manifestation of Mutual Accountability to the One,
      Apostolic Faith   171

Ecumenical Attitudes and the Unity of Church and Humankind   209
Conclusion: Mutual Accountability—An Intrinsic Element
    of Conciliar Fellowship   220

Chapter 4. Mutual Accountability and the Church as *Koinonia* (until 1998)   223

Mutual Accountability and the Coherence of Ecumenism   224
Mutual Accountability and Unity as *Koinonia*   244
The Role of Mutual Accountability in the Faith and Order
    "Ecclesiology" Study (1998)   266
The Report from the Faith and Order Study
    on Hermeneutics (1998)   274
The Common Understanding and Vision of the World Council
    of Churches   283
Summary: Mutual Accountability as Required Attitude
    toward Unity as *Koinonia*   297

Chapter 5. A Systematic-Theological Evaluation   303

A Brief Evaluation of the Outcome of the Analysis   303
Mutual Accountability as Ecumenical Attitude   306
"Relation" as Supplement to "Faith" and "Order"   324
A Definition of Mutual Accountability as Ecumenical Attitude   333

Bibliography   335

PROLOGUE

What do we, as churches from around the world in fellowship, owe to each other? Does our communion imply, even compel, a measure of accountability to each other, to the traditions and authority we inherit, and to the wider world we serve?

In this work, I try to show that, emphatically, mutual accountability has been and remains a vital element of the ecumenical movement, its quest for unity, and its ethical relevance today. Without a sense of, or the attitude of, mutual accountability, how can there be an ecumenical relationship between us?

Mutual accountability refers to the quality of relations between and among people in community. It refers to an attitude of active responsibility that must characterize any authentic relationship, the profoundly moral dimension of life together. In the ecumenical movement, I therefore argue, mutual accountability is a matter of how we seek the truth together by sharing insights into the truth we carry. The truth of the Gospel can only be sought in a sense of accountability to what is given to us as the faith through the ages, and in a sense of accountability to those whom the Gospel addresses today, in their context, in their time, in their search for hope.

Ultimately, the truth we owe one another is an accounting for our hope. We are as churches and followers of the crucified and risen Christ called always to be ready to give account of the hope that we carry. This is the criterion of our Christian witness. This is the criterion of being Church: Are we giving hope to others, real hope? This is also the criterion of what it means to be human, created in the image of God: How do we give hope to the other?

We cannot free ourselves from the accountability we carry together for sharing the treasure of the Gospel as liberation and hope, in each period and in any context of the Church. How would we know the truth if nobody had shared it with us? And how should we know more of the truth, if we are not giving account to one another for what the Spirit has shared with us? Accountability for the hope we have means that there is a truth of the resurrection that we have to share, and an openness to the world that God has created to see what this hope means today and tomorrow. The ecumenical movement is indeed a privileged context for making this account rich and real.

Several reasons impel publication of my study of mutual accountability, done some years ago. The first is the most pragmatic and obvious reason: Many have asked me where the text is available, and I had to tell them that it was only available in photocopied versions in some libraries. My original text, "Mutual Accountability as Ecumenical Attitude: A Study in Ecumenical Ecclesiology Based on Faith and Order Texts, 1948-1998," was submitted to the Norwegian School of Theology for the Degree of Doctor Theologiae in November 2001 and defended in a public disputation in May 2002. My Doctorvater was Professor Em. Dr Torleiv Austad. The ordinary opponents were the late Professor Dr Anton Houtepen from the Netherlands and Professor (now Emeritus) Dr Viggo Mortensen from Denmark. In addition to them, Professor Em. Dr Turid Karlsen Seim and Prof Em. Dr Kjell Olav Sannes offered relevant and challenging questions to my work during my studies and at the disputation. I owe them all again my heartfelt thanks for guiding me and my questions toward texts and perspectives of high relevance for my ideas.

The study was received as a significant contribution to the understanding of the work of Faith and Order, but also to the debate on ecclesiology and ethics in the ecumenical movement. New commitments and appointments postponed for too long my intention to rewrite the dissertation for another circle of readers, so I have decided to instead to make the study in its original form available for those who are interested.

The deeper reason that motivates me to publish this text is that I quite simply find that several findings of my study are relevant to the present discourse about ecumenism and ecclesiology. In my work and service for the World Council of Churches today, as WCC general secretary, I hardly experience any day in the office or in meetings or visits elsewhere in the world without addressing the need for mutual accountability. In defining and pursuing mutual accountability, we are developing and improving the quality of human relations in all their dimensions, particularly in relations among people of different confessions, religions, cultures, geographic or ethnic backgrounds, but also in the task of building justice and peace in the world of today.

The World Council of Churches has through its multilateral dialogues as well as in its institutions and great ecumenical gatherings been serving the visible unity of the Church, and through its many initiatives and programs for witnessing and serving justice and peace together, exercised many dimensions of mutual accountability since its very beginning up till today. At some crossroads, and in some particular studies and discussions, this has become even more clear. Some of those texts are carefully analysed in my study, to explore what mutual accountability means, whether the terminology is used or not. Already the discussions about the ecclesial character of the council, as well as the significant theological study about the Tradition and the traditions of the Church, indirectly raised these questions. The famous study of *Baptism, Eucharist and Ministry* (BEM) is the most significant exercise and document showing how it works as the heartbeat of a serious and constructive ecumenical methodology. There are also other studies I have analysed that have gone deeply into the issues of truth and accountability that should not be ignored.

Another dimension of mutual accountability is elaborated in the studies around ethics and ecclesiology. In these studies the terminology is used more often in an explicit way. However, there have not been many efforts to develop a clear definition of the concept. The context in which the concept is used is in reflection about the moral dimension of being Church together. It is not an option to seek unity, it is a moral duty. Furthermore, accountability has to be expressed in taking the quest for unity into the mission of the Church and its service in the world for unity, peace and justice. The documents from the "Costly Unity" studies, analysed in chapter 4 here, deserve further attention, not least in our reflection on what a pilgrimage of justice and peace means today.

To elaborate the definition of mutual accountability, I made use of a theory of ethics. The theory of "attitudes" (Norwegian: *holdninger*) developed by my teacher, Professor Em. Dr Ivar Asheim, was a very useful tool to define mutual accountability. It leads to further reflection on the qualities that define relations and that are required in a fellowship defined as Church or between churches. These qualities are also of great relevance for the relations we need to build in any multicultural or multi-religious context.

The dynamic approach to the unity of the Church that can be pursued by the concept—and structures—of mutual accountability is shaping our daily work and objectives in the World Council of Churches and in the wider ecumenical movement. Building trust through a higher sense of transparency and accountability among all partners is a basis for all serious ecumenism. Attitudes of openness, constructive critical and self-critical approaches, repentance, reliability, commitment to the common calling and tasks, faithfulness, sharing, and indeed hope—these are all genuine and necessary attitudes in a fellowship that follows the crucified and risen Christ.

The truth we owe one another lies in both our insights and our true life in community, defined by the attitudes of faith, hope and love. And greatest among them is love.

In love for the ecumenical movement and all its gifts, and even more in love and appreciation to all the colleagues and partners with whom I live and work in mutually accountable relations, I submit my findings for anyone interested in reading my reflections. This is part of the truth I myself owe as a result of my studies but also as affirmed through many succeeding years of work in the ecumenical movement in general and in the World Council of Churches in a special way. For all of it I give thanks to God.

CHAPTER 1

Introduction

The Scene, Perspective, and Focus of This Study

The Recommendations of Mutual Accountability and Their Context

The locus of this study is the work of Faith and Order, the most comprehensive, established theological ecumenical forum in the second part of the 20th century. I have looked at the major results of the work of Faith and Order toward unity among divided churches, particularly in regard to a common ecumenical ecclesiology.

My study focuses on one feature of Faith and Order's work. In several documents from approximately the last decade I find a recurring motif: a recommendation of more *mutual accountability*.[1] This recommendation appears at crucial points in deliberations about the current challenges to the ecumenical movement. Sometimes the recommendation sums up an analysis of the present state and the tasks ahead; sometimes it conveys an impression of embarrassment at not being able to be more specific when identifying the relevant tools for the ecumenical work or the "cure" for its failures.

Here I will try to answer some questions related to these recommendations and explore what contribution the perspectives implied in "mutual

---

1. Cf. ch. 4.

accountability" have made to the ecumenical endeavour. Why ask for more mutual accountability? What does this mean? How can it, eventually, be pursued? Has this perspective been important before, too, in other guises? What kind of perspective is this, really?

At this point I will only give some responses to the last question to indicate the direction of my task and procedure. The call for mutual accountability corresponds to the *calling to the churches* to manifest the unity the triune God has given to the Church. Hence, there is *a moral perspective* to the communion of the churches. The appeals refer to a standard for interchurch relationship, a *quality of relations* to be promoted or maintained. This moral dimension of mutual accountability can be seen as a duty or obligation to give account to one another. I will, however, dwell on another side of this moral dimension of the interchurch fellowship: the *attitude* required by mutual accountability. Corresponding to the duty of giving account or being accountable, there must be a willingness to do so, an openness and ability to live in a relation characterized by being accountable to one another.

Recommendations of mutual accountability do not exclude other theories, models, or concepts of the unity of the Church. They are, rather, a *supplementary perspective*. Although these recommendations occur in contexts of hermeneutics and ethics, I find it most adequate to anchor them primarily in ecclesiology; to be more specific, *ecumenical ecclesiology*.

This combination of scene, perspective, and focus is certainly not the only starting point for exploring ecumenical ecclesiology or for a study of the work of Faith and Order. But it is a useful way of getting into a study of ecumenical theology at the present moment of the ecumenical movement.

Everyone seems to speak well of mutual accountability. For this reason, it has not been adequately explored.

The Insufficiency of "Models of Unity"

The modern ecumenical movement has as its main basis the assumption of a given unity in Christ. Therefore, the efforts of the ecumenical movement have been to pursue manifestations of this unity of the Christian Church in a situation of diversity, even division and conflict, between churches. The efforts have been met with approval and dissatisfaction. Evaluations are, of course, dependent on how one defines the goal of the ecumenical movement.

A converging understanding of the goal and of the proper ways toward that goal has led to definitions of *models* of the unity of the Church. Some of these models are focused mainly on the *goal* or the result of the process.[2]

---

2. Introductions and presentations of ecumenical theology usually give an overview of such models, but under different titles. With some exceptions they present the same models/concepts. E.g., Beinert 1987:169–73 is talking about "*Modelle christlicher Einigung*"; Frieling 1992:257–65,

Some models are focused on patterns or structures of interrelations between churches—not only a definite goal, but also the *process* of ecumenism.³ Seen from another perspective, each model emphasizes at least one particular *principle* of ecumenism, defining theologically what is important for the unity of the Church: the visible unity, the doctrinal basis or requirement of unity, the episcopal succession, the Church as an organic entity, unity in diversity, and so forth. Consequently, even the focus on *koinonia*-ecclesiology in the 1990s can be described as an ecumenical model, although it is now perceived as a shift *from* a focus on unity toward focusing on communion or fellowship.⁴ Actually, the *koinonia*-ecclesiology can be interpreted as an alternative to the concept of "models" of unity, and does signify a relative decline in interest in that concept after its prevalence in the 1970s and 1980s. In the 1990s, models of unity were not the crucial point of any Faith and Order study.

The impact of such models on ecumenical efforts is not minimized when pointing to their limitations and insufficiency. Indeed, they have even been seen as obstacles to unity, for several reasons.⁵ There are models of unity developed through experiences in the past. Some are conceptualized in the specific ecclesiology of one or more churches or church families and confirmed and theologically defended from that position. Other models are elaborated through ecumenical dialogue, and thus they still have certain features from already existing fellowships of churches. This is both their strength and their weakness as configurations of interchurch fellowship. They are relying on theological foundations of well-established church traditions, and have shown how unity

---

"*Einheitskonzeptionen*"; Meyer 1996 and Neuner 1997:281–96 are writing about "Ökumenische Zielvorstellungen." Tjørhom 1999 also presents the models primarily as concepts of the *goal* of the ecumenical efforts. The Lutheran/Catholic report *Facing Unity* (1985:8–20) gives a presentation under the title "Concepts of Unity and Models of Union." Among the models focusing particularly on the *goal* of unity, the models of "organic union" or "organic federation" played a significant role already in the deliberations at the establishment of Faith and Order in Lausanne in 1927 (cf. Frieling 1992:257–65). The concept of "corporate union" has particularly been used as description of the goal in the Anglican–Catholic dialogue (essential consensus on questions of faith and a joint episcopal constitution). This model focuses on the goal of the process, too. The same can be said, although it is a different definition of the goal, about the model of "church fellowship through agreement," e.g., the Leuenberg Agreement, 1973 (cf. *Facing Unity* 1985:13f.).

3. Maybe the most typical in this respect is the model of "reconciled diversity," defined as a model of unity by the Lutheran World Federation in Dar-es-Salam in 1977. Some even see the concept of "unity in tension" ("Ökumene in Gegensatzten") also as a model of unity (Neuner 1997:291f.; Frieling 1992:264f.).

4. Neuner 1997:292ff.: "Es erschien wesentlich realistischer, als ökumenisches Ziel eine Gemeinschaft von Kirchen anzustreben als deren Einheit" (293).

5. Frieling 1992:257: "Es lässt sich nun zeigen, dass die unterschidlichen Vorstellungen von der Einheit der Kirche vielleicht das grösste Hindernis für die Einheit der Kirche sind."

can be established and preserved.[6] But they might therefore be insufficient as tools or guiding principles to establish new relations, because they represent too much one particular tradition, sometimes offending other traditions.[7]

Another limitation of the models of unity is the tendency to focus on the end of the process, making it difficult to characterize theologically the not-yet-full unity that exists during the process leading toward the goal. Maybe the most significant reason of the insufficiency of these models for the dynamic of ecumenism is the proclivity toward focusing on certain principles of ecumenism to the exclusion of other important theological aspects of the unity of the Church. The concentration on one model also abstracts ecumenical theology from the situation in which the churches have been historically and are now in the contemporary context.

A Supplementary Perspective: The Quality of Relations

In this study there will be no attempt to make a comprehensive evaluation of the ecumenical movement, nor its models or its goals. Rather, I will focus on *the quality of relations between the churches*. Whatever the model and goal of

---

6. The model of "visible unity" has become particularly important in the Anglican tradition, focusing on the historical episcopate as the visible sign of apostolicity and unity. The model of "organic union" can have its basis in the organic communion of the hierarchical communion of bishops led by the successor of Peter in the Roman Catholic Church (Frieling 1992:262f. even calls one model "*Gemeinschaft mit dem Papst*"). The model of "concord" depends on an understanding of unity as unity in doctrine, which is a dominating aspect in Protestant churches, particularly in the Lutheran tradition. How the church traditions have coloured the goal of unity becomes transparent in the problems of translating "council," "conciliar fellowship," or "conciliarity" between English and other languages, e.g., German. In the Protestant tradition "council" could be "*Rat*," "*Synode*," as well as "*Konzil*." A dominating problem of this model of "conciliarity" has been that the Roman Catholic Church and the Orthodox churches have a definition of "council" exclusively as "*Konzil*," as a representative gathering of (mainly) bishops from all churches, according to the tradition of the Old Church. Thus, the ambiguity in the name of the model reveals the ambiguity of the model.

7. A typical example of this problem can be seen in the efforts to promote church fellowship among Anglican, Lutheran, and Reformed churches in Europe. The Anglican standard of visible unity expressed through a "reconciled episcopate" becomes an obstacle to "full communion" with Reformed churches, which theologically and traditionally have chosen a church model other than episcopacy. Consequently, Reformed churches do not have and do not want their church presidents (in Hungary and Romania titled as "bishops" for political reasons, however) consecrated in Anglican episcopal succession. A majority of Reformed and Lutheran churches in Europe have signed and dedicated themselves to the establishment of church fellowship through agreement on the basic theological understanding of the gospel and the sacraments (The Leuenberg Concord). The historical episcopate as sign of unity, if defined as a condition and requirement of church fellowship, could in this context become an obstacle of church unity. Cf. the report from a conference on "compatibility" between the Porvoo, Meissen, and Leuenberg agreements, Liebfrauenberg 1995.

unity, the issue at stake is the relation between the churches. The purpose of the ecumenical movement includes improving the *relations* between the churches. The quality of these relations cannot be isolated from the question of the basis and the form of the unity, but it is a supplement to the dominating perspectives of "faith" and "order," and deserves attention in its own right.

Of course, the respective ideas or principles for the goal of ecumenism color the understanding of what improved relations might be. Therefore, the issue of quality of interchurch relations should not and cannot be isolated from the question of models or concepts of unity. It might seem, then, that I am playing the same game under a different name. I intend to demonstrate that it is something more.

My study reflects a tendency in several ecumenical documents from recent years to ask what is lacking in the quality of ecumenical relations. In the reflections on the status of the ecumenical movement in general, and in the World Council of Churches particularly, there has been a growing awareness of the importance of this perspective.

Attention to quality of relations is not an alternative, but a supplement to the quest for a common doctrinal foundation for interchurch relations and a common structure of the churches. According to common ecumenical tradition, as documented in Faith and Order texts I will analyze, the Church is a fellowship created by the triune God in the image of the relations within the triune God. If this is true, the question of the quality of relations is a matter of the doctrinal basis of the Church, though it is also a matter of church structures, of church order. But it goes through and even beyond the discussions of what is the structure of unity in the Church. It is a matter of quality, whatever the structure of the relations might be (hierarchical, episcopal, synodical, congregational, and the like).

The doctrinal dialogues have given many results in consensus and convergence documents. Some of them have led to agreements of fellowship between churches. But this has not reduced the need to focus on the required quality of relations. That question is not fully answered through declarations that doctrinal condemnations are no longer applicable, or through agreements on the understanding of unity and some common structures to serve interchurch relations.[8] These types of agreement can be seen as results of improvement of relations between representatives from the involved churches.

My interest in quality of relations has not only to do with critical attention to unfulfilled tasks of the ecumenical movement. One important motivation for choosing this perspective is a presumption that what has already happened

---

8. The Leuenberg Agreement (1973) and the Roman Catholic–Lutheran Joint Declaration on the Doctrine of Justification (1999) are both examples of the potential and the limitation of the first type of agreement. The Porvoo Agreement is an example of the latter.

in the ecumenical movement must have made a difference in the understanding of what the unity of the Church can be. In my view, the real development of interchurch relations must be taken into account in our reflecting theologically on what it means to be one Church in the apostolic tradition. The pursuit of the ecclesial status of the World Council of Churches might be seen as a fruit of the demand for self-reflection of the relations established through the ecumenical movement.[9]

Whatever the evaluation of the ecumenical movement of the 20th century might be, it has—in the perspective of a century—changed the relations between the churches.[10] It is a matter of fact that the churches, through their members, have had numerous opportunities for contact and to exchange all kind of resources since the turn of the 21st century, opportunities unimaginable earlier. The changed relations are, however, more than a matter of numbers and frequency of interchurch contacts. Rather, they are institutionalized and formalized in several ways: ecumenical councils and organizations; ecumenical dialogue commissions; agreements of church fellowship and even united churches; joint ecumenical projects of material aid and struggle for peace, human rights and preservation of creation; joint efforts in mission and ministry to the world. Through the ecumenical movement most churches have been involved in relations to churches of other confessions, traditions, nations, cultures, and so forth. For a majority of churches today, to get into and stay in some kind of manifested relation to other churches has become an important and not negligible aspect of being a Christian church.

Changed relations between the churches require new theological reflection on what it means to be a Christian church. The ecumenical movement has provided significant experiences of great importance for ecclesiology, and these experiences have been evaluated and reflected in conferences, studies, and statements from ecumenical settings. This process goes both ways. There is no reason to doubt that the changes of relations have incited a corresponding revision of ecclesiology in the churches.

Theologians have gained common insight in ecclesiology through their encounter with one another in a mutual exchange and struggle with theological

---

9. Cf. the discussion of the ecclesial quality and status of the World Council of Churches raised through the process of the "Common Vision and Understanding of the World Council of Churches," culminating at the Harare assembly. This process will be discussed below; cf. ch. 4, pp. 308-322.

10. In this study *Church* (with a capital "C") means the one, holy, catholic, and apostolic Church in the theological sense, as this notion is used, for instance, in the Nicene Creed. The local churches, organized as national, regional, or confessional bodies, are here designated as *church/churches*. Officially, these churches—to a large extent—have been both the subjects and recipients of the work done in ecumenical organizations, although, in practice, the acting subjects of the ecumenical movement are *persons* representing their churches.

questions of the basis, nature, and purpose of the Church. The common insight of ecclesiology formulated in ecumenical documents is something else and something more than these theologians could have had if they had worked in splendid isolation or in cooperation with representatives from their own church tradition only.

Seen against this background, reflections on ecclesiology from ecumenical endeavours deserve attention and theological analysis. More than that, they require an adequate approach, taking into account the particular context of ecumenical dialogue.

Ecumenical Ecclesiology

The theological framework of this study is *ecumenical ecclesiology*. There is a need for reflection on ecclesiology that can be applied to different ecclesiological traditions and to new configurations established as a fruit of ecumenical relations. A presentation of ecclesiology can, in many cases, be an apology for one particular church tradition. Ecumenical ecclesiology should go beyond this. The perspective of "ecumenical ecclesiology" should convey a wider perspective than the concepts of unity. Any aspect of the Church, its life, and its purpose can be seen in the perspective of unity, not only those aspects having to do with the respective model or concept of unity. Therefore, the framework of "ecumenical ecclesiology" can more directly and effectively link the specific question of interchurch fellowship to other contexts (that is, other than the specific ecumenical contexts) where fellowship and unity in the churches are discussed.

The intention here is not a kind of pragmatic ecclesiology dominated only by the daily agenda of the ecumenical organizations, without the classical theological questions of what it means to be one, holy, apostolic, and catholic church. But these principles for ecumenism should not be discussed in abstraction or theoretically. Considering the *quality* of interchurch relations can give *direction* to the development of ecumenical relations. The quality of interchurch relations should be discussed in the perspective of these classical themes in order to make those themes relevant for the everyday interchurch relations. *The quality of interchurch relations is an important aspect of what it means to be a church in the apostolic tradition.*

Therefore, this is a study of *ecumenical ecclesiology*, understood as follows:

a. An ecclesiology which intends to pursue the question of what it means to be one, holy, apostolic, and catholic church;

b. An ecclesiology which takes into account the experiences and the reflections of the ecumenical movement of the 20th century, making them relevant for ecclesiology in general;

c. Ecclesiology aspiring to be a common ecclesiology for the churches, at least to some extent reflecting a consensus in issues of ecclesiology; this is ecclesiology pursued in constant dialogue with other churches, or as a reflection of the already finished dialogue between churches;

d. Ecclesiology pursued under the "ecumenical imperative," focusing particularly on why and how to overcome those divisions of the Church which hide or contradict the unity of the Church granted by the triune God and given a model in the relations between the persons of the Trinity;

e. Theological reflection on why and how the Church can believe, live, and act as one in a certain diversity, as well as why no communion could be called "church" if it in principle and in practice is isolating itself from other churches.[11]

This definition of ecumenical ecclesiology presupposes that ecclesiology *must be* ecumenical, because of the axioms of ecclesiology. However, my particular interest in this study is not a general ecclesiology, but to analyze and discuss ecclesiology which can be relevant for the task of establishing and making perceptible the unity between churches. Texts from the ecumenical movement are of special significance in this regard, since they rely on ecumenical

---

11. The terminology "ecumenical ecclesiology" is the most familiar, although reflections on ecclesiology under one or more of these five perspectives is rather common among theologians exploring ecumenical theology or ecumenism. The English ecumenist Gillian Rosemary Evans uses this concept in her book *The Church and the Churches: Toward an Ecumenical Ecclesiology* (Evans 1994a). She discusses the theme under the thesis "Ecumenism cannot proceed without an ecclesiology" (ibid., 3). She has registered that the most difficult issues are what she calls "ecclesiopractical" (ibid., 16). Dealing with what are classic Faith and Order themes, she tries to indicate points of coherence and requirements that go beyond the traditional alternatives.
One of the most experienced North American Roman Catholic ecumenists, George H. Tavard, gave one of his books, *The Church, Community of Salvation*, the subtitle *An Ecumenical Ecclesiology*; cf. Tavard 1992. In the introduction to this book he follows Paul VI in his encyclical *Ecclesiam Suam*, and takes his "departure at this point: being Church means sharing a distinctive self-awareness and, on the basis of this self-awareness, engaging in a multisided dialogue" (ibid., 10). He uses Vatican Council II (where he served as conciliar *peritus*) as a genuine expression of Catholic tradition and ecclesiology. He takes as an axiom that a church must be in internal and external dialogue, and that ecclesiological reflection must take into account the outcome of ecumenical dialogue. Cf. his chapter "The Ecumenical Horizon," in ibid., 191–208. Thus, particularly my point *b* corresponds to Evans's concept. Further, my points *b–d* correspond to Tavard's understanding of "ecumenical ecclesiology." My focus on ecclesiology in diversity is to some extent integrated in his book, too. He focuses in his study particularly on the ecumenical movement manifested in the Roman Catholic Church from the 19th century (from Möhler and Newman) and the documents from Vatican II. I will concentrate my study on material mostly from the World Council of Churches.

experience, dialogue, and motivation, and thus convey insight not really accessible through other channels.

Nevertheless, I am also interested in how the experiences and reflections of ecclesiology coming out of the ecumenical encounter can be relevant for ecclesiology in general. If the churches are called to live as one, in relation to each other, the ecclesiological principles for that communion should be relevant for any relation in any church fellowship. The concern for ecumenical ecclesiology is not a matter of specialized interest for ecumenists. The quest for the unity of the Church is founded in the identity of the Church. Thus, ecumenical ecclesiology is a matter of intrachurch as well as interchurch relationships, and is relevant at any level and for any kind of fellowship in the Church. But the key issues of ecumenical ecclesiology have been raised and elaborated on extensively in the efforts to establish relations *between* churches through the ecumenical movement of the 20th century. Therefore, theological reflection on the premises and results of this quest for unity among different churches is the *primary* perspective of this study. Only after an elaboration of the specific issues of interchurch relationship can these findings be discussed in regard to their relevance for ecclesiology in general.

Because the perspective of this study is the quality of relations between churches as a matter of ecumenical ecclesiology, the core question will be, What is an *adequate category* for this? This question implies a moral dimension to ecumenical ecclesiology besides the questions of doctrine and order: What is a (morally) right relation between churches?

The quality of relation between churches is a profound theological issue when the Church is defined as a *koinonia,* a participation in the life of one another through the participation in Christ. One important perspective in the ecumenical dialogues has been the *visibility* of unity or the visibility of the *koinonia,* given in Christ. The discussions have to a large extent focused on structures and ministry, particularly the importance of the historical episcopate. These discussions of visibility tend, in my opinion, to be rather formal debates about principles, like historical episcopate versus synodical/presbyterial structures. But if visibility of unity is a manifestation of *koinonia,* visibility of unity cannot be conceived only in terms of structures. The meaning of a communion or a fellowship is not only the agreement about basis, goals, and structures. No less important are the values of the relations themselves. But then we must also ask how to define and evaluate such values of fellowship in the Church, between the churches. This leads to a reflection on required *attitudes* for the *koinonia.*

Attitudes as a Matter of Ecumenical Ecclesiology

To promote, establish, maintain, and improve a fellowship, certain *attitudes* are required. Some are common for any kind of human fellowship; some are specific for each particular type of fellowship. These are important elements in the theory of ethics of attitudes developed by Norwegian Lutheran theologian Ivar Asheim.[12] I find his theory relevant and helpful to establish an understanding of attitudes to be applied in this study, for several reasons.

Asheim offers a brief definition of attitude: "A firm, conscious and consequent position or behavior (in a certain occasion, in a certain case)."[13] He argues that the notion of "attitudes" (Norwegian: *holdning*) has a cognitive and an affective component, as well as a constitutive component of behavior. Asheim explores attitudes within the frame of the ethics of virtues (Norwegian: *dyder*).[14] He finds a great deal of coherence, but also important distinctions, between the traditional concept of "virtues" and his definition of "attitudes."

To focus on attitudes means to emphasize the goodness and righteousness in the relation between persons, not the excellence of the character of each person—as most often happens in the perspective of virtues. Asheim is critical of the traditional understanding of virtue (*dyd*) as the excellence, the goodness of a person, and the attractive quality of one individual. Corresponding to Luther's critique of Aristotelian ethics of virtue, Asheim emphasizes how the goodness or righteousness of a person must be demonstrated in the *relation* between this person and others. Who we are by ourselves as righteous persons can only be defined in a theocentric perspective.[15] A *relational and communal* aspect of attitudes should therefore, according to Asheim, replace the intro-

---

12. Cf. Asheim 1991:87–117; Asheim 1994b:116–30; and, in his most comprehensive work on the theme, Asheim 1997. Asheim writes in Norwegian, and discusses the Norwegian word *holdning*, which I here translate as "attitude." In my use of Asheim's theory, I will use his definition of *holdning* as my definition of attitude. He finds a large degree of coherence between the English and Norwegian terms, although possibly with more emphasis on the aspect of behavior in the Norwegian terminology (cf. Asheim 1997:24–26). Asheim has presented his theory in a German article (Asheim 1998), on the basis of one part of his analysis, namely the role of virtues in Luther's ethics. There he uses the terminology of "*Haltung*" and "attitude" (in the English Summary, 260) as translations of *holdning*.

13. Asheim 1997:22; trans. mine. Cf. the Norwegian quotations in the succeeding footnote.

14. Asheim 1997:36–39, et passim. He argues that *dyd* should be defined as a positive attitude that serves the fellow human being and preserves the fellowship: "Heller enn som egenskap som kjennetegner positiv selvutvikling bør dyd derfor defineres som *positiv holdning (='fast, bestemt og konsekvent stilling eller opptreden') som tjener medmennesket og bevarer fellesskapet*" (Asheim 1997:283). Consequently, he can talk about "*relasjonell dydsetikk*" as a synonym to "*holdningsetikk*" (Asheim 1997:284).

15. Asheim 1994b:116–20. The profile and relevance of Luther's concept of virtues is the major focus of the article from 1998.

spective, *reflexive* aspect of the ethics of virtues. The tendency toward narcissism in recent approaches to virtues can thereby be overcome.

These distinctions underscore the relevance of Asheim's theory for a study of interchurch relations. In his theory, attitudes go beyond the internal, introspective, and individual perspective; attitudes are relation-oriented and manifested in the common life—from the smallest to the largest scale. The sense of fellowship is developed in basic, intimate, and close relations, but is flexible and adaptable. The sense of belonging to a fellowship or unity can be widened to a universal perspective without changing character; Asheim even explicitly mentions the ecumenical movement to illustrate this.[16]

Attitudes can be perceived through analysis of what is said and done, through an analysis of "position," not by an analysis of personality as such. When a group of persons is involved in fulfilling the same goal, a certain standard of attitude is a precondition to get somewhere. Therefore, the framework of *institutions* corresponds to attitudes at the level of social ethics. Attitudes presuppose and are realized through structures; structures are not principles or standards of ethics in themselves, but need qualification through attitudes.[17] Asheim mentions a wide scale of illuminating examples of this correspondence in families, school classes, institutions for public health, international negotiations for disarmament, and so forth.[18] In respect to the last example, he unveils how traditional concepts of virtues in fact are understood as collective attitudes.

To establish attitudes as values for a fellowship, the attitudes must be explainable and somehow possible to perceive. This requires agreed-upon criteria of how the partners are accountable to one another for what has been done or not.[19] Reliability, stability, and duration of a relation are such significant attitudes for the preservation of a fellowship. Asheim maintains that where certain basic attitudes are missing, there is no fellowship in a real sense.[20] Fellowship can, to some degree, be defined in terms of attitudes. One significant

---

16. Asheim 1997:27, 291f.

17. This is his main concern in the chapter "Er rammene likegyldige?"; Asheim 1991:118–39.

18. Asheim 1994b:123; Asheim 1997:266f. Here he concludes his analysis in this respect as follows: "Prinsipp-og regeletikk (deontologisk etikk) trenger holdningsetikk som en komplementær innfallsvinkel. Det samme gjelder også verdi-, konsekvens-, og formålsetikk (teleologisk etikk). Holdninger er nødvendige forutsetninger for verdirealisering. For at felles målsettinger skal kunne forfølges, må elementære holdningspremisser være til stede."

19. Asheim 1997:267. He specifies: modesty must be shown as withdrawal to defined geographical points, credibility as concrete steps to ratify an agreement, openness as admittance of foreign inspectors to arsenals, etc. Asheim elaborates more comprehensively in his theory the need for differentiations of forms of fellowship and a corresponding differentiation of required attitudes (ibid., 284ff.).

20. Asheim 1994b:120–22.

example is "friendship." The attitudes of friendship such as openness, loyalty, faithfulness, reliability, confidence, trust, and the like are not means to achieve a goal, but values deciding whether this is friendship or not, whether it is a good friendship, and so forth.[21] This raises interesting questions in respect to ecclesial fellowships and interchurch relations in general: To what extent, and how, can these relations be defined according to attitudes? Is the goal of an ecumenical fellowship—at least in some ways—to promote and maintain certain attitudes?

Although Asheim is promoting a theory of general ethics, his approach is relevant for ecclesiology. This is a theory for how to define values, standards, purposes, and goals of communities in general. The specific problems of ecclesiology and ecumenical relations are not his major focus. However, he has made some efforts to elaborate the challenge of ethics for a church fellowship as well.[22]

Since the perspective of my study is on the *quality* of interchurch relations, I find this theory of attitudes to be a useful tool for the analysis of texts that deal with premises, methods, models, and goals of the ecumenical movement. A church and its representatives, through positions taken in principle and in practice, in respect to internal as well as external matters, do reveal their attitudes to other churches. This perspective of church fellowship has not always been a point on the agenda of ecumenical theology, where the common basis in faith, the structures, the models of unity, and the common task have been the most dominant issues.

Neither have attitudes been a prominent theme in standard presentations of ecclesiology.[23] But it should be nothing particularly remarkable to suggest that certain attitudes can improve the quality of interchurch relations. Here a reflection by Asheim on the relatively small attention paid explicitly to attitudes in the discussions of ethics can be illuminating for the situation in ecumenical

---

21. Cf. Asheim 1997:271f.

22. In a textbook for the study of theology, Asheim dedicates one chapter on ethics for "church life" (Asheim 1994a:273–99). Here he elaborates the ethical dimension of participating in a church fellowship locally and universally, emphasizing the relevance of attitudes of mutuality. He dwells particularly on the demand of building confidence and mutual trust (Asheim 1994a:281). He explicitly discusses the significance of ethics with respect to the task to manifest and make visible the unity of the Church, not as a matter of establishing or creating unity (which is a gift of God) (Asheim 1994a:288). In a specific exploration of the task and authority of ordained ministers, he emphasizes the attitude of mutual loyalty, openness, and willingness to accept critique from one another—as premises for living with diversity in a Lutheran church where the highest authority is Scripture, and no definition of doctrine by a magisterium (cf. Asheim 1980:56f., 83).

23. One interesting exception is the recent study and apology of hierarchy in the Church by the Roman Catholic theologian Terence L. Nichols. He redefines a church hierarchy as a "participatory social hierarchy," which demands certain attitudes from those in power, e.g., "an authority of virtue rather than of force" (Nichols 1997:305f).

theology.²⁴ The tendency to handle attitudes as somewhat self-evident, even as a banality, can be observed in both cases. Ecumenical texts talk about trust, commitment, love, faithfulness, openness, and so forth without relating them specifically to ecclesiology.

Asheim discusses the ethics of attitudes in relation to the tension between individual freedom and communal responsibility. Individual responsibility, in a proper sense, grows in a fellowship and presupposes recognition of the significance of the dimension of community.²⁵ The potential for constructive critique in the Church presupposes the attitude of loyalty and willingness to be criticized oneself by the fellowship.²⁶ This, we will see later, corresponds to the attitude of mutual accountability, the focus of this study.

Hence, if the quality of relation is an important issue of ecumenical ecclesiology, then the required attitudes of Church fellowship deserve much more attention than they have been given so far in reflections on ecumenism as well as on ecclesiology. My points of interest in this study are, therefore:

a. What kinds of reflections there have been on the role of necessary attitudes in general, and of mutual accountability particularly, in the ecumenical theological reflection of Faith and Order;

b. Why attitudes seem to have become a more important aspect of ecumenical theological reflection in recent years; and

---

24. "Weil haltungsethische Fragen banal wirken können, werden si weithin aus der Ethik ausgeblendet. Das heisst: Sie werden schon einleitend kurz erwähnt (indem man nunmehr einsieht, die Ethik habe zu sehr das ethische Subjekt und die notwendige Integration der Normen in die Persönlichkeit versäumt) und sodann eventuell auch am Ende berührt, wo nach Klarlegung dessen, was zu tun ist, die Notwendigkeit entsprechender Handlungskampagnen betont wird" (Asheim 1998:256f.).

25. "Bare for en overflatisk betraktning er det en motsetning mellom ansvarlighet og felleskapstanke. Ansvarligheten vokser frem innen fellesskap og forutsetter . . . erkjennelse av fellesskapsdimensjonens betydning. . . . Radikalt oppgjør og eventuelt brudd er ikke i strid med fellesskapstanken, men tvert imot kjennetegn på at fellesskap tas på alvor. Et fellesskaps kvalitet kjennes på i hvilken grad fet gir rom for gjensidig personlig integritet" (Asheim 1997:275f.).

26. "Når rammene om problemene er et kirkelig fellesskap, medfører dette at det må kunne stilles etiske krav til begge parter I en mulig konflikt. Kravet til *det kirkelige fellesskap* og de som representerer dette, må være at skrifttolkningen i prinsippet må være fri, slik at bekjennelses- og kirkekritiske synspunkter kan komme til orde. Dette er nødvendig for at det skal kunne foregå en permanent prøving av kirke og bekjennelse i forhold til Skriften. Samtidig må det imidlertid stilles som *krav til en mulig kritiker* at vedkommende viser seg villig til å åpent drøfte sin skrifttolkning med det kirkelige fellesskap som helhet, slik at også *den* kan bli kritisk overprøved. . . . Dette har implikasjoner både med hensyn til måten kritiske synspunkter fremsettes på, valg av fora for drøftelser og fremfor alt holdningen hos dem som fremsetter dem. Vedkommende må vise seg *beredt til og i stand til* konsensus" (Asheim 1994a:290f.).

c. Which attitudes are—according to the ecumenical theological reflections of Faith and Order—most necessary for the particular type of relations that interchurch relationship does represent.

Attitudes required for the improvement of an ecumenical relation must be in concord with the basis of any church fellowship, its specific character and task, and take into account its theological, historical, sociological, and cultural diversity. This requires a theological interpretation of these attitudes. Such attitudes should correspond to the fact that this kind of fellowship has its common identity based in the apostolic tradition. The same apostolic gospel of Jesus Christ and the common apostolic faith in the triune God are the common basis for any church fellowship.

This common apostolic tradition can be used and understood differently, which is the presupposition and the problem of the ecumenical movement. The attitudes of this kind of fellowship must convey a dynamic toward improving the relations and better manifesting the God-given unity, according to the call to unity formulated in Scripture. Besides this, the required attitudes should care for the integrity of all kinds of members of this fellowship, which also means a constructive approach to differences and diversity.

The theme of attitudes seems to have been paid increasingly more attention in ecumenical documents over the last 10 to 15 years. Several statements recommend a set of attitudes that can be subsumed as *mutual accountability*. To some extent this specific terminology is used, but not always. It sounds immediately plausible and adequate to recommend an attitude of mutuality and accountability to handle the challenges of the ecumenical movement. The same seems to be the case for many authors of texts where mutual accountability is recommended; only a few of them do attempt to discuss comprehensively what mutual accountability really means. This type of recommendation deserves further analysis and discussion.

The Material and the Method of This Study
The Selection of the Texts to Be Analyzed
The analysis will be limited to what I have called "Faith and Order texts" from the last half of the 20th century. This means reports from larger conferences and major study projects, particularly those that appear to have relevance for this type of analysis. Documents from some of the commission meetings are included in the analysis, but only as far as they appear to be important for understanding my theme. This material will be supplemented by some important documents from the work of the World Council of Churches (WCC)

from the same period dealing with theological premises for the field of Faith and Order regarding the unity of the Church. In many cases these are documents prepared for the WCC by Faith and Order.

The work of Faith and Order deserves, for several reasons, attention in any theological discussion or analysis of ecumenical ecclesiology. Faith and Order's purpose is to give a theological foundation to and promotion for the processes toward unity among the churches. The movement of Faith and Order went through an important change into a more institutionalized life after becoming a part of the WCC in 1948. Its task has been to reflect and stimulate the process that can lead to a deeper and more clearly expressed visible unity; a matter of *order* on the basis of *faith* within the worldwide framework of the WCC. These two perspectives, since the establishment of Faith and Order in Lausanne in 1927, have been supplemented and to some extent also challenged by the focus on the common *life and work* of the churches. In some cases there have been attempts to coordinate and integrate the doctrinal, ecclesiological, and ethical concerns of the ecumenical movement in the studies of Faith and Order.[27]

The dynamic of the encounters of Faith and Order (and the World Council of Churches) has stimulated theologians to find new perspectives and themes in the quest for the unity of the Church. The documents from the study programmes, commission meetings, and conferences are, therefore, a unique contribution to the theological reflection on the unity of the church. Theological analysis of the task of the ecumenical movement and of the actual state of the relation between churches has been the main occasion for the production of these texts.

Moreover, these documents reflect encounters of theologians from a wide range of churches and traditions. The Faith and Order movement can be seen as the most representative forum for ecumenical theology. The documents from Faith and Order can, therefore, be analyzed not only to find what happened in the ecumenical movement, but also as a unique source of theological reflection on ecumenical ecclesiology.

Since the agreement in Toronto in 1950 not to make the World Council of Churches dependent on any particular ecclesiology and not to demand that any church involved in the WCC question or give up her own ecclesiology, a comprehensive, broad-scale study of ecclesiology was not pursued in the study processes of Faith and Order until nearly fifty years later.[28] Nevertheless, several

---

27. Cf. chs. 3 and 4, pp. 227-39, 244-89.

28. See the Toronto statement of 1950, in Documentary History 1963:167–76. The Faith and Order study of ecclesiology after Santiago 1993 has so far resulted in one document, *Nature and Purpose* (1998). This is one of the first attempts in Faith and Order to proceed toward a common ecclesiology.

themes of relevance for ecumenical ecclesiology have more or less been integrated in all study processes.

Although these texts were made in different situations, by different people, and under different type of leadership, they represent continuity through the constant purpose of Faith and Order. To some extent there is a tradition within this movement, both thematically and personally.[29] Other studies of this material serve as arguments for the relevance of regarding these documents as one corpus.[30]

The term "mutual accountability" was introduced in Faith and Order texts during the 1990s, at points where it serves as a contribution to how the churches can proceed in the most urgent task of the ecumenical movement. The term appears in contexts where there is an attempt to harvest the fruits of the work done and reposition them for the present and coming challenges.[31]

The immediate recommendation of this attitude, without great efforts to define what is meant, can indicate that this applies to reflections and tendencies in earlier Faith and Order texts, in ways not previously articulated. Thus, I find it useful to study the Faith and Order texts from a period prior to the theme when "mutual accountability" is explicitly mentioned. The main results of Faith and Order since the establishment of the WCC can illuminate in a wider perspective the significance of an ecumenical attitude first defined as "mutual accountability" in the texts from the 1990s.

An interpretation of the documents of Faith and Order must take into account the rather specific context and dynamic in which they were produced. It makes no sense to expect from them the same consistency, clarity of concepts, or continuity as in a corpus of literature from one author or one clearly defined group of authors. An analysis of these documents should, therefore, aim at identifying the specific contributions from this type of text, looking for the new questions and concepts, the tendencies, the convergence of understanding and agreement on basic issues, and new challenges of the ecumenical movement. The Faith and Order texts should be read as indicators of a wider range of theological reflection on ecumenical ecclesiology, as well as catalysts for further work on the bilateral level of ecumenical dialogue.

Thus, I have selected the Faith and Order texts to enlighten the theme of mutual accountability as an attitude for interchurch relations because of the general relevance of these texts as contributions to ecumenical ecclesiology, and

---

29. E.g., the text from Toronto 1950 has played an important role in the discussions at the fifth World Conference in 1993 and in the Faith and Order contributions to the study of the Common Understanding and Vision of the World Council of Churches in the 1990s.

30. E.g., Brinkman 1995.

31. This is rather typical in the documents from Santiago 1993.

the possibility granted here to identify an important tendency in ecumenical reflection.[32]

The Method of the Study

This is a systematic theological study, pursued on the basis of an analysis of Faith and Order material, treated in chronological order. The *systematic theological approach* can be derived from the two-sided intention of the study: (1) to discuss the significance of mutual accountability as ecumenical attitude; and (2) to contribute to a proper theory and definition of this attitude in the framework of ecumenical ecclesiology.

This intention is carried through by a systematic-theological approach to the texts.

> a. Because the analysis of the texts will aim at a *discussion of a particular theme*, it will not be a study of the history of Faith and Order as such. I will not pretend to give a complete picture of what happened in the study processes, nor will it offer a complete analysis of all Faith and Order documents in the period analyzed. However, if this is an important aspect of the reflections of Faith and Order during the last five decades, my analysis could be one contribution to the history of Faith and Order.
>
> b. The study will be done to find support for my assumption of the significance of the perspective of "mutual accountability" in these texts, and, therefore, for ecumenical ecclesiology generally.
>
> c. The analysis is made to find relevant elements to *establish a definition or theory* of mutual accountability as ecclesiological attitude.
>
> d. I want to discuss and *show the relevance of the dimension of the quality of relation and proper attitudes* for the unity of the Church, emphasizing the dimensions of "faith" and "order." I will discuss whether "relation" should be a third, supplementary perspective in this context.

Since the main purpose of this study is to work toward a theory of mutual accountability as an important attitude of interchurch relations—hence also of ecumenical ecclesiology—I want to develop such a theory of mutual accountability in a wider perspective than the meaning of the terminology of "mutual accountability" in just a few of the Faith and Order texts. I do not want to be too dependent on the object language in the youngest texts. Therefore, it is important to see if and, eventually, how this has been a theme in the whole

---

32. I have defined the end of analysis of texts by the Faith and Order documents published in 1998, i.e., before the 1998 WCC assembly in Harare. This is the endpoint of my study.

period of Faith and Order after the establishment of the World Council of Churches. This will give a better understanding of the developing—or changing—interest in attitudes in theological reflections on the unity of the Church.

Some tools are needed to analyze the earlier texts in the perspective of attitudes and mutual accountability. The theory of attitudes referred to above will serve as one important tool for these analyses. Further, it is necessary to establish a preliminary definition of the concept of "mutual accountability." The explicit recommendations of mutual accountability occur mostly in the texts of Faith and Order from the mid-1990s. These latter texts could, therefore, have been the starting point of my analysis, to develop an analytical language of "mutual accountability" on the basis of the object language in these texts. However, I will let my analysis of the later Faith and Order texts wait, to make them one part of an analysis in a longer perspective. Thereby I hope to avoid reducing them to an "answer book" for the analysis of the whole bulk of texts. Consequently, I will try to establish a preliminary definition of "mutual accountability" in a more general perspective than the Faith and Order texts, to have a somewhat wider reference when establishing the analytical language for the further analysis. This will be presented at the end of this introduction. This definition can then serve as an analytic tool for the texts in which the terminology does not occur.

My analytical approach to the texts will be conducted on a double track:

a. How and where do we find arguments in these texts for proper attitudes of ecumenical relationships that can be subsumed under the concept "mutual accountability"? How do the texts show an awareness of what I am focusing on in this study? How and why has there been a growing interest in these attitudes?

b. What can be identified as the most relevant elements of a definition of mutual accountability as the attitude significant for the quality of interchurch relations?

The analysis will be presented in chapters 2 through 4. These chapters are defined according to what I find to be an adequate ordering of the material according to my theme. In the final chapter I will discuss my thesis on the basis of the previous summaries, and establish some parameters for a theory of mutual accountability in the framework of ecumenical ecclesiology. I will also try to look at this theme in a wider perspective of ecumenical endeavours and general ecclesiology.

The Thesis

With this background, I formulate the thesis for my study as follows:

The attitude of mutual accountability is vital to improve and maintain the quality of interchurch relations. It is explicitly and implicitly recommended in Faith and Order texts (and Faith and Order-related WCC texts) from the period from 1948 to 1998. The quality of "relation" is a supplementary perspective to the dimensions of "faith" and "order" in the quest for the unity of the Church. There are significant theological reasons why "mutual accountability" should be an important element in ecumenical ecclesiology.

It might sound somewhat abstract to discuss "ecumenical ecclesiology" and to announce mutual accountability as an "attitude" in this context. To bring my arguments into higher relief, I will briefly point to some alternatives, maybe even *anti-theses*.

First of all, if the churches are not mutually accountable or should not make any effort to be so, they can pursue their own theological traditions and confessions best in isolation from differing points of view. This is the core of the definition of a *sect*. But it is also a feature in some of the *confessionalistic trends* in confessional churches. In such cases, the doctrinal basis of a church and its practice becomes clearer and more reliable the more its profile is sharpened against alternative perspectives. Paradoxically, those rather close to the point of view defended by a particular church will be the most threatening and therefore to be condemned.

A doctrinal condemnation is not necessarily representing an anti-thesis to mutual accountability. It can be the only possible solution after a struggle with what appears to be directly opposed to the basis of a Christian church, a necessary "no" to be able to confirm the common "yes" of confession to the triune God and protection of human lives. But to *stay with* doctrinal condemnations as a necessary paradigm of identification of the Church can be an argument against any real mutual accountability to other churches, if the underlying thought is this: Why bother about taking the point of view of others seriously? Why give any apology for our church?

In this sense, there is a paradoxical similarity between isolationistic, fundamentalist tendencies, on the one hand, and more liberal and pluralistic approaches, on the other hand. None of them corresponds to the attitude of being mutually accountable in the relation to other churches. A presumed anti-thesis to mutual accountability to other churches can be to state that the only and real accountability of the church is to God. However, that could easily be a defense for being accountable only to one's own tradition and doctrine, immune to contributions from others. Mutual accountability as a matter of ecumenical ecclesiology means that to be a church implies being mutually accountable to other Christian churches. The deepest theological issue in mutual accountability can be identified in this question: Does a church need to be mutually accountable to other churches to be accountable to God?

Mutual Accountability: Toward a Preliminary Definition

What do the dictionaries say about the terminology "mutual accountability"? Can we get clues from its use outside the specific contexts of ecumenical texts from Faith and Order?

Dictionaries by and large give a twofold definition of being "accountable." This adjective means either to be subject to an obligation to report, explain, or justify something, or to be able to explain or to be explicated.[33] The former meaning can be related to a formal, maybe even juridical, relation in which the subject is positioned; the latter focuses more on the capacity and ability of the subject (not necessarily a person). The adjective can mean not only to be made accountable by someone but also to be capable or willing to give an account, to be account-able. In this study, this latter meaning predominates.

Accordingly, "accountability" (the noun) is the state of being accountable, to have the duty to give account or to be answerable. Corresponding to the meaning of the adjective, it can designate the ability, or the moral attitude, of acting openly and responsibly, having a readiness to give account at any time; or being accountable in the sense of "reliable." The dictionaries are inclined to refer to situations of subordination, implying obligations or charges on somebody, not optional or mutual relations. They give, nevertheless, some openings for a general state or mode of "being accountable," which is something beyond formal relations.

---

33. *The Random House Dictionary of the English Language* (New York: Random House, 1983), defines "accountable" thus: "1. To be subject to the obligation to report, explain, or justify something; responsible; answerable. 2. Capable of being explained; explicable; explainable," (13). Similar definitions appear in the *Webster's II New Riverside University Dictionary* (Boston: Riverside, 1984) as well as *The Oxford English Dictionary*, vol. I, A–B (Oxford: Oxford University Press, 1933). The latter (65–66) gives five meanings of "accountable": "1. Liable to be called to account, or to answer for responsibilities and conduct; answerable, responsible. Chiefly of persons. A. to a person, for a thing. B. Also without *to* or *for*. 2. To be counted or reckoned for. 3. Able to be reckoned or computed. 4. To be reckoned or charged: chargeable, attributable to. 5. Able to be accounted for or explained; explicable. Also with for." This dictionary gives examples from older literature on "accountability" or "accountableness," which means the same: "The quality of being accountable; liability to give account of, and answer for, discharge of duties or conduct; responsibility; amenableness."

Some examples from the use of terminology in contemporary English can show the oscillation between the external and formal obligation imposed from outside and accountability as ability or attitude. The latter meaning, less related to formal structures, also tends to be more oriented toward aspects of *common* accountability, mutuality, and reciprocity.

A check in library indexes shows that this terminology is mostly used in contemporary English in the field of civil bureaucracy[34] and education.[35]

In a study by the Dutch scholar Mark Bovens on responsibility in complex organizations, we find some interesting reflections on the meaning of the word-field of responsibility/accountability. He tries to restrict the meaning of "accountability" to the first of the two meanings we find in the dictionaries. It is, in his definition, one of several meanings of "responsibility," namely, ". . . in the sense of political, moral, or legal liability (or in all or some of these sense) for the results, mostly harmful, of a given form of behavior or event."[36] This corresponds to his distinction between passive and active responsibility.

---

34. In the U.S. context of public life it is used for the (semi-) legal obligations to give reports or accounts of what has been done. Annually, the government departments present their "Accountability Acts" to the Congress. A typical example is the Clinton administration's suggestion to rationalize bureaucracy, in order to increase the accountability of bureaucracy. That means improvement of transparency in the lines of giving and receiving accounts of what has been done. This can be in tension with the flexibility and creativity of public managers. Cf. use of this terminology in a discussion on this problem in Khademian 1996:1ff.

35. A field in which the term *accountability* is very much used the last years is the effort to establish a system of common evaluation of results for schools in the United States; cf. Darling-Hammond and Snyder 1992: "In recent years, the term 'accountability' has been used nearly synonymously with mandates for student testing and standard setting. The idea of many legislated accountability initiatives is to bring rapid order to the educational system by setting high goals and making students, teachers, and administrators responsible for meeting them" (14). These authors are concerned about how the liable accountability should be also an integrated attitude of being accountable to the superior task of education. Thus, it can serve as an illuminating example of the double level of "accountability": "We argue, however, that accountability requires much more than measuring narrowly defined student outcomes. An accountability system is a set of commitments, policies, and practices that are designed to create responsible and responsive education. Each aspect of an accountable school's operations should aim to (a) heighten the probability that good practices will occurs for students; (b) reduce the likelihood that harmful practices will occur; and (c) provide internal self-correctives in the system to identify, diagnose, and change courses of action that are harmful or ineffective." The authors continues by claiming that in most enterprises in society there are at least five types of accountability mechanisms: political, legal bureaucratic, professional, and market accountability (14f.).

36. Bovens 1998:25. He describes "responsibility" as a "container concept," which can be clarified best by making a sketch which Wittgenstein called "a family resemblance." The meanings are related, but cannot be reduced to one essential meaning. Bovens suggests five forms: responsibility as cause, as accountability, as capacity, as task, and as virtue (24–26). The distinction made in the English translation between "responsibility" and "accountability" corresponds to the words in the Dutch title: "*Verantwoordelijkheid*" and "*aansprakelijkheid*" (ibid., preface, xii).

The former is the case only when these four criteria are fulfilled: transgression of a norm, causal connection, blame-worthiness, and the relationship with the agent. This is a digital sense of accountability: you are either accountable or you are not. But accountability has not only a formal or juridical aspect. The forum for this passive responsibility can be anything from one's internal conscience to an international court for crimes against humanity. Although accountability can have four forms (corporate, hierarchical, collective, and individual), it is still a matter of being held accountable by a forum. It is the sense of the question of "how" or "what."

The active responsibility is defined as a virtue, and demands an answer to a question of "why." This latter form could, therefore, better be described as "a sense of responsibility."[37] Bovens concludes, however, that "accountability" and "responsibility" are closely interrelated. Being (passively) held accountable is a precondition for becoming responsible in the active sense. On the other hand, the blame or the call for account does not have a meaning by itself, only as a way to mature in a deeper sense of being responsible in a community.[38] What Bovens discusses here as active responsibility is close to the definition of "attitude" above.

There might be good reasons to make this kind of distinction between "responsibility" and "accountability." Nevertheless, the difference between them is fluid in less scholarly use, and "accountability" can appear in both the active as well as the passive meaning of "responsibility." The interrelation between them is important. To become actively responsible/accountable, there must be something making the sense of being so, and this must be some kind of forum or standard.[39]

---

37. Bovens 1998:32–38.

38. This constant interchange between accountability and responsibility is necessary for a community to maintain: "Norms are reproduced, internalized, and, where necessary, adjusted through accountability. . . . Giving account of oneself is therefore one of the most important means by which we can try to maintain the fragile public sphere and to make sure that the way in which society is arranged does not at crucial points slip through our collective fingers. In the course of this process, control and prevention, accountabilities and virtues, go hand in hand" (Bovens 1998:39). It is not necessarily a legal conduct that causes this effect; it can also be just to tell one's story to clear the air. The important matter is whether the accounting process leads to those involved, and others in a parallel situation, learning from the mistakes made. Accountability is a matter after the event; active responsibility can convey control before potential deviance (Bovens 1998:39–42).

39. One obvious example: then-U.S. Senator Walter Mondale demanded a much higher degree of "accountability" from the president of the United States to the Congress, according to the U.S. Constitution. After Watergate, this was necessary to establish a new confidence among Americans that the president was an "accountable" person. Legal, constitutional obligation as well as a moral virtue of accountability was highly recommended. This should be achieved by improving the accountability to the constituency through open contact via media, etc. (Mondale

If we look at some examples of the use of "accountability" in church-related texts, we find several examples of the oscillation between the active and passive meanings. Too formal standards of accountability can lead to nonaccountable attitudes in important relations, because only the most flattering are presented, and not the total reality.[40]

The impression that the terminology of "accountability" and "mutual accountability" in many cases has a connotation of attitude is confirmed through its use in contexts describing dynamics in small groups.[41] It can, for instance, be used to describe the covenant interrelation between people committed to nurture their mutual growth in sanctification and discipleship in congregations in the Wesleyan/Methodist tradition.[42]

1975). "This book represents my effort to describe what I believe the Congress, other institutions, and we as Americans must do to respect our system and our liberties from the encroachment of an unaccountable Presidency" (ibid., foreword, vii). Chapters 5 and 6 are devoted to the relation of the president to Congress; the last chapter has the title "The Presidential Personality and Public Leadership." The double aspect of accountability flows together in a passage like this: "A healthy President must be capable of earning the trust of the American people. He can do so only if he tells the truth, obeys the law, and respects the American public and their right to an accounting of his leadership" (ibid., 259).

40. In an article on "accountability in priesthood," the standards and routines of juridical accountability generally practiced is referred to as a given fact (accounts to the local Ordinary, the parish council, and other ecclesiastical bodies), according to canonical law. But the point to be discussed in this case is how counterproductive a mere formal meaning of accountability can be. The aim should rather be "account-ability," a mature relationship of trust in which the priest is able to deal with his own vulnerability. This demands some kind of mutual accountability, to avoid destructive self-defense. Thus, the structures of accountability in priesthood should aim at developing "genuine accountability" in confidence and cooperation, i.e., "accountability" as a virtue making the priest able to serve and to learn, not a sole formal procedure of accountability (cf. Whitehead 1992, particularly 36–45).

41. Cf. Lawson 1994: "Creating mutual 'accountability' among group members is the chief means by which home fellowship groups are intended to solve the pastoral problems of congregational size and geographical dispersal" (91). "The trust, honesty, and compassion that small-group intimacy engenders create 'accountability'. Group members are accountable to each other for the ways in which they apply God's word in their lives, which they learn to do by collectively 'fleshing out the Sunday sermon" (95).

42. In a study on Discipleship Groups as a variant of the Methodist "Classes," emphasizing a *koinonia* structure according to a "roundtable" model, "mutual accountability" is used as a principle. It seems to have some connotation to "forum," but is directed toward building up the mature disciple of good virtues, e.g.: "Mutual accountability within a small group is foundational for the building up and growth of The Church. Sometimes difficult and even painful questions need to be asked of others about the table, always in the spirit of love. . . . The formation of disciples is an ongoing, even life-long process, which incorporates both heart and mind, emotion and cognition, risk and certainty. It is not only learning what Jesus said and did, but how that shapes and forms the values and ethos of the individual believer, as well as the broad scope of the community of believers" (Earley 1996:51–52).

There is a change in connotation when "accountable" or "accountability" is linked to "mutual." This word, according to dictionaries, can be rather neutral, describing persons having the same relation each toward the other. Mostly, however, it has a positive connotation of respectful reciprocal relation, sharing without profiting one from the other. It has a more positive connotation than "common."[43]

The expression "mutual accountability" does not occur in standard English dictionaries. It has been used, however, in several contexts dealing with the proper relations between partners. Some of them are regulated by more or less official agreements, such as the small-group commitment mentioned above. It can go all the way to a large scale, to obligations according to documents or standards for international politics and employer/employee relations.

In conclusion, we find that mutual accountability is the state of being asked to give an account in a mutual setting, where the questions can be asked both ways and "about the table," in a mutual way. It presupposes some kind of community with *some common standards* to which the different members can be held accountable. The meaning of "accountability" is, however, oscillating between this and another meaning: to have the attitude of *being account-able*. In connection with "mutual," it means to be able to be open and willing to give and take account in a setting of mutual commitment and trust. It requires a mature fellowship. But confidence and maturity are also, to some degree, the goal of this kind of fellowship, too.

In the analysis of the role of mutual accountability in ecumenical texts, it is my interest to study which of the two basic meanings is preferred and, eventually, how they are interrelated. It will be relevant to analyze how much and what kind of formal accountability can be demanded in interchurch relationship and how important it might be to nurture attitudes.

From the reflections above, it is possible to sum up a preliminary definition of what kind of attitude is recommended when using this terminology.[44] I here define mutual accountability as *one* attitude with several aspects. These aspects can, isolated, be defined as attitudes too, but there is a fluid border between them.

1. Openness, transparency in a mutual relation, not to keep thoughts, intentions, actions, or initiatives secret or hidden.

2. Readiness to take responsibility for what is done and should be done.

---

43. *Random House Dictionary of the English Language* (1983), 1270.

44. In this study I will sometimes make distinctions between the terminology ("mutual accountability"), the concept, idea, or notion ("mutual accountability"), and the (real) attitude (mutual accountability), but only when it is important for the meaning in a context. Where I find such distinctions more distracting than illuminating in the text, I will omit them.

3. Reliability, in the sense of staying firm to what is common, traditions, standards, and agreements.

4. The willingness to make each other mutually responsible, even in a critical way. This includes, in a mutual relationship, readiness to receive critical evaluation and take critique seriously without threats of sanctions.

Summary

Interchurch relations have changed through the efforts of the ecumenical movement over the last half century, and so has the focus of theological reflection within the ecumenical endeavours. There is a tendency in Faith and Order texts toward a stronger focus on the quality of relations, at the cost of attempting to define models of unity. This has led to a higher frequency of recommendations of certain *attitudes* as necessary for the improvement of interchurch fellowship. "Mutual accountability" has become a crucial concept in this respect.

The purpose of this study is, therefore, to raise the question whether and in which sense a certain type of attitude is particularly important for interchurch relations. To be more specific, I want to identify and discuss the theological meaning and significance of mutual accountability as a necessary attitude for the quality of interchurch relationship. This I will do according to the thesis I want to test and, if possible, to confirm through this study.[45]

I find that a theory of attitudes as a third, supplementary perspective (to the ethics of duty and the ethics of purpose) formulated in the studies of Norwegian theologian Ivar Asheim is particularly relevant to identify the role of attitudes in these texts.

The study will be pursued in five chapters. In the following three chapters, the ecumenical documents from the Faith and Order movement (and some related texts from the WCC) from the period 1948–1998 will be analyzed. I will focus on how the attitude of mutual accountability (according to the preliminary definition above) has been an aspect in these texts all the way, and how it has become an increasingly important issue of ecumenical ecclesiology. Through this analysis I am also searching for elements of a theory of mutual accountability as an attitude for ecumenical relations.

In the last chapter, I will make a systematic theological appraisal of what I've found. I will particularly discuss "relation" in dialectic to—respectively— "faith" and "order." This last chapter will be an attempt to formulate a theory of mutual accountability as a necessary attitude for interchurch relations,

---

45. See above, p. 20.

particularly in regard to what kind of necessity is implied. Mutual accountability will be discussed as an important attitude to improve church relations dominated by diversity, division, and even tension, and the ecclesiological horizon and relevance of this concept should not be limited to the efforts of the ecumenical movement. But questions and material from the Faith and Order texts will be the focal point of this study.

CHAPTER 2

Ecumenical Attitudes and Premises for Ecumenical Ecclesiology

From Amsterdam (1948) to Montreal (1963)

The Significance of Attitudes in the Premises for the World Council of Churches

The Role of Attitudes in the Ecclesiological Premises for Establishing the World Council of Churches

Amsterdam 1948

The importance of proper attitudes to pursue the ecumenical task is explicitly emphasized in the texts of Faith and Order in the last part of the period I will analyze. In this chapter I will scrutinize texts reflecting on the unity of the churches from the early phase of the World Council of Churches (WCC). The purpose is to see whether this is a new aspect of ecumenical theology in the last decade or so, or whether it has its roots in the theological reflections of the pioneering time of the ecumenical movement after the Second World War. This is not a question of mere curiosity, but based on the assumption that ecumenical theological reflection in the 1990s must be seen in the context of the issues at stake earlier.

To be able to understand theological ecumenical reflection, it is necessary to see both continuity and change. It is also my presumption that comprehensive and solid theological work was done energetically and with fresh questions and open eyes. Therefore, attention to the early phase, when the new field of ecumenism was breaking open, might stimulate creative ecumenical theological reflection in a time like the present, when only a few questions are raised for the first time.

What I am particularly looking for in the texts is a reflection of the need for certain attitudes to establish an interchurch relationship, and signs that the recommended attitudes correspond to what has been subsumed as "mutual accountability" in chapter 1. I will start the analysis of texts from the event of transformation of movements among people deeply interested in the unity of the Church for the sake of mission into an institutionalized fellowship of *churches*.

The texts from the first assembly of the World Council of Churches in Amsterdam in 1948 and the important document on the "ecclesiality" of the World Council of Churches from the Central Committee meeting at Toronto in 1950 present a framework for reflection on the ecclesiology of Faith and Order after 1948. The themes raised were discussed substantially within Faith and Order before and after the meetings.[1]

According to the first general secretary of the World Council of Churches, Willem Visser 't Hooft, one important goal of the WCC was to urge the churches themselves to take responsibility for ecumenism, and not to leave it to the continuation committees of the different conferences. His comments highlight the relation between institutionalizing and focus on attitudes: "All churches had to consider whether they would accept responsibility for, and commitment to, an ongoing organization which would be the expression of their will 'to stay together' and which would be controlled by them."[2]

This reference to responsibility might also mean taking upon themselves certain financial and organizational obligations, but the context certainly points to the attitudes required from the churches as the dominant perspective of "responsibility." "Accepting responsibility" refers to an attitude corresponding to the duties and contracts involved. Further, "commitment" of the churches and their "will to stay together" refers to an attitude of reliability and trustworthiness to the process. The shift from a movement of personal

---

1. The parts of the Amsterdam report and the Toronto report I analyze here are found in Lukas Vischer, ed., *A Documentary History of the Faith and Order Movement 1927–1963* (St. Louis: Bethany Press, 1963), 75–84, 167–76.
2. Visser 't Hooft 1970:7.

initiatives toward an institution for institutions (churches) did not, therefore, mean leaving behind the need for adequate attitudes, but shifting the subject of the required attitudes.

Since the churches are the subjects in mind, the attitudes are defined in an attempt to establish a dialectical relation to institutional formalities. This becomes particularly clear in the report of the Policy Committee.[3] It carefully balances the churches' "earnestly seeking fellowship in thought and action" with reassurance that the council

> disavows any thought of becoming a single unified church structure independent of the churches . . . or a structure dominated by a centralized administrative authority. The purpose of the Council is to express its unity in the attitude of "love." This should be the real "binding" force. The theme of bounds and the binding purpose of the World Council of Churches is comprehensively elaborated in precisely this perspective. The Biblical expression of this attitude is described as 'bearing one another's burdens and so fulfilling the law of Christ.'

Thus, the attitude required is some kind of mutual responsibility, sharing one's burdens and readiness to carry the burdens of others. Church unity requires the *willingness* to be involved in binding relations to other churches. At this point the binding element is defined in theological terms ("bound together in Christ") as well as in a moral perspective ("bearing one another's burdens"), more than a structural one. But the dynamic interrelation between theology, structure, and morality is important in this text.

The Message and Reports of the First Assembly in Amsterdam 1948 has a strong christological focus, and was to a large degree concerned about the role of the World Council of Churches and the churches in the pursuit of *responsibility*.[4] The interchurch relations are seen in the light of God's given unity in Christ. The question of attitudes is not made a subject as such in the report, but in the exposition of dominant themes there are several indications that attitudes are required. The churches should be responsible in the divided world, taking upon them their responsibility for the unity among themselves.[5]

---

3. Amsterdam 1948:127f. This text from Committee II on Policy became a stepping stone for the further discussion of the "ecclesiality" of the World Council of Churches in Toronto in 1950.

4. Only the first of four subsections deals primarily with the interchurch relations as such (Section I: "The Universal Church in God's Design"), but the emphasis of the *responsibility* of the Churches is characteristic of the whole report. Within the assembly theme of "Man's Disorder and God's Design," the subtheme "The Responsible Society" became a slogan. It was an important theme of, e.g., Section III: "The Church and the Disorder of Society."

5. The report of Section I starts like this: "God has given to His people in Jesus Christ a unity

The christological focus of this time of ecumenism—"in seeking him we find one another"—is elaborated as a process described as *covenanting* ("we have covenanted with one another"), a deliberate intention, recommended for any local congregation in their relation to other congregations.[6] The dialectic between institutionalized obligations and attitudes can be seen here, and even more at the end of the report of Section I. The theme is exactly *mutual responsibility*, defined as being together in Christ as one body:

> The World Council of Churches has come into existence because we have already recognised a responsibility to one another's churches in our Lord Jesus Christ. Therefore we cannot rest content with our present divisions. Before God, we are responsible for one another. We see already what some of our responsibilities are, and God will show us more. But we embark upon our work in the World Council of Churches in penitence for what we are, in hope for what we shall be.[7]

The status of being accountable to God, expressed as "before God," implies that a mutual responsibility for one another is an obligation. But this responsibility also appears as something to be developed as attitudes of uneasiness with the present divisions. The responsible way of handling divisions is not to hide them, but to act in the forum of the World Council of Churches in responsibility to the churches that have sent the delegates.[8] The proper ecumenical attitude is the balance between "false claims" and "faithless timidity."[9]

This multifaceted theme of responsibility to God and to one another is related to the exposition of three themes of great importance in this text: (a) the failure of adequate interchurch attitudes as a *moral* problem; (b) the need for *openness* regarding the differences between the churches; and (c) proper *awareness of the other* churches as a prerequisite for ecumenism.

The question whether the division between churches should be designated as *sin* is a delicate one. In the report of Amsterdam, it has deliberately been given a prominent position.[10] It is to some extent described as the bad and destructive attitudes to one another, which have more or less permanently affected interchurch relations. The guilt of the "fathers" of the times of split and

which is His creation and not our achievement" (Amsterdam 1948:51).

6. Amsterdam 1948:9 (Message).

7. Amsterdam 1948:57.

8. Amsterdam 1948:56.

9. Amsterdam 1948:57.

10. This is a crucial theme in the Message and in the first part of the report of Section I (cf. Amsterdam 1948:9f., 51). It was emphasized through interpolations in the text; cf. the report of the conversations in the plenary (Amsterdam 1948:57).

division is played down in relation to the present hostile attitudes of churches. To some degree these attitudes have been expressed in acts of strife between "lands," showing clearly the postwar atmosphere and theme and the close relations between church and nation.[11]

Another type of sin as unacceptable attitude is injustice and racism, these "evils of the world [that] have so deeply penetrated our churches." A third type of bad attitude is the way the churches have done their business. This is described as lack of awareness of the need of the world, and preoccupation with internal affairs. There are also destructive attitudes between the ordained servants and the ordinary members of the church, and they therefore share their guilt. The churches have been dominated by "ecclesiastical officialdom, clerical or lay, instead of giving vigorous expression to the full rights of the living congregation and the sharing of clergy and people in the common life in the Body of Christ."[12]

As an alternative to these attitudes that are counterproductive for ecumenism, the report suggests desired attitudes for an ecumenical fellowship. The report articulates and encourages *frankness and openness* about the differences between the churches. The proper ecumenical attitude for the new relations inaugurated by the WCC is "loving one another in Christ" and at the same time facing "our deepest difference."[13] This corresponds to a willingness to be humble and open for mutual critique, and at the same time speak boldly against injustice and oppression, to say both "yes" and "no" with conviction and love.[14]

The third type of attitude relevant for interchurch relationship is the awareness of being part of the body of Christ, the fact of being in relation to the other churches. The churches have to relate to each other because of the differences, not only because of the similarities.[15] This understanding of relations within the body of Christ is spelled out in the report. One clear example is "the

---

11. "We come from Christian churches which have long misunderstood, ignored and misrepresented one another; we come from lands which have often been in strife, we are all sinful men and we are heirs to the sins of our fathers" (Amsterdam 1948:51).

12. Amsterdam 1948:56. Cf. also 81: the Church has "reflected and then by its example sanctified the racial prejudice that is rampant in the world."

13. Amsterdam 1948:51. Cf. the whole argument under the titles "Our deepest difference" and "Common beliefs and common problems," 51–54.

14. Cf. Amsterdam 1948:9–10 (Message).

15. "We cannot ignore one another, for the very intensity of our difference testifies to a common conviction which we drew from him. The Body of Christ is a unity which makes it impossible for us either to forget each other or to be content with agreement upon isolated parts of our belief whilst we leave the other parts unreconciled" (Amsterdam 1948:55).

ecumenical sense" which should be found in any Christian group, reminding itself of being part of the worldwide Church.[16]

In the section reports dealing with the contribution of the Church to the restoration of "God's order" in society, there is no clear emphasis that the *interchurch relations* should be an *example* of the attitudes required for the restored society. Rather, the dominant perspective is the witness of the individual Christian and clear words from the Church's leadership.[17] There is a deep sense of guilt for the failure of the churches and the Christian community to stand against racism and antisemitism, but these problems of attitude are not seen as a specific *inter*church matter, but a problem in the midst of any church.[18]

On the other hand, the distinction between principles for interchurch fellowship (within the WCC) and for the life together between nations and states seems to blur. In his address to one of the public meetings, Bishop Eivind Berggrav of Oslo described the work of the "foe" this way: "He loves to divide." The iron curtain is then mentioned as a division between states as well as churches. Most interesting for our theme is Berggrav's description of "victory" in terms of attitude of solidarity, a solidarity shown precisely in accepting mutuality in responsibility: "God's order is realized by the recognition of mutual respect, mutual rights and mutual responsibilities. This is the solidarity which fills the vacuum revealing the coming victory."[19]

Therefore, to mature and develop attitudes were seen as integral aspects of the process of institutionalizing the ecumenical movement, not as something belonging to the time of personal initiatives of ecumenism. The crucial role of attitudes was acknowledged for the churches' contribution to the restoration process of society as well as interchurch relations.

To be more specific: the recommended attitudes are the sense of being related to each other in Christ, being open for constructive critique in love, carrying the sense of being responsible for one another and to one another. The balance between humility and proper boldness is the repeated melody. Therefore, we can conclude that at the beginning of the World Council of Churches there was an awareness of the need for mutual accountability in interchurch relations established through this organization.

---

16. See the report of Section II (Amsterdam 1948:67f.).

17. The role of the individual: "The Church can be most effective in society as it inspires its members to ask in a new way what their Christian responsibility is whenever they influence public opinion, whenever they make decisions as employers or as workers or in any other vocation to which they may be called" (Amsterdam 1948:82). The role of churches as deliverer of moral premises: "The churches have an important part in laying that common foundation of moral conviction without which any system of law will break down" (Amsterdam 1948:92).

18. See Amsterdam 1948:80f., 161.

19. Amsterdam 1948:182.

Toronto 1950

The establishment of the World Council of Churches raised several critical questions, particularly on the issue of the ecclesial status of the new organization. The identity of the WCC was discussed in a paper adopted by the Central Committee in Toronto in 1950. This document is divided into two parts, establishing a dialectic as to what the WCC should or should not be. To a certain degree this became also a dialectic between ecumenical structure and ecumenical attitude.

The "no" was basically a refusal to define the WCC in terms of an ecclesiological structural perspective, and definitely not as a "super church." The Council is "not the Una Sancta of which the Creeds speak."[20] This "no" to a magnificent universal structure was balanced by a "no" to defining the WCC only in terms of a spiritualized ecclesiology of "the invisible church."[21] But then the question remained: What were the basic components of the ecclesiological identity of the WCC, since it obviously had some structural components and was based upon theological affirmations?

The "yes" is "the positive assumptions which underlie the World Council of Churches and the ecclesiological implications of membership in it."[22] This formulation was an attempt to define a new category of ecclesiology. It is based on the relevance of the WCC for ecumenical ecclesiology, and has two basic pillars taken from the Amsterdam resolution: (a) a theological reflection on the implications of the Church as the body of Christ; and (b) an elaboration of the need of (what I here will define as) ecumenical attitudes. Although there are some indications how these two pillars should carry the house, much is left open to how this in practice could become an ecclesiology of the new phenomenon of the WCC. And it certainly did not answer the questions in terms of the ecclesiology held by some of the member churches. The Toronto statement has, therefore, been criticized as being an obstacle to the development of the ecclesial status of the WCC. Thus, the significance of the negative affirmations has been greater than of the positive.[23]

---

20. Toronto 1950:169.

21. Toronto 1950:171. This accusation is presented as a critical remark from the Roman Catholic Church, referring to the encyclical *Mysteri Corporis*.

22. Toronto 1950:171.

23. Cf., e.g., Aagaard 1993:133f. Anna Marie Aagaard evaluates the Toronto report as a static element in the identity of the WCC and an obstacle for further development of the ecumenical movement, implying that the churches only are "looking at, not accepting new developments." She refers also to Van Elderen 1991:140, who discusses the questions raised about the adequacy, scope, and status of the Toronto statement. Van Elderen regrets that it has been given too much weight as a dogmatic formulation (especially by the Orthodox churches).

In the attempts to develop a new understanding and vision of the WCC in the late 1990s, however, more attention has been paid to the positive affirmations, and in this context we find recommendations of mutual accountability.[24] There might, therefore, be a common focus on attitudes in ecumenical theological reflections of 1950 and the 1990s, which increases my interest in an analysis of the Toronto statement. But did the Toronto statement claim mutual accountability as an attitude important for the ecumenical fellowship of churches, while not using that terminology?

The most significant reflection on attitudes in the positive affirmations is related to the term *recognize*. It means in this context more than accepting a fact or taking something for granted; it is used to describe a collective, active, conscious approach to the fellowship, expressing a positive affirming attitude to the others.

First, the text says that all churches recognize that the Church of Christ is more than one single member church. The ecumenical movement should, in contrast to traditional attitudes in the churches, convey the willingness to seek fellowship with those belonging to the "mystical body" if the Church, but not yet belonging to "the same visible body."[25]

Second, the text proposes that the member churches accept that differences of faith and order do exist, but that they face this situation with "mutual respect," "recognizing one another as serving the One Lord."[26] Quite remarkably, there is a distinction between this kind of recognition not able "to accept each other as true and pure Churches," and those churches "which recognize other Churches in the full and true sense." In this way the text expands the use of the term *recognize*, from signifying a standard of full acceptance and fellowship to mean also an attitude of regarding other churches as belonging to the same fellowship in spite of differences. This maneuver has its cost in terms of losing the most distinct meaning of "recognize." But it introduces as an ecumenical attitude the ability to regard churches not fully recognized as nevertheless partners with whom one should be open and respectful. This is meant to be more than a general sense of kindness and tolerance: "The Member Churches of the World Council recognize in other Churches elements of the true Church. They consider that this mutual recognition obliges them to enter into a serious conversation with each other in the hope that these elements of truth will lead to the recognition of the full truth and to unity based on the full truth."[27] Thereby the text lays the theological foundation for

---

24. CUV 1997:8.14f.; cf. 6.
25. Toronto 1950:172f. It is added here, quite noteworthily: "Including the Church of Rome."
26. Toronto 1950:173.
27. Toronto 1950:174.

ecumenical dialogue, recognizing these elements as "powerful means by which God works." (The preaching of the word, the teaching of the holy Scriptures, and the administration of the sacraments are mentioned here.)

The characteristics of this dialogue are important for our theme. It should be a "frank and brotherly intercourse for the realization of a fuller unity," in which the churches "will be led into fuller unity." The Toronto statement thereby says that the churches in their dialogue toward the fullness of truth have the attitudes of mutual respect, accepting God's work through the *vestigia ecclesia* in other churches, being frank and brotherly in their conversation. This should be seen together with the forestalling of any accusation that the WCC fosters a lack of interest in finding the truth, mere tolerance, or what is called "latitudinarism."[28]

The Toronto statement further agrees that the member churches are "willing to consult together" for the sake of the common witness of Christ. This attitude is necessary for common mission.[29] Further, they "should recognize their solidarity with each other."

> Within the Council the Churches seek to deal with each other with a brotherly concern. This does not exclude extremely frank speaking to each other, in which within the Council the Churches ask each other searching questions and face their differences. But this is to be done for the building up the Body of Christ. This excludes a purely negative attitude of one Church to another. The positive affirmation of each Church's faith is to be welcomed, but actions incompatible with brotherly relationships towards other member Churches defeat the very purpose for which the Council has been created.[30]

Behind this statement lies the answer to the quest for an ecclesial status of the new fellowship of churches, the World Council of Churches. The total picture of the attitudes required for this fellowship has much in common with our preliminary definition of mutual accountability, particularly in what is said about the sense of belonging together in spite of differences, of being willing to participate in an open, respectful dialogue where the goal is to give an account of one's own treasures and to listen to the others. The crucial point is the balance between being humble, open to learn, but consequently frank and not indifferent. The conclusion can therefore be drawn that the Toronto statement

---

28. Toronto 1950:170. This attitude is described as claiming the equality of all Christian doctrines and conceptions of the Church, ignoring the matter of truth.

29. Toronto 1950:174.

30. Toronto 1950:175. The need to express attitudes in actions or to abstain from certain actions is an important element of Asheim's theory of attitudes. The same argument is explicitly used in the Toronto statement.

requires the attitude of mutual accountability, understood as a condition for the existence for the WCC as well as for bilateral dialogues. We find here an attempt to give a theological argument for the ecclesiological relevance of ecumenical attitudes when no common ecclesiological structure is at hand. It is more than simply pragmatism in the difficult situation of not choosing one particular ecclesiological model to define the WCC.

At some points, the distinction between attitudes and duties is not quite sharp, certainly not as clear as in studies of principle ethics (like Asheim's). In one case the attitude implies an obligation: "They consider that this mutual recognition obliges them to enter into a serious conversation with each other in the hope that this will lead to the recognition of the full truth and to unity based on the full truth."[31] In another case the duty implied in the given unity is described as the task to show the attitude of openness and willingness to seek fellowship with other churches.[32] These examples show how the Toronto text promotes the dialectic between ecumenical duty and ecumenical attitude in respect to ecumenical ecclesiology. The required attitudes are derived from the basis of the ecumenical fellowship; the attitudes required contribute to a better understanding of the basis, the form, and the goal of the ecumenical effort.

Throughout the Toronto statement, the Church as *the body of Christ* defines the ecclesiological situation of the ecumenical fellowship. The unity is given in Christ. Therefore, the churches somehow belong together if they participate in the gifts of Christ, and therefore are accountable to enter into dialogue and show solidarity with each other.

The image of the body of Christ is combined with the image of the "temple of God" to argue that the church "needs constant renewal."[33] The body of Christ is in a building process. "It is at the same time a building which has been built and a building which is being built." To pursue the building process, the churches should help each other in the growing process by "mutual exchange of thought and experience." What one church has does not belong to it alone. The churches are accountable to the fellowship: "Whatever insight has been received by one or more Churches is to be made available to all the Churches for the sake of 'building up the Body of Christ'." The mutual respectful and open conversation should be pursued in the expectation of the guidance of the Holy Spirit toward full unity in Christ.[34]

This is more than a romantic understanding of a colorful exposure of diversity. It must also be taken as a serious theological argument that a mutually

---

31. Toronto 1950:174.
32. Toronto 1950:173.
33. Toronto 1950:175f.
34. Toronto 1950:173.

accountable "recognition" of difference and diversity can convey richness and is fruitful for the growth of the Church. The emphasis on ecumenical attitudes is a consequence of the christological understanding of the fellowship of churches: because we are one in Christ, we should have an attitude to one another like this or that. This is an attempt to take seriously the different confessional ecclesiologies, but also a serious attempt to take one step further away from the struggle between them. There is both a reference to a Lutheran perspective on unity, understood as a fellowship in word and sacrament, and a reflection of the meaning of the Church as the mystical body of Christ, significant for Roman Catholic ecclesiology. The alternative is presented as an outline of a common ecumenical ecclesiology (body of Christ), based upon the common tradition from the Scriptures and the creeds. It is not a general pluralism but a theologically defined common frame for useful plurality.

The argument of the Toronto text for the necessity of attitudes confirms what we found in the Amtsterdam report: that this perspective is not new in the documents from the 1990s. It is also significant for my thesis that this perspective was important before the ecumenical movement had its most blooming period and before the great bulk of bilateral dialogues was established and their results were presented to the churches. The recommendation of mutual accountability is a perspective established to start and promote the ecumenical dialogue and fellowship among churches. It is not a perspective that belongs only to the critical evaluation of ecumenical efforts and the reception of them.

But we may ask at this point whether the relatively strong criticism and disregard of the significance of the Toronto text undermines the conclusion that the attitude of mutual accountability is important for interchurch fellowship. We notice that most of the critique against the Toronto text has been directed at the limits and passivity of the first part of the text; hence the assessment of the status of the text has been based mainly on that part. The conclusion of Marlin Van Elderen,[35] that the "negative affirmations have stood the test of time better than its 'positive' one" can be challenged. The positive ones have not been tested to the same extent.[36] But the Toronto text has not been sufficient as a platform for saying what is the ecumenical ecclesiology of the WCC. Nevertheless, I conclude that arguing for new attitudes has been important and was given a theological basis.

35. Van Elderen 1991:140.

36. E.g., in the study of the Common Understanding and Vision of the WCC in the 1990s (CUV; see ch. 4 below, pp. 308-22), the positive affirmations have been confirmed in terms of fruits of the WCC. In my opinion, it can hardly be contested that the WCC has become a forum for mutual exchange of traditions and resources, a forum for learning (e.g., about the social ethical responsibility of the churches) and a forum for mutual solidarity. Thus, the World Council of Churches has promoted a certain degree of mutual recognition between the churches. The ecclesial "status" of this type of recognition seems, however, to be one of the difficult questions.

These premises for a new type of dialogue between the churches played a significant role later on in the first Faith and Order World Conference after the inclusion of Faith and Order in the WCC.

The Importance of Attitudes for Interchurch Relations in the Report from Lund (1952)

The third Faith and Order World Conference in Lund in 1952 continued some of the trends of Amsterdam and Toronto, particularly the christological focus in ecclesiology. The report from Lund gives the impression of a confidence in the ecumenical processes, which permitted deeper penetration into the differences that divide the churches and into the background of these differences. This confidence also led to the formulation of a principle of ecumenical conduct (the so-called Lund principle[37]), a belief in a new ecumenical methodology (away from the comparative method), and a formulation of the goal of ecumenical processes. The Lund report makes clear that attitudes are not enough for church union or communion at the Lord's Table,[38] but the theme of proper attitudes plays a remarkable role in reflections on the principles of conduct, methodology, and goal.

In what was later called *the Lund principle*, the second part of the sentence is most often quoted. However, the entire sentence gives a clear impression that the argument is based upon a requirement of proper attitudes that are necessary for a better dialogue as well as common action: "Should not our Churches ask themselves whether they are showing sufficient eagerness to enter into conversation with other Churches and whether they should not act together in all matters except those in which deep differences of conviction compel them to act separately?"[39]

The attitude required in this sentence runs like a thread through the report. It is, for example, elaborated in a reflection on the phenomenon of *schism*.[40] The text accepts that churches to some extent highly regard the origin of their divisions. But the schisms also arose out of unacceptable attitudes such as impatience, lack of understanding and vitality, and refusal to reform. The maintenance of the divisions is regarded as reciprocal guilt. In other words, an attitude leading in the opposite direction is required to overcome the reasons for division, whether or not they are acceptable reasons. Consideration of differences in *worship* concludes a clear recommendation to go as far as possible in

---

37. Cf. the reference to this principle, e.g., in the message of the fifth World Conference of Faith and Order (Santiago 1993:227).

38. "It is of the utmost importance that all unions find their basis in the teaching of Scripture and be tested by conformity to the Word of God" (Lund 1952:117).

39. Lund 1952:86.

40. Lund 1952:96f.

common worship, so as to foster "the cultivation of a sympathetic and reverent attitude by all Christian people toward all forms of worship."[41]

In the Lund report we also find a discussion of "non-theological factors," with a request for more self-critical attention and accounts of how such factors have shaped worship life; "a re-examination of its attitude to that of others."[42] Another significant example of how the attitude of the Lund principle should be practiced is the strong recommendation of a self-critical approach to the confessionally based obstacles to a higher degree of intercommunion.[43] Self-critical examination means to be able to go into a process of giving an account of theology and practice in a mutual setting. The text implies that proper self-criticism and self-accounting can only be pursued in an ecumenical setting fostering this attitude.

Already in the first lines of the report, the Lund conference articulated the end of the so-called method of comparison.[44] To proceed in ecumenical dialogue and relationship, it is necessary to accept the consequence of the common heritage and participation in Christ. The christological dimension should lead to a more committed attitude to the difficult process of criticizing, being criticized, and being open for changes. "The mutually self-critical attitude is a fruit of the relation to Christ: When we place ourselves in our Churches under His judgment and in obedience to His calling and sending, we shall know that we cannot manifest our unity and share in His fullness without being changed."[45]

The text then gives a remarkable description of how churches of different types, according to confession and tradition, have something to learn from the "fullness" represented by the other churches. Thus, the text provides a unique example of what mutual accountability under the accountability to Christ could lead to. Some examples:

> Some of us who have been assured that we possess the true order and the true sacraments will find ourselves called to give its rightful place to the preaching of the Living Word. Some who have neglected the sacraments will be

---

41. Lund 1952:106–114; quotations from 114.

42. Lund 1952:114.

43. Lund 1952:122f. Without naming the groups of churches, obviously the Lutheran and Anglican churches are particularly requested to "carefully re-examine their practice" toward a more open communion. Other churches, satisfied with a principle of Mutual Open Communion, should "examine the objections" to their practice. (The Orthodox churches were not members of the WCC at that time. The Roman Catholic Church has participated in the work of Faith and Order since Montreal 1963.)

44. "We have seen clearly that we can make no real advance toward unity if we only compare our several conceptions of the nature of the Church and the traditions in which they are embodied" (Lund 1952:85).

45. Lund 1952:91.

> confronted by Him who humbled Himself in Baptism and broke bread and shared the cup to make us partakers of His passion and death.... Churches which have valued little His prayer that the oneness of His people be made manifest to men will be summoned to make His prayer their own. Churches complacent in the face of racial divisions in the Body will be brought to repentance by Him in whom bond and free, Jew and Gentile, Greek and barbarian, are one.... Those who are ever looking backward and have accumulated much precious ecclesiastical baggage will perhaps be shown that pilgrims must travel light and that, if we are to share at last in the great Supper, we must let go much that we treasure....[46]

It is not easy to distinguish between what Christ will teach and what will be taught the churches in the open encounter between them. Obviously, the mutually accountable relations, as I will call them, are coincidentally understood as an accountable relation to Christ. "We cannot know all that shall be disclosed to us when together we look to Him who is the Head of the Body. It is easy for us in our several Churches to think of what our separated brethren need to learn. Christ's love will make us more ready to learn what He can teach us through them."[47]

The Lund report attempts to formulate the goal of the ecumenical process, under the eschatological perspective:

> In summary, the nature of the unity towards which we are striving is that of a visible fellowship in which all members, acknowledging Jesus Christ as living Lord and Saviour, shall recognize each other as belonging fully to His Body, to the end that the world may believe. In His own day Jesus Christ will gather His scattered people to live in eternal union with Him.... With light that pierces the Christian conscience that day of our Lord illuminates the solemn responsibility of every contemporary communion to prepare itself for unity.[48]

It is striking how the text here speaks about the churches as subjects, as if they were persons, which gives sense to our talking in terms of attitudes. The crucial verb for the effort leading to the goal of the ecumenical process is "recognize." By bringing in the theme of recognition in this way[49] (compare how it was used in Amsterdam and Toronto), the attitudes of mutual respect, acceptance, and openness to learn are highlighted as crucial for the ecumenical

---

46. Lund 1952:91.
47. Lund 1952:90f.
48. Lund 1952:105f.
49. Lund 1952:102.

project. The formulation of the ecumenical goal carefully combines two ecumenical principles: the task of making unity visible and manifested, and unity as something given because of common participation in Christ and the gifts of Christ. The active link between these two principles is the attitude expressed in "recognition," an attitude that flows from having Christ as Lord and Saviour. It is the adequate attitude for the relations toward all churches who for exactly the same reason (having Christ as Lord and Savior) belong to the one Church, designated as the body of Christ.

Therefore, we find here in this crucial passage of the Lund text a formulation of the importance of an attitude that has much in common with my definition of mutual accountability. It is linked to a formulation of the theological basis for any ecumenical relation ("belonging fully to His Body") and a formulation of the goal of the ecumenical process ("recognize each other as belonging fully to His Body"). This shows how highly regarded the qualities of relations and an attitude resembling mutual accountability was regarded already in 1952. It also shows the theological basis and significance of this attitude, required to express a christological ecclesiology.

Summary

Analysis of texts from Amsterdam, Toronto, and Lund confirms that attitudes play a significant role in the reflections on how to develop interchurch relations in the framework of the WCC. There are explicit and implicit references to attitudes and their importance for the ecumenical fellowship, positive as well as negative effects. One dominant requirement of attitudes is related to the perspective of "recognition," which in the context means the ability and willingness to regard the other churches as true churches, and, therefore, to establish permanent and improved relations with them. The attitude of openness to receive and give constructive critique is also highly esteemed. My conclusion is that the attitude of mutual accountability is important for the ecumenical process already at this pioneer stage. In the first years after World War II and the establishment of the WCC, the quality of relations in the body of Christ was paid remarkable attention.

Besides the conclusion that mutual accountability is an important perspective in these texts, it is of interest how the required attitudes are given a christological basis and profile. The first years after the establishing of the WCC have been regarded as a period when the ecumenical movement was dominated by a christological understanding of the unity of the Church. That is reflected in the way that proper ecumenical attitudes are described.

The reference to Christ is not connected to a historical discussion of the christological dogma of the old church, or to the debate on the historical Jesus.

It is mostly related to a dogmatic concept of the Pauline image of the Church as the body of Christ, saying that the churches are what they are because of their participation in the work of Christ, having Jesus Christ as their Lord and Savior. From this consequences are drawn: how they come closer to each other as they draw closer to Christ and vice versa; and how much they have in common with other churches having the same relation to Christ. The other churches should for this reason not be ignored, the relation to them should not be destroyed, and the division between them cannot be accepted.

The image of the body of Christ is used to argue for the proper attitude in three ways. First, the churches should follow the example of Christ. Second, the churches have to recognize other churches as expressions of Christ in this world; not only one's own church carries that identity and task. The time of negative attitude and disregard has to come to an end. This is the interpretation of the Pauline image that is closest to the way Paul uses it. Third, the churches *together* are the fullness of the body of Christ. Therefore, they are accountable to one another in the sense that they learn from one other what it means to be the body of Christ.

These reports raise an important question for the analysis of other Faith and Order texts: How is the recommendation of the attitude of mutual accountability given a christological basis and perspective?

The Ecumenical Attitude of "The Fully Committed Fellowship": The Statement on Unity (New Delhi 1961)

The statement of unity from New Delhi is reminiscent of the reluctance to go into definitions of ecumenical ecclesiology in Toronto 1950. But serious work on the goal of unity made it possible to launch a statement that became a basis and pattern for subsequent statements of this kind.[50]

The famous slogan of New Delhi, "one fully committed fellowship," can to some degree be understood in terms of ecumenical attitudes. A reasonable interpretation of what it means to be fully committed is to have a certain attitude toward a task, a programme, an idea, but most of all toward another person or other persons. In this statement of unity this reference to the attitude of

---

50. The background of the statement is presented this way in the report from the section of unity in New Delhi: "[The statement] . . . is based upon a statement worked out by the Commission of Faith and Order, accepted by the Central Committee of the WCC in 1960 and sent to the churches for consideration and comment" (New Delhi 1961:145). Harding Meyer regards this statement as significant, "ein Entscheidener Schritt, den man in seiner Bedeutung für die Entwicklung der ökumenischen Bewegung nicht hoch genug veranschlagen kann" (Meyer 1996:55).

(mutual) full commitment is even regarded as *a hallmark* of the fellowship.[51] This crucial point in the argument appears when seen in the context of the entire sentence:

> We believe that the unity which is both God's will and his gift to his Church is being made visible as all in each place who are baptized into Jesus Christ and confess him as Lord and Saviour are brought by the Holy Spirit into one fully committed fellowship, holding the one apostolic faith, preaching the one Gospel, breaking the one bread, joining in common prayer, and having a corporate life reaching out in witness and service to all and who at the same time are united with the whole Christian fellowship in all places and in all ages in such wise that ministry and members are accepted by all, and that all can act and speak together as occasion requires for the tasks to which God calls his people.[52]

In the report each part of this statement is elaborated in a section of explanatory comments. The context within the complicated sentence, together with the explanation of "fully committed fellowship," convey significant perspectives of this ecumenical attitude.

The commitment is not presented as some sort of a social contract, but *defined theologically*. The theological significant terminology of *koinonia* is used to define "fellowship," to say that this is "not merely an institution or organization."[53] The statement itself says that the attitude of full commitment makes visible the unity of God's will and God's gift. It is the unity given through participation (through baptism) in Jesus Christ. The Holy Spirit brings the attitude. Thus, the attitude of full commitment is given nothing less than a trinitarian explanation and dimension. The direction of the attitude is toward Christ and to one another, the second as a consequence of the first. "They are thus 'fully committed' to him and to one another."[54]

This commitment finds its form in theologically significant manifestations of unity. The dimension of full commitment is, however, something other than the expressions of unity. It is a dimension of all of them or, better, a dimension

---

51. It is rather common to refer to the statement of New Delhi as a statement about the unity "all in each place" and "in all places," a statement focusing the locality and the catholicity of the Church. This is adequate when referring to the last part of the statement. Nevertheless, the hallmark common to all succeeding descriptions of the features of the unity is the *full commitment*. Harding Meyer has pointed clearly to this, and argued that the "fully committed fellowship" is the most profound description of the goal of ecumenism (cf. Meyer 1996:57, 180).

52. New Delhi 1961:144f.

53. New Delhi 1961:148.

54. New Delhi 1961:148.

of unity that is and should be expressed through all of them. This interpretation is confirmed by the following explanation, which clearly describes attitudes or expressions of a certain ecumenical attitude:

> Such a fellowship means for those who participate in it nothing less than a renewed mind and spirit, a full participation in common praise and prayer, the shared realities of penitence and forgiveness. It means mutuality in suffering and joy, listening together to the same Gospel, responding in faith, obedience, and service. They are joined in the one mission of Christ in the world, a self-forgetting love for all whom Christ died, and the reconciling grace which breaks down every wall of race, color, caste, tribe, sex, class, and nation. Neither does this "fellowship" imply a rigid uniformity of structure, organization, or government. A lively variety marks corporate life in the One Body of one Spirit.[55]

If not all, at least some of these attitudes resemble what I have preliminarily defined as mutual accountability. There are features of a "renewed mind and spirit," which might be called signs of *mutual reliability*. This becomes even more apparent in the German tradition of the text: "eine völlig verpflichtende Gemeinschaft."[56] The perspective of mutually binding relations is important for the whole argument. It runs through the aspects of openness in listening and responding, support, sharing, and participation, the mutual responsibility for each other and the common task. There is not a focus on mutual openness and self-critique, as in the study of tradition, but the aspects of willingness to renew, change, and even to break barriers are expressions of a mutually accountable attitude.[57] The aspect of full commitment also means that the fellowship is not to be identified with any particular structure. This, too, reinforces the understanding of the aspect of attitude, as it is relevant for any structure or government.

Discussing the implications of this statement for local church life, the report comes to the difficulties of a really open and serious dialogue. The commitment must find its expression in "abiding commitment for each other." The dominance of the christological dimension is apparent when it is said, "that Christ is present among those to whom we cannot, on the grounds of our differing convictions, grant the full meaning of the word 'church'." The situation of barriers and skepticism calls for attitudes of responsibility that care not only for the borders of the churches, but are willing to take risks. The following

---

55. New Delhi 1961:148.
56. Cf. Meyer 1996:55.
57. Cf. ch. 2, pp. 49-80.

question might be one of the most profound expressions of an attitude of accountability that is really mutual: "In this situation are we not constrained by the love of God to exert pressure on the limits of our own inherited traditions, recognizing the theological necessity of what we may call 'responsible risk'?"[58]

Concluding my analysis of this statement, I find it noticeable how crucial the idea of "fully committed fellowship" is for the understanding of unity. It is also remarkable how strong a theological basis the statement tries to give this idea, and how it is a dominant feature of all signs of unity. It is surprising that the New Delhi statement by and large has not been treated as a statement of the importance of ecumenical attitudes. The reasons for this are not quite clear. It might be that this aspect is regarded as too obvious to be discussed, or overshadowed by the focus on "in all places—all in each place." Nevertheless, in light of the later focus in Faith and Order texts, it deserves attention. The text recommends mutuality in commitment to the fellowship of participation (*koinonia*), which means mutual openness and reliability—attitudes that can be integral elements in a theory of mutual accountability as ecumenical attitude.

The Significance of Ecumenical Attitudes in the Preparations and Reports from Montreal (1963)

The Purpose, Scope, and Result of the Study of Tradition

The Lund conference responded to a need to approach the ecumenical problem in a new way, with new methodology as well as new themes for ecumenical theological studies: the common—not only the separated—histories and dogmas of the churches should be explored.[59] The Theological Commission appointed by Faith and Order after Lund understood its task to lead the work beyond the "method of comparative ecclesiology."[60] The result was a study

---

58. New Delhi 1961:153f.

59. "We propose the establishment of a Theological Commission to explore more deeply the resources for further ecumenical discussion to be found in that common history which we have as Christians and which we have discovered to be longer, larger, and richer than any of our separate histories in our divided Churches. Such a study would focus not only on the hard cores of disagreement between us, but also on the positive discoveries there to be made of the various levels of unity which underlie our diversities and dividedness" (Lund 1952:15).

60. This profile and potential of the method, and the feeling of its insufficiency, is described well in the report of the Theological Commission Appointed: "'The method of comparative ecclesiology'; that is, the effort of separated Christians to explain themselves to each other in the hope that they would thereby remove stultifying misconceptions and also discover hitherto unregistered areas of agreement. Most of the participants in such ecumenical discussion were familiar enough with their own denominational histories, and with the history of Christianity construed in the light of those respective histories. Thus the experience of mutual comparison of

done by a highly qualified commission of theologians.[61] It became a deeper exploration of the ecumenical problem and a more critical definition and reflection on the theological problems implied in the work for the unity of the Church than had been presented until then through the work of Faith and Order. After some discussions, there was wide consensus that the core of the study had to be the theme of "tradition." Not surprisingly, to study ecumenical historiography became too ambitious a project. Although "tradition" had become a well-known theme, it was remarkable that it became the focus in the attempt to find a new theme for the ecumenical movement, a reminder that the issue of Scripture and Tradition has been a classical dividing issue between Roman Catholic and Protestant theology. A study of the theme was desired even among the basically Protestant-dominated Faith and Order Commission. There was already in the second World Conference on Faith and Order (Edinburgh 1937), an understanding that "tradition" was an ecumenical concept of great potential. Through the influence of Eastern Orthodox theologians, "tradition" was defined in a more dynamic way for the ecumenical endeavour:

---

these separate histories in the context of a common concern for authentic unity was the first step towards the transcendence of partisan history. In a sense, it was the beginning of a rudimentary sort of ecumenical historiography. Nevertheless, 'comparative ecclesiology' soon reached a point of diminishing returns. Even at its best, it could scarcely do more than clarify the actual issues in disagreement; at its (normal!) worst, it allowed for self-justification in moods that varied from smug intransigence to pious truculence. It is now widely recognized that Lund marked the final flood and the first ebbing of this pattern of ecumenical theologizing" (TCTT 1963:7).

61. The commission had two sections; one North American section, moderated by Prof. A. C. Outler, Methodist, and one European, moderated by Prof. K. E. Skydsgaard, a Danish Lutheran. There were not financial resources available to fulfill the intention that the two sections should cooperate. The North American section concentrated on the aspect of history, while the European section focused on the theme of tradition in Scripture and the history of dogma. The minutes of the meetings present serious difficulties and tensions in the groups, according to Gaybba 1971:16–25. Each group presented one interim report (Old and New 1961) and one final report (TCTT 1963), used as basis for the deliberations of the fourth World Conference of Faith and Order in Montreal in 1963. These reports, together with the section report from Montreal, and the reports presented from the rather modest continuation of the work on this theme, represent the basic material for our analysis here. It was regretted that the sections were not able to work together. Their reports, nevertheless, complement each other. The establishing process and the work of these commissions are described in Old and New 1961:12–19 and in TCTT 1963:7–13. Brian Gaybba has made the most extensive analysis of the study project (Gaybba 1971). This analysis of the project is done from the perspective of the Roman Catholic–Protestant discussion on the understanding of Scripture and Tradition. He writes that the decision to implement this project "caused both Protestant and Catholic theologians in contact with the ecumenical movement to sit up and take notice" (ibid., 1). He gives a brief summary of the whole study process (ibid., 16–25) to which I am indebted in my understanding of the process leading up to the final reports. I find it to be sufficient to scrutinize only the final reports as the most relevant for my purpose here.

"By tradition is meant the living stream of the Church's life."[62] If tradition was defined as "the living stream," somehow common for the churches, it naturally had to be studied as something more than a matter of division. The theme of tradition had been "taken up with astonishing vigour,"[63] but mostly within the confessional churches and families in the decades between 1930 and 1960.[64]

The three most important theological results of the study are these:

a. A theological argument for an adequate historical approach as a necessary supplement to dealing with the theological problems of ecumenism merely in terms of dogmatics and "order";[65]

b. A theological proposal: ". . . this Tradition which is the work of the Holy Spirit is embodied in traditions (in the two senses of the word, both as referring to diversity in forms and expressions, and in the sense of separate communions);"[66]

c. A new approach to the classical problem of Scripture and Tradition.[67]

My questions to these texts are: Did the aspect of attitude (like mutual accountability) play any significant role in these reflections aiming at this new

---

62. Edinburgh 1937:229.

63. Skydsgaard 1961:20. He refers to a "not at all exhaustive" list of 210 books and articles. Lukas Vischer wrote in his introduction to TCTT 1963 that this theme had "even found a place in the columns of the daily press—a privilege rarely given to theological problems" (3). The importance of the focus on this theme at the Second Vatican Council, especially under the inputs from Yves Congar, should not be ignored here.

64. Cf. the introduction to the report by Lukas Vischer (TCTT 1963:3f.).

65. The North American section concluded this way: "Our point, rather, is that if we succeeded at all in identifying 'Tradition and Traditions' as a genuine problem with a bearing on all dogmatic issues, then it is up to the WCC to muster the requisite resources for bringing church history and historical theology into effective partnership with biblical and systematic theology in all prospective ecumenical study." "In the endeavor to reach this level (i.e. according to the previous sentence, where separated churches are in actual, albeit mysterious, process of conversion), a reverent, critical, ecumenical historiography might well be a prime power" (TCTT 1963:26f.).

66. Montreal 1963:52.

67. Section II even formulated a principle of *sola traditione* in their first draft: "Our starting-point is that we are all living in a tradition which goes back to our Lord and has its roots in the Old Testament, and we are all indebted to that tradition, inasmuch as we have received the revealed truth, the Gospel, through its being transmitted from one generation to another. Thus can say that we exist as Christians *sola traditione*, by tradition alone. Tradition then in this sense includes the preaching of the Word and worship, Christian teaching and theology, missions, and also witness to Christ in the lives of members of the Church" (so David M. Payton, in "A Montreal Diary," in Montreal 1963:23–25). Although this principle was omitted in the final version, it shows the direction of the deliberations.

approach to the ecumenical problems? If so, was there a christological or any other theologically argument related to such references to attitudes?

The answer is, briefly, that the perspective of attitudes is integrated with the reflections on why a new hermeneutical and ecclesiological approach to the ecumenical problem is necessary, and is not raised as a subject as such. In the study report and the further discussions of it in Montreal there are some contributions important for the exploration of what kind of attitude is needed to promote the ecumenical endeavour and the theological problems involved. I will present them successively in relation to the two sections of the final report and the report from Montreal.

The North American Report

The first part of the final report, from the North American section, gives evidence that attitudes are included in this new approach in its two main themes, namely, the need for an adequate historical approach to the ecumenical problem and the question of what tradition is. The understanding of tradition is brought to a useful and illuminating threefold definition:[68]

1. "Tradition" in the lower-case singular form is defined as the general category, which includes both the process of transmission (*actus tradendi*) and also the substantive contents of whatever is transmitted (*traditum*).

2. "Traditions" in the lower-case plural is defined as denoting "the several, yet specific, patterns of traditioning by which the separated churches, and church families, have come to be distinct and distinguishable one from another . . . a phenomenological term for the various concrete *forms* actually taken by the traditionary *process*." In the Montreal report it is explicitly said that this means "both the diversity of forms of expression and also what we call confessional traditions."[69]

3. "*The* Tradition" is not so easily defined. A first glance at the paragraphs discussing this problem makes it quite apparent that this is a crucial question in the whole study project. In the North American section of the report, the problem of defining this is openly admitted. Although they say that this is "not because we are more doubtful of its referent but because it *is* a doubt as to its proper use in critical historical parlance," the text nevertheless includes a discussion on what its referent might be, even in theological terms. It is something that is beyond the historical

---

68. Cf. TCTT 1963:15–18.

69. TCTT 1963:17, and Montreal 1963:50. The tradition in this sense might also be in the singular; the TCTT text mentions "e.g. the Puritan tradition, the Orthodox tradition."

phenomena defined in the two first definitions. It gives an impression of piling up everything important, central, crucial, and genuinely christological in all the traditions. To give an example:

> 'The Tradition' is a term that refers to our living Lord in his Body since Pentecost, to his intercession for the Church on earth today, to his continuing presence among his people in heaven and on earth, to his promise that he will continue to renew and renovate his Church . . . in sum, we have come to virtual consensus in this usage: *The Tradition is the self-givenness of God in the self-giving of Jesus Christ, 'for us men and for our salvation'*.[70]

The report speaks several times about the urgent need to overcome "partisan"[71] approaches (which certainly must be defined as an attitude) to church history. This was a real danger when using comparative methodology, presenting oneself in some kind of apologetic role. The first part of the report concludes with a remark on the need to work on a level where attitudes are also involved, *from conversation to conversion*. To get there, serious work on history with the proper attitude is required.

> The ecumenical movement has passed beyond the stage where the "togetherness" of disparate Christians is any longer a good thing in itself. If it is to continue to justify its existence or to serve its avowed ends, it must press behind and beyond its formula of "churches in conversation" to a new level where separated churches are in the actual, albeit mysterious, process of *conversion*. In the endeavor to reach this level, a reverent, critical, ecumenical historiography might well be a prime power.[72]

Two factors have stimulated the partisan attitude pointed out in this text: (1) the history of the churches had been told and used to confirm the denominational history, and (2) the ecumenical conversation has been focused on the issues of dogmas and order, not history. This is in reality a postulate that the accountability required for a real ecumenical dialogue should include a critical and open study of one's own church's history, seen as a part of the total history of the one Church. It is not enough to give account of the doctrinal positions and the structural principles of a church in comparison to parallel contributions from others. The idea of "nontheological factors" is deeply misleading in a historical understanding of theology and goes against the perspective of

---

70. TCTT 196:18.

71. Italics mine.

72. TCTT 1963:27.

incarnation.[73] An adequate approach for "ecumenical historiography," according to the report, requires a certain mood: it is "neither more nor less than a mode and method of historical study which operates on the assumption that the Christian community *is* a reality; that this community has some sort of identity and continuity in time and space; and that its perimeter is roughly indicated by some such radius as the so-called Basis of the WCC."[74]

The required "mood" should be characterized by accountability to this basis, and by openness to "diversity and relativities."[75] It is an alternative to any "sentimental view that 'somewhere' in the Christian past there was an actual ideal image of the unity we seek today and may achieve tomorrow."[76] This acceptance of diversity must include openness for a historical, critical approach to one's own church and theological tradition. We should not read history as partisans.[77] Attitudes are here closely related to what later is discussed under the title of "hermeneutics."

The historical inquiry, governed by the attitude of "historical realism," cannot locate The Tradition, but it can be used to reveal illusions and inadequate attitudes. "Here again, a relativistic historiography can be a salutary safeguard against bigotry. Historical inquiry cannot be used to locate or establish any single historical tradition as *the* Christian tradition. However, if it is sufficiently objective, it exercises a useful veto power over anti-ecumenical absolutisms of various sorts—biblicist, ecclesiastical, ideological."[78]

The historical approach can do away with any attempt to absolutism, challenging any claim that one particular tradition is exclusively The Tradition, for instance, by a postulate of representing an apostolic succession. There is not only one strain of tradition that can be followed back to the only original Tradition. There were many traditions already in the early church, documented, for example, by the differentiated Gospels. [79]

---

73. TCTT 1963:7–9. "For if theology is, in some sense or other, reflection upon the biblical witness to God's sovereign grace in the history of our salvation, then every aspect of human existence viewed in *this* perspective is theological in context if not in content. Christ's fully human incarnation in the historical milieu of Israel and the Augustinian principate forbids the relegation of human history and politics to some limbo of the non-theological" (8).

74. TCTT 1963:15.

75. TCTT 1963:15.

76. TCTT 1963:15.

77. "We have found ourselves in unforced agreement that no doctrine of tradition, or of 'Scripture and tradition' can be adequate unless it is informed and reformed by a critical sense of history" (TCTT 1963:23).

78. TCCT 1963:13.

79. TCTT 1963:18f. Ernst Käsemann—in his famous lecture given in Montreal—exposed this plurality.

But when the argument says that historical inquiry can exercise a useful "veto-power over anti-ecumenical absolutism," it really takes a further step. To say what The Tradition is not, is implicitly to say that it is known to the historian what it is. There is here a contradiction between the requirement in principle of historical realism in studying the diversity of Christian traditions, and the position that there is a common identity of all Christian traditions. This problem is handled in the text by postulating that the church historian working for the ecumenical project must have two sets of identities, one as a historian (committed to relativistic historiography) and one as a Christian (believing in one God and one Church).[80]

This is not the place to try to solve this classical problem of academic theology. What is interesting for me is how this text urges that certain positions must be accompanied by firm attitudes, to promote the ecumenical process. One of those positions is that there is a unity of the Church in the many historical church traditions.[81] This latter position is a presupposition described as an attitude of mutuality, a willingness to "recognize and acknowledge each other *as Christians*."[82] This must be shown as attitude in two regards: (1) willingness to give up any attempt to define one's own tradition more or less exclusively as The Tradition, and (2) willingness to seek and find The Tradition in the many traditions.[83] The intention is apparently to warn against the inadequacy of absolutism.

But the report is alert to the opposite alternative, a radical skepticism, which not only might exclude not only confessionalistic absolutism but also exclude the possibility to get at all ". . . a describable common tradition in all existing communities which call and profess themselves as Christians."[84] The report warns that a definitely negative response to that question "would finally undercut the present basis of ecumenical study and action." This is based on the presupposition that unity requires that The Tradition can be defined. But the real conclusion of the North American report is that The Tradition cannot

---

80. TCTT 1963:19.

81. TCTT 1963:11–13.

82. TCTT 1963:18.

83. "The Church, living as she does by *the* living Tradition, still cannot make the slightest claim to possessing it by right or merit; must never pretend that she can, or would even wish to, confound it with the manifold of traditions" (TCTT 1963:27).

84. The question was raised by the Orthodox theologian Georges Florovsky (cf. TCTT 1963:13). According to Brian Gaybba (who refers to the minutes of the 1959 meeting of the North American section, kept in the WCC archives in Geneva) the section undertook a phenomenological examination of the transplantation of the Christian traditions and the mutations that occur thereby, especially the case of Christianity in America. The consequence was that "the painful obvious reality of history seemed to rule out any possibility of a unifying tradition on which all other traditions depended" (Gaybba 1971:21).

be defined in the mutually exclusive ways denominations traditionally have done it.

It is exactly the interrelations between the different levels of tradition that bring in the element of attitude. The search for The Tradition in the encounter with other traditions demands a critical openness beyond what had been familiar to churches and theologians. Representing one tradition within *The* Tradition implies being accountable for how this common Tradition is used and preserved. Therefore, the question of "the criteria of authenticity" is raised.[85] Those criteria might be discerned, but the Church cannot define them exhaustively once and forever. The attitude of reverence for the common Tradition means, first of all, an acceptance of being corrected and judged (as *traditiones interpretativae*) by the *traditio constitutiva*, that is, *The* Tradition.[86] This reverence cannot exclude reverence for the tradition of other traditions. This brings us to the core of the theological argument of this report.

Quite remarkable in the definition of "tradition" is the attempt to theologically qualify *The* Tradition as something else than the faith or succession of one church or tradition. To make sure that such an identification is impossible, *The* Tradition is identified as Christ or, more precisely, "*The Tradition is the self-givenness of God in the self-giving of Jesus Christ,* 'for us men and for our salvation'."[87] The christological perspective from Amsterdam, Toronto, and Lund is here carried further into the theological problem of tradition. It has an impact on the issue of ecumenical attitudes in these ways:

a. The Tradition is described as the self-giving event and process of God. To be in conformity with this tradition requires first of all the ability to receive.

b. The Tradition, understood this way, means that any tradition representing it is pointing beyond itself to "their common source and head."

c. The Tradition is therefore somehow embedded in all churches where Christ is present, and will be present. It is "the living history of all

---

85. TTCT 1963:20. This given but not static common Tradition resembles what later (in the study of the apostolic faith in the 1980s) was called "the apostolic tradition." ". . . fidelity to the self-presentation of God in Scripture; loyalty to the central core of faith and order in an ancient Church; the continuity and legitimate development of the Christian message in and through the great focusing of the Christian mind; the experiences of the renewing power of the Holy Spirit, as resident Governor of the Church."

86. "All *traditiones interpretativae* are each and every one under the judgment and jurisdiction of the *traditio constitutiva*; and the 'charter' for this *traditio constitutiva* is uniquely and decisively present in the Scripture's witness to God's sovereign grace in Jesus Christ our Lord" (TCTT 1963:27; cf. TCTT 1963:18).

87. TCTT 1963:18.

history, gathering up the history of Israel, centering in the history of Jesus Christ, and continuing in the history of the church, in *saecula saeculum.*"[88] It is both "event and advent." The proper attitude to the churches where this Tradition is present must, therefore, be both reverent and critical. The temptation to identify one tradition with the Tradition is always at hand. Thus, the churches are accountable not only to *The* Tradition, but to the many traditions—since *The* Tradition is to be found there. This section report does not elaborate the theme of mutual accountability as an ecclesiological problem beyond giving these kinds of premises, but they themselves might very well have been significant for the further processes of ecumenical dialogues and the openness for the other churches in those processes.

The European Report

The European section tried to take a new step in dealing with the classical theological problem of tradition through a reflection on tradition as phenomenon, "tradition as an essential element of human life."[89] After the collapse of the old way of life after the two wars, the trends of modernism with "a hostile attitude to everything 'traditional' grew up" and challenged the whole idea of reverence and responsibility to traditions. This affected the churches, whose identities to a large degree are defined by traditions from the past.

The report discusses this as an ecumenical challenge to the churches to revise and reformulate the relation to tradition as phenomenon. This involves the attitudes of the churches, demonstrated in their conceptualization of "tradition," and in their attitude to other Christian traditions and their understanding of tradition. Tradition can neither be denied as a phenomenon nor regarded as an absolutely fixed entity. Tradition must be understood properly as a *living tradition*, in the sense of a living word in a living community.[90]

---

88. TCTT 1963:18.

89. This was the title of the first part of the European report (TCTT 1963:33).

90. Although Luther's consequent critique of "traditions" as "*Menschensatzungen*" has led to difficulties in discussing this theme, Luther's definition of the gospel as the spoken and heard *viva vox* is used to define what a living tradition is. The report elaborated the difference between this understanding of "living tradition" (as the original tradition made living and relevant in a living community) and the idea of development of tradition, confirmed by the magisterium, articulated by the Roman Catholic theologians of the 19th century, John Henry Newman and Johann Adam Möhler (cf. TCTT 1963:37–41). Skydsgaard has elsewhere discussed this concept of "living tradition"; cf. Skydsgaard 1955:167ff.: "Die Lebendige Tradition ist Wirksamkeit des Heiligen Geistes, der die ganze Bewegung besselt und inspiriert, sowohl im gläubigen Volke als—und ganz besonders—im magisterium hierarchiae, im Episkopat und im Papsttum. Tradition ist hier Entfaltung, Explication und Evolution" (167). Skydsgaard describes this as

Although it is not discussed comprehensively, nor was it a theme of the agenda, the core of the report argues that in order to preserve and use the Christian tradition, certain attitudes are required. These attitudes must be ecumenical and characterized by adequate responsibility.

The basic understanding of tradition is summarized this way: "The word 'tradition' signifies a movement in which something from the past is transmitted to the present which receives it and hands it on to the future. In every tradition there is a substance, *traditum*, and an act of tradition, *actus tradendi*. Between these two there is an intimate relationship."[91]

The report shows a clear interest in overcoming the modern critique of tradition as traditionalism by describing the inner dynamic and sense of tradition in the terminology of modernity: "The only way of preserving what is valuable in tradition is to progress. . . . Tradition without movement is something fossilized and dead, movement without tradition—that is, without a substance which is handed on—makes no sense. . . . History, freedom and tradition belong together."[92]

These perspectives on tradition imply a focus on the giver as well as the receiver. It involves a concern for the attitude, the ability, and virtue by which the whole effort is pursued. Tradition is necessary for human beings to survive, "as something on which our life depends for its true and free development. . . . Tradition is the substance of history." But it can only make sense when it includes some acceptance of the modern critique of authority and tradition as mere repetition and preserving of the past. "Tradition and continuous renewal are complementaries. . . . Tradition is *not* traditionalism."[93]

This phenomenonology of tradition is relevant also for theology. The report demands a *via media* between the understanding of tradition from the

---

"gewaltige Realismus . . . was 'wirklich' geworden ist, ist wahr." His critique to this is not a challenge of the authority, but the claim that there has been executed less authority than necessary, too much has been uncritically accepted (168). Instead of this perspective of evolution on the "living tradition," Skydsgaard argues for another meaning of "living tradition" on the basis of the phenomenon of tradition, the *actus tradendi*, "*wie* die Tradition sich vollzieht": "Indem die Kirche je und je, oft in grosser Anfechtung und in Unsicherheit hinsichtlich vieler Dinge, in actu verkündigt, lehrt, Zeugnis ablegt, tauft, Abendmal feiert, lobsingt, geschieht die Tradition. Hier ist strengsten Sinne von einer *lebendigen* Tradition die Rede, nicht als Entfaltung oder Entwicklung, nicht als Wachstum oder religiöse Vitalität, sondern in dem Sinne, dass hier etwas *geschieht*: nämlich dies, dass der lebendige Herr selbst tätig gegenwärtig ist. Der Geist ist eben die Gegenwart des lebendigen Christus in deer Gemeinde. Und der Umstand, dass der Geist, der eins ist mit dem Herrn (2. Kor. 3,17). Die überlieeferung beherrscht, bewirkt, dass die eigentliche Tradition, um die es schliesslich allein geht, nie mit der geschichtlich fixierten Tradition identisch sein kann, wenngleich sie auch nie ohne diese existieren kann" (176).

91. TCTT 1963:33.

92. TCTT 1963:34.

93. TCTT 1963:33f.

"traditionalist school" of the 19th century and a modern liberalism. The first is described by a one-sided answer to the question: "What have you that you have not received?" The latter emphasizes that each human being has an independent relation to God, without being bound to the doctrine or any mediator.

According to the conclusion of the report, tradition is a matter at the "the very center of the ecumenical mystery."[94] There have always been different forms of Christian tradition, because it is a human phenomenon. Therefore, it is a matter of culture and context, of human diversity. The process of tradition can be a false alteration of the gospel if it is a "slavish reiteration."[95]

If the process (act) and the content (substance) of tradition cannot be separated, it is certainly theologically relevant to discuss how this relation really should be understood. To give account of the Christian faith means to acknowledge "Christianity has entered history." This problem is discussed explicitly for Christianity as tradition. The process is even understood as a prolongation of the incarnation: "Because Christ is the living Lord, the Gospel incarnates itself in different forms."[96] Then the problem can be formulated this way: "If, in this way, Christianity enters history, will not the original event in its absolute significance disappear in the process of history? Will it not perish in the maelstrom of history?"[97]

---

94. TCTT 1963:63.

95. There was a striking awareness in this report of the problems raised later in different types of "contextual theology." "This early tradition was not divine in a 'docetic' way, a 'theophany' miraculously separated from any human form. Tradition does not exist, so to speak, as an 'antiseptic' divine tradition purified from every human element." "Genuine Christian tradition always passes through the living medium of the faithful. Because of their human character there exists *various* traditions understood as interpretations of the same Christ-event. . . . The delivery of the Gospel is never a monotous recitation of the Scriptures, but a living proclamation, the *viva vox evangelii*. This announcing of the Gospel is in itself an historical event, taking place at a specific time and at a definite place within specific situations. Man is never a *tabula rasa*, nor is the Gospel a ready-made once-for-all-worded manifesto, but a proclamation in a form proper to the actual condition in which men are living, shaped to some extent by the particular situation in time and space. . . . Each age must 'translate' the Gospel. This translation does not mean altering it. On the contrary, a slavish reiteration of one wording or form would certainly be a fatal alteration of the living Gospel. Indeed, the New Testament involves a rich variety of preaching and interpretation of revelation" (TCTT 1963:45). The Christian tradition could, received in freedom and responsibility, be linked to—even integrated in—different traditions. Christian spirituality as tradition is described as one of three pillars of Western culture, together with Greek philosophy and Roman order. But this combination is not the only possible one; in other contexts the use of Christian tradition can be combined with other elements: "But such processes of synthesis may just as well take place between Christianity and other cultures, e.g. the Chinese, the Indian, or the African cultures" (TCTT 1963:44).

96. TCTT 1963:45.

97. TCTT 1963:46f.

But how to avoid the process of tradition changing the content of tradition into contextually bound variations, with little or no continuity with the origin of tradition? What is rather interesting for my study is how the report argues that this type of problem, whether it is about tradition in general or about Christian tradition particularly, must be handled by *freedom and responsibility*.

> History, freedom and tradition belong together. Tradition is the coherence of the past with the present and the future: but not an automatic and blindly irresponsible coherence. Tradition does not continue automatically from the past to the present, but is received in freedom and responsibility. . . . Without this free answer to what comes from the past there is no real continuity. Tradition and personality by no means need to be contraries. What is handed down from the past is received in freedom and responsibility. Continuity and renewal are not contrasts but complementaries. . . . Tradition is not only transmission of peculiar and strange ideas and ceremonies, but renewal of life through such manifestations.[98]

The specific question about Christian tradition is this: How can the Christ-event then (*illic et tunc*) be significant for what is happening now (*hic et nunc*)? The answer is that the decisive moment of *kairos* must break through the running *chronos*. The *kairos* is the "unique moment with its responsibility and inescapable decision," in the time of the Christ-event and now. This is an event in which the Spirit works; still, it is a matter of personal responsibility.[99] "Responsibility" here, in the combination with freedom, is to be understood as a matter of attitude. The question would then be: Responsibility for what and to whom? The answer is not given directly, which again strengthens the emphasis that this is a matter of attitude more than a matter of jurisdiction. Although it is elaborated as a personal responsibility, it is here discussed in the context of churches and as a matter of mutual responsibility.

Under these perspectives, the report reflects on "tradition" as an ecumenical challenge and problem. This theme has several aspects: How to handle the different understanding of the word *tradition*?[100] How to find the Christian tradition when there are so many traditions that have become contradictory and mutually exclusive? What is specific in a Christian "tradition"? These reflections are interwoven in the text.

The report tries, on the basis of the ecumenical dialogue behind it, to promote an attitude of *openness and self-criticism* in regard to how the different

---

98. TCTT 1963:34.35
99. TCTT 1963:47.
100. TCTT 1963:36.

church traditions have handled their concept of tradition. The report in itself is more accountable in its presentation than many other reports of this type. There is no attempt to conceal that the Danish Lutheran theologian Kristen Skydsgaard wrote it.[101] He particularly criticizes the Roman Catholic idea of the history of dogma as a "development," and sees in the dogma of the Assumption that "the theory of development seems to have reached its fatal culmination."[102] But there is no less reason for a self-critical approach on the Protestant side regarding their claim of the principle *sola scriptura*, a claim that also represents a system of tradition and interpretation.[103] The report refers to some examples of hope that there is a growing ability to adopt the required self-critical approach to the problem of Scripture and Tradition in both camps.[104]

This theme of self-critique corresponds to the theme of mutual critique and correction. Accountability to what each church is really thinking and doing can be fostered in a real living encounter. The question of "Tradition and tradition" demands attitudes, both courage and patience.[105]

In this text there is a noticeable emphasis on the legitimacy of and need for real encounters and confrontations between theologians and churches. Common dialogue work on the theological problems of tradition is, therefore, in itself a way to preserve and renew the Christian tradition.

> There is no thing such as an "intra-mural theology", a "real" theology, as distinct from a theology directed outwards. . . . When we take an interest in the theology of another church, we do so not only to get acquainted with it, or perhaps to argue against it. All controversial theology is genuine theology, that is to say profound consideration of the Christian faith. If it is not, it is without importance to the other party. And all "intra-mural" theology must constantly invite the other party to join in theological consideration, through reciprocal question and answer. If this does not take place, it is hardly theology at all.
>
> Our present situation is one of confessional disunion. We have inherited it from past history, and to close our eyes to this is to shirk a common distress, a common responsibility—and a common promise. Emancipation from this

---

101. Only Skydsgaard signed the report.

102. TCTT 1963:39.

103. TCTT 1963:46. "Each 'tradition' represents a particular system of knowledge and convictions, self evident to its adherents and validated in its often relatively short history. The appeal to Scripture, perhaps under the catchword *sola scriptura*, does not overcome the dilemma, because the ways in which we represent the Bible are bound to the tradition in which we have received the Scripture as our authority" (Outler).

104. See TCTT 1963:42–46.

105. See TCTT 1963:42.

solidarity is bound to lead to a lack of theological depth. If we take the other party seriously, not only as opponents, but as neighbours given to us by God, theology will acquire a dimension of depth, which is not possible while we remain within our own boundaries. Controversial theology is genuine theology. It is a theological dialogue for the theological scholarship's own sake, a *fides quarens intellectum*, in which both parties share.

Even disagreement has its blessings. The continued existence of the disagreement indicates that it is of importance. Otherwise there would be no respectable reason for keeping it up. Disunion is not done away with the efforts to bridge the gulf which arrive at a merely pragmatic form of unity. The only way of progressing is increased occupation with the matter over which there is disagreement. Unity will grow up through persevering work and dialogue—or else (and this possibility must be taken into consideration) the disagreement will continue, and perhaps deepen. . . . Nobody must give up the hope of unity on the foundation of truth before every possibility has been exhausted.[106]

This is a description of much more than a technical arrangement of further and official dialogues. Dialogue, with the proper attitudes, is a source of insight that theology cannot do without. It is a matter of the real identity of theology.

Here we find a significant presentation of what kind of accountability is required for ecumenical progress. First of all, it is an ability to discuss and reflect openly with other positions, giving up any idea of an "intramural theology." There must be a real "reciprocal question and answer," which, of course, means the ability to be asked and to give an account that can be understood and discussed. The situation of disunion should be a demonstration of solidarity, not the responsibility of one part only. The classical approach *fides quarens intellectum* here is understood as mutual questioning, not the individual asking for herself or himself. The asking faith is directed toward the other that shares the same faith, but in a different way. This responsibility for disunion is not expressed properly by lazy pragmatism, but through resilient and patient work to make the matter of difference clear. This ecumenical attitude cannot, according to the report, solve the ecumenical problem alone. It is necessary for substantial ecumenical dialogue to proceed, even though it might make the disunion even worse.

These attitudes are particularly necessary, however, in the search for a common Christian tradition, or *The* Tradition, because, according to this report, the substance of this Tradition is Christ and because this Tradition is embodied in so many traditions. The core of the argument is the combination of these two points: "Therefore Jesus Christ is the substance of this handing on through

---

106. TCTT 1963:50f.

the generations. God's self-giving in Jesus Christ is mediated to us by the apostolic testimony in the canonical scriptures and by the continuing action of the Holy Spirit in the people of God through all the visible elements of the Church. The apostolic tradition is this *tradere Christum*, and in this sense there is only *one* Tradition—although in different forms and wordings."[107]

The christological reflections play here a significant role in the understanding of the particularity of Christian tradition as change and continuity. The words of Jesus broke the Jewish rabbinical tradition and concept of tradition.[108] The death of Christ as a victim of the religious tradition of the people was at the same time a fulfillment of that tradition.[109] Ultimately, the new tradition of Christ's resurrection breaks the concept of tradition from within. The report not only reflects on the particular and special origin of the Christian tradition, but continues by defining the content and phenomenon of the Christian tradition as something totally different from other traditions. The new tradition ". . . was not merely the tradition about Jesus in the past, not only a tradition with an unique religious content. Tradition is the servant of the living Lord himself, who acts and speaks as one present in his people. No tradition of doctrine can comprehend this reality. Here, if anywhere, the ordinary concept of tradition is broken so emphatically, that it must be asked whether the word 'tradition' can be used at all as an expression of this reality."[110]

This break of a general concept of "tradition" becomes an argument for the need of certain attitudes in the Church. The only way to answer how the Church both can have a tradition in the "traditional" sense of a definite content, and at the same time can say that this tradition is the same Christ now as then, is: "We believe in the Holy Spirit."[111] To get one step further in answering this difficult question, the report reflects again on the necessary attitude: "This means that the Church's action in relation to tradition must express her recognition of the Spirit's lordship and freedom. Here, above all other places, the Church must be 'in the form of a servant.' When she fails to have this attitude, she ceases to be guided by the Spirit and falls victim to her characteristic sin of traditionalism."[112]

---

107. TCTT 1963:36.

108. TCTT 1963:47.

109. "The *paradosis* of which he is the substance, the *paradosis* of the new Messianic people, is the tradition of him who was delivered up and killed by the old tradition and its bearers. . . . A strange clash between two meanings of *paradosis*! . . . But here too, Jesus completed and fulfilled the true Old Testament tradition, the tradition of the suffering Servant. The fulfillment could only take place through a rupture" (TCTT 1963:48).

110. TCTT 1963:48.

111. TCTT 1963:49.

112. TCTT 1963:49.

This christological understanding of tradition corresponds to the dimension of attitudes in two ways: first, Christ as the substance of tradition means that the Christian tradition implies a dynamic interaction between Scripture and the attitude of faith. The attitude expressed by "recognition of the Spirit's lordship and freedom" and "to be guided by the Spirit" is a description of a trustful, receiving faith. It is the opposite of the attitude of "traditionalism." Second, it is a matter of having the attitude of Christ ("In the form of a servant"; cf. Philippians 2).

The christological argument for the unity of the Church is brought further in this report than in the previous Faith and Order documents. I notice for the relevance of my study that this christological dimension leads to an argument for the necessary ecumenical attitudes to other Christians and churches. To believe in the Spirit's guidance as to how Christ is present in the Church means to learn from other churches: "No church can be so completely confident of its own ability to interpret and obey the Spirit that it can assert without qualifications that its own particular tradition is entirely free from some weaknesses and that it has nothing to learn from the others."[113]

Learning from the reformers what adequate criticism might be, a balanced concept is described this way:

> There is a certain criticism of tradition which is only "revolution", and which therefore means dissolution and retrogression; there is another criticism of tradition which, it is true, means a process of elimination, but whose chief element is concentrating on the essential, and which therefore means progress in the understanding of the revelation of God. Such criticism is not hostile to tradition as such. On the contrary: it is necessary for the true Tradition. This is true of any church, even the church which takes a firm stand on the criticism of tradition, but which, nevertheless, is continuing unconcernedly in its "un-traditional" traditionalism![114]

This relation between Christology and mutually accountable openness to the other is most profoundly expressed in the conclusion of the entire report:

> Christ is so consistent and so real a person that it is impossible to have anything to do with him without finding oneself in conversation with the other people who have also found him, and without this conversation being a form of his grace. . . . [The conversation] invites all confessions and all Christians to ask themselves to what extent "their" particular traditions serve (or fail to

---

113. TCTT 1963:49. According to the report, this is a quotation from a paper presented to the commission by Professor Daniel Jenkins.
114. TCTT 1963:49.

serve) *the* Tradition which Christ wished to create, by entering history, by delivering himself to men, by his incarnation and his cross, while remaining their Lord through his resurrection.[115]

Thus, both acknowledgment of the continuity in and unity of the Christian Church and openness for criticism and even for legitimate break can be expressions of a christological approach to the concept of tradition. Both positions are expressions of attitudes, which, according to this report, foster the unity in the Church. The proper attitude of openness, faithfulness, mutuality, and accountability has a dimension of Catholic consistency and Protestant change. Tradition is, according to the report, still shaped by the phenomenon of tradition, giving a *depositum fidei* from generation to generation. But the Church is not totally in control of it.

The issue of *Scripture and Tradition* plays a significant role in the report. I will not deal comprehensively with this theme as such. The report attempts to formulate a new approach, overcoming the dichotomy between the Catholic and Protestant approaches to Scripture and Church. In this context the report formulates an interesting correspondence between being under the radical questions of the word of God and being in a dialogue between churches that can perform the proper self-criticism.[116]

Toward the end, the report discusses three dimensions of critique of the Church or, in my terminology, three dimensions of accountability.[117] They are: (1) the critique from tradition, between the earlier and the later; (2) the critique from the word of God; and finally (3) the eschatological critique, "the last."

Within Scripture, "the earlier" is understood in light of "the later." This is the case for all Christian tradition, too, whether it is admitted or not. And it *should* in a certain sense be so, too. This hermeneutical problem is not in contradiction to the need to "ensure that the 'original' remains in all its validity." The accountability to Scripture cannot be isolated from the accountability to the situation in which Scripture is used.[118]

---

115. TCTT 1963:63.

116. TCTT 1963:53f.

117. TCTT 1963:51–55.

118. Although critical to Newman's concept of development, the report admits, ". . . in its true context it is a legitimate concept." Christianity is a ". . . living historical reality in which there is 'development', because a continuous interpretation of the biblical words takes place, an interpretation in which the present situation necessarily plays a part in the act of understanding. . . . Every new situation places the Church before a *tentatio* and a *promissio*. The temptation is that the message may be altered according to the situation, the promise that a new insight will be given into the gospel of Jesus Christ, which—without anything being added to the Gospel—is necessary if the Word of God is to have authority and clarity in this particular

The Bible as a book is historically after the Church, but as the bearer of the word of God it is superior to the Church. It is always challenging the Church's attitudes—to the word of God and to others in the Church. "The Word of God is always radically asking the Church and its different offices whether they really are servants and not lords." This fundamental question can be asked and answered only in an open and real conversation between churches. This practice of the attitude of mutual accountability is necessary for the Church to remain in truth: "Every Christian church must keep on confronting itself with the question whether its own doctrine and preaching is not being mistaken for the living Word of God which is above and before every tradition. In the realms of preaching and theology, the churches can and must help each other to perform this self-criticism together."[119]

The ultimate critique of the Church is described in terms of escathology. Any "later" tradition is judged by its correspondence to the "last," the end. This is present in the Church, which is "the place on earth where the end, both as judgment and as salvation is present among men, here and now."[120] Only the awareness of this end can enable the Church to distinguish between essential and unessential. In this way the report emphasizes that the Church is accountable first of all to the criterion of God's purpose for tradition: the kingdom of God.

The Montreal Report

Section II at the fourth World Conference on Faith and Order in Montreal in 1963 received the two parts of the report from the Theological Commissions. In their report, they repeat and dwell on most of the ideas presented above. They do not bring any radical new perspectives, either on the issue of tradition or on proper ecumenical attitudes. But the broad confirmation of the insight gained in the study process behind the Montreal report is significant, particularly since this conference had participants from other parts of the world besides Western Europe and North America, and also had Roman Catholic guests/observers. The Orthodox positions and the questions of "younger" churches were raised more clearly, to some extent supplementing the focus on denominational history and doctrinal debate on Scripture and Tradition dominating the report from the Theological Commission.[121]

---

situation" (TCTT 1963:52).

119. TCTT 1963:51f.

120. TCTT 1963:55.

121. The concluding remarks about the Orthodox and Roman Catholic traditions are typical of the attempt to include their concerns: "In none of these cases where the principle of interpretation is found elsewhere than in Scripture is the authority thought to be alien to the central concept of Holy Scripture" (Montreal 1963:53).

This means that the historicity of any theology or tradition is accepted. Scripture as well as Tradition is discussed from the perspective of its christological content. The main focus is *The* Tradition as the content of Scripture and the life of the Church: "Historical study and not least the encounter of the churches in the ecumenical movement have led us to realize that the proclamation of the Gospel is always inevitably historically conditioned. . . . We can speak of the Christian Tradition (with a capital T), whose content is God's revelation and self-giving in Christ, present in the life of the Church."[122]

The Tradition is regarded as the key concept of Christianity altogether. Although the paragraph explicitly mentioning "*sola traditione*" was omitted, the focus in the relation between Scripture and tradition is on Tradition with the capital T.[123] The question is defined as the problem of Tradition and Scripture, rather than Scripture and Tradition. The fact that Tradition precedes the formation of Scripture is noted, but the continuity of Christ present in the Church as an organic relation between the origins of Tradition and "we" plays a more significant role in the argument. It brings all actors and partners in this discussion into the same position, in a combination of Protestant kerygmatic theology, a Roman Catholic emphasis of the role of the Church for guarding the Tradition, and an Orthodox perspective on the living tradition in the life of the Church. This is formulated very clearly in Montreal:

> Our starting-point is that we are all living in a tradition which goes back to our Lord and has its roots in the Old Testament, and are all indebted to that tradition inasmuch as we have received the revealed truth, the Gospel, through its being transmitted from one generation to another. Thus we can say that we exist as Christians by the Tradition of the Gospel (the *paradosis* of the *kerygma*) testified in Scripture, transmitted in and by the Church through the power of the Holy Spirit. Tradition in this sense is actualized in the preaching of the Word, in the administration of the Sacraments and worship, in Christian teaching and theology, and in mission and witness to Christ by the lives of the members of the Churches.[124]

---

122. Montreal 1963:51f.

123. Paton 1963:24f. From the suggested formulation: "Our starting point is that we are all living in a tradition which goes back to our Lord and has its roots in the Old Testament, and we are all indebted to that traditon, inasmuch we have received the revealed truth, the Gospel, through its being transmitted from one generation to another. Thus we can say that we exist as Christians *sola traditione*, by tradition alone. Tradition then in this sense includes the preaching of the Word and worship, Christians teaching and theology, missions, and also witness to Christ in the lives of members of the Church." According to Paton, both Max Thurian and Ernst Käsemann could accept this formulation, but warned against due to the risk of "serious misunderstanding" (ibid., 25).

124. Montreal 1963:51f.

The focus of discussion has shifted from Scripture/Tradition to how *The Tradition* is "embodied" in the traditions: "But this Tradition which is the work of the Holy Spirit is embodied in traditions (in the two senses of the word, both as referring to diversity in forms of expression, and in the sense of separate communions). The traditions in Christian history are distinct from, and yet connected with, the Tradition. They are the expressions and manifestations in diverse historical forms of the one truth and reality which is Christ."[125]

Hereby the need for an ecumenical attitude of mutual accountability, found in the commission report, is confirmed in a profound way. The christological definition of the Church is still important, but there are some more references to the role of the Holy Spirit. However, the Montreal report does not deal comprehensively with the issue of attitudes. But there are some important concepts and reflections in this report also for my theme of ecumenical attitudes.

The report draws the line from the acceptance of traditions as expressions of The Tradition to the need for a criterion to define The Tradition; further, to the necessity of interpretation of Scripture, to the help of the Holy Spirit, ending up with a definition of the need for a "hermeneutical principle." In considering the diversity of such principles, the report recommends a serious study of Scriptures and the Church fathers "in the light of our ecumenical task." And then finally: "Does not the ecumenical situation demand that we search for the Tradition by re-examining sincerely our own particular traditions?"[126] The arguments—or the lack of argument—for a "hermeneutical principle," concludes with a recommendation of a scrutiny done in an ecumenical attitude of sincerity and self-criticism. A similar conclusion is reached in the reflection on how a "history which is ecumenical in its scope and spirit" can help the ecumenical process. And the proper attitude is identified when churches are admonished to recognize how the Holy Spirit enables churches to preach and serve different cultures, to "avoid the dangers of developing a 'ghetto mentality'."[127] The ecumenical attitude can be developed through the work of the WCC, and this attitude is necessary for the search for the truth.[128]

---

125. Montreal 1963:52.

126. Montreal 1963:52–54.

127. Montreal 1963:55, 58.

128. "The content of the Tradition cannot be exactly defined, for the reality it transmits can never be fully contained in propositional forms. . . . This basis of membership safeguards a position from which we may seek constantly to grow in understanding of the fullness of God's revelation, and to correct partial apprehensions of the truth" (Montreal 1963:58).

One important aspect in the Montreal report is the way it understand the problem of Tradition/tradition in terms of "*catholicity*":

> It is in the wholeness of God's truth that the Church will be enabled to fulfill its mission and to bear authentic witness. The traditionary process involves the dialectic, both of relating the Tradition as completely as possible to every separate cultural situation in which men live, and at the same time of demonstrating its transcendence of all that divides men from one another. From this comes the truth that the more the Tradition is expressed in the varying terms of particular cultures, the more will its universal character be fully revealed. It is only with all the saints that we come to know the fullness of Christ's love and glory (Eph. 3. 18-19). Catholicity, as a gift of God's grace, calls us to a task. It is a concept of immense richness whose definition is not attempted here. It can be sought and received only through consciousness of, and caring for, the wholeness of Christ's body, through witness for Christ's lordship over every area of human life, and through compassionate identification with every man in his own particular need. . . . All must labor together in seeking to receive and manifest the fullness of Christ's truth.[129]

Two aspects here bear on the theme of my study. First, catholicity can only be sought and received by a certain attitude: the consciousness of the wholeness of Christ's body. This remarkable description of the required ecumenical attitude corresponds to a standard description of the relation between grace and faith. Catholicity is even called "a gift of grace" that "calls us." Second, there is a remarkable mixture of the perspectives of quality and quantity in respect of "catholicity." The quality of the Christian tradition ("the fullness of Christ's love and glory") is reached only through the richness of the universal church. This implies awareness of "Christ's lordship" and "compassionate identification with every man in his particular need."

The report goes beyond the Church to define the category of accountability of the Church. The Tradition should be transmitted both in "everyday language" and for "contemporary thought."[130] Thereby the relevance for the world of the work for unity in the Church is raised as a theme implicit in the theological understanding of Tradition.

---

129. Montreal 1963:59.

130. Montreal 1963:60; cf. the expression "dual responsibility." This theme was elaborated later in the study of *Giving Account of the Hope* and the study of *Unity of the Church—Unity of Mankind*. See below, ch. 3, pp. 128-56, 227-39.

Two Studies and Two Section Reports on Ecclesiology from Montreal 1963

After the Lund conference, the Commission on Faith and Order initiated two studies in ecclesiology, one on "Institutionalism" and one on "Christ and the Church." Both resulted in two final reports presented as part of the preparation process for the Montreal conference.[131] Although these studies work through the field of ecclesiology, the issue of ecumenical attitudes as a dimension of ecclesiology is not nearly as much in focus here as in the study of tradition. In fact, neither of the studies directly addresses the issue of interchurch relationship. They were laying the groundwork for a common understanding of important ecclesiological problems rather than discussing how different churches should relate to one another. These studies were made in a period before there were many results of interchurch dialogues to provide a platform for new configurations of interchurch relations.

Also, the studies address questions urgent at that time for mutual recognition between churches of different traditions, particularly tensions that can roughly be labeled as "high-/low-church" differences. The study of institutionalism was struggling to find a combined sociological and theological approach that would the personal aspect and the focus on the ordained ministry, Episcopal succession, sacraments, and institutions of the Church.[132] The study of Christology and ecclesiology tried to balance these traditions through the dialectic relation between form and freedom, institution and event, and the Church as essential and provisional. Parallel to this is the balance between emphasizing the identity of Christ and the Church as one body, and, the emphasis on the superiority of Christ as head over his body.[133]

The issue of the Church as the body of Christ is discussed under those perspectives and under the perspective of the Church as human and divine, serving the world under the same conditions as Christ did: sent by God, opposed in the world. The image of the body of Christ is not used, as it is in the study of tradition, to define interchurch relations, with one exception: the distinction between accepted diversity and division is specified by the difference between "diversity [which] may contribute to the health of the body" and "real fractures . . . [which] represent a force of evil which militates against the saving purpose of God."[134]

---

131. Institutionalism 1963 and Christ and the Church 1963.

132. E.g.: "Theological reflections on our subject matter are often predicated on the assumption of a polarity between the personal fellowship of believers and, on the other hand, the institutional structures and arrangements of the Church" (Institutionalism 1963:19).

133. Cf. esp. Christ and the Church 1963:25–30.

134. Christ and the Church 1963:32.

Nevertheless, in these studies there are three types of reflections relevant for the issue of ecumenical attitudes. First is the strong emphasis on the urgent need for *self-criticism* in each church, particularly significant in the study of institutionalism. The intention behind the report was to evoke an adequate self-appraisal, based on proper accounts of the sociological aspects giving shape to a church tradition (so-called nontheological factors). This should improve the understanding of one's own church and the other churches.[135] Second, attention is paid to attitudes forcing unity and disunity, like those mentioned in the study of tradition.[136]

Third, we find the most explicit reflection of the need for an attitude of mutual accountability in a passage dealing with *theological hermeneutics*. An ecumenical attitude is required in the dialogue process, a process going on *within* the Church as the body of Christ. Christology, hermeneutics, and ecclesiology are linked together by the proper attitude of being open to give account and receive the account of how the other is "thinking." To get to the truth of Christ, "his mind," the theologians must be in a listening position to one another, in the Church:

> Christian discipleship is the disciplined habit of thinking and acting in Christ. The Church must let his mind be its mind, and its understanding must be continually renewed and transformed in him, its whole structure determined by his truth. Here is its theological task. Theology is not primarily a function of individuals but of the Church, in which Christians are called to think together and learn from one another. Christian thinking is ecumenical thinking in which we share with one another and refuse to run off on private byways of our own.[137]

The Montreal world conference had *two sections* that in a special way addressed ecclesiology from the perspective of interchurch relationship, Sections I and V.[138] Their respective reports carry the titles: "The Church in the

---

135. "The chief task of the Commission was to help the churches become self-critical of the manifold ways in which their institutional structures and procedures, in interaction with one another and with society, may either obstruct or support the quest for unity" (Institutionalism 1963:5).

136. E.g., Institutionalism 1963:10, and Christ and the Church 1963:50 (where we do find a paragraph with the title "The Church is a communion of love").

137. Christ and the Church 1963:50.

138. Sections III and IV discussed ecclesiology under the titles *Baptism, Eucharist and Ministry*. I will return to the question of ecumenical attitude in respect of those issues in the analysis of the BEM document; see ch. 3, p. 156-85.

Purpose of God" and "'All in Each Place': The Process of Growing Together."[139] In these reports we also find some evidence of the challenges for the churches as they are relating more closely to each other in the ecumenical processes, and how these challenges demand responses in the realm of attitudes.

The report from Section I considers the impact of understanding the Church as "the body of the crucified-risen Lord" in terms relevant for ecumenical attitudes: "Even as Christ's glory is revealed in his self-humilation, so in Christ the Churches are called and enabled to manifest the 'new creation' in obedient discipleship and faithful servanthood in the world."[140] The Church as new creation, as the body of Christ is an ethical dimension of the Church, obeying his Lordship and having "in view the world for which he died."[141] But all is based on the new freedom, "released from every enslavement to be truly human." This freedom "leads to a new solidarity with all God's creatures." This theme is then actualized through several questions for ecclesial self-reflection and evaluation, most of them a reflection on what Jesus Christ did and how he met all kinds of people, ending up dishonoured "outside the camp." "Barriers which separate men today, whether east and west or black and white" are not possible to accept for the Church whose Lord has "broken down the wall of partition." The attitude of *solidarity* with all is a matter for the Church's concern for the world and for the unity of the Church, because it is the body of the new creation, Christ.

The image of the Church as body of Christ is used to make a distinction between an organization with different "parts" and the living organism of the catholic Church. They are related to each other "by an identity of existence in Christ." The congregation gathered by word and sacraments "is therefore a manifestation of the Catholic Church."[142] This has an impact on the criteria for what a Christian Church is: it must be found "in the nature of its faith and worship and its resultant witness." Even more interesting for my study: the consequent "renewed self-awareness of the churches," gained through this theological approach, "must involve profound changes in their thinking and perhaps also in their structure." The image of the body of Christ should be applied in the life of the churches as changed attitudes to other churches.

In light of the difference between the term *council* in the meaning of the ancient councils and the World Council of Churches (referring to the difference in German: *Konzil/Rat*), the WCC is called to have a role of renewal and enrichment both of the Christian existence as well as the attitudes toward other churches. The themes of Christology, unity, and attitude are thereby

---

139. Montreal 1963:41–49, 80–90.
140. Montreal 1963:42.
141. Montreal 1963:42–44.
142. Montreal 1963:45f.

brought into a more concrete problematic of councils and conciliarity, which was elaborated during the coming one-and-a-half decades of the ecumenical movement.[143]

In the report from Section V on "growing together," the "catholic" approach of New Delhi is present already in the title. The report sums up the basis, sense, and task of catholicity, describing the attitude of "striving in faith and obedience," open to be "corrected and enriched" in a profound way:

> The treasure of traditions and experience, of knowledge and insight, which have been given to the whole Church, are available to the local church. A congregation cannot effectively witness amid contemporary challenges and confusions unless it is always striving in faith and obedience to enter into the wholeness of the truth, which the Church everywhere proclaims. In this activity the congregation is both corrected and enriched, and may also make its contribution to the understanding of Christian truth by its own fresh insights and experiences. The growing ecumenical fellowship is making the riches of common Christian truth more easily available to all Christians, and this places upon us the obligation to share more fully in the life of the whole Church.[144]

The report also describes the *obstacles* to the growing together in terms of attitudes. A balanced evaluation of denominations is presented, but they nevertheless "have caused rivalries among local congregations," sometimes destructive "denominational fragmentations." "The Christian community is often divided by rigid denominationalism." The unwanted attitudes are not the only reasons for the problems that the structures themselves also came to be questioned. But there is no way forward unless the attitudes of the churches are changed into ecumenical attitudes: "The churches are called to overcome inertia and denominational pride, which alienate believer from believer and hinder the proclamation of oneness in Christ."[145]

In the perspective of attitudes we can understand what is meant by "unity is the fruit of Christian discipleship." Discipleship is shown in protest against injustice and in willingness to cross barriers, and not least in a wider participation in prayer and worship.[146] All this can be summed up as the "responsibility" of the churches, shaping their relations to other Christian communities and churches.[147]

---

143. Montreal 1963:48f.
144. Montreal 1963:83f.
145. Montreal 1963:85f.
146. Montreal 1963:87.
147. Montreal 1963:87f.

A Word to the Churches from Montreal

In addition to the section reports, the Montreal conference presented its results in the document *A Word to the Churches*.[148] Although they in many ways repeat the study of Tradition as presented above, these texts bring some other elements to the question of ecumenical attitudes. In the first we find important signs that the perspective of attitudes plays a role in the general understanding of the ecumenical task. It was a time of breaking new ground of "ecumenical reality," getting into open and deeper dialogues, for which the study of "tradition" had established important premises. It was also a time of growing awareness of the world as one; as common opportunity and common destiny and under threat of nuclear weapons: "[God] is shaping a world which cannot deny that it is one world, except by self-destruction."

First, the effort of mutual challenge is described as the only sure method of getting deeper into God's purpose for the unity of the Church. "We still find it hard to know what God calls us to keep or to abandon and what he calls us to venture. But we do know that we must continue to challenge each other in the light of God's will for us."[149]

The churches are then addressed by five challenging questions; all opened by "Will you . . ." The five questions present key points of the conference in the form of a challenge to take steps toward an ecumenical process, which demands that certain attitudes be demonstrated. The five questions combine the concern for more information, insight, and wisdom with the proper attitude to foster the processes leading to the goal. The goal itself is a changed attitude, a new type of courage, boldness, and ecclesial self-esteem, born out of another relation to the other churches. The goal is to become "the one people of God in each place, and prepared to realize this new and bold venture of living faith."

To achieve this goal, the questions require what I call "the sense of catholicity." The wholeness of the Church must be discovered. Through a better understanding of others, "we discover fellowship with other Christians throughout all time as well as throughout the world." The sense of catholicity must be shown as mutual recognition of the insight and gift of others, and taken advantage of in sharing of insight "to learn more of him who is the God of ages." The sense of catholicity must also be practiced in relation to other churches and within each church, as recognition of the "whole ministry" of the "whole Church." Particularly in worship the churches can learn from each other.

Most of all, the questions are hallmarked by a call to humility, shown in willingness to reassess and change ecclesial self-estimation and the evaluation of others, particularly the history of other churches, through "going deep

---

148. Montreal 1963:39–40.

149. Montreal 1963:39.

together." This call is given a christological framework; Christ is the Lord of judgment, working through the mutually accountable encounter.

This recommendation of attitudes, shown in a new approach to the other churches, is a way to "manifest openly the unity of life which is hidden with God in Christ." This unity is a matter of faith, and it is a matter of faith how far it can be made manifest. "Today we see openings which only faith could discern yesterday."

Summary

In this phase (before and during the Montreal 1963 conference) of developing new theological and hermeneutical premises for ecumenical dialogue and interchurch relations, we find substantial reflections on the ecumenical attitudes. Some of the features of what I have defined as mutual accountability belong intrinsically to these premises. The elaboration of "tradition" implied focus on the appropriate accountability between the churches in respect of how The Christian Tradition is received, interpreted, used, given reverence, preserved, and handed over between generations. This focus on the matter—not the terminology—of accountability had several aspects.

The classical controversy on *Scripture and Tradition* (which indeed has much to do with criteria of accountability) was explored. Accepting that tradition is a *phenomenon* of the Church (even before Scripture), always present in any use and interpretation of Scripture, the study of tradition could exercise a self-critical accountability on behalf of the different Christian traditions at this point. This seems to have had a great impact on the discussions, and made it possible to take both concepts of "Scripture" and "Tradition" as seriously as they deserved. The accountability to Scripture as origin and remaining standard of the authentic apostolic tradition of Christ is not the same as an idea of Scripture being "alone" in the Christian tradition. It is involved in a process of tradition as source and matter of interpretation, for which any church can and must be accountable.

The study of tradition illuminated that no church or group in the churches ever was and ever will be "alone" in their understanding and use of Christian tradition. Therefore, *how* to relate to other churches (a matter of ecclesiology) becomes a crucial question of hermeneutics. The perspective of attitudes appears at the core of the arguments about hermeneutics as well as interchurch relations and links those issues together. This happened even though "attitudes" were not the topic on the title of the discussion.

The concept of "tradition," particularly when in a search for "*The* Tradition," becomes in this ecumenical setting something other than a matter of denominational self-manifestation; it becomes rather a matter of self-critique, even "conversion." There is a connection between taking the *position* that *The* Tradition is embodied in the traditions and the *attitude* of mutual accountability to the traditions.

This study project emphasized the importance of *historical* accountability.[150] The common tradition is "embodied" in a theological and cultural diversity, and has always been so. Historical awareness means taking account of the historical and contextual circumstances under which the Christian tradition has been shaped. The one Tradition is diversified, and should be accepted as such. That *The* Tradition is one cannot, therefore, be claimed through identification of one of the traditions as The Only Tradition. Thus, the *ecumenical* aspects of accountability are diachronic as well as synchronic.

This implies that a *critical* approach to all traditions is necessary, and that it can be achieved only through a well-balanced combination of mutual critique and self-critique. This conclusion is a result of historiography as well as doctrinal reflections. The first is more or less a description of historical facts. The latter is a result of the *christological* definition of the substance of *The* Tradition. If Christ is present in other churches, the accountability of a church is not only directed toward the "fathers" of the Church. The fullness, the *catholicity* of *The* Tradition can be found only in the open and accountable encounter with others, not by "traditionalism" or self-defense.

Through an open and transparent encounter the churches could be supplemented or corrected. The ecumenical encounter is a privileged setting for this exercise, sometimes even described as an opportunity to gain new insight on our faith. The study combined a Protestant principle of critique and the impossibility of making tradition at any stage or in any form an absolute criterion) with a Catholic concern for the sense of "catholic substance" in tradition. Thus, in this study the tradition of the Church was not ignored, but set under adequate mutual critique.

The quest for *The* Tradition thereby helped to shift the focus from the comparative method of ecumenism. To touch *The* Tradition, not as the little

---

150. At the meeting in Aarhus in 1964, the Faith and Order Commission authorized a study on the hermeneutical problem. Three reports are presented in the report from the commission's meeting in Bristol in 1967, under the title "Scripture and Tradition" ("The Significance of the Hermeneutical Problem for the Ecumenical Movement," "The Significance of Patristic Study for Ecumenical Discussion," and "The Importance of the Conciliar Process in the Ancient Church for the Ecumenical Movement"); see *Studies* 1968:32–59. The study of biblical hermeneutics elaborated the problems raised in the tradition study, particularly the need for historical critical exegesis and the importance of acknowledging the unity in diversity within Scripture. It did not bring any particular new aspect to the issue of ecumenical attitudes, nor did the study of the patristic texts. Still, these studies confirmed the relevance of mutual critique and confrontation within the Church. The Christian tradition was at time a living tradition, "a critical process in which the question of truth was raised ever anew" (ibid., 46f.). The third report about the councils will be discussed below, together with other texts about conciliarity.

minimum of common elements, but understood as a long, rich, and living tradition, always renewing itself, encountering new situations and cultures, requires processes of mutual accountability.

Because *The* Tradition is in its nature directed toward entire humankind, the circle of partners to which the churches are accountable has to be seen in that perspective. Maybe paradoxically, but to preserve the Christian tradition adequately, it should be constantly renewed and supplemented through a constant encounter with new cultures, generations, and groups of people.

The participants in the work on tradition (before and in Montreal) were reluctant to establish formal criteria for defining *The* Tradition. The question was not left behind, however. A *christological* focus and a definition of *The* Tradition as Christ, given to humankind and for humankind, present in the Church though the Holy Spirit, have implications for an understanding of what kind of accountability the carriers of this tradition have. The center of Scripture in Jesus Christ cannot be out of focus if the concern for The Tradition is to be maintained. The christological focus is also a critical standard for what is relevant and useful in the manifold traditions developed after the establishment of Scripture.

The core of the "living tradition" is defined as the living and present Christ. This implies that the accountability to Christ cannot be understood only as accountability to the texts about Christ. The presence of Christ is several times in these texts defined as his saving presence. Accountability for *The* Tradition, which is the presence of Christ, can therefore not be separated from the concern for those who shall be saved and renewed and will live by *The* Tradition. Mutual accountability is not directed only toward an accountable persistence of the historical accounts. It also has an eschatological dimension.

Christian unity requires that Christians and churches follow Christ in his humbleness and attitude of openness and servanthood. To learn from one another in the body of Christ is the way to learn what is the mind of Christ. The ecumenical interchurch relations are the privileged situation to come closer to Christ, to learn more about Christ's will, and to be shaped in his image. In these texts, it is mostly related to hermeneutical issues, in the sense of finding the truth and mind of Christ. The description of these attitudes has much in common with what I have called the attitude of mutual accountability. This has to be understood also as an eschatological accountability. The evaluation of the "later" versus the "earlier" always has to be under the judgment of the "last."

In all these reflections, the questions of hermeneutics are pushed toward an *ecumenical ecclesiology*. The accounts of each denomination should get beyond the "partisan" and confessional histories of their own traditions. These accounts have to be supplemented through living encounters. The method of comparison was left behind in search for new common ground and a dawning concern for *dialogue*. The diversity or even differences acknowledged between the different confessions and theologians were tentatively understood in the frame of a diversified universal Church.

In the report from Montreal we find some descriptions of the significance of ecumenical attitudes (echoing the studies before Montreal). The attitudes are not developed as a theme of ecclesiology, rather as a matter of proper hermeneutics within the framework of interchurch ecclesiology. The attitudes required are humbleness, willingness to learn, to accept critique and make reassessments, even to repent and undergo "conversion." Therefore, openness and frankness in the mutual encounter is necessary to develop the sense of catholicity in regard of the wholeness in *The* Christian Tradition, historically and universally. These dimensions of mutual accountability are complemented by the concept of mutual commitment in the declaration of unity from New Delhi. The dominant perspective in respect to ecumenical attitudes is what was needed at this entrance into deeper interchurch dialogues.

The ecumenical attitudes were not discussed primarily as an ethical or sociological approach to interchurch fellowship. They were most of all—in these Faith and Order-related texts, *seen as a matter of theology*, concerning the fellowship of the Church as *koinonia* with a christological basis (being the body of Christ) and pattern (following Christ). Required ecumenical attitudes were described as expressions of the *catholicity* of the Church, having a sense of the accountability to the whole Church. The aspect of *conciliarity* was also paid some attention, a sign of what would be on the agenda in the years after Montreal.

Summary: Ecumenical Attitudes as Premises in the Pioneer Phase of the WCC

We can conclude that ecumenical attitudes were important when the premises were laid for the life together in a new ecumenical phase in this period from Amsterdam to Montreal. A new type of interchurch institution was inaugurated (the WCC). The accountability to one another demonstrated during the wartime became a model of ecumenical fellowship. The fellowship of churches in the WCC required more accountability than the former "movements." The impossibility and inadequacy of efforts to establish a new Church had to be compensated by affirmations of belonging together, recognizing one another as churches, and willingness to do together what was possible. Such recommendations and affirmations were partly articulated in terms of what I have called ecumenical attitudes. They were to a large extent defined as the attitudes corresponding to being the body of Christ, as this Pauline image was interpreted: mutual love, respect, acknowledgment, being aware of one another in love and care.

In this period we also find a strong attempt to explicate The Tradition common for the churches, making it possible to relate to the traditions represented by the different churches and denominations. This approach required critical as well as constructive attitudes. A critical approach to the history of each Church and tradition, as well as to the former methodology of interchurch affairs and disputes, was articulated. Christ as the living tradition in all churches makes it necessary to be mutually accountable to one another.

Thus, the texts from this first decade and a half confirm the importance of ecumenical attitudes and the relevance of mutual accountability, without using that terminology. This can be seen as a sign of the inevitable role of attitudes when overall premises for interchurch relationship should be defined. The qualities of relations in terms of attitudes were not presented as substitutes of issues of Faith or Order, but as premises to proceed in those fields. Whether this is the case in the succeeding period of addressing more specific ecumenical problems will be the question in the next chapter.

CHAPTER 3

Mutual Accountability and Conciliar Fellowship

From Montreal (1963) to Canberra (1991)

A Universal Council, Conciliarity, and Conciliar Fellowship

Background, Procedure, and Terminology

After the first decade and a half of studies and reflections on the identity of the fellowship established as a "World Council," focus of Faith and Order reflections on unity in the 1960s turned to the notion of "a universal council," "conciliarity," or "conciliar fellowship."[1] These terms became together a model of the goal as defined both before and in Montreal: a committed fellowship truly united and a fellowship of churches with their traditions sharing the same

---

1. The idea of an "ecumenical council" or "universal council" was first mentioned in the report of a Faith and Order study on the importance of the conciliar process in the ancient Church for the ecumenical movement. New Delhi had called for a "fresh general study, among the member churches, of the conciliar process in the Church of the early centuries." The study was initiated in Montreal (1963) and presented in Bristol (1967). See Ancient Church 1968:57f.

Tradition. In this chapter I will explore the relevance for a theory of mutual accountability in the work on the premises for conciliar fellowship.[2]

The real launch of the quest for conciliarity in the framework of the WCC and Faith and Order was the fourth assembly in Uppsala in 1968. In the statement of the previous assembly in New Delhi in 1961, the attitude of mutual commitment was, already, a key notion:

> The ecumenical movement helps to enlarge this experience of universality, and its regional councils and its World Council may be regarded as a transitional opportunity for eventually actualizing a truly universal, ecumenical, conciliar form of common life and witness. The members of the World Council of Churches, committed to each other, should work for the time when a genuinely universal council may once more speak for all Christians, and lead the way into the future.[3]

The tendency to define the goal of unity in terms of an ecumenical council was, obviously, influenced by the convocation of the Second Vatican Council as an ecumenical council. There was also an increasing awareness of the urgent need to formulate a model of the goal of unity that could bind the churches closer together than could the dialogues and the membership of the WCC.[4] The entrance in New Delhi in 1961 of the Orthodox churches into the membership of the WCC and Faith and Order and the Roman Catholic Church's participation in the work of Faith and Order after Montreal (1963) injected an emphasis on their concepts of conciliar fellowship as an "indispensable part of the nature of the church" into Faith and Order reflections.[5]

Fascination with this idea of a council was also a result of the fact that many churches at this juncture acknowledged both the legitimate diversity of

---

2. In this section I will present my analysis of the most significant Faith and Order documents on conciliarity. That means some smaller studies after Montreal and before Uppsala, and of the assembly reports from Uppsala (1968) and Nairobi (1975), a German study report that was to some extent adopted as a Faith and Order study (Conciliarity 1974), a report from a Faith and Order consultation on the definition of unity (Salamanca 1973), and of the reports from the Faith and Order plenary commissions in Accra (1974) and Bangalore (1978).

3. Uppsala 1968:17.

4. On this background, Lukas Vischer, in his address to the Central Committee of the WCC in Cambridge in 1969, recommended "a universal council" as a criterion for the ecumenical efforts. "The word 'dialogue' is quickly losing the magic it had till quite recently and there is even some uneasiness about its use. . . . For dialogue between the separated Churches to be a credible and meaningful enterprise, therefore, it must aim resolutely at the establishment of fellowship; and at the time may have arrived for the Churches to envisage together this goal more explicitly and concretely than before" (Vischer 1970:97f.).

5. Cf. Keshishian 1992:4f.

the churches and the demand for genuinely democratic structures and procedures in the life of the churches. The concept of "organic union" could be too static and not suitable to bridge the gap between the visions of the pioneers and the probable results of the efforts.[6] This double line of motivation for developing the idea of an "ecumenical council" toward more binding structures (Ger.: *Verbindlichkeit*) and more ability to handle diversity and plurality properly became significant for the development of the concept. This double line is also important for my approach to these discussions of "conciliarity."

The culmination of the significance of the model of "conciliar fellowship" was the Nairobi assembly, which on the basis of the report from a Faith and Order consultation in Salamanca in 1973 defined the goal of ecumenical endeavours this way:

> The true Church is to be envisioned as a conciliar fellowship of local churches which are themselves truly united. In this conciliar fellowship, each local church possesses, in communion with the others, the fullness of catholicity, witnesses to the same apostolic faith, and therefore recognizes the others as belonging to the same Church of Christ and guided by the same Spirit. As the New Delhi Assembly pointed out, they are bound together because they have received the same baptism and share in the same Eucharist; they recognize each other's members and ministries. They are one in their common commitment to confess the gospel of Christ by proclamation and service to the world. To this end, each church aims at maintaining sustained and sustaining relationships with her sister churches, expressed in conciliar gatherings whenever required for the fulfillment of their common calling.[7]

The 1978 meeting of the Faith and Order Commission in Bangalore in many ways ended the era of explicit discussions of definitions of "conciliar fellowship." It was difficult to find a sufficient agreement on what "conciliar fellowship" was. The idea of a universal, ecumenical council seemed somehow to have become obsolete as a goal of the ecumenical movement, too. Nevertheless, Faith and Order continued to pursue efforts toward a conciliar fellowship after 1978 according to the three main requirements of church unity that it had been repeatedly defining: (a) consensus in the apostolic faith; (b) mutual recognition of baptism, eucharist, and ministry; and (c) structures making possible

---

6. Cf. Raiser 1971:203f. He also found that the proposal of a universal council was "put forth at a very critical moment in the development of the ecumenical movement," experiencing a "widening gap between vision and reality which is in danger of leading into resignation."

7. Nairobi 1975:60. This text is a quotation from the Salamanca report; cf. Salamanca 1973:121.

common teaching and decision making.[8] Therefore, studies and reports related to these themes could be seen as efforts to establish conciliarity, without spending too much energy on the task of finding a consensus in definitions.

The problem of establishing a common terminology followed the project as a shadow. The study on councils and conciliarity has been troubled by ambiguous terminology in the English language. The English word *council* can designate two different concepts that are distinguished in other languages, including Latin, French, and German. On the one hand, it can be *concilium* (*Konzil, concil*); alternatively *consilium* (*Rat, conseil*). The difference is generally defined this way: the first is mostly referred to as the original meaning of a Church council, the representative gathering of the one, united Church, which describes the goal of the ecumenical movement. The ecumenical councils of (mainly) bishops in the ancient Church are often mentioned as the typical examples of this meaning. The second is often defined as the looser or more provisional fellowship of more or less divided churches, which do not necessarily have eucharistic fellowship. These are councils established at the local, regional, national, or global levels, like the World Council of Churches. In the texts they are usually positively defined as a preconciliar phenomenon.[9]

This terminological ambiguity is not a linguistic matter only. How absolute or definite the difference between the two meanings should be is a crucial issue of the documents discussing conciliarity. The need for this distinction shows also that there is an important interrelation between them. This becomes even more apparent when the more generalizing, abstract concept of *conciliarity* is discussed. *Conciliarity* or *conciliar fellowship* designates the kind of fellowship between and in churches that corresponds to a council. Therefore, to some extent the same ambiguity can be found here. Most often it is linked to the first meaning of "council."[10] It is, however, generally not limited to the situation when a *concilium* is gathered, but designates the fellowship in which

8. Cf. Bangalore 1978:243.

9. Cf. Vischer 1973:29f.; Salamanca 1973:121; and Bangalore 1978:240f. Cf. also comments to these types of definitions in Bouwen 1991:336; Best 1991:231f.; and Keshishian 1992:1f.

10. The use of the term *conciliarity* in the ecumenical movement as the most profound expression of unity in the Church is coloured by the entrance of the Orthodox churches into the World Council of Churches and into the Faith and Order movement. They represent a concept of "council" as the highest authority in the Church, most often as a gathering of bishops. It is also relevant to refer to the interest in the ideas of the "conciliarity movement" within the Roman Catholic Church. This movement was a result of the controversy in the Church in the West in the late Middle Ages, which has become significant for the connotations of "conciliarity." After two popes each laid claim to legitimate authority, the Council of Constance in 1415 claimed to have its authority from Christ himself to settle the matters of faith and to end the schism. Even popes were bound to obey it. This doctrine was contested from the time of the Council in Florence (1438–39), and certainly opposed by the First Vatican Council (1870), but played an important role again in the Second Vatican Council.

such a gathering is possible. This means that "conciliar fellowship" can be used to define (a) a concrete gathering in and between churches, or (b) a model of unity and goal for the ecumenical movement,[11] and thus (c) a criterion for the ecumenical movement.[12] Therefore, conciliarity is a criterion corresponding to the standards of a council. This means that the role of councils in the second meaning (*consilium*) is important for the establishment of a conciliar life in the first meaning (*concilium*). The qualities of the first can (at least to some degree) be realized already in processes related to a *consilium*.

In deliberations on different levels of conciliar life, reflections on presuppositions, premises, procedures, and responsible relations could be expected to touch central elements of a definition of mutual accountability. Is mutual accountability an attitude typical for the goal (*concilium*), for the provisional state (*consilium*), or is it rather describing a common feature for both? If it is the latter, reflections on conciliarity could give important elements to a theory of mutual accountability. The dimension of ecumenical attitude could contribute to the concept of conciliarity in such a way that the preconciliar levels of ecumenical fellowship cannot be disregarded as null and void compared to the ideal goal of an ecumenical council.

Some Theological Dimensions of Conciliarity in Respect of Ecumenical Attitudes

Catholicity

The theological significance of the *catholicity* of the Church became an important basis for launching conciliarity as model of the unity of the Church. This attribute of the Church has several aspects important for the dimension of ecumenical attitude.

Catholicity as the universality of the Church was a dominating feature in the Uppsala report, which announced the idea of a "conciliar form of common life" and a "genuine, universal council." In its explanation of what catholicity means, the Uppsala report reflects on attitudes as an important dimension of the *quality* of the Church:

> Since Christ lived, died and rose again for all mankind, catholicity is the opposite of all kinds of egoism and particularism. It is the quality by which the Church expresses the fullness, the integrity and the totality of life in Christ.... Members of the Church should reflect the integrity and wholeness which is the essential character of the Church. One measure of her internal

---

11. This is the basic view of Aram Keshishian; Keshishian 1992.
12. See Vischer in his interpretation of the Uppsala report; cf. Vischer 1969 (World Council of Churches/CC):183f.

unity is that it is said of believers that they have but one heart and one soul (Acts 4:32; Phil. 2:1-12). There are then two factors in it: the unifying grace of the Spirit and the humble efforts of the believers, who do not seek their own, but are united in faith, in adoration, and in love and service of Christ for the sake of the world. Catholicity is a gift of the Spirit, but it is also a task, a call and an engagement. . . . So to the emphasis on "all in each place" we would now add a fresh understanding of the unity of all Christians in all places. This calls the churches in all places to realize that they belong together and are called to act together. . . . But the clearest obstacle to manifestation of the churches' universality is their inability to understand the measure in which they already belong together in one body.[13]

As we can see, there are two types of attitudes corresponding to the catholicity of the Church. First of all it is the sense of belonging together, the opposite of egoism and particularism. It is the attitude of searching to be one heart and soul. This is closely related to the second, humility. This is also the way Uppsala 1968 continues the understanding of unity from New Delhi 1961, as an exploration of what it means to be "a fully committed fellowship."[14] This attitude is defined as something different from solidarity only with selected groups, which might be the background for discrimination and racism. The Uppsala report explicitly describes the attitudes expressed in "racism of every kind" as "a denial of catholicity." That some are excluded on the basis of racial segregation when gathered in Christ's name demands a firm attitude from the Catholic Church: "the most passionate rejection."[15]

Conciliarity and the Quest for Reconciliation in Eucharist

A constantly repeated theme in the texts regarding a universal council is the role of eucharist: Is it a means toward a council or the goal of the ecumenical efforts? There seems to be a wide consensus that the conciliar fellowship must

---

13. Uppsala 1968:13. 17.

14. Cf. the quotation above, referring to the fellowship of the WCC as churches "committed to each other" (Uppsala 1968:17). Lukas Vischer pursued this perspective when he elaborated the theme of a universal council for the WCC Central Committee in 1969, reminding of the universal solidarity required in the Church. "A fellowship of holding a council further presupposes a definite sense of universal solidarity. The churches cannot reach valid conclusions unless they are aware that in Christ they belong together for better of for worse as one body and are responsible for one another." "Modifying a sentence by Bonhoeffer one could say: To make demands and then inwardly or outwardly to separate off is the way of 'cheap' renewal. To accept the fellowship in all its weakness and to venture forwards on this weak ground, is costly renewal" (Vischer 1970:101, 106).

15. Uppsala 1968:14. 18.

be a fellowship of unity, and therefore a eucharistic fellowship.[16] The dividing question seems to be what is required, in respect to eucharistic fellowship, to call something a conciliar fellowship in the proper sense.

There was no disagreement on the importance of the close relation between conciliar fellowship and eucharistic fellowship, or on the importance of eucharist as a sign and place of developing the ecumenical attitudes corresponding to solidarity: trust, responsibility, and mutuality. The problem was the premises on which a eucharistic fellowship can be established. It is not so clear in the ecumenical texts themselves, but more so in some comments: the Orthodox churches and the Roman Catholic Church understand the conciliar fellowship as a fellowship among those who share the eucharistic fellowship that is defined as the communion of bishops in the historical episcopate.[17]

Conciliarity and eucharistic fellowship belong together in respect to ecumenical attitudes. This is a dialectic relationship: common eucharist presupposes mutual participating in the gifts of the gospel, namely reconciliation with God. The goal of eucharist is the mutual reconciliation expressed in conciliar fellowship. Thus, there are, obviously, important links between establishing a common sharing of eucharist and ecumenical attitudes. The churches should in conciliarity be ready to practice the attitude of mutual, universal solidarity and accountability, "taking account of the other in all of one's thinking and acting."[18]

---

16. Cf. Councils 1968:5; Raiser 1971:208. "Conciliar fellowship cannot but be eucharistic fellowship" (Salamanca 1973:122). In the definition of the goal of unity as conciliar fellowship, it is explicitly said (as in New Delhi) that unity finds its expression in sharing in the same eucharist (Nairobi 1975:60).

17. Keshishian is very clear about this in his analysis of the ecumenical texts and his own formualtion of "conciliar fellowship" as goal and model of the unity of the Church (Keshishian 1992:35–41). "In other words, eucharist, episcopate and conciliarity are inseparable dimensions of the church. Conciliar fellowship is essentially the communion of local bishops and churches" (ibid., 41). This understanding is common for the Orthodox churches and Roman Catholic Church. Keshishian represents the Orthodox tradition, and emphasizes that these churches do not acknowledge the Roman pontiff as *primus inter pares*. Thus, they do not accept the communion with the Roman Patriarch as a prerequisite for conciliar fellowship as an episcopal communion, more than communion with any other local bishop. In an article by Pierre Duprey (Duprey 1978), Under-Secretary of the Vatican Secretariat for Promoting Unity, the Roman Catholic understanding of conciliar fellowship is spelled out in comparison to the definition of the Nairobi assembly, Section II, article 3 (see above, pp. 1-15). It can serve as a comment of great insight in this document. Duprey can very well accept it, particularly due to the passage about eucharistic community. He also agrees that this can be a fellowship in diversity, and therefore needs to be a fellowship in solidarity. Nevertheless, or exactly for that reason, it must be a communion under the central authority in the Roman Catholic Church. "If a conciliar fellowship is to function, it must be clear who is the first, the head, and he must be recognized as such" (Duprey 1978:134–36, at 136).

18. Raiser 1971:208.

These discussions often show a remarkable tendency to elaborate the eucharist as a meal of reconciliation, promoting and demanding certain ecumenical attitudes, no matter which criteria for eucharistic fellowship are used. It is emphasized that the ancient councils as eucharistic gatherings were convoked in times when clarification and reconciliation were demanded, although some of them caused a split in the eucharistic fellowship.[19] This theme is explored in the German study on conciliarity. After saying that "conciliarity is primarily designed to preserve the area of *shalom* in the Christian community," the report describes the potentiality of conciliarity to reconcile conflicts as the *open* room where conflicts are dealt with. This is theologically defined as the celebration of eucharist. This aspect of conciliarity certainly demands a change in the understanding of eucharist and the attitudes to be demonstrated in the eucharistic fellowship. The conciliar fellowship gathered at eucharist is the reconciled and reconciling fellowship:

> If in earlier centuries it was assumed that church conflict set the limits of eucharistic fellowship, the question for us today, with the benefit of critical hindsight, is whether the very opposite is now the case and whether church conflict must not now finds its limits in eucharistic fellowship. . . . As a conciliar fellowship the churches can anticipate and reflect in the meal of reconciliation what God has promised for that day when he will gather a united human race around him.[20]

This corresponds to the first study of eucharist conducted by Faith and Order, presented in Bristol in 1967, initiated as a parallel to the first studies of conciliarity. That report focuses particularly on the "catholic Character of Eucharist," showing an attitude of belonging together with the whole Church. This dimension of catholicity is closely linked to the "agapeic" character of the eucharistic meal. This agape of the eucharist is described as an attitude of willingness to recognize and live in mutuality and accountability to one another. It is the mutual love in a covenantal relation:

> By sharing the common loaf they show their unity with the Church catholic, the mystery of redemption is set forth, and the whole body grows in grace. . . . Catholicity welcomes that "particularity" which renounces self-realization at the expense of others and which has allowed itself to be converted by the

---

19. "Councils may not be understood as organizational super-structures, but always are connected to the nature of the Church as the eucharistic assembly. In any case, the principle intention of all of the councils was to preserve the fellowship of the Church in the Eucharist. They met in the eucharistic fellowship and sought to strengthen this bond" (Ancient Church 1968:52).
20. Conciliarity 1974:9, 19–21.

Gospel, so that it dies to self and lives to Christ. . . . The term agapeic here signifies a covenantal relationship in which the members of the community both recognized their common existence in Christ and pledged to live for one another's total welfare according to, and as they were involved in, God's servant-love in Christ.[21]

The Bangalore report from 1978, at the end of the explicit Faith and Order discussions on conciliarity, is more reluctant to define the role of eucharistic fellowship in relation to conciliarity.[22] The text is only descriptive, saying that some understand the eucharistic fellowship beyond confessional traditions in terms of "organic union," and others accept a unity in "reconciled diversity" as a transformation of confessional identities, in which full sacramental fellowship is possible.[23] The intention of defining the eucharistic, conciliar fellowship as a common goal seems to have come to an open end here; this is a "challenge to all churches."[24] The Bangalore report redefines the vision of visible unity in the most elementary theological categories. What is required is nothing more and nothing less than the attitude of love, shown in the proper attitudes of discipleship: "The love which is in Jesus Christ holds us together. Therefore, it is a matter of grateful and obedient discipleship not to acquiesce in the divisions but to engage constantly anew in the struggle to break old and new barriers which separate us from one another."[25] This focus on love, the most profound and basic attitude of mutuality and accountability, can be interpreted as a sign of resignation in the face of inability to achieve a common understanding of "conciliarity." On the other hand, it can be seen as the essence coming out of the reflections of what conciliar fellowship really means, presented as a lasting reminder for reflection at any stage, whether it is preconcilar or conciliar fellowship.

The Image of Christ and the Attitudes of Conciliarity
This was said in the context of Christology. Love is the hallmark and fruit of the ". . . communion (koinonia) with Christ and of Christians with one another, . . . those whom Christ has brought together in his body through his suffering and death on the cross, and trough his resurrection."[26] The attitudes corresponding to belonging together are found in several references to the Church as the body of Christ, a theme that has been central to the ecclesiology

---

21. Eucharist 1968:62–64.
22. Bangalore 1978:235–42.
23. Bangalore 1978:240.
24. Bangalore 1978:239.
25. Bangalore 1978:238.
26. Bangalore 1978:237f.

of WCC and Faith and Order since the establishment of the WCC in 1948. Although the interest in "conciliarity" might represent one aspect of a move toward "horizontal" perspectives of ecumenism, there were several attempts to anchor the concept of "conciliarity" in a christological understanding of the Church. The perspective of attitudes links Christology with the concept of "conciliarity."[27]

This concept was launched in the 1968 Uppsala report in the framework of entering "a fresh and exhilarating understanding of the Body of Christ." This was more than a stepping stone. It was followed by a theological reflection on the interrelation between the work of Christ, catholicity, and the perspective of proper attitudes. "Since Christ lived, died and rose again for all mankind, catholicity is the opposite of all kinds of egoism and particularism. It is the quality by which the Church expresses the fullness, the integrity and the totality of life in Christ."[28] The inner dimension of the unity of the Church is in this way closely intertwined with the need for external, structured, and visible forms of unity in terms of "a truly universal, conciliar form of common life." Catholicity is understood as the pursuit of the mystery of "incorporation into Christ," in which the proper attitudes can mature. In this way, the Church can be a sign of God's purpose of unity.[29]

The same attempt to base reflections on unity and conciliarity in Christology, we find also in the Salamanca report and Lukas Vischer's preparatory paper. In the famous definition of unity as conciliar fellowship, adopted by the Nairobi assembly, it is emphasized that the Church is founded by Christ and

---

27. Visser 't Hooft articulated his concern for the ecumenical movement in his address at the Uppsala assembly in 1968. He declared that the adequate combination of Christology, ecumenism, and fostering the *appropriate attitudes* was essential for any task of the ecumenical movement: "The crisis is a crisis of motivation, of fundamental attitudes." True solidarity could only be ensured if Christians were true "followers of Christ." Visser 't Hooft had learned through the ecumenical movement not to "identify unity with acceptance of one and the same church order," but "that it belongs to the very nature of the people of God to live as one reconciled and therefore united familiy" (Visser 't Hooft 1968:317–21). He emphasized the christological approach as the only possible one in the new agenda for the churches to be a force toward the "unity of mankind." The time of the assembly was adequately called a "postecumenical" age if the ecumenical movement forgot that "a Christianity which has lost its vertical dimension has lost its salt and is not only insipid in itself, but useless to the world." Christ is the manifestation of God's love for mankind. Christians can be working for humanity only because the Son of God died for all humankind: "No horizontal advance without vertical orientation." Visser 't Hooft maintained that the ecumenical movement should pursue responsible unity among *churches*. It could not remain as a movement of enthusiastic persons and organizations without becoming a "castle in the air." He accepted, though, that the task of unity of humankind was a genuine task of the ecumenical movement.

28. Uppsala 1968:13.

29. Uppsala 1968:11–18, at 13.

has a unity in the confession of Christ in the world.[30] Vischer says that precisely because it is "grounded in Christ," the Church should be directed toward "the whole of mankind." To be catholic means to have the attitudes that come from being in Christ, "the fullness of truth and love and, at the same time, continually be advancing into new areas of human life." Loving openness is a Christ-given attitude.

In the elaboration of conciliarity, for instance, in the German report, additional correspondences between Christology and ecclesiological attitudes are noted. The fellowship of the Church is understood as the fellowship drawn together by Jesus Christ. From the Lordship of Christ it follows that the Church must carry the attitude of searching for unity. To ignore this "responsibility" (in this context I understand "responsibility" both as task and attitude) may even lead to a heretical understanding of the Church. "Jesus Christ draws believers together into a committed fellowship of brothers and sisters, a fellowship subordinated to His will alone. . . . Just as the Church knows that it has only one Lord, so too is can only really live in unity. Individuals or groups who simply shrug off this responsibility lapse into heresy."[31]

One important biblical reference in this context is Matthew 18:20, dealing with the presence of Christ among those gathered in his name, a theme of significance also in the ancient church. This goes along with the invocation of the indwelling of the Holy Spirit. Together these dimensions theologically qualify the fellowship gathered as an assembly worthy of mutual respect and confidence.[32] The relation to one another is also seen as a common life under the cross, in which mutual humility and empathy have been its role. "As we draw closer to the cross, we draw closer to one another." This is something other than making a plan of unity together.[33]

The Bangalore report, concluding the debate of conciliarity, tried to reaffirm the importance of the visible unity of the Church on the basis of Christology. To have the requested attitude of love of Jesus Christ to proclaim the gospel of the work of Christ to the world, the Church must be in communion with Christ and with one another. This summarizes a common basis for the understanding of conciliarity. On the form of conciliarity, however, there was no consensus.[34]

---

30. Salamanca 1973:121. Cf. Vischer 1973:22.

31. Conciliarity 1974:11.

32. Conciliarity 1974:9.

33. Cf. Moltmann 1977:42f.

34. Bangalore 1978:237f. The attempt to formulate a common confession in Bangalore got a striking christological framework and substance, representing some kind of a refreshed christological approach in the work of Faith and Order.

The christological dimension seems to have been easier to expose in terms of proper attitudes than in the elaboration of conciliarity as a model of church unity. But the perspective of attitudes links the christological emphasis in the ecumenical movement with the concern for conciliarity. It is the attitudes of following Christ and being his body which could make the interchurch relationship a truly conciliar common life.

Ecumenical Attitudes of Conciliarity in the Dialectic between Verbindlichkeit and Diversity

Verbindlichkeit

The German terminology *Verbindlich/Verbindlichkeit* is a key notion to describe one very important aspect in the efforts to establish the universal council or conciliar fellowship as the goal of the ecumenical movement. An English equivalent could be "fully committed," "authoritative," or "binding," although none of those are quite satisfying translations.[35] *Verbindlichkeit* is an important dimension of the preliminary definition of mutual accountability I presented in chapter 1.

The concept of "concilarity" should convey a dynamic process, from dialogues and gatherings toward more binding features of the ecumenical movement. This implies that the churches have to be open to changes corresponding to the new bounds of conciliarity. Such changes should be accepted when the churches are convinced they are following the truth that way, not as a concession to indifference.[36] On the basis of the study of councils in the ancient Church, the claim of the councils of authority, by making decisions that "demanded obedience," has been regarded as one important feature of the councils (not the same for the *conseil/Rat*).[37]

"To accept conciliarity as the direction in which we must move means deepening our mutual commitment at all levels," says the Louvain report, and continues: "The acceptance of a Council as a true Council in the full sense implies that its decisions are accepted by the Church as authoritative."[38] The Salamanca consultation also emphasized that conciliar fellowship is not a loose, arbitrary kind of fellowship. "The conciliar fellowship requires organic

---

35. Cf. New Delhi 1961:144. The study "How Does the Church Teach Authoritatively Today?" (Teach Authoritatively 1976) carries in German the title:"Verbindliches Lehren der Kirche heute" (Verbindliches Lehren 1978)

36. This is made particularly clear in Vischer's contributions to launch and define the idea of an ecumenical council; cf. Vischer 1970:97f., 103f. The request of more binding structures followed the line of those emphasizing the difference between *concilium* and *consilium*. Vischer's emphasized the need for changes in the churches, resembling the Reformed *semper reformanda*.

37. Cf. Ancient Church 1968:55.

38. Louvain 1971:226f.

union." This implies attitudes of willingness to be bound together, to learn from one another, to take responsibility for human need together, and to find a new common identity.

> The vision of such conciliar fellowship will, therefore, become a reality only as the churches are prepared to face, at all levels, the implications and challenge of organic union. . . . Union has repeatedly become the occasion for Christians discovering a deeper identity; it has proved again and again to be a dynamic concept with a capacity to respond to new expressions of human need, making possible the growth of a more inclusive identity and fellowship.[39]

This corresponds to an interesting reflection on the meaning and significance of a binding consensus. Consensus is understood as a part of a process, which is actually described by attitudes required for a fellowship searching for an ecumenical council:

> It is vital that consensus be understood as part of a process. It is like a single frame taken from a motion picture: the attitudes seen in it indicate the direction of movement but they are fully intelligible only when the whole picture is shown in motion. . . . The process preceding and following up the establishment of consensus provokes that fermentation of thought and discussion which is essential to the preparation of a future general ecumenical council. A process of true consensus derives from and moves towards Jesus Christ.[40]

The structural perspective of *Verbindlichkeit* conveyed in the Faith and Order reflections of conciliarity was not necessarily understood as stiffness, rigidity, or limited ability to accept changes; indeed, it meant the opposite. Nevertheless, some of the major problems disclosed in the discussion of "conciliarity" were related to what kind of structured authority should dominate the understanding of this concept. This is most clearly reflected in the Accra report. Some wanted conciliarity to be more clearly defined as structure, criticizing the Salamanca report for presenting a "remote idea which has little bearing on present realities"; others find that it describes "the nature of the Church in an external way."[41]

---

39. Salamanca 1973:123f.

40. Salamanca 1973:127. Here the Salamanca report plays on the same features in the word *attitude* as Asheim does in his theoretical contribution. "Attitude" is, in its original sense, a description of the *position* of the body, displaying ("posing") intentions, relations, moods, and convictions; cf. Asheim 1997:22f.

41. Accra 1974:114.

It is important to notice that *Verbindlichkeit* of conciliarity has *both an external, structural aspect and an inner quality*, a matter of motivation, theological accent, and mutual attitudes. The structural element is complicated, not at least because of the role of the WCC as conveyor of the ideas but also an insufficient example of what the churches should aim at. This complication might mean that the aspect of attitudes in the reflections on "conciliarity" might assume an even more important role in a longer perspective.

This double dimension of the *Verbindlichkeit* of a council is important in the issue of *representativity*. This is, in many regards, a matter of accountability. Those participating in a council are doing it on behalf of others, their churches, and groups of churches or groups within churches. It is a matter of accountability to the mandate and the constituency represented. In the study of the councils of the ancient Church, the starting point is the need for conciliarity, defined as "the fact that the Church in all times need assemblies to represent it." Conciliarity is the "necessity *that* they take place, is a constant structure of the Church, a dimension which belongs to its nature." The Church as assembly locally or at other levels needs "representative assemblies in order to answer the questions which it faces."

While it is clear that this conciliarity cannot be spoken of *in abstracto*, but only through studies of all types of councils and conciliar life, it matters further what attitudes those representing the churches in such councils really have.[42] This is an issue of geographical representation. But the report rightly says that the absence of some parts of the Church became a problem mostly because of an "inadequate representation of certain theological positions or ecclesiastical interests." "The ecumenicity of a council does not finally depend on representation of the 'whole world', however; rather it is an inner quality which must show itself in the reception."[43] The representativity of a council depends not only on how the representatives are accountable to their constituency, but also on the extent to which the participants are mutually accountable to one another and their traditions and, not to forget, to the variety of traditions and positions held in the Church for which it is a representative council. The binding character, the authority, the representativity, and the significance of a council have much to do with the kind and extent of authority its decisions gain in the process of *reception* in the churches.

In the study of the significance of the Chalcedon council, reception is a crucial point. The status of reception or nonreception of this council in different churches illustrates very well the importance of the issue of reception for understanding schisms in the Church. Hence, it is a matter for the ecumenical movement. The Chalcedon report describes this also as a matter of attitudes:

42. Ancient Church 1968:50.
43. Ancient Church 1968:53f.

"Dealing with the Council of Chalcedon raises the general question of the Churches' attitude towards the authority of the councils in general."[44]

Consequently, the interrelation between the churches today, particularly between those whose interrelation is governed by their evaluation of Chalcedon, becomes a matter of re-reception. This becomes a question of mutual accountability toward the other churches when this re-reception happens in contact with other churches:

> As the Churches live together in the ecumenical movement in which they experience a re-reception of their traditions the question becomes relevant when they study their attitude towards the Councils: Are the churches ready to contribute to this emerging of re-reception of Christian tradition today by placing their reception of the Councils in the context of re-reception? . . . It is to be hoped therefore that this mutual re-examination will contribute to overcoming problems about the reception of a particular Council.[45]

One dimension of interchurch divisions is the difference in reception of statements and traditions from the whole Church. If the churches are involved in a conciliar fellowship, they cannot isolate their individual accountability to their particular tradition from the accountability and common re-reception of the Tradition embedded in other traditions. The conciliarity of the Church must therefore involve a process of mutual reception, not only of one's own confessions.

One widely accepted premise of "conciliar fellowship" of a common apostolic faith received from the past. It is usually described not only as accountability to a formula of faith or the canon of Scripture as such, as defined by one or more councils; there is supposed to be, as well, a dynamic relation between apostolic tradition, decisions made by councils in the past, and reception of these in the conciliar fellowship of our time. The mutual attitudes of a conciliar fellowship cannot, therefore, be separated from the common accountability to what is given in the traditions from the past.

This theme appears on several occasions in discussions of "conciliarity." The study of Chalcedon ended with an important reflection on "how we are to understand the place of Councils within the whole process of Tradition and how *that* understanding relates together Tradition, Unity and Truth."[46] By this conclusion, accountability to the past and mutual relations to other churches today are twinned together in the perspective of reception. Taking up a point

---

44. Chalcedon 1971:24.

45. Chalcedon 1971:29f.

46. Chalcedon 1971:33.

from New Delhi ("committed fellowship . . . in all ages and all places"), the Louvain report on conciliarity and the future of the ecumenical movement reflected on the "temporal dimension" of conciliarity. Without repeating the past, the proper attitudes of open and real dialogue necessary for mutual relations today are also required for an adequate relation to the past. "It is an essential part of our growth into full conciliarity that we should be continually engaged in a process of 're-reception' of the Councils of the past, through whose witness—received in living dialogue, the same Holy Spirit who spoke to the Fathers in the past can lead us into His future."[47] This theological argument from the work of the Spirit can be, of course, rather flexible. Nevertheless, it is noticeable that the work of the Spirit is not limited to the past councils, and that the encounter with the work of the Spirit should not mean servile acceptance, but "living dialogue," whether encounter with the past or with contemporary expressions. I understand this reference to living dialogue as a parallel to the many requests elsewhere in the texts for proper attitudes of mutuality, trust, and responsibility.

The Salamanca consultation discussed the relation between identity, change, and unity as a problem all churches are facing together in a mutual encounter in this preconciliar situation. Parallel to the reference to a living dialogue, the Salamanca report focuses on the "living tradition." It is defined as "the ultimate and normative reality in Jesus Christ" in which the churches are living and facing the past as well as contemporary challenges. Hence, the argument is that matters of "faith" have to be handled in a proper "order" qualified by ecumenical attitudes (conciliarity).

> In this living tradition we are one with the Church throughout history and at the same time we are liberated to articulate our witness within the conditions and demands of our present historical moment. Identity and change are not therefore opposed or contradictory. Rather our present identity is to be found as, from within its whole tradition and out of its solidarity with the needs and hopes of the world, the Church undertakes to manifest the Gospel of our Lord Jesus Christ in thought, life and action. In this effort, the traditional expressions of our identity as confessions and communions are gratefully received as witness of the ever faithful leading of the Spirit, but they are also time-bound in their terms of reference and relevance. They have helped us to enrich our understanding of the Christian faith and they should also help us in accepting the change that the present moment demands.[48]

---

47. Louvain 1971:227.

48. Salamanca 1973:126. Cf. also Vischer's definition: "Conciliar fellowship is fellowship in the truth of the Gospel" (Vischer 1973:30).

The German study of conciliarity specifies several grounds for a council to be regarded as *authoritative*.[49] None of them are objective, however. The authority of a council's claim to speak the truth will always remain subject to future correction and revision. The never-really-finished reception is therefore an integral element in the conciliar process. This becomes again and again a question of willingness to take a self-critical approach, and a question of ability to receive a decision or text from a council in accountability to other churches represented in the council. The relation to a council is, therefore, a matter of relevant attitudes of "certitude (*certitudo*) but never for certainty (*securtias*) about the truth reached and defined." [50]

Diversity and Ecumenical Attitudes

The study of "tradition" legitimized diversity as a feature of unity. *Verbindlichkeit* required for a conciliar fellowship implies going beyond confessionalism or other barriers, to change inter- and intrachurch relations. Thus, there is a significant correspondence between the attitude of accountability in the sense of *Verbindlichkeit* and the attitude of openness to the position and tradition of others. This is a striking tendency in most of the texts discussed in this chapter, which call for pursuing binding conciliar forms of life as something different from uniformity or suppression of diversity.

The Uppsala report continued this line by integrating the "quest for diversity" into the "quest for continuity," leading to "conciliar form of common life" and "a genuinely universal council" as manifestations of "the quest for the unity of the whole Church." According to Uppsala, this is the way the "catholicity" of the Church can be taken seriously: "Diversity may be a perversion of catholicity but often it is a genuine expression of the apostolic vocation of the Church."[51]

In Louvain (1971) the possibility of developing the looser fellowship of the WCC toward a "fully committed fellowship" was discussed. It would require, among other things, that the WCC became an arena for really challenging and open encounters, in which the member churches could develop understanding and recognition of each other. This is described in terms that make it natural to talk about attitudes and accountability: "The World Council [should] be recognized as a place where the great issues on which Christians are divided may be faced—even at the risk of severe conflict, so that it may in a measure

---

49. The cooperation of gifted church ministers, the representative character of the church delegates, the appeal to the work of the Holy Spirit, agreement with the witness of Holy Scripture (apostolicity) or with church tradition or with the *sensus fidelium* (*sensus ecclesiae*) (Conciliarity 1974:16).

50. Conciliarity 1974:16.

51. Uppsala 1968:15–17.

fulfill the ancient function of a Council as a place where Christians can be reconciled together in the truth; . . . member Churches [should] be encouraged to re-examine and (when appropriate and possible) interpret anew their polemical statements against each other."[52]

After a discussion of how much "organic union" corresponds to "conciliarity," the Accra report concludes that the relation between organic union and diversity finds its balance in "conciliarity" when it is understood in terms of proper ecumenical attitudes: "Conciliarity can be a way of describing a certain kind of church life—at every level—in which a total mutual acceptance is combined with a deep respect for the 'otherness' of those who share the same fellowship but fulfil its obligation in different ways."[53] Conciliarity is both a gift and a task, demanding proper attitudes. This is reflected in the German study report. Faithfulness corresponds to the aspect of gift. Willingness and ability to take the risk of being in fellowship with different convictions corresponds to conciliarity as task. These two—faithfulness and risk—resemble the double dimension of mutual accountability as willingness to be bound and open at the same time. "The Church will only be able to accept this risk as it trusts the Lord's promise that whoever loses his life will save it, and it knows that we can do nothing against the truth."[54]

This discussion, whether "conciliarity" should be understood with an emphasis on an authoritative, structured organic union or more in the direction of providing space for legitimate diversity, is relevant for a theory of ecumenical attitudes. This question was elaborated in a Faith and Order staff paper, presented by Lukas Vischer at the Salamanca consultation in 1973.[55] The paper provided important premises for conciliar fellowship as the model of unity, later confirmed by the Nairobi assembly.[56] This reflection on diversity uses explicitly the terminology of "mutual accountability" to indicate how this can be handled properly in a conciliar fellowship.

---

52. Louvain 1971:229.

53. Accra 1974:115.

54. Conciliarity 1974:12.

55. Vischer was in many regards the promoter of the concept of "conciliarity" as a *model* of church unity in his capacity as director of Faith and Order. He presented papers on this theme as preparations for or inputs to most of the Faith and Order and WCC discussions on it: ; Louvain 1971; Salamanca 1973; Accra 1974; Nairobi 1975; Bangalore 1978; et al. This particular paper was his opening address in Salamanca, contending "in revised form much of the substance of the staff preparatory paper for the Salamanca consultation" (Salamanca 1973:7n.1). Hence, it carries a status beyond being his personal remarks.

56. Vischer 1974:29–31.

Conciliar fellowship means that not only the individual members but also the local communities in each place realize their mutual responsibility. They are not free to ignore one another. The conciliar fellowship requires them to answer to one another for themselves and their understanding of the Gospel. *This mutual accountability* is especially important in a period in which situations change rapidly and new problems are constantly arising. It is no accident that the practice of conciliar relationships has been especially intensive in periods of upheaval in church history.[57]

First of all, the text settles the matter by defining conciliar fellowship as "a much closer association than the somewhat loose fellowship established in ecumenical structures so far," while not disregarding the present status. The present ecumenical bodies are *consilia*, not *concilia*, still they are "pre-conciliar."[58] Therefore, between the two expressions from Uppsala (universal council/conciliar fellowship), the latter is the more important. The universal council is "an exceptional event" showing what should be the common feature of all church life, at "all levels," namely "conciliar fellowship."

But what, then, is the goal of the ecumenical efforts? The text displays here a significant confusion. On the one hand, conciliar fellowship is the goal: "The goal of the ecumenical movement, therefore is not primarily the calling of a universal council but the achievement of conciliar fellowship." On the other hand, conciliar relationships are the means to an end: "Because what is sought in conciliar relationships is a common apprehension of the truth, their goal is the unity of the Church." This shows how "conciliarity" is understood as a hallmark of both the goal and the process of ecumenism. This also shows how the "goal" or "model of unity" is insufficient for ecumenical reflection if they are understood only as an end of the efforts, something to be reached in the future. They make sense as a description of the indispensable features of the unity the churches are searching for. Consequently, such models are meaningful if they help to define the quality of relations pursued at any level. This becomes particularly clear in the quest for a definition of "conciliar fellowship."[59]

---

57. Vischer 1974:30; italics mine.

58. Cf. the definitions below, pp. 128-30.

59. Cf. my reflections on pp. 2-5 on reasons for shifting focus from models of unity toward attitudes. Models of unity can be insufficient for the ecumenical efforts if they primarily focus on the structure (or lack of structure) of unity. The discussions of "conciliar fellowship" show, however, that in the concept of one model of unity there can be a significant element of reflections on the quality of relations and/or ecumenical relations. Nevertheless, the *difference* between structures (episcopal representation, etc.) and quality of relation became a crucial point in the difficulties of establishing "conciliar fellowship" as the shared model of unity.

The text emphasizes the constant aspects of conciliar fellowship: close association, the truth of the gospel, conciliar fellowship as eucharistic fellowship because "it must be in a position to appeal to this common ground, especially when unity is in danger." Within this frame, conciliar fellowship "includes a dynamic concept of diversity in the Church." "Unity is reconciled diversity or diversity on the way to reconciliation." The legitimate diversity is described here as different expressions of the gospel in "different cultures and situations." There may be a tendency to harmonize differences here (as in many and other ecumenical texts). Severe tensions in conflicts or disagreements are not discussed. This might be a sign of superficiality. However, it could also be that these texts take the character of such tensions seriously, that they cannot be handled or solved in a general way. Whatever matter lies behind the general reference to "differences," the texts on conciliarity reflect on the appropriate *context and atmosphere* in which differences can be handled.[60]

With this background, we can understand the significance of references to the appropriate attitudes of a conciliar fellowship. There are several such references, which together outline a terminological field. First of all, the texts proclaim: "Conciliar fellowship presupposes complete mutual recognition. It is unity." This can be interpreted as a prerequisite for calling something a conciliar fellowship. But it can also be seen as a description of the core of ecumenical fellowship on its way *toward* unity. Mutual recognition is what is needed and what is worked for, true conciliar fellowship means "complete" mutual recognition.

A succeeding paragraph of the text focuses on ecumenical hermeneutics, the common search for the "truth of the Gospel." This is hermeneutics of a fellowship in diversity, even conflict. It is a search for truth that is given, yet at the same time a truth that must be found. It must be preserved as the basis of the Church's life. But this can happen only through proper interrelations between local churches (not simply discussions between individual theologians or church leaders).

This statement is followed by other definitions of required attitudes: "Conciliar fellowship will always be characterized by the will to unity." "Full mutual commitment is just as much a condition of conciliar fellowship as it is of organic unity."

---

60. The Faith and Order texts are usually raising ecumenical problems that also are treated more in specific terms in confessional dialogues. This might be read as superficiality in the Faith and Order texts. However, the bilateral dialogues have profited from the more general multilateral dialogue in several cases, maybe because of the possibility to see one interconfessional problem in a wider perspective. The most significant example of that might be the *Wirkungsgeschichte* of the BEM document in bilateral dialogues.

We might say that conciliarity or conciliar fellowship is a principle of mutual counseling, criticizing, testing, committing oneself to another, in order to give the fellowship of churches a visible, binding common structure that has a regulative, authoritative significance for them. "Mutual accountability" can also be defined as a "principle," but becomes more intelligible as a required *attitude* to realize conciliar fellowship. To be mutually accountable in this context means, therefore, to be committed to the others, to be open, reliable, and willing to be accountable to contribution and critique from the fellowship. It also means the willingness to deal with, even live with, diversity, and to some extent also tensions, without breaking or leaving the fellowship.

The Salamanca report confirms the staff text, particularly its suggestion that developing a conciliar practice is more important than a discussion of how and when a universal council could be established. The standards of conciliar fellowship should be pursued, and are also adequate in a preconciliar phase. But there is some more emphasis on the close relation between organic union and conciliarity.[61]

A passage in the German study report provides a similar expression to support my understanding that mutual accountability, as ecumenical attitude, is a dominant feature of conciliarity. Reflecting on the relation between catholicity and conciliarity, the texts convey the sense of what kinds of attitudes are required for a conciliar fellowship, both as a goal of unity and in its anticipation at any level on the way toward the goal. It is a profound combination of the attitude of mutual recognition and the willingness to be involved in a real process, being accountable to the contribution from the other without losing accountability to one's own profile and position. The churches should anticipate the conciliar fellowship they are seeking, finding a way to handle the task of unity in diversity without becoming indifferent:

> One element in this anticipation is the churches' present recognition of one another as churches. They are compelled to this mutual recognition by the realization of their own poverty, by the realization that they can be the Church and fulfil the task of the Church only as they consult together. . . . Conciliar fellowships are dynamic in character. They are created in order to strive for, deepen and make real the unity to which the Church is called, in a permanent process. They press beyond the consensus already reached at any given moment, because they are willing to discuss, criticize and receive the claims, questions and advances of the partners with whom they do not yet have direct contact, in order in this way to become the fellowship which can sponsor a universal council. . . . Conciliarity is a provisional framework of unity within which the diverse contributory elements can rub up against each

---

61. Cf. Salamanca 1973:passim, esp. 123: "The conciliar fellowship requires organic union."

other and mutually enrich each other. In the process a common tradition is born which moves towards the complete unity of the churches, without eliminating enriching diversity.[62]

The Faith and Order reflections on conciliarity take for granted that churches can learn from their history and from each other how they can develop an interchurch fellowship that is at the same time mutually authoritative and hallmarked by mutual openness. In the many reflections on structures for such a fellowship, surprisingly few remarks note how this project has a parallel in modern democracy. Quite remarkably, there are rather meager reflections on how the principles of mutuality and the required attitudes should be set into practice in a real conflict of diverging interests and struggle for power. In the German study report, however, there is one strong recommendation of learning from secular institutions to develop conciliar processes. It is even given a theological reason: "Christians have no monopoly either of religion or of love of the neighbour." However, we do find a warning following immediately: conciliarity should not be mistaken for being "rationalistic concept of tolerance," or "an ecclesiastical form of pragmatic conciliatoriness."

Without solving this distinction between, on the one hand, an ecclesial desire to achieve consensus in a pluralistic but authoritative conciliar process, and, on the other hand, a need to learn from secular institutions, the report ends with a recommendation to study further the potential of the concept of *hierarchia veritatum*.[63] This sounds theologically reasonable. There must be some basic agreement for a fellowship that shall live with diversity and plurality, and some differentiation of the importance of the issues to be discussed. Still, much more should be said about how a conciliar fellowship could learn from principles of democratic structures and studies in sociology of power sharing. This could have helped the ecumenical movement to be more specific about what is required to pursue conciliar fellowship, in which mutual relations could be developed in accountability to one another and to the common living Tradition.

Summary

In the analysis of the texts on "a truly universal council"/"conciliarity"/ "conciliar fellowship," I have found that ecumenical attitudes are an important aspect of attempts to define the goal of unity by these notions. There are similarities between the meaning of these terms in the texts and my preliminary definition of mutual accountability. There are significant differences, too, and

---

62. Conciliarity 1974:18f.
63. Conciliarity 1974:21f., 24.

both are important for the task of formulating a theory of "mutual accountability" as ecumenical attitude.

The most important likeness is how the elaboration of conciliarity as a model of church unity needs definitions of a basic mutual commitment, described as attitudes. This mutual commitment aims at binding and structured responsible interchurch relations where the partners take into account the identity and tradition of the others. In the way toward this framework, the attitudes of mutual openness and frankness must be combined with the attitudes of reliability and seriousness. These attitudes are also derived from the description of the goal; they are not only interim values on the way toward a goal. They fit rather well into the preliminary definition of "mutual accountability."

In spite of differences in definitions of "conciliar fellowship," there seems to be a common recognition that "conciliarity" requires some kind of structure. These structures should foster mutual accountability by safeguarding a certain amount of representativity in the conciliar fellowship and the conciliar organs. It is a matter not only of numerical or geographical representativity, but also of taking into account the different opinions and traditions in the fellowship. This can be done if there are structures conveying openness and processes of reception.

The combination of emphasis on a structure and emphasis on the needed inner quality of relation in terms of attitudes is significant for both the discussion of conciliarity and the definition of mutual accountability. Parallel to this, both combine the dimension of *Verbindlichkeit* and openness toward a legitimate plurality. The ecumenical documents I have analyzed tried to find a way to combine these two dimensions of "conciliarity." In these texts we found that the attitude of accountability can be fostered in interchurch relations if there is an element of structured mutual commitment. To develop accountability as attitude, a structured framework is required, setting standards by which the level of accountability can be tested. This is also, in many ways, the core of the idea of conciliarity.

Both conciliarity and mutual accountability imply a dimension of quality of relations between persons or personal attitudes. The structures are not in themselves sufficient. These personal qualities have a theological basis: awareness of being members of the body of Christ, being open, listening to the Holy Spirit, and most of all, the commandment to love one another.

The *christological* dimension in the understanding of the unity of the Church is important for the concept of conciliarity, too. The link is, actually, ecumenical attitudes requested by the *catholicity* of the Church: the Church should develop a conciliar way of common life because those belonging to the body of Christ could and should be open, loving, and acknowledge the other. Conciliar life is the opposite of egoism and particularism. Unity in the

Church is the unity given in Christ, and, therefore, a unity in following Christ in humility, and a searching for the unity of the Church and the unity of humankind.

The image of the body of Christ is supplemented by the understanding of the Church as a *gathering* in the name of Jesus (Matt. 18:20). Some participants in Faith and Order emphasized that the dimension of humility in life under the cross must be a dominating perspective for the understanding of Church unity as a source of real renewal. "The living tradition" as the presence of Christ is an important element also in the concept of conciliar fellowship.

The christological aspect, however, is not as dominating in these texts as in the earlier. The focus had, to some extent, shifted from the personal interrelation between those in Christ toward the churches and their principles and forms of structured, conciliar life. But the christological dimension is not absent. Conciliarity is a matter of proper relations and personal attitudes in faith and love.

The *differences between conciliarity and mutual accountability* are significant, however. The most important is that conciliarity requires mutual accountability, but not vice versa. Conciliarity is a model of the unity of the Church that presupposes the pursuit and the practice of the ecumenical attitude of mutual accountability. Mutual accountability is here understood as an attitude incorporating the "field" of attitudes referred above: mutual recognition, mutual trust, reliability, openness, frankness, representativity, willingness to be self-critical, and being open for diversity and changes. The pursuit of ecumenism cannot be done without the dynamic given by relevant attitudes. Therefore, the attitude defined as mutual accountability can be seen as the inner dynamic of the goal of unity as well as any level or stage within the ecumenical process.

The debate on "conciliarity" stopped because of major divergence in defining what structural elements are required for a conciliar fellowship. There were clear differences in the understanding of what a proper conciliar fellowship would be. The neuralgic point seems to be the relation between "conciliar fellowship" and "eucharistic fellowship," and the necessity of the historical episcopate for acknowledging the eucharist and the representatives from a certain church. Mutual accountability cannot be an ecumenical attitude without any kind of church structure. It is even to some extent an attitude requiring structural bounds between churches. Mutual accountability could be an ecumenical attitude relevant also apart from conciliarity as a model of church unity. The attitude of mutual accountability and the need for structures fostering this attitude are not limited to that model. In a hierarchic structure as well as a flat, democratic, or spiritualistic church relationship, mutual accountability is required. It is a principle of the standards of mutual relationship required in any intrachurch or interchurch relation. The concept of conciliar fellowship is, however, in many regards closer than other models of unity to the notion of "mutual accountability."

Mutual accountability combines the perspective of binding, committed relation and openness to diversity. Quite often, the dimension of ecumenical attitudes becomes the link between these two dimensions of conciliarity. To enter into a binding and authoritative relationship with other churches, willingness to take the others seriously for what they are and represent is required. The responsible commitment to a conciliar fellowship implies mutual love, which can accept diversity and plurality. On the other hand, if the conciliar fellowship is a binding relation, it could imply that the churches have to be willing to change. In this atmosphere of mutual recognition, mutual trust, and reliability a conciliar fellowship can grow even to the stage of being able to hold a "truly universal council."

Hence, the ecumenical attitude of mutual accountability is necessary to develop conciliarity to combine "organic unity" and "reconciled diversity." Conciliarity needs a structural element and a perspective of mutuality and accountability, understood as attitude: the willingness, the readiness, the reliability, and the commitment to consult, to search for insight, and to show both humility and firmness.

Bangalore 1978 articulated the end of the discussion on the definition of conciliarity but not the end of the quest for a conciliar fellowship. The succeeding studies in Faith and Order should be interpreted as efforts to lay premises for the realization of conciliar fellowship, according to the definitions of premises for conciliar fellowship established at Bangalore.[64]

Authoritative Teaching in Mutually Accountable Relations

A Small Study on a Large Theme

The dimensions of the themes raised in the study "How Does the Church Teach Authoritatively Today?" are not proportional to the relatively modest study programme pursued. The study touched on crucial questions of theological hermeneutics as well as some of the most difficult issues of ecclesiology, namely, the problem of authoritative content of teaching, and who should carry the authority to define the teaching of the Church.

---

64. "Again and again three requirements were mentioned: a) consensus in the apostolic faith; b) mutual recognition of baptism, the eucharist and the ministry; c) structures making possible common teaching and decision making" (Bangalore 1978:243).

The title of the study leans toward the *activity* and, therefore, the institution or ministry of teaching. In combination with the adjective *authoritative*, it easily could lead to an emphasis on the structure of power for making definitions and giving instructions, and the right to demand obedience. But this classical ecclesiological problem, of great significance for the divisions between the churches, did not become the most basic perspective of the study. From the beginning this study intended to widen the scope, to raise more fundamental questions of the meaning of "authoritative teaching," particularly the sense of "authority," a matter of quality of the relations between those teaching and those receiving teaching. This also implies questioning the quality of the institutions, the persons, and the fellowship (the Church) claiming to have an authoritative message as the basis for their existence and service in the world.

The theological importance of the theme of this study is easier to grasp in German. "*Lehre*" (synonymous with "dogma") has a more theologically significant connotation than "teaching."[65] However, in the study the official statements of Church doctrine do not become the focal point, but the manifold aspects of the *task* of teaching in the Church. To "teach" should mean ". . . the multiplicity of ways in which the Church as a community communicates authoritatively the apostolic truth to its members and to the world—statements, models of action, forms of worship, and so on."[66]

The texts of preparation and the report from the study give substantial contributions but not comprehensive solutions to the difficult problems of ecumenical theology in these highly important issues. Some of the proposals from this study are indeed relevant for a theory of ecumenical attitudes.[67]

---

65. The German title of the publication of the final report from the study is "*Wie lehrt die Kirche heute verbindlich?*" Cf. DÖSTA 1978.

66. Cf. Odessa 1977:79.

67. The Faith and Order Commission, meeting in Accra in 1974, made a conspectus of a study on the teaching authority of the Church. It was pointed out as a crucial theme for the ecumenical movement in earlier studies pursued in the period between Montreal and Louvain, particularly the study on the significance of the Council of Chalcedon. In Zagorsk (1973) the working committee recommended a study like this as one conclusion to their discussions of the study "Giving Account of the Hope" (Minutes Accra 1974:91–95; Zagorsk 1973:39. The Nairobi assembly approved the idea, and a short study process was initiated. A small consultation in Geneva in 1976 made a working paper for the study process (Teach Authoritatively 1976). After national groups had worked on the issue, a larger international consultation reviewed the discussion on the basis of their reports and a survey made by Dr. Anton Houtepen (Houtepen 1977; Verbindliches Lehren 1978). The report from the consultation in Odessa, in the former USSR (Odessa 1977), was discussed at the Bangalore commission meeting in 1978. In Bangalore this theme became an important perspective as the third of three requirements for visible unity as a conciliar fellowship: "agreement on common ways of teaching and decision-making"; cf. Minutes Bangalore 1978:40–42 (the two others were a common understanding of the apostolic faith and the full mutual recognition of the baptism, the eucharist, and the ministry). This theme was not followed up according to the Bangalore formulation. Faith and Order was reminded on

Authoritative and Mutually Accountable Teaching

There are two dimensions in this field that appear more or less directly related to the issue of mutual accountability as ecumenical attitude. First of all, to ask for authoritative teaching is to ask for *reliable* teaching, teaching which can claim to be trustworthy, convincing, relevant, and responsible in today's situation. In other words, to discuss what is "authoritative teaching today" is to ask what is accountable teaching.

When "accountable teaching" is considered in an ecumenical setting as the teaching of *the Church*, one must ask how it can be a *common, mutually supported* teaching. Consequently, authoritative teaching in the Church includes being open, listening and learning from one another. This second dimension is explicitly defined as a matter of mutual accountability:

> Finally, the question arises because the fellowship among the churches is growing. Obviously, they are not yet sufficiently united to speak authoritatively with one voice, but increasingly there are occasions when they are capable of bearing common witness; and even if they continue to teach separately, it is becoming more and more recognized that each church, in its teaching, needs to take into account the teaching of other churches. Though they are not yet one, they have committed themselves to the search for unity and for common witness, they need to act with a sense *of mutual accountability*. They face the question of how, in their partial fellowship, they are to fulfil responsibly their task of teaching.[68]

The entire text confirms that the terminology of "mutual accountability" was not just an accident. Already in the working paper (1976), the definitions of the substantial questions to be raised in the study signaled the concern for accountability as well as mutuality.

---

this unfinished task in Vancouver in 1983 (Vancouver 1983:50). Although these themes were to some extent included in the studies of ministry in BEM and in the later study of the apostolic faith, they were not discussed as such before the study of hermeneutics after Santiago (1993). Günther Gassmann said it was foreseen that the Faith and Order World Conference in 1993 would give it a new direction in a study on ecclesiology; cf. Gassmann 1993:205. These texts from the 1970s have, however, only to some extent become "authoritative" in the ecumenical movement. The German ecumenical study commission DÖSTA worked on this theme from 1975 to 1978, and published a report ("Arbeitsbericht"; cf. DÖSTA 1978). This report was (in German) published in one volume together with the Odessa report and Houtepen's study. After an inductive analysis and comparative presentation of how the respective church traditions understand their authoritative teaching, the report presents theological principles and a few theses.

68. Odessa 1977:78; italics mine.

Each Church needs to re-examine its understanding of authoritative teaching and to assess the effectiveness of its practice. . . . All Churches, in fact, are aware that their ways of authoritative teaching are to a certain extent in crisis. The practice reveals weaknesses in their approach. Each could learn from the other and it is vital for all that not only dialogue but actual exchange of experience take place. Openness is particularly difficult in this field, however, because, for many Churches, the way of exercising authority has become almost the symbol of their confessional identity.[69]

We find here that a basis for this study is manifested in the coherence between strengthening the authoritative teaching and the emphasis on mutual, open critique of the existing ways to exercise authority. The focus on these aspects of mutual accountability is a result of ecumenical experiences. It is interesting to note that there is a felt need to define the proper ecumenical pursuit as more than "dialogue." This can be interpreted as a critique of ecumenical encounter that has no deeper level than information and contributions to mutual understanding. Without using the words, the text is here appealing for more accountability in the sense of more real openness, which means more real willingness to be mutually confronted at the most neuralgic points of confessional identity.

The working paper continues by raising the issue of "Authoritative teaching in ecumenical solidarity," and exposes a dimension of authoritative teaching that conveys a very important aspect of ecumenical attitudes: How can churches gain (or lose) authority in the sense of reliability in a difficult situation by showing (or abstaining) from real solidarity with one another? According to this text, ecumenical relations must be really accountable if the aim is being the Church together.

The crowning example is the Barmen Declaration and the churches expressing solidarity with the Confessing Church in Germany, which is regarded as being of unique significance because it is seen as

> . . . one of the decisive reasons for the growth of the ecumenical movement. It has placed the tentative fellowship of Churches before the definite choice between truth and error. The ecumenical movement had to make up its mind whether it wanted to be simply a forum of exchange and mutual enrichment or whether, in its decisions and pronouncements, it aimed at being the Church. The moment of expressing solidarity with the Confessing Church was, in a certain sense, a moment of exercising teaching authority ecumenically.[70]

---

69. Teach Authoritatively 1976:232.
70. Teach Authoritatively 1976:233f.

This profound example of solidarity as ecumenical attitude could very well be defined as mutual accountability. Hence this understanding of mutual accountability cannot be an indifferent acceptance of diversity, but a mutual, reliable solidarity in faithfulness to the truth and to one another.

The text expresses hope for avoiding a destructive contradiction between facing ecclesial diversity, the result of being involved in the life of one another, and together taking an accountable stand in difficult issues.[71] The way forward is previewed as facing the common "challenge of particular magnitude" in a way that forces the churches to respond together.

The connection between authority and quality of relations is a dominating perspective in the study Anton Houtepen did at the request of Faith and Order.[72] He suggests that the issue of "infallibility" plays a remarkably important role as an aspect of authoritative teaching.[73] He warns against exaggerating or underestimating this issue, or letting it be an internal debate of the Roman Catholic Church only. Corresponding to the use in the early Church, most churches of today claim the primary dimension of "infallibility," namely the *reliability and trustworthiness* of the teaching of the Church. That is simply due to the fact that this teaching presupposes that the triune God is the source and the object of faith. This corresponds to a second meaning of "infallibility," namely, the reliability of Scripture and the apostolic preaching, creeds, and practice in continuity with Scripture. "Originally it meant the firmness and trustworthiness of God's providence and promises, of his Word in the Scriptures and in Tradition, mainly in the articles of faith."[74]

The Church has to claim that she teaches authoritatively and is right when proclaiming the gospel of God's "magnalia of the past," because the Church proclaims a message of *salvation*. All Church teaching must serve this basic

---

71. Teach Authoritatively 1976:234.

72. Anton Houtepen elaborates the problems defined for the study far more comprehensively than the working paper and the final report, in his theological survey (70 pages + 20 pages of notes) of this theme, presented on the request of Faith and Order as preparation for the consultation in 1977. Hence, his survey can serve as a useful basis to identify and discuss some of the most relevant aspects from this study. Therefore, I focus on aspects in his text that are echoed in the few common texts from this study, not neglecting how they are given a specific approach in the Odessa report.

73. He uses here reflections developed in his own study of "infallibility" and hermeneutics (Houtepen 1973), and the famous debate on "infallibility" related to the book of Hans Küng. Houtepen gives an interesting historical and ecumenical review of the problem of "magisterium" and "infallibility" to pinpoint the more abstract theme of "authority." Although he has a dominating Roman Catholic perspective on his discussion of the theme, he shows the relevance of the debate in the Roman Catholic Church for the ecumenical discussion.

74. Houtepen 1977:41.

certainty given in the works of God—and in the "anamnesis" of these works.[75] Houtepen here elaborates the definitions of "authority" from the working paper of Faith and Order: "Teaching is here not only the attempt to understand the truth conceptually and to communicate it to the believers. The term stands for the efforts which are required within the Church to make the gospel of Jesus Christ alive to the Church."[76]

Therefore, according to my terminology, Houtepen says that the teaching of the Church has to be accountable to be authoritative. This accountability depends on its reliability in conveying the memory of God's work, and reliability in the use of the primary witnesses of these works, the apostolic teaching. This is the essence of teaching authoritatively.[77] Consequently, I would add, this must be the essential condition of what it means to be an accountable Church.

Houtepen insists that church teaching is not authoritative because of repetitions of texts from the past or by exercise of certain offices.[78] Actually, the content of the teaching as a message of hope requires that the Church be creative and address its message of hope for this and the coming life to the different situations in which people live today.[79] The churches must listen to and

75. Houtepen 1977:37, 41, 45f., and 60ff.

76. Teach Authoritatively 1976:220.

77. Concluding his analysis of the papal or conciliar "infallibility," Houtepen finds that the decisions of those institutions ". . . participate in the trustworthiness of the revelation transmitted to us by Scriptures and Tradition. This participation does not imply 'irreformability' in the sense that no other formulations could be chosen in the future to express the same truth of revelation. Dogmatic decisions, either by council or by the pope, cannot be 'fixed' as the Scriptures are, because they are dependent on this first witness, exactly as secondary witnesses, which must act situationally in the course of history and therefore need constantly new words and concepts to serve the truth of the gospel" (Houtepen 1977:45).

78. "This 'memorial function' of ecclesiastical teaching authority does not mean the reiteration of the teaching from the past through quotations of former formulations or through a jurisprudence on former canonical decisions" (Houtepen 1977:61). In this passage he almost gives a caricature of the Protestant principle sola scriptura and the magisterium of the Roman pontiff.

79. This is a dominating idea in Houtepen's reflections. The following passage is typical: "This holy certainty of faith and efficacious, purposeful acting and living which results from it should fade away in any living Christian community. It must be the basis of its commitment. It transcends confessional diversity and division (to apply Gal. 1:6-8 on confessional divisions sounds rather blasphemic). Each church lives from this gospel and cannot claim it for herself, because it transcends, by God's own primacy, all concrete ecclesiastical forms, confessions, formulations, signs, structures and codes of behaviour. This 'certainty of faith,' based upon God's own 'efficacy' and 'providence,' is the basic content of the oldest meaning of 'infallibility,' as we have seen. If Church teaching is called 'infallible,' it is because of this divine infallibility which bears all 'certainty of faith.' It belongs to the category of 'promise-words,' though it is incorrect to say it has only an eschatological meaning. God's promises do generate hope for this time and history. The authority of the Church's teaching participates in this hope and could, therefore, participate in God's own efficacy and 'infallibility.' . . . Now in our time, churches have recovered the

integrate the gifts of prophecy in order to discern the signs of the time and to promote a real *reception* of teaching. The authoritative teaching must integrate critical perspectives toward the churches and their traditional teaching, sometimes even new perspectives.[80]

The authority of the teaching is dependent on the relation that is created through the teaching and the reception of it. According to Houtepen's study, not even in the Roman Catholic Church's claims of infallibility should authoritative teaching be understood as a unilateral proclamation of "irreformable" statements of truths.[81] The teaching must be *communicative* to be authoritative. The focus is shifted from *determinatio fidei* toward *communicatio fidei*, which I would call a shift also toward mutual relations of a certain quality.

The dominating perspective in this regard (in Houtepen's study) is the necessary *reception* by the community of faith, and the importance of the *sensus fidelium*. The authority of teaching must aim at learning the faith more than calling to obedience, invitation rather than sanctions, without losing the basic authority implied in the message itself.

The perspective of communication is integrated in the Odessa report, albeit in slightly different terminology and by other examples. The required ability to communicate is described particularly in terms of "credibility," under which heading the Odessa report pursues the understanding of the nature and importance of *reception*. Reception is described in the context of change, plurality, and participation. Authority is described in terms of credible and open

---

wholesome function of the conciliar process as a structure for the *basic creativity* which is needed to bring the Gospel, not only into all nations and countries, but also into all times and generations. Acts 15 could be our guiding model in deciding upon the opportunity or the necessity of such a conciliar process; every time the content of the Gospel becomes unclear because of new situations" (Houtepen 1977:60f.).

80. Houtepen finds the "new hermeneutics" to be a necessary correction to somehow narrow confessional viewpoints in discussions of truth and consensus; cf. Houtepen 1977:61f., focusing the need for "infallibility of hope"/"authority of hope" and the gift of prophecy. Cf. also p. 50: "Only if Tradition (taken as the most comprehensive term for the totality of the interpretation process) is considered as the ongoing life and history of man and mankind, can a given 'consensus' have authority."

81. His analysis of Vatican I reveals that the deepest concern was neither to "dogmatize" the teaching of the Church as authority besides or over the revelation in Scripture, nor to "teach an absolute unchangeability of the doctrinal formulations of faith." This keeps, according to Houtepen, the door open for necessary new formulations of the faith. The deepest concern of Vatican I was to guarantee the freedom of Christian teaching over against secular dominion. This was realized through a decision of *where* in the Church the supreme authority of Church government and teaching authority was to be found. Cf. Houtepen 1977:42–47; and Houtepen 1973:367–78.

communication, accompanied with openness to change. However, "change" is not merely "innovation and betrayal" but a way to "be faithful witness to the past." Authoritative teaching must be in active "interaction with the world." This implies that authority demands a legitimate openness for plurality, in contrast not only to rigidity and "juridicism," but also to "indifferentism" and "relativism." The text unveils the tensions implied in these matters. It actually does this by defining the proper attitude of listening. This attitude implies openness to learn, be corrected, and challenged to say "no" even to something embedded in the traditional teaching of the church. There is nothing automatic here, but matters must be dealt with in a way close to my definition of "mutual accountability": "Obedient listening and the desire to teach aright call for the recognition that sometimes the line between truth and error must be drawn. The churches cannot teach authoritatively unless they recognize that they are not automatically preserved from heresy."[82]

Thus, credibility in maintaining teaching authority in intrachurch and interchurch relations demands real participation. This is described, for example, by the terminology of "taking into account" the experiences of persons and groups not usually queried in defining the official teaching of a church. A fundamental theological reason is given why no church can afford to repress active and wide participation in these important processes. Wisdom and insight should not be lost by ignoring somebody: "Such participation is theologically based on the fact that the gift of the Spirit is given to the whole Church and that, therefore, the discernment of truth needs to take place through the interaction of all members. Participation is a way of expressing the *sensus fidei fidelium*."[83]

Reception, as an aspect of participation, is understood as a process of testing as well as of appropriation. It is not only a matter of formal reception through certain structures or institutions. The thread through this understanding of reception is how anybody in a position of implementing reception should act according to the attitudes explicated above. The full authorization of the teaching of the Church cannot be prestructured. The teaching must be "digested into the life and liturgy of the community," aiming at a "participatory reception of the entire body of Christ."[84]

These perspectives turned the focus away from a mere formal or juridical understanding of authority (of ministry as well as content of teaching) toward a personal and relational perspective, in which attitudes are significant. Authority is not described in terms of attitudes but in terms of relations that in reality

---

82. Cf. Odessa 1977:87.

83. Odessa 1977:88.

84. The idea as well as the reference to the German terminology *Anegnung* and *Bewährung* to define "reception" is taken from Houtepen's text into the Odessa report; cf. Houtepen 1977:51, 53; Odessa 1977:88.

require certain attitudes. The attitudes required are openness, willingness to involve the whole Church, ability to adjust and be adjusted, reliability, credibility, and authenticity. The dimension of proper *relations* definitely makes these attitudes more than internal qualities in individuals.

The Odessa report explicitly discusses the problem of handling plurality in terms of attitudes. The churches can get stuck in dissents due to the commitment to new ecumenical relations, but the churches also face the temptation to withdraw from authoritative teaching by avoiding controversial, important matters of faith and justice. These temptations demand an attitude that combines openness as well as firmness:

> Controversy within the Church and conflict with evil in the world may be inevitable if the Church is to be faithful to the Lord. As the churches engage in the ecumenical movement, they must continue to teach the Gospel. The ecumenical movement must not lead to a loose attitude to the truth of the Gospel. What in fellowship with other churches has been heard must in common be proclaimed. How can the churches, in the ecumenical movement, assist each other to teach more effectively in fidelity to the apostolic heritage?[85]

Consequently, authority must be seen in the perspective of *catholicity* in the sense of universality. No truth can be true only for a few, but the truth cannot be confined in general and common formulations. The proclamation of truth requires sensitivity to the context as well as loyalty to the universal fellowship. This combination of attitudes is important for a theory of mutual accountability.

The importance of *relevance today* for authoritative teaching is highlighted and further explored by several examples.[86] These examples could, in my terminology, be seen as arguments for the need to be accountable to the specific problems and given conditions in certain contexts to gain reliability. For instance, in East Asia a church is considered to be authoritative if it shows "faithfulness to the Gospel and demonstrates spiritual strength in adverse social and political situations." In the German Democratic Republic (that is, the former East Germany) the churches had learned that "authoritative teaching must have the character of missionary witness," a credibility that makes the Church understood, providing people "perspective on the meaning of life and the event of history" that "helps them to act responsibly." Therefore, the witness "must involve all church members." The report even responds to the fear of losing authority if there is a contextual variety in the teaching of the Church. "The

---

85. Odessa 1977:89.

86. Odessa 1977:83–86.

variety rather manifests the richness of the tradition as well as its capacity to respond pertinently to different situations."[87]

Hence, the Odessa report gives an important dimension to mutual accountability, already mentioned by Houtepen. The churches are accountable to their own tradition, consciousness, or leadership. They are also mutually accountable to the people living in their contexts, primarily the church members and their *sensus fidelium*. And, finally, they are also *accountable to any human being* who needs the hope of the gospel. Only this way can the churches have an authoritative word of the gospel to speak.[88]

This corresponds to the important distinction made in the Odessa report between "authoritative teaching" and "*authentic* teaching." "Teaching proclaimed 'authoritatively' by the Church could turn out to be untrue (sometimes even after having been enthusiastically received)." The report is rather feeble when trying to define what "authentic teaching" is and does not add much new reflection to the general statement: "Authenticity depends on the inspiring and sustaining power of the Spirit."[89]

After mentioning four types of definitions of authentic teaching in different confessional traditions, adding the conclusion that "there is no single criterion for judging the authenticity of teaching," the report ends up with a proposal for a potential contribution to "ways of verification" from the ecumenical movement. It is, quite noteworthy for my study, an elaboration of the requirement of "mutual accountability." The report suggests that there is no way toward preserving and proclaiming authority in the Church while avoiding mutually accountable relations with other churches. "Can churches be strengthened in their witness by the teaching of another church, even if that church has received it as authoritative in a way which differs from their own? Can the churches, by striving to perfect their ongoing teaching within the framework of their tradition but in dialogical relation to each other, move step by step to greater unity and thus more fully the catholicity of the Church?"[90]

The churches should be able to listen to those not always regarded as authorities, those raising new and critical perspectives, sometimes even from marginalized positions. Houtepen refers to the insights of new hermeneutics, which shows that the truth should be sought in discontinuity as well as

---

87. Odessa 1977:86.

88. This argument raises hermeneutical problems that are not really discussed in the Odessa report. A short comment in the report shows that they were not ignored, although they were not discussed comprehensively: "The sharper awareness of variety raises, however, in a new way the question of the relationship between teaching addressed to the whole Church and teaching formulated on behalf of the whole Church in particular situations" (Odessa 1977:86).

89. Odessa 1977:79.

90. Odessa 1977:83.

continuity, through human "value centers" according to "the will of the people." "We learn about the directive goal of history from our *'contrast experiences'*."[91] This corresponds to the awareness in the Odessa report of appropriate address to the difficult and challenging situations of today, for instance, the needs of oppressed people.[92]

There is a remarkable lack of emphasis on *structures or institutions of authority* in the Odessa report. The focus is on the conditions for and relations of a real church authority, as referred to above.[93] This is a sign of how difficult it is to agree on what kind of structure of authority should be pursued in ecumenical relations, which the study of conciliarity disclosed, too. In the Odessa report we find some signs of how this theme touches the identity of the churches in a delicate way. Although Houtepen pays attention to the specific problems of institutions and the ministry of the "magisterium," he, too, primarily lays a foundation for understanding authoritative teaching as credibility and relevance for what the teaching may concern. Houtepen's text shows the necessity of a theology of authority in relation to ecclesiology and hermeneutics, not based only on one structure and/or only a few principles of authority constituted in rather special circumstances, both contextual and historical.[94]

There is a noticeable openness in the common text from Odessa to *learn from secular patterns of democratic authority*. This has at least two dimensions. First, there is a general tendency to legitimate the values of democracy in terms of wide participation, accountability to one's own constituency, acceptance of plurality, and so forth. This corresponds to the principle of theological affirmation, that is, of taking into account a wide spectrum of contributors, listening to the voices of the people of God. Second, there is some reflection on how the Church could adjust sympathetically or critically to civil powers, according to a higher calling of the Church. This is exemplified in some notes on solidarity with those carrying a unique experience of resistance against oppression and injustice.[95] The matter of truth is a matter of authenticity, faithfulness, and quality, not quantity.

91. Houtepen 1977:50; italics mine.

92. Odessa 1977, esp. 79, 88ff.

93. Even in the passage which lists the different approaches in "various times and various ways," emphasizing respectively personal credibility, ministerial authority, and corporate teaching authority, the Odessa report stresses that authority must be rooted in the *consciousness of the people of God* (Odessa 1977:81).

94. To some degree Houtepen draws the line from his principal understanding of the authority of communications to a critique of the hierarchy of the Roman Catholic Church. For example: "A 'catholic community' will be found where all members are accepted in a non-discriminatory fellowship, where no hierarchy of dignitaries decides about the right faith, but where the examples of a faithful life distinguishes people with Christian dignity and authority" (Houtepen 1977:63).

95. This is not meant as a servile subjugation under patterns of civil authorities, rather the

The text confirms the problem following from the fact that patterns of authority in the churches often developed together with or under the influence of the patterns of civil powers, but did not change with them.[96] Nevertheless, the text really only touches the problem of adapting the principles of democracy in the Church to ensure a credible and accountable exercise of authority. The relation between legitimacy, authority, accountability, and majority is only touched, not solved.[97]

The particular problem of *common, authoritative teaching* for churches together is the crucial point when applied in the particular ecumenical setting. We do find some reflections on the role of mutual accountability (although without the terminology). Although the German study report is made in a wide ecumenical circle, the reflections are implicitly and explicitly coloured by the experiences from the German context, particularly the Confessing Church (Barmen 1933) and the—at that time—fresh result of the Reformed–Lutheran dialogues (Leuenberg 1973).[98] The Leuenberg Agreement serves as a model for the argument, particularly in the emphasis on a common, binding basis, namely the gospel. This basis should serve as the point of reference to which any church must be mutually accountable.[99] Second, the Leuenberg model serves as an example of how churches can be mutually bound and accountable to one common basis of teaching and still have a differentiated or multidimensional way of expressing the gospel.[100]

---

opposite. An example of how the Church should adapt its style of teaching to the context is the recommendation to emphasize "freedom and participation in decision-making processes" in an authoritarian society. The principle of the "option of the poor," which later became a common ecumenical heritage, was not articulated here, although there were some openness for that perspective both in the text of Houtepen and in the Odessa report; cf. Odessa 1977:84 (a reference to Korean Christians' courageous witness and defense of human rights); 87 (in situations of injustice the church may take a "critical revolutionary approach and develop a style of teaching which seeks to manifest the identification with the oppressed classes"); and 91 (a principal reflection over how "the Cross of Christ is the supreme act of identification with suffering humanity").

96. Odessa 1978:86f.

97. The working paper warned against uncritical use of a majority rule in the reception processes of the Church. Those claiming authority in the capacity of their positions, their presumptive wisdom as well as their great majority, can go astray or accept false teaching; cf. Teach Authoritatively 1976:231. Cf. to this point also Houtepen 1977:63.

98. DÖSTA 1978, esp. 18f., 27.

99. The churches must be convinced "vom Primat des Evangeliums." "Da die Treue zur Wahrheit des Evangeliums für die Kirche konstitutiv ist, muss sich jede Kirche nach diesen Voraussetzungen und ihren Implikationen für die verbindliche Bezeugung des Evangliums befragen lassen" (DÖSTA 1978:23).

100. Cf. DÖSTA 1978:18: "Diese Kirchengemeinschaft hebt die Gültigkeit der Bekentnisse der beteiligten Kirchen nicht auf, versteht sie vielmehr als Hilfe für die Verwurzelung verbindlicher Verkündigung in der Heiligen Schrift. In dieser Tendenz nötigt Kirchengemeinschaft zu

This leads to the third point, which is common with the experience from Barmen: common binding (*verbindlich*) teaching is necessary when facing particular challenges or a particular situation. Then the churches must be able to be accountable to the problems of the world by formulating the gospel together in new ways. This implies giving mutual account of what has been taught and a process of mutual testing.[101] Church fellowship demands, according to this report, a common content (but not totally common formulation) of teaching. But this is not to be realized without an attitude of *Verbindlichkeit*, both as being accountable to a common basis and as being accountable to new, common ways of teaching.[102]

Toward the end, the Odessa report discusses several aspects of *common teaching* today. Affirming the need for common authoritative teaching when facing injustice and oppression, the report discusses the importance of "sharing in the teaching" and a mutual "receiving" of one another's teaching. The encounter between churches can shake the churches and create "new understanding and commitment."[103]

There is in the Odessa report a particular emphasis on the need for a binding, authoritative reception of multilateral ecumenical agreements, implying both a comprehensive and representative response. "In order to make decisions representative, the community as a whole should be part of the process. Churches will need, therefore, to promote responsible discussion of ecumenical findings within their own ranks. . . . In order to make consensus real in the churches, the weight of decisions needs to be comparable."[104] All these comments can be seen as recommendations of more mutually accountable procedures between the churches to give their common efforts a sense of being more than a play of ecumenism, but expressions of authoritative teaching.

Finally, one comment on *the terminology describing the content of the teaching*: the working paper of 1976 varies without any discernible purpose between

---

gemeinsamer verbindlicher Lehre." See also ibid., 27.

101. "Die Wahrheit des Evangeliums fordert von der Kirche eine verbindliche *Formulierung* der Wahrheit in den wechselnden Welsituationen. . . . Die Wahrheit des Evangeliums fordert von der Kirchen unbeschadet legitimer Vielfalt eine möglichst grosse Gemeinsamkeit der Bezeugung in Wort und Tat. Dieser Forderung entgegenstehende kirchliche Eigenheiten und Traditionen soziokultureller art unterliegen daher notwendigerweise einer ständigen Überprüfung danach, ob und wieweit sie das Evangelium eher verdecken statt im Rechnung tragen" (DÖSTA 1978:24).

102. The Barmen experience might be one explanation why this report seems to be rather optimistic in respect to formulating a common basis *and* formulating the gospel anew according to the present challenges.

103. Odessa 1977:89ff.

104. Odessa 1977:92f. The necessity of official representative reception was highlighted in the response process to BEM. See pp. 158-64.

"the gospel," "the truth," "the faith," and "the true Tradition of Jesus Christ."[105] A Protestant, somewhat kerygmatic approach can be traced ("gospel"/"faith"), as well as an awareness of the significance of including the terminology of "Tradition." There is a sliding use of terminology between the content given (the message) and the believed faith. In the Odessa report, "the Gospel" is used to describe the content of authoritative teaching.[106] This can be seen as setting a standard of critique for any claim to "authoritative teaching": it must convey the apostolic gospel of God's work in Jesus Christ. It also signals that the authoritative teaching must be a "good message," bringing hope and faith.[107] Thus, some ambiguity between *fides quae* and *fides qua* has been replaced by a focus on the first. The question of how the content can be integrated in those receiving the teaching is addressed through the emphasis on credibility and relevance of the teaching.

Houtepen's survey seems to deliberately play on a wide register of such terms. After referring to some crucial ecumenical texts defining the question of content, he concludes with a differentiated approach: the written authorities (the oldest meaning of the Latin "*auctoritas*") are secondary to the revelation in the *events* of history. However, though holy Scripture has the highest normative value in the Church as original witness, it is not in its totality as such "the Gospel." The teaching of the Church is handed over in a variety of forms, more or less corresponding to the four or five keywords from the New Testament for this study (*didaché, exousia, parrhesia, martus, kerygma*).[108] Different expressions have been and can be used in specific theological traditions or agendas.[109]

---

105. Teach Authoritatively 1976:216 ("the gospel of Jesus Christ," "the content of the gospel," "the meaning of the gospel"); 218 ("the Gospel of Jesus Christ"); 221 ("the Gospel" and "the gospel"); 222 ("the truth of the Gospel"); 225 ("the truth"); 227 ("issues of faith," "Christian faith"); 234 ("convictions of faith"); and 227 ("the true Tradition of Jesus Christ"). Cf. also 235f., referring to the conclusion from Montreal.

106. Odessa 1977:passim. "The truth of the Gospel" is used here, too; cf. 85, 89.

107. An interpretation of these expressions in a strict classical Lutheran scheme of law/gospel is not quite to the point, particularly if that means excluding ethical themes in teaching. However, there is an emphasis of the liberating power and the joyful dimension of the gospel, which should not be neglected. On the other hand, exactly the liberating power for oppressed people has a social ethical dimension. Cf., e.g., Odessa 1977:89.

108. Houtepen 1977:19f., 23ff.

109. Houtepen 1977, e.g.: "rule of faith," "the gospel" (27); "the authority of the tradition in an objective sense, i.e. the scriptures, the symbolum, the canons of the Church, the liturgical books and the writings of the Fathers," "the formulations of the faith" (29); "the living voice of the Gospel," "the Word of God in Scripture" (41); "the faith," "the revelation transmitted to us by Scripture and Tradition," "the truth of the Gospel" (45); "The continuing event of Christ" (47); "the Gospel of the Kingdom" (60); "promise-words," "God's *magnalia* of the past," "*memoria Christi et Dei*" (61); "the content of the Gospel," "(not) propositional truths," "faith and morals" (62); "the Gospel itself" (64); and "dogma," "the mystery of Christ," "Tradition" (67f.).

The traditional picture of "authoritative teaching" limited to official statements of church leadership needs to be *supplemented*, particularly in respect to *how* the teaching becomes authoritative. But reflection on the process involves also deliberations on the content of what can be authoritative teaching. He emphasizes both the "basic continuity" with the trustworthiness in the work and word of the triune God, that is, how this word of God can be authoritative only through a processes being accountable to a wide range of human experience.[110] He mentions the role of independent prophets, the experiences of marginalized people, and the manifold variety of expressions.[111]

When defining the specific role of the "ministerial teaching authority," Houtepen says, "The content of their teaching cannot be another content than the content of the Gospel itself." They "deserve audience because of their mission and responsibility."[112]

The texts of this study show that the terminology of the content of authoritative teaching deserves attention, as it can convey significant theological points. The approach in this study, emphasizing "authoritative," demands a correspondence between how something becomes authoritative teaching and the definition of the content of authoritative teaching.[113]

Summary

Authority requires certain qualities of relation. The perspectives of authority conveyed in the study of authoritative teaching could be understood as *principle, quality,* or *attitude*. The terminological field applied to the concept of authoritative teaching can be described as a network of "principles": credibility, authenticity, reliability, trustworthiness, faithfulness, communication, reception, relevance, openness, critique, and the like. Some of them can be conceived as "intrinsic qualities" of persons involved. But even these might better be understood as matters of relations, or, more precisely, as descriptions of qualities that can be realized only in certain relations. Therefore, I find it relevant to apply the definition of "attitudes," introduced in chapter 1, to the dimensions of authority presented in these documents. To some degree

---

110. Houtepen 1977:61f.

111. Houtepen 1977:61. He mentions imagery, poetics, reflection, ethical imperatives, action for justice, renewal and reformation of old forms, formulations, and structures.

112. Houtepen 1977:64.

113. The later study of "The Apostolic Faith" discussed more intensively the *content* of teaching, particularly the meaning of "apostolic teaching" and "the apostolic faith." Houtepen has in later publications (together with other authors) promoted two expressions to elaborate the correspondence between given faith and ever-new formulations of faith: "The living tradition" and "The faith through the ages"; cf. Houtepen 1995a, 1995b.

I also find this to be the most relevant terminology, because of the dominating perspective of defining proper relations. These qualities are perceivable in efforts, actions, statements, and patterns that are important for interrelations. The authority of the Church becomes real in certain attitudes required to make the message of the Church credible.

These qualities of relations, or attitudes, can to a large degree be seen as expressions of accountability. Because of their relational dimension, the accountability required can be subsumed under the notion of "*mutual* accountability," as said explicitly in the Odessa report.

These texts emphasis that the authority, reliability, and accountability of the content of the teaching is the basis for any teaching's claim to be authoritative. The authority of the message rests on nothing other than representing the trustworthiness of God's promises. The reliability of the teaching implies, therefore, "infallibility" in the sense of having a message of the truth of God's magnificent acts and love.

The focus of this particular study was the conditions for becoming *authoritative* teaching, and in this respect, the integration of three dimensions is important: authoritative teaching means presentation of a reliable message in a reliable way in reliable relations. The interrelation of these three points is at stake when teaching is authoritative *today*. The understanding of the interrelation between them will, naturally, have consequences for what will be the most proper terminology for the *content* of the teaching. This study did not, however, focus on the definition of the content of teaching or on the appropriate terminology for describing this content. These texts, in a remarkably open way, confirm that to make *the received* reliable, persons, churches, and institutions must be reliable and credible. This accountability of authority is understood as a combination of mutual openness and reliability. It is important that there should not be a contradiction in terms between them. There is no reliability or trustworthiness in isolation. Mutuality is a condition for gaining insight from one another to be able to face the challenges of the churches today.

The study of authoritative teaching left open the question of the structure of "magisterium" or ministerial teaching, but made contributions to a deeper understanding of authority. The principal reflections of the content and credibility of authority in the Church are critical memoranda for any definition of structures of authority. The structures as such are mostly not described as an obstacle for being mutually accountable in exercising authority, although some structures are regarded as pursuing that standard more effectively. *This study shows how attitudes subsumed under "mutual accountability" are of great significance to create relations and structures in which the teaching of the Church can have authority.*

The study of authoritative teaching deals in different ways with this question: *To whom* is the Church accountable when exercising authority? The study shows there is a potential of richer and better authoritative teaching if partners in the churches and the churches between themselves become able to learn from one another in a conciliar process.[114] The authorities in the Church should emphasize reception, as the structured, serious listening to the faith of the people of God (*sensus fidei fidelium*). Thus, the conciliar processes cannot be limited to institutions and ministers. This is a dominant dimension in the texts from this study.

However, the reflections as to whom the authoritative teaching should be accountable did not end there. It is a matter of *being accountable to anybody for whom the message of the Church should be authoritative* in bringing salvation and hope. The different directions and types of accountability—and the relations between them—is implicitly discussed in the texts. It is theologically significant to be aware of the difference, but also the coherence between (a) accountability to other churches and their institutions, ministries, and traditions of authoritative teaching, (b) accountability to the reception among the faithful in the people of God, and (c) the general accountability to anybody. Accountability to the churches cannot be in opposition to the accountability to those who need the gifts in the hands of the churches, freedom, salvation, and hope. The texts, quite properly, bring these perspectives together. To pursue a theologically relevant theory of mutual accountability as ecumenical attitude, it is important to include this concern for coherence.[115]

The christological dimension is not explicitly dominant in the text. The approach of rewinding the issue of authoritative teaching back to the content and the credibility in the total life of the "teacher" indirectly says that these two dimensions cannot be separated. As these dimensions were integrated in the ministry of Jesus Christ, they should be in the ministry of the Church. Authority, therefore, becomes a matter of faithfulness to the authoritative teaching of Jesus Christ (both his teaching and the teaching about him), and the credibility of acting in correspondence to the image of Christ.

The relative weight given to proper mutual relations, understood in terms of qualities of accountability such as trustworthiness, openness, and relevance, is indirectly a critique of a strong focus on authority and legitimacy in terms of certain structures, for instance, structures of succession. But the question

---

114. The Odessa report adopted and quoted the Salamanca/Nairobi definition of the unity of the Church: "The fellowship among the churches today is still preliminary and 'preconciliar,' but it anticipates and heralds the future goal. The churches are called to advance step by step to full conciliar communion. In particular, through their acts of teaching they should prepare the way to that unity which is capable of common conciliar decisions" (Odessa 1977:88).

115. Cf. pp. 244-51 and 341-42.

of structure is not neglected. The strong emphasis on proper relations presupposes some structures, but not which.

For churches in an ecumenical setting to pursue common authoritative teaching, a definite common accountability to a common basis and mutual accountability to the new formulations of the gospel is demanded. In this case, the binding aspect (*Verbindlichkeit*) is the dominating perspective of accountability. It is interesting to see how the texts combine this dimension with the need for openness to and ability for self-critique.

The problem of *the terminology of the content* of the authoritative teaching is not given much attention in this study. Nevertheless, the terminology used shows that this is an important question. In some parts of the texts the terminology describes the richness of aspects in authoritative teaching. In other passages of the texts—notably in the final report—the terminology used ("the Gospel" or "the Gospel itself") expresses a common standard for critical evaluation of anything claimed to be "authoritative teaching." These texts demonstrate that the definition of the content cannot be isolated from *how* the church is teaching authoritatively. The good message of the gospel requires accountability in presenting God's trustworthiness. It requires mutual accountability to prevail credibly in a wide circle and to get as much insight and authority as possible.

The study of authoritative teaching leaves many questions open. But it makes quite clear that to gain authority the Church must be accountable when proclaiming a message of hope. The impact of this demand is elaborated in the parallel study of "Giving Account of the Hope That Is within Us."

Giving Account of Hope—in Accountability to Other Churches

Titling a study of Church unity "Giving Account of the Hope That Is Within Us" raises an expectation of finding relevant material for a theory of mutual accountability. The material from the study gives a picture of a stimulating but controversial study process.[116] Something happened to those involved in the process. There are several signs that the study challenged their attitudes and

---

116. I.e., documents of initiation and invitation to the study, reports from consultations, some of the collected "accounts" and responses, and common reports from Faith and Order. I will concentrate here on reports from the debate in the phase of initiating the study (Louvain 1971), on the invitation to participate (Invitation 1972), on one report from an exploratory conversation (Giving Account 1973), on reports from the commission meetings (Accra 1974, Bangalore 1978), and on some texts from the debate on methodology raised through this study (Method Accra 1974, Ecumenical Methodology 1976).

strengthened their accountability. However, when asking whether the particular approach announced in the title of the study provides elements for a theory of mutual accountability as ecumenical attitude, the answer is both "yes" and "no." But even the negative answer is relevant for establishing such a theory.

The study, pursued in the period between 1972 and 1978, can be seen as Faith and Order's attempt to deal with the "new" themes on the ecumenical agenda set after the conference on Church and Society in 1966 and the WCC Uppsala assembly in 1968.[117] The new social ethical awareness is announced

---

117. The director of the Faith and Order Secretariat, Lukas Vischer, proposed this study project at the commission meeting in Louvain in 1971. The report (Louvain 1971) has several documents in which this study is discussed: Lukas Vischer: "Report of the Secretariat to the Commission on Faith and Order," 200–211; "Reports of Committees. Committee I. II. 'Giving Account of the Hope that is in Us'," 215–16; "Conspectus of Studies to be Carried Out (revised in the light of the discussion in the plenary), I. Common Expression of Faith (giving account of the hope that is in us; cf. 1. Peter 3:15)," 239–40. The project was intended as a follow-up to the fourth assembly of the World Council of Churches in Uppsala in 1968. Faith and Order was challenged to follow up the work on the common hope of Christianity and humanity. Uppsala had confirmed the social-ethical challenges and involvement of the ecumenical movement as a focal point. One answer to this challenge from the Faith and Order Secretariat and Commission leaders was the launching of the study on "Unity of the Church—Unity of Mankind" (Louvain 1971:200ff.); see pp. 227-39 below. This was already formulated as a theme in the Bristol meeting in 1968 (Bristol 1968:132ff.). Another answer was the study process on the Christian faith as contextual, accountable accounts of hope ("Giving Account"). Both were introduced, discussed, and approved as new study programmes of Faith and Order in Louvain. Another problem thereby taken into account was to do something to overcome the gap between the doctrinal dialogue work of Faith and Order and the Life and Work-oriented part of the ecumenical movement.

After further preparations by the secretariat, the plan and the invitation to participate in the "Giving Account" study were finalized at the meeting of the Working Commission in Utrecht in 1972 (Minutes Utrecht 1972:115–18.33-38). The next year's meeting of the Working Committee reflected on the amazing wide responses to the invitation and great interest for this study. It also continued the reflections on the scope of the study. "An Invitation to Study: Giving Account of the Hope That Is in Us" was published and distributed, e.g., in Study Encounter 8, no. 4 (1972) (4 cover pages, unpaginated). At the Utrecht meeting a reflection paper marked by a strong personal involvement was presented by Lukas Vischer (Vischer 1972b). The study was discussed again in 1973; cf. Zagorsk 1973:9–11.37-42. The full commission meeting in Accra, Ghana, in 1974, gathered under the theme "Uniting in Hope." The report of the conference carries the title of this study project: "Giving Account of the Hope That Is Within Us." According to Vischer's preface, the study was obviously not finished in Accra, but "remain[s] a major concern of the Faith and Order Commission for several years" (Accra 1974:vi). The report from Accra should therefore serve as an invitation to further participation in the study. The gathering of accounts should in this way stimulate others, through these accounts, to give accounts themselves. This was a major concern in the decisions made for the further work on this study; cf. Minutes Accra 1974:84.

It was also decided to bring some of this material into the preparations for the forthcoming fifth assembly of the World Council of Churches. Inputs from this Faith and Order material became important elements in the discussions and work on the theme "Confessing Christ

in the emphasis on "hope." The status of being challenged, even charged, is signaled through the word *account*. The churches had to answer new questions. The ecumenical movement required new material for their work and new methods to get it. The contextual, inductive approach was launched as a supplement to, even as a substitute for, the traditional methodology of dialogue on the basis of biblical and confessional texts.

In the same period, developing forms of conciliar life was high on the ecumenical agenda.[118] The intention to initiate a conciliar process leading toward a common statement of the Christian faith as hope was quite explicit. The tension in this enterprise between the emphasis on a contextual, social, and even political approach and the aim of a new, *common* expression of faith became difficult to handle. The common texts from Accra and Bangalore were notable achievements in combining the new approach and a common expression of the given faith, but they had not been received or used as ecumenical breakthroughs. Nevertheless, they indicated the need to face new questions and develop new ecumenical methodology. My analysis of the study is not an evaluation of its success or lack of it, but an exploration of how the issue of ecumenical attitudes was addressed.

Independent and Contextual Accounts

Although we can trace a continuous stream of admonitions to pursue unity by making a *common* statement of the Christian faith, a new, contextual approach implied a strong *eccentric* force. The study project invited the churches to formulate accounts of hope primarily for their own context. The Faith and Order

---

Today." In this way the concerns and methodology of this study were confirmed as a central element in the ecumenical endeavour. Some of the most significant expressions of the report of Section I (Nairobi 1975:41–59) shows this: "In confessing Christ and in being converted to his Lordship, we experience the freedom of the Holy Spirit and express the ultimate hope for the world" (§17). The concern of being accountable to the gospel in accountability to the real need was described in a comprehensive way, interpreting and extemporizing how "the whole Church" should fulfill a slogan of the discussions: "'The whole gospel for the whole person and the whole world' means that we cannot leave any area of human life and suffering without the witness of hope"(§18). To achieve these goals, the churches were given the recommendation to "encourage and promote broader participation on all church levels in ecumenical studies pertaining to confessing Christ, such as the study 'Giving account of the hope that is within us'." (§73.8).

Through newsletters and the like the churches were encouraged to continue the work. Two volumes of accounts were published and distributed (Giving Account 1972, 1975, 1976a, 1978). The first week of the Faith and Order Commission meeting in Bangalore, India, in 1978, was dedicated to work on accounts of this study project and an attempt to make a common text on these discussions (Bangalore 1978/Minutes Bangalore 1978). This became the final station of the work of this project. The work of gathering accounts of faith was, however, continued in publications of similar material, cf. "Confessing Our Faith I–IV" (1980–85).

118. See the analysis of the studies of "conciliarity," pp. 83-109.

Commission and its secretariat in Geneva formulated the request for these accounts. The accounts should be sent to the wider community of churches, represented by the Faith and Order Commission. But it was stressed that real accounts of hope had to address the actual, contextual problems of local communities.

Certain dissatisfaction and uneasiness was articulated: Should the focus be on unity in faith as matters of doctrine continue? The critics of the more traditional approach claimed that more contextual accounts were needed even to get hold of the really believed faith. There also seems to have been a rather wide acceptance of the significance for unity of profound contextual statements of faith and hope (e.g., the experience with the Barmen Declaration, 1934).

In this study (and the parallel planned study of "Unity of Mankind—Unity of the Church") a debate on ecumenical methodology was raised, particularly through a document presented at the Accra meeting in 1974, which articulated a skepticism toward any claims of "universal truths."[119] Theological, philosophical, and political reasons were presented for not aiming at a united statement. According to this hermeneutical approach, a general common statement could not get the same meaning in every context.

The study initiated accounts that could have social and political power in their contexts. This social-ethical orientation focused on the duties of the churches to take a stand in conflicts against injustice and oppression. The accounts of hope should represent alternatives of witness as action. In many respects, but not in all, this was a shift from doctrinal issues as matters of ecumenical dialogue and common statements toward ethical issues. The character of ethical problems at stake, however, invited more concentration on categories of duties, actions, and consequences than of the traditionally more personal dimensions of attitudes or virtues, although the latter definitely were not absent, as we will see.

At the particular time of this study, the freedom of former colonies and the awareness of the problems of the "Third World" became crucial issues for the churches and the ecumenical movement. For churches and theologians in the Third World, this meant that the time of more independence from the "mother churches" had come, the time to formulate a theology that could be accounts of hope for these churches, accounts that could no longer be clothed in the traditional Western theological language. It was, of course, more than a matter of independence and language. To some extent it became a conflict of interest. The reality could even be described as "hope encounters hope."[120]

---

119. Method Accra 1974.

120. That the hope of growth and wealth of the countries in the northern hemisphere has become a matter of despair, not hope, of people, for instance, in Africa, was explicitly said in Accra in the address of Mr. Bola Ige: "Ghana's independence dashed the hope that was contained

Another strain in this study programme can also be seen as a tendency against making the *churches* accountable. The invitation to the study emphasized the importance of making "new groups" active in formulating accounts of hope. This was, of course, an indirect critique of church leadership. Consequently, the study process did not involve officially responsible church officials as such, but the tendency was to handle the gathered material as representative for the churches. This confusion of the subject of the accounts was not really addressed explicitly. This might be one reason why the results from this study were not taken into account in the churches nearly as much as the later BEM study was.[121]

All these aspects show that this study of giving account of the hope tended to strengthen the attitude of being independent rather than of becoming mutually accountable. However, this was not the only direction in this study in regard to ecumenical attitudes.

Making One Another Mutually Accountable through Giving Accounts

Account and Accountability

Making the political/social-ethical dimension of hope relevant was, at that time, pursued also outside the circles working with a particular *ecumenical* dimension. Nevertheless, the project of giving account of hope in an ecumenical setting raises certain questions of significance for the ecumenical movement and for theological reflection in general. Although the focus on contextual accounts led to more differences and stressed the moral obligation for the churches to provide (political?) acts of hope, some emphasis on the quality of interchurch relations can be observed in this study programme, too.

First of all, the approach of "giving accounts of the hope that is within us" conveyed the demand of *authenticity and credibility*. The aim was coherence between the preaching of hope and the acts of hope in a particular situation. This was a dominant feature in the argument for this study. The title of the project showed that it was meant to focus on one particular aspect of the content of the Christian faith (hope). But this focus on hope was combined

---

in what our plunderers called 'the civilizing mission'. . . . And even now in 1974, one can hear Vorster and white South African intellectuals clutching that fond hope which reasonable people all over the world have abandoned, if for no other reason than that black Africans have falsified it" (Minutes Accra 1974:52). The same point is reflected in the following: "A desire for an expanding economy in one country can cause poverty in another. A necessary struggle for power in one country may appear to contradict the responsible use of power in another. Some even say: 'One's hopes become another's despair'" (Bangalore 1978:3).

121. See pp. 156–85.

with a definite interest in *how* the churches present their message, and how this presentation corresponds to the core of the message.

Although the title of the project presumed that questions of accounts of hope were explicitly raised to the churches from outside, the project itself should be done on the initiative of the churches themselves. Thus, it was more an exercise of showing how the hope was integrated in the churches than an external question-and-answer process. This makes it relevant to interpret the endeavour as a focus on the *attitude* of accountability, more than on a formal or juridical external aspect of accountability. This dimension is also emphasized through the words "that is within us."

Making the Churches Accountable to One Another

The project of gathering the contextual accounts had, of course, the purpose of strengthening the unity of the Church. The Faith and Order movement, not only the churches, felt the pressure of giving credible and relevant statements from their work in a time when the meaning of the ecumenical endeavour for "life situations" was challenged.[122] Faith and Order had to show the results of its work as an "account of that which they as Christians have received together and are charged to offer." Otherwise, their studies might be in "danger of perpetuating the dialogue without pressing on to the point at which we give account of what we have in common in our faith."[123] This had to be done by making one another more *mutually* accountable.

The churches should present what was beyond the traditional creeds and confessional statements. The invitation to participate in the study formulated positively what was wanted: "What we have in common in our life together, prayer and preaching is in advance of what we are able to define together in matters of doctrine. Therefore we should endeavour to express what is the content and meaning of our life and prayer and proclamation."[124] In the preamble of the invitation to the study the ambitions are rather high: "Will you take part in a world-wide effort of Christians to say together what it is that they believe?" Although the result of 40 years of work of Faith and Order was that "wide agreement has been reached on such matters as baptism, eucharist and the relation between Scripture and Tradition," there was more to be accomplished: "The churches cannot rest content with what has been achieved. They must

---

122. To achieve a common expression of the Christian faith for all churches was in the planning process explicitly articulated as the ultimate goal of the project; cf. Louvain 1971, particularly the introduction to the study by Lukas Vischer, pleading for "A coherent account of the hope that is in us! A common statement of our faith!" (ibid., 210). The conspectus for the study, defined by the commission, was given the title "A common expression of faith" (ibid., 239).

123. Louvain 1971:215.

124. Louvain 1971:215f.

move forward to a fuller statement of the faith they share. For the agreement already reached is not yet an adequate exposition of the Gospel. We must accept the challenge to go beyond the limitations of our present agreement and try to state together the full Gospel which we believe."[125]

Thus, the invitation to the study programme presumed that there was another consensus of hope that the churches already shared, accessible only through a shift of focus and attitudes (more restlessness). Whether this presumed latent unity was a fiction more than a reality was really questioned during the study process. The desired ability could be seen as an external matter, in the sense of being able to address new themes. Nevertheless, the programme of mutual "challenging" was to make one another able and willing to give account for more than before (corresponding to my understanding of accountable as "account-*able*"). The study obviously aimed at improving the willingness to open the gates between the churches to make it possible to see the life of the churches better.

There is also another implication in what is said about the presumed "full Gospel which we believe": the gospel is described as a common treasure that the churches in a way own together. Or, more correctly: it is a treasure given them to be stewarded as something belonging to all of them, even to all humankind. Therefore, the churches must give account of this hope. This is a duty. In this context the duty corresponds to the attitude of willingness to share mutually accounts of hope: "We have the duty to give witness of our Christian hope to the world. We are captives of this hope. Merely by existing, we continually either testify to it or deny it. Since, therefore, we cannot escape this obligation, we must seek out the ways and means of rendering account."[126]

The churches should be forced to take a stand on new issues, new for Faith and Order and to some extent new for some churches. To achieve this, the churches should challenge one another throughout the *process* particularly on the "new themes" of social ethics, which the ecumenical movement had brought to the table. Therefore, the process documented through the reports of the study is important. Not only the formulated common accounts of common beliefs are of interest when observing the changes in focus on attitudes of relationship.

Contextual Diversity Demands a New "Discipline of Fellowship"
The entire study implied an impetus to make the Christian faith understood and received as one common hope for the one world.[127] It was not the inten-

125. Invitation 1972:1 (cover).
126. Accra 1974:45.
127. The focus on the unity of (hu)mankind was settled in Uppsala in 1968. Attempts to launch studies of the relevance of church unity for the unity of the "one world" was made already in

tion to widen the gap between the churches by strengthening of differences and separatism. The deeply interwoven *tension* between reinforcing contextually oriented expressions of Christianity and the work for unity was, however, felt and articulated in a typical way already at the first "exploratory conversation" in this programme. It was called a "pilot experiment," bringing together 15 theologians from different continents to answer The Question of Christian theology in a contextual framework: "Who is Jesus Christ—for you?"[128] "They were not to give general and ready-made answers but should make the effort to express the faith in and for the situation in which they find themselves. In a second stage their different answers were to be compared. Is our confession in substance one and the same? If not, can the differences exist side by side in one and the same fellowship? How is the oneness in Jesus Christ to be understood and expressed today?"[129]

After a presentation of six different cultural approaches to Christology, and after an affirmation of the theologians' benefit from listening to each other, they addressed the difficult question of how these approaches lead to rather different expectations with regard to the Church. Although discussed in a friendly manner and regarded as complementary, the different answers led to "different styles of life and different patterns of identity." The problem was formulated as a real theological dilemma: when believing "that Christ himself unites us," the problem of diversity is brought to another level. If the unity of the Church is given in Christ, and the identities we have in Christ are so diversified, does this mean that the churches are "condemned to live with our different christologies and our subsequent divisive ecclesiologies?"[130]

This sharpening of the problem of unity led the theologians to address the challenge to develop and change the *quality* of relations in order to be able to pursue unity.

> They [the differences] raise questions about *the discipline of fellowship in the whole Church, within each Church and between churches.* . . . Our study speaks of a *common account* more than of a common hope and that is the problem to which we address ourselves now. The common account requires a relationship between the different identities we have been describing and therefore leads us

---

Louvain in 1971; cf. Louvain 1971:171–99, 240. This was to some degree a parallel, even a doublet, of the "Giving Account" study. Several perspectives were tried, but a final outcome of the "Unity of [Hu]mankind" study was not reached until the report "Church and World" was published in 1990. See pp. 227–39.

128. This happened in Bangkok in January 1973. The report was presented as a contribution and inspiration to the local study groups, published in Giving Account 1973.

129. Giving Account 1973:1.

130. Giving Account 1973:15.

into the conflict these identities have produced and are producing.... In our discussion three models of relationship came up: Some said that we need for some time a *moratorium* on interdependence so that different identities can be developed and acquire sufficient strength for a true fellowship in which all are on equal footing. Although nobody disputed the need to develop strong identities, the question was *asked how, in this model, independence can be saved from isolation*. The latter, we all agreed, is destructive.... A second group plea for a strategy of communication for the period during which the identities are developed.... An important element in this idea is that it allows for the enrichment of different cultural groups, *enabling mutual critique and a sharing of success and failure*. A third group searches for a relationship which also leaves cultural identity intact, *but stresses interdependence in a creative confrontation, in order to strengthen identity within the fellowship*.[131]

The theologians refrained from proposing answers to the problem of diversity "verbally," and tried to turn the attention to a deeper discussion of "worship," which hardly gave any clarity to the issue here. The more general reflection on the need to get other forms of communication, to find a better relation between independence and interdependence, seemed more to the point.

As the italicizing of some passages here suggests (see the note), these theologians saw the relevance of discussing perspectives of relationship for progress in this programme. Their experience of giving one another accounts of their contextual witness to Christ, and their reflections on this experience, led them to a discussion of relations in terms that come rather close to my preliminary definition of mutual accountability ("discipline of fellowship"; independence-interdependence; openness with mutual critique and support; "creative confrontation," etc.) The clear and interesting answer from this report was that the task of establishing independent accounts of hope needs a certain room of freedom, but could suffer from isolation.

Two Attempts to Formulate a Common Account of Hope: Accra 1974 and Bangalore 1978

The two main reports from this study, from the commission meetings in Accra (1974) and Bangalore (1978), reflect both the process and the conclusions. They have to some degree a common structure. After defining the problem and challenge, the reports formulate a common statement of the given Christian faith before the specific challenges and problems raised in this study are addressed. Toward the end they both propose steps to give further account of

---

131. Giving Account 1973:14f. Except for the terms *common account and moratorium*, italics have been added by the author.

the Christian faith, maintaining the tension between faith in Christ and the reality of this world. Although the more classical statement of Christian faith must have been difficult to formulate, more interesting (in respect to my questions here) is how it becomes apparent that the accounts given have been a matter of mutual challenge between those involved in the process.

The Accra report is in itself a report of just these mutual challenges and the responses given in the process. The representatives from the African churches made the churches of the former colonial powers accountable for the problems of giving a credible account of hope in Africa. But they also asked for an attitude of humility, openness, and mutuality—in a wider sense than had been practiced in the ecumenical dialogues.

> We feel, therefore, that all the expressions of the Christian faith up to now, from whatever area of the Christian Church . . . do not speak to us at the depth of our situation, past, present and future. . . . The sin of the Church in the past has been that each particular expression of the human understanding, made according to local histories and situations, has claimed to be the *One* and *Only*. To us, this is blasphemous self-idolatry. Hence our disgust with the socalled ecumenical dialogue and encounter so far.[132]

The European answer was made in deep self-critical humility. Over 40 years after, the document can be seen as a sign of a new and shaking experience, and of the fear of losing the contact with the new and vital churches in Africa of that time. Indeed, it is a witness of how this study challenged and developed the ecumenical attitudes. If the representatives from the churches of "the Northern hemisphere" had not been accountable for their heritage before, they now expressed an almost exaggerated attitude of self-criticism and accountability forced upon them in this mutual encounter. It can, nevertheless, serve as a significant example of what the encounter between the churches means when the gates are wide open to give contextual accounts of both hope and despair:

> Europeans have brought the Gospel to Africa in Western garments. Some of them were unavoidable, since the missionaries had to speak their own language, the only language they knew. Some could have been avoided if there had been less European arrogance. Some of these garments were authentically Christian, since Jesus is also the root of European culture. Many, however, came from definitely other than Christian sources, good or bad (for instance, the influence of Greek/Roman metaphysics, and later of science and technology on Christian theology and thought). . . . African Christians have the right to find their own, and to them meaningful, expressions of the faith.

---
132. Accra 1974:33f.

> In this situation, it is a painful wrench to leave them alone. It is even more agonizing to be left alone by them. . . . Might it not be that a church which lives today in some sense in the first century can be much closer to the truth than one which lives in a post-Reformation period and stage? . . . The conviction, so much alive with our African brothers, that God is today a living God challenges our doubts and our dwelling in the past. Have we made ourselves an image of God according to the paternalistic fashions of past centuries? Is this why we can no longer convey the idea of God to our children? . . . This document is written in a time when the conviction of European theological superiority which dominated our thoughts consciously, or, even more, unconsciously, has been shaken by the rebellion against it of Christians in other continents as well as of our own youth. Praise be to the Lord if we are being humbled and made poorer in spirit and less arrogant![133]

These paragraphs show how the contextual approach opened the way for a real, mutual critique. The Western churches were charged and made accountable: You are guilty! But they could not pay a reparation or be punished for their guilt. The mutual encounter provoked a new insight into the problems, which was shown in a specific attitude. It even changed the perspective on one of their domestic problems, the challenge of credibility in handing over the tradition between generations. Hence, the study process fostered a new humility and a new kind of attitude important for fellowship and openness. The "African response" was a plea to God "for all mankind, Father forgive."[134] Here we find mutual accountability in attitudes of openness, frankness, humility, and trustworthiness, combined with an ability to accept *vulnerability*, too, acknowledging the wounds of others, accepting attack by legitimate critique in a way that displays one's own weaknesses. Toward the end of the Accra report we find an important theological reflection on unity in regard to the diversity explored and the insight obtained through the process so far.[135]

The "one hope of Christ" or "the proclamation of the Gospel of Hope" is regarded as a given unity, given in a legitimate articulation of diversity corresponding to the diversity of gifts of the Spirit. From there the text continues by making all varieties "valid" for everybody in the fellowship:

> Giving account of the hope is the communal act par excellence because, though hope is expressed in a given context, each individual, when acting, is bound through his particular charisma with the other members of the community. What is valid for each one of the charismatic members of the ecclesial

---

133. Accra 1974:35f.
134. Accra 1974:36.
135. Accra 1974:45–47 (the following quotations are from 45f.).

community is equally valid of the different confessions and Christian tradition. . . . Only through their exchange of their gifts of grace can they give account of their common hope in the Spirit. This is especially true when one of these isolated communities finds itself in a hopeless situation.

Here is one important aspect of becoming mutually accountable: one part of the Church cannot ignore the accounts of hope given by others. They are "valid" for all in that sense. Accounts of hope make the churches responsible for bringing hope together in solidarity. But there is another dimension of this mutual accountability in hope, integrated in the study and elaborated above, which might be hidden if the former perspective is the only one. Diversity cannot be only a romantic picture of "manifold richness." The accounts of hope must be tested in a mutual encounter. This might have been intended by formulations, such as: "Hope cannot be acquired by one individual alone. Nor can hope be expressed by one individual alone." But it could have been more clearly stated.

The report from Bangalore articulates even more explicitly how the real and open encounter between accounts of hope should affect the mutual attitudes of interchurch fellowship. The encounter is in itself a room to become self-critical and to experience the judgment of Christ over selfish wishes:

> The encounter has been *humbling* because of the provocation to become more self-critical. It is necessary to distinguish hopes from desires and wishes. Some of our expectations are little more than unexamined desires and wishes, or expressions of fears and anxieties. And these often contradict one another. . . . But we refuse to believe that the hopes of humankind are ultimately contradictory: God-given hopes are many-faceted and complementary. But human hearts are sinful, and their desires can be false. They need to be judged and purified. Christ is the judge of human hopes. He weighs our desires.[136]

This principal statement is continued in a reflection on ecclesiology ("The Church: A Communion of Hope").[137] The church is the community in which the triune God gives "the power to share with each other." This power is defined as the power of *love*.[138] This attitude is shown in acts that correspond to the demands of the New Testament: "We can rejoice with those who rejoice and weep with those who weep. We can bear one another's burdens. It is in this communion we also learn to share one another's hope. This encounter of hope

---

136. Bangalore 1978:3.

137. Bangalore 1978:5f.

138. There are good reasons to regard "love" as the fundamental attitude of Christian life. See, e.g., Asheim 1990:108f., 116.

in itself has been made by God to be a sign in every situation and place: Christ our hope, the power of love!"

The text attempts to verify that the attitude of love is the power that has been experienced through the open, mutual giving of accounts in the communities of hope in the churches. It is here even explicitly elaborated as a community that makes the participants "accountable to each other." This mutual accountability is crucial for a theological ecumenical understanding of the Church as a communion of hope in love:

> Of this power among the churches we are witnesses. We do have hope for this communion. And we believe that this communion, incomplete as it is, can become a sign of hope for others. Communion in Christ provides the possibility of encounter across the barriers. It reestablishes relations in mutual respect without sacrificing convictions. It can be a testing ground for the witness that each church bears. *Without being pressed into conformity, churches can become accountable to each other*. It is also a source of hope because as they live by God's forgiveness, they can extend forgiveness to other churches as well, and find in the witness and commitment of others an enrichment of their own. Finally, communion in Christ is a source of hope when it anticipates the reign of God and does not acquiesce in things as they are.[139]

The particular combination of attitudes is significant. The mutually loving communion, accountable to each other, is a fellowship that reestablishes mutual respect without sacrificing convictions. There is a fine balance between being challenged and not being pressed into conformity. This particular point is important for a theory of mutual accountability.

The Bangalore report continued the process of gathering accounts toward the formulation of a common account of hope. It does not expose the mutual confrontation as openly as the Accra report, but conveys the reflection after such encounters. The report focuses particularly on how the churches in solidarity should face the common threats to humanity, no matter in what context they occur.[140]

The report concludes by proclaiming the need for another attitude: the willingness to take a *risk*. But is this an attitude that corresponds to the attitude of mutual accountability? The risk is described as willingness to be challenged by new and other contributions from other cultural contexts, to risk self-criticism as the channel of renewal, to risk dialogue, cooperation with those from whom we differ, to risk new forms of community between women and men, to risk scorn and even death. It "can be a costly witness" of hope. This attitude

139. Bangalore 1978:6; italics mine.
140. Bangalore 1978:6–8.

of taking risks is to be demonstrated through the living encounter of openness and self-criticism. The real encounter in dialogue, according to the report, should not be primarily a matter of passive self-defense, but active, open, and reliable *willingness to pay the cost of fellowship*. These are indeed important distinctions for a definition of "mutual accountability" as ecumenical attitude.

The "Giving Account" study did not succeed in establishing a common agreement in faith of lasting significance for the ecumenical movement.[141] However, the Bangalore statement deserves more attention than has been paid to it. One reason for the meager reception could be that it is not well enough formulated to be some kind of creedal statement or common confessional document, parallel to what some churches already had. On the other hand, the concluding statement might not be specific and contextual enough to function as a confession in that particular contemporary situation, either. It did not address one particular problem or crisis, but several, and in a rather general way. The situation of the writing of the statement (a meeting of theologians in the Faith and Order Commission) was somewhat arbitrary and artificial for establishing a Church confession. The status of accountability was not clear. A comparison, for example, with statements made during World War II, immediately exposes this striking difference.[142]

The Discussion of New Methods and Ecumenical Attitudes

The "Giving Account" study was initiated to pursue unity through *new methods*.[143] Although it did not solve the methodological problems, the study con-

141. Lukas Vischer already in his announcement of the "Giving Account" study saw that a common statement would not be as important as the process itself: "The attempt to produce a common account of the hope that is in us would probably not result in any conclusive findings. It might never be more than an attempt. It will probably show that statements can only be made along the way, with repeated fresh attempts, always proving inadequate. This does not make the attempts worthless" (Louvain 1971:210). Already in Bangalore a new initiative was taken to make a common statement of what the Christian faith is, with a christological starting point and done with more traditional, deductive methodology than in the "Giving Account" study. See Bangalore 1978:243–46.

142. Cf., e.g., the Barmen Declaration. Another example of the importance of the context for the content, form, and status of a confessional text is the confession of the Lutheran Church in Norway, *Kirkens Grunn* ("The foundation of the Church"). See Austad 1974:229–32 (German Summary 233–40), who defined this statement as a temporary and particular confession (Norwegian: *"temporær bekjennelse"/"partikulær bekjennelse"*).

143. Already in Louvain in 1971 a redefinition of the methods of Faith and Order work was recommended; cf. Louvain 1971:241f. In Accra in 1974, "Reflections on the Methods of Faith and Order Study" was presented and discussed (Method Accra 1974). The Faith and Order Commission published some material discussing these issues in *Study Encounter*. The "Statement from the Theology Committee of the Church of Norway" on "Ecumenical Methodology" and an article by the Australian theologian Richard Campbell on "Contextual Theology and

veyed an awareness of the hermeneutical problems of the quest for unity, which had not been exposed to that extent before.[144] The hermeneutical discussion (partly as a result of the "Giving Account" study) in ecumenical texts from these years touches the problem of quality of relations in which these problems of diversity should be solved. The discussion on hermeneutics cannot, of course, be fully considered here, but only some perspectives to illustrate how the problems of mutuality and accountability were affected by this discussion.

But what is the relevance of looking for the issue of *mutual* accountability when the tendency was to emphasize new, contextual approaches, independent of the former framework of Western theologians? The answer is implicit in the context of the effort: because of the ecumenical framework of the questions, focus on the accountability of theology done locally and contextually had to be intertwined with the underlying question of how theologians and churches are accountable to other churches, too.

The Accra document on methodology proclaimed the need to penetrate behind the confessional problems and to take on board the new hermeneutics in a fresh approach to theology. It was not a matter simply of new logic and techniques. It affected the self-understanding and the basic relations of the theologians, not only the theological statements. New hermeneutics "have shaken the theological self-confidence which characterized much of the earlier debate." The questions of purpose, place, and sources of theology were raised radically.[145] The new hermeneutical awareness meant to "recognize the context, the experiential situation in which theological statements are formulated as a constitutive factor for theological reflection itself." [146] This recognition could dawn in a mutual encounter focusing on the responsibility of the churches: "The question: What is the place of theology? It cannot be answered in a general way. Neither Church nor theology can freely choose the place they want to occupy in a given culture and society. Ecumenical theological discussion, however, in exposing the churches to each other, makes them aware of their 'localization' and its implicit dangers as well as responsibilities."[147] All these

---

its Problems" illuminate quite well the problems at stake and their relevance for my interest in ecumenical attitudes in terms of mutual accountability.

144. Already in Louvain the implicit critique of Western theologians was raised: "How could new theological traditions outside the West and theological insights from outside the academic community be fruitfully included in Faith and Order studies?" (Louvain 1971:242). Due to the definite shift of methodology after Bangalore, confirmed in Lima in 1982, the inductive, contextual method was put on a sidetrack (except in the "Unity and Renewal" study, see pp. 227–39) until it became a hot issue in Santiago in 1993.

145. Cf. Method Accra 1974:68, 70–73.

146. Method Accra 1974:68f., 71.

147. Method Accra 1974:71.

expressions show that the attitudes of the churches and the theologians were challenged, in respect to their relations to one another, to their context, and to themselves. This impression is reinforced when the texts talk about the burning issues of diversity and consensus more as a matter of how to relate to one another than a logical crux.

This Accra text has some relevance for the question of "mutual accountability." When discussing the issue of the *sources* of theology, the question is formulated like this: Tradition or situation?[148] The report denies that this is a real antinomy:

> Of course, no theology can reasonably claim to be independent from the Tradition of the Christian faith, not the least from Scripture itself. Equally, it would be a misunderstanding of Tradition if one were to oppose it to experience and situation. The process of Tradition represents the permanent attempt to reinterpret and develop anew the Apostolic witness in the light of a particular, given situation and its interpretation in philosophy, science, the arts etc. All theology moves between the two poles of Tradition and situation.[149]

The text argues that theology has to be accountable both to the given Tradition and to the insight into the "experience and situation," conveyed by others and other disciplines. The Christian confessions have chosen differently between these poles as the starting point in their methodology. Now the task to be accountable both ways is maintained. The "growing consciousness of change, of a definite break in the historical continuity, of alienation from all tradition" raised the problem of diversity more intensely than before, according to the text, particularly in Africa, Asia, and Latin America. "Ecumenical discussions have to take it into account," is the preliminary and laconic summary of that insight.[150] Therefore, in this document on ecumenical methodology in 1974, it became important that this double accountability should be developed in a framework of an ecumenical, mutual accountability.

According to the Accra text, the situation calls for "inter-contextual method." This method requires "interdisciplinary collaboration," "a new awareness of the ideological implications of our discussions on the unity of the Church," "an empirical method, in the sense that it recognizes the life-situation in which statements are being formulated as a constitutive factor for the formulation itself."[151] These types of mutuality and accountability between contexts

---

148. "Tradition" is here understood in the meaning elaborated in Montreal in 1963, and does not mean one part of the classical dichotonomy of Scripture/Tradition.

149. Method Accra 1974:72.

150. Method Accra 1974:72.

151. Method Accra 1974:77.

should, according to the text, be "spelled out" in a conciliar process centered on Christ. The following passage illustrates how these claims led to reflections on criteria for unity in faith that presuppose mutuality and accountability:

> Conciliar unity [that] implies that there is ample space for diversity and for open mutual confrontation of differing interests and convictions. This confrontation is bound to take place once the difference of live contexts which determine and influence the formulation of our theological statements is actually taken into account. . . . This center [Jesus Christ] certainly is accessible only through the different interpretations of the Apostolic witness. . . . The growing awareness of the differences between particular social, political and cultural contexts in which Christian life and theological reflection take place puts the Churches under the urgent demand to give a common expression of their faith in Jesus Christ. . . . The purpose cannot be to arrive at consensus statements and common formulae. The emphasis will rather lie on developing ways of comparing and relating different accounts to each other. Thus criteria might emerge which could guide mutual criticism. The more specific such an account will be, the more fruitful the comparison will also be. How far can an account go in onesidedness and specificity without running the risk of being incommunicable and thus not comparable?[152]

The text attempts to be realistic about the given premises for doing theology, being aware of the danger of onesidedness. It emphasizes the active, mutual critical fellowship as a condition for the churches to adequately engage in the process of tradition.[153] Actually, *the* way to handle old and new types of unavoidable diversity and to give a basis for mutual *Ideologiekritik* is described as a mutually accountable process.

Not everybody found the Accra text satisfying and acceptable as a solution for ecumenical methodology. An analysis of two examples of critique, published by Faith and Order, can illuminate important problems of this study. A statement from the Church of Norway criticized particularly a tendency to give the contextual approach, experience, and empirical knowledge a role as primary criteria in the ecumenical encounter.[154] The critical questions of

---

152. Method Accra 1974:78f.

153. The Accra text to some extent makes a point out of the difference between "theologians" and "churches," whether the theologians should do theology primarily inside and in accordance with the churches, in an academic context, or in a wider public context (Method Accra 1974:70f.). The document itself speaks mostly indiscriminately of "theology" and "theologians" parallel to "churches" as subjects in this respect, too. The lack of clarity of who are the subjects in the ecumenical dialogues might be a structural problem in the Faith and Order endeavours. It is difficult to analyze, if possible at all.

154. Ecumenical Methodology 1976.

methodology are formulated in accordance with the major themes of Faith and Order and the World Council of Churches at that time: catholicity, conciliar consensus, ecumenical methodology. [155]

The statement does not question the relevance of the mutual, critical encounter as a way toward unity. Despite the clear interest in the doctrinal problems of ecumenism, the statement cannot be seen as narrowly confessionalistic. The committee was aware of the need (articulated in several documents of the early 1970s) for relevant self-critique to proceed in the ecumenical dialogues in a conciliar process toward consensus in faith. The critical point is—to remain in my analytic terminology—*what* the churches should be mutually accountable *for* (or what should "bind" them), not whether they are mutually accountable or should be so. The following passage of the statement shows this critique.

> In other cases the method itself is misleading: it tends to bind Christians to what is historically arbitrary, instead of liberating them from it. The method takes the form of a demand or pressure on Christians in different cultural settings to conform, in their faith, to their particular cultural pattern, since only that which is specific to the actual culture or situation can be genuine. Naturally, the Christian is bound to take his own life situation seriously. He is sent out into the world, and has to live "in the world." But he should not be "of the world," and the contextual method, in its pure form, does not seem to take this kind of situation into account.
>
> At this point there is an almost imperceptible but fatal shift in the criteria for what is genuinely Christian. They tend to be culture-oriented, not Christian-oriented. What is "genuine" or "authentic" is what's seen from a cultural viewpoint as native or functions in socio-cultural manner. This imperceptible shift of criteria is extremely dangerous. In a confused spiritual situation such as ours, it is crucial to preserve the criteria for what is authentically Christian. And that means that these criteria should be taken exclusively from the Holy Scriptures, the foundation and the norm of the Church. The values of meeting representatives from other cultures in an ecumenical setting should consist in this, that one learns to lay aside the specifically cultural in one's own faith, and distinguish between what is an arbitrary historical form and what is essential content.[156]

---

155. Cf. the titles of the subsections: "An inter-cultural or an ecclesiological catholicity?"; "An empirical or a biblical point of departure?"; "What constitutes the Church's unity, and what divides it?"

156. Ecumenical Methodology 1976:30.

This text did indeed confirm that the churches should be accountable in the context in the sense of being "genuine" and "authentic." It even confirmed that this is a matter of mutuality. The churches should learn the most theologically significant lessons in the cross-cultural ecumenical meeting. But which lessons are to be learned is somewhat different from the picture the other documents from this study programme gives. It is not the integration of local culture; contextual approaches are, rather, in danger of being "arbitrary." In a polemic style, the text maintains most emphatically that churches should learn in the mutual encounter "to lay aside the specifically cultural in one's own faith." Here the warning is: real Christian authenticity is the opposite of conformity to the context. Contextual theology as such is not accountable as specific *Christian* theology.

The churches should in their mutual, critical encounter, get help to hold on to the criteria of Christianity from the holy Scriptures and to leave what is "historically arbitrary." "Giving Account" could become a case study in which human experiences got the status of a second source of revelation in addition to Scripture. The question of method that should be raised is, "An empirical or a biblical point of departure?"[157] It cannot be a matter of what is effective for unity, at the cost of dismissing what is "theologically valid."[158] According to the statement, the contextual method could be reversing the growing consensus on what is central and what is peripheral in Christian doctrine.

Hence, this text sharpens the definition of what mutual accountability in a mutual giving of accounts of contextual theology should be. The statement raises four important questions of accountability: (1) How could the churches be accountable to "the foundation and norm of the Church"?[159] (2) How could the churches be accountable in the context as critical instances, not adapted conformists? (3) How could the churches help one another to see how they have corrupted this norm in the way they consciously or unconsciously have adapted the context in which they live? (4) How should the churches be accountable to the ecumenical dialogue and really receive and turn into practice what has been accepted in the dialogues?[160] These four questions could be

---

157. Ecumenical Methodology 1976:32.

158. Ecumenical Methodology 1976:27f.

159. I see this question as a parallel to the question of The Tradition or The Dogma. In the deliberation of the third part of this document, "What constitutes the Church's unity, and what divides it?" (34ff.), there is a christological and sacramental definition of the basis of unity, which preclude a "biblicistic" interpretation of the statement's emphasis on Scripture. However, some of the problems in the statement might be caused by a weak awareness of the hermeneutical problems involved in the use of Scripture in different contexts.

160. Theology is described as "a *scientia practica*, in other words, a science which is not concerned with the purely theoretical plane, but with the real life of the faith in the fellowship of the Church." This is where doctrine "should be reflected in the life of the Church." Applied to

theologically relevant and important reminders in any endeavour of exercising mutual accountability. The first three questions are raised more sharply here than in many of the other documents analyzed so far. The sense of being accountable for something different in the cultural context, should, according to this text, be strengthened in the ecumenical fellowship. Seen in the context of the contemporary ecumenical debate at that time, these critical questions were relevant in discussions such as how to be a credible church behind the Iron Curtain and how to address racism in the churches and in society.

The problem with this type of critique is apparent, however, when analyzing it from the perspective of mutual accountability. Discussions of method in Faith and Order demonstrated the lack of awareness in Western churches how they transported to other parts of the world what could be in conflict with local cultures. This export is now regarded even as potentially being in conflict with the "foundation and the norm of the Church." Although the principle of mutual critique is accepted, it is here *a problem of self-reference*. The problem is twofold. One aspect of this problem becomes apparent in the statement's use of the terminology from the Gospel of John: "in the world"/"not of the world." The concern for the legitimate and valuable elements of the manifold cultures of the world (as God's creation) is here indiscriminately discarded, using the term *world* to describe the God-denying, sinful "world." That terminology conveys a disputable theological evaluation of culture. Culture is seen less as an expression of God's creation than as the sinful existence of human beings. There is, however, no theological possibility for an exclusive choice between the two alternatives.[161]

Second, the theological problem at stake is more complex than the alternatives *either* Scripture *or* situation, either text or context. It is a burning issue of theological hermeneutics: Can there possibly be a common, neutral biblical exegesis, free from what is "historically arbitrary"? How can any attempt to establish unity be without historical, contextual elements? In this respect the statement exaggerates its point when claiming the need to learn lay aside what is "specifically cultural" in the faith. Any theologian must do theology in the world in a certain context, bound to the elements of the culture (language, history, traditions, etc).[162]

---

the ecumenical endeavours, the question of practice is formulated: "How many of the 'results' obtained from inter-confessional dialogues will ever reach the practical level?" This question is directed both to the ecumenical dialogue and those responsible for its reception in the churches (Ecumenical Methodology 1976:32).

161. This analysis can be confirmed by a reference to how the Statement itself explicitly criticized the attempts to include theology of creation on the ecumenical process: "The question of unity has been wrongly placed in the context of creation" (Ecumenical Methodology 1976:31).

162. The problem is illustrated in the text itself. As argument against "empirical reality as source

The same points and problems are apparent when analyzing the use of the notion of *catholicity* in the same document. We find a strong critique against tendencies to blur the unity of the Church with the unity of the world by a movement toward "a catholicity whose peculiar quality was an open, communicative solidarity and which had the stamp of a universal culture." The possibility of Christian unity could be reduced to the potential for intercultural communication.[163] The alternative is formulated as the conclusion of the statement: "The conclusion, then, is that we consistently and resolutely take the line that ecumenical method is centered in doctrinal dialogues on the basis of holy Scripture. We must first of all dig deep into the Gospel, as it is given us in the word of the Scriptures. This is the way to a true catholicity of the Church."[164]

These comments sharpen the awareness of what is really meant by "catholicity" in ecumenical dialogue. "Catholicity" is indeed a notion that must be theologically defined as more than a formal category. It is more than mere "universality." Abandoning its theological "fundament and norm," theology will be arbitrary and lose both relevance and interest. But development of a sense of catholicity in the churches, as a tool toward unity and as a description of the goal of unity, cannot ignore the problem of self-reference and cultural heritage in theological hermeneutics. These problems of accountability are not solved by a call for more Bible studies, either.

A glance at a totally different opinion can contribute to this analysis of the impact of mutual accountability for ecumenical methodology. The Australian theologian Richard Campbell reflected on his experience in Accra in 1974 in an article published by Faith and Order together with the Norwegian Statement. Responding to the debate in Accra, he argues that it raised a fundamental problem of theological methodology. It was "not a mere flourish of anti-colonialist rhetoric, nor even a point about the need for greater sensitivity in the way the Church impinges on a non-Christian culture."[165]

---

of Christian knowledge" is used the Lutheran distinction between faith and works, where experience and empiri is theologically classified as "works" (33). This and other examples show how even this text claiming a common noncultural platform is very much bound to a historical, confessional, and contextual discussion between Catholic theology and Protestant theology about the meaning of "faith," "love," "experience," "works," and so on. The Roman Catholic–Lutheran dialogue, pursued in a classical theological style and presented in "Joint Declaration on the Doctrine of Justification" (signed 1999), shows the insufficiency in an absolute distinction between faith and work in a description of Christian life in this world.

163. Ecumenical Methodology 1976:30–32. The committee noticed with satisfaction a shift in this tendency at the Nairobi assembly in 1975: "We hope that trend has now been arrested."

164. Ecumenical Methodology 1976:40.

165. Campbell describes the debate as a "conflict [that] grew out of the unshakeable insistence of the third world delegates on the necessity for theological activity to reflect the particular and local character of the different human contexts in which it occurs" (Campbell 1976:11).

The problem, according to Campbell, is how the Platonic idea of "eternal truths" has dominated Western thought, theology, and even the ecumenical dialogue. He attacks the programme of "moving away from the partial and inadequate propositions we hold as opinions and uncovering the hidden delineations of unchangeable reality."[166] Since no existence can be proved from logic or definitions alone, the Christian doctrines cannot be safeguarded this way, either.[167] The perception that all human existence, action, and speech are historical is in some sense rather new. But Campbell argues[168] that the Western consciousness of truth has gone from a Greek to an Old Testament idea of truth (*emeth*). "*Emeth* is not at hand once and for all as a timeless, binding state of affairs. Rather, it must occur again and again. It means the reliability, the unshakeable dependability, of a thing or word, and thus also the faithfulness of persons. In this ways *emeth* involves a future confirmation of a current expectation, and operates accordingly in an historical dimension."[169]

As he elaborates the concept of *emeth* as "reliability" and "faithfulness," he brings the questions of quality of relations, attitudes, and accountability into the heart of the theological discussion. He even argues that this concept of truth corresponds to the dimension of hope in the "Giving Account" study: it is through historical experiences that the correspondence between what is said and done can be confirmed. Tested attitudes raise hope. Thereby he argues that these qualities are not only matters of ecclesiological structures, but belong also to the center of theological hermeneutics as it is exercised in ecumenical dialogue.

The consequence of this position is that the concept of *authority* must be reconsidered in terms of these attitudes. It is "doubtful whether any church can claim that its own authoritative doctrine attests to the fullness of truth." The possibility is not definite judgments once and for all, but "authentically Christian expression—of speech and deed—in a given historical and social context."[170] At this point he conveys the "*living* tradition" as the alternative approach. The living traditions (also in plural!) are here understood as the category for authenticity and unity, in terms that have much in common with

---

166. Campbell 1976:13.

167. Campbell 1976:13–16. He understands the Roman Catholic doctrine of infallibility as an intention of being able "to present the eternal truth of God." (This is not the case if the dogma of Vatican I is understood historically, according to Houtepen; see pp. 111–24.) He also argues "the same concept of truth underlies Protestant scholasticism" (ibid., 16).

168. With an unspecific reference to "Pannenberg" (Campbell 1976:17).

169. Campbell 1976:17.

170. Campbell 1976:18, 22. These attitudes were connected with an understanding of authority in the study of "Teaching Authoritatively Today." Campbell here proposes a fundamental theological and philosophical argument for this understanding of authority.

my preliminary definition of mutual accountability. "Rather the living tradition, or living traditions, must be constantly adapting, criticizing, correcting, venturing. But insofar as there is a church, it will need to have some way of expressing and ensuring faithful, unified action from its members, and that will require the existence of some form of authoritative teaching."[171]

This approach raises, of course, the issue of relativism and historical skepticism. Campbell is aware of this, and formulates an alternative to that as well as to ideas of absolute, eternal truth. In his attempt to find a way out of this dilemma, his argument for the possibility of ecumenical dialogue hangs on the significance of attitudes as *mutual solidarity in terms of sensitivity and acceptance*. He makes the problem of intercontextual theology a matter of hermeneutics developed in a moral and ecclesiological perspective:

> Far from necessarily preventing a person from penetrating the "thought-world" of another, sensitivity to the way his own content conditions his concepts, outlook and concerns can free him from the limitations of his own intellectual horizons and enable him to enter the self-understanding of someone in a different context. Indeed, I would go further, the recognition of one's own relativity, that is, of how one's own self-understanding and one's grasp of truth is conditioned by and only authentic within one's own particular "thought-world," is a *pre-condition* for recognizing the self-understanding and grasp of truth of another in another context. It is precisely those who tend to absolutize their modes of self-description and values, and their associated truths, who fail to appreciate the authenticity of others who live in a different cultural or historical context. . . . No matter how much the language, the implicit ideologies, the styles, the ethos, and the apparent implicit doctrines in different churches operating in different contexts may differ, only on the basis of mutual acceptance of one another as each in its way striving to present a faithful (i.e. true) presentation of Christian thought and practice can ecumenical dialogue proceed.[172]

Recognition of the historicity and contextuality of theological statements, when taken seriously into a reflection of potential unity, leads toward an understanding of dialogue where attitudes play a crucial role. Campbell particularly elaborates the need for an honest self-reference "of one's own relativity."[173] We

---

171. Campbell 1976:22; italics mine.
172. Campbell 1976:23.
173. This was the most problematic point according to my interpretation of the Norwegian Statement above.

find here a remarkable connection between sensitivity, openness, self-awareness, self-criticism, and mutual acceptance. It is a picture of a gentle but deeply honest and serious dialogue. This, not the tough, academic confrontation judging one another, is regarded as the way forward.

Campbell's point about the Platonic heritage in theology hits to some extent the argument of the Norwegian committee. It might be regarded as tough and one-sided. Theologians are not necessarily presupposing Platonic truth when they try to develop a common understanding of biblical theology as a basis for unity in the Church. A more plausible philosophical heritage for the attempts to establish one common expression and formulation of the Christian faith is a reflex of the project of modernity. As Campbell himself also shows, the biblical texts are not to be understood primarily from a Greek context.

Although both Campbell and the Norwegian Statement emphatically speak of the need for what I would call a mutual accountable encounter, there is a remarkable difference in the style and—attitude—that they recommend for these encounters. Campbell is tough against traditional doctrinal theology, but speaks with great sensitivity to the context of the Third World. He refers to what he had learned about the lack of self-reference as the weak point of "Western theology," through reflections on the history of church and theology in Australia.[174] The Norwegian Statement promotes a classical conceptual method based on biblical and doctrinal "truths," and is tough against promotions of what might be "historically arbitrary." Both demands in reality an attitude of humility and self-critique. But they speak from different contexts. The Norwegian Statement seems to take the academic dispute as model for the recommendations of "learning to lay aside" and to act accordingly. The Accra text on methodology and Campbell's article convey the need for mutual critique, but appeal strongly to solidarity as sensitivity, acceptance, and confirmation of what might be different. These texts reflect more the need for attitudes of humility and sensitivity, taking into account that those cultures overruled and not accepted by Christian mission, and maybe even by ecumenical dialogue, do not have the same academic language, background, and style. It might also be seen as more adequate in a situation when the ecumenical movement was

---

174. A typical example of his reflections: "Contextual theology in Australia is conspicuous by its absence. It is perhaps significant that the Church arrived in Australia in the person of the military chaplain—on the side of established authority—and has been dominated by sectarian rivalry and bitterness carried over unchanged from the 'old country'. . . . The task indeed is doubly difficult: we need first to uncover those basic concepts in terms of which Australians understand themselves, and then to develop theological models which genuinely speak to people in this situation" (Campbell 1976:19).

increasingly hearing the voices of those who had been living in oppressed and marginalized cultures.

This shows that a principle of "mutual accountability" can be applied in different ways. Openness and self-critique is common to both of them. But there are different approaches to how the mutually accountable encounter in itself is a theologically significant point of hermeneutics. The notion of "mutuality" can be understood as a matter of open, critical, but fair and balanced dialogue. It can also have a connotation of empathy and sensitivity in favor of the other. In Campbell's perspective, the proper ecumenical attitudes are presuppositions for a fruitful learning process of the truth; by developing the living tradition, true new insight and contributions can be found. In the Norwegian Statement the mutually accountable encounter is primarily seen as a tough, cleansing process, in which the contextual should be sloughed off. For a theory of mutual accountability it is relevant to discuss both perspectives.

Summary

This study programme combined the traditional Faith and Order agenda of establishing unity among the churches with a programme to elaborate expressions of Christian faith as relevant, credible contextual statements of hope. The intention was to bring these accounts together in a mutual exchange, challenge, and enrichment to develop the model of conciliarity and to formulate a common account of hope. The study unveiled, not surprisingly, several tensions. It exposed the difference between theologians working within a classic, Western, academic theological paradigm, pursuing a modern concept of unity as common concepts, expressions, and forms of Christian faith, and more cultural, political, and contextual approaches to theology. In this postcolonial period it was time to be outspoken about how Christian mission had not always represented hope for local people and cultures in the Third World. The situation could even be described as "hope against hope." The study also revealed a tension between those who would pursue unity by healing the divisions in this world and those theologians concerned about the classical confessional divisions.

In these attempts to exercise new methods, to unveil differences and tensions, and to realize conciliar fellowship, we find important reflections on the discipline of fellowship and the attitudes required to handle these challenges: to balance the legitimate diversity and the concern for unity; to combine independence and interdependence; to focus both contextuality and communality.

The specific contributions from this study toward a theory of mutual accountability are most of all the recognition of the need for "discipline of fellowship," if the ecumenical fellowship should give account of the differences it really represents. To be able to give account is to some extent described as an attitude. To be able to let the account be heard, even examined in a mutual fellowship, requires mutual accountability. This implies a sense of being a steward, taking care of and giving account of how the common treasure of Christian tradition is stewarded when facing particular contextual challenges. Further, it means a willingness to pursue not only mutual encounters of accounts of hope, but to work toward common expressions of hope.

The two reports from the commission meetings in Accra and Bangalore are attempts to formulate a common account of hope. There we find important examples of the relevance of opening the floor for mutual critique and learning. After Accra (1974) the ecumenical fellowship could not ignore the problems of how the same texts and message could be used both for liberation and oppression, both to give hope and to remove hope. The report of the process might be as important as the final formulations. The attitude of love, with the reference to the biblical images of what that is, became a fundamental ecumenical issue. This love should combine mutual respect for diversity and ability to maintain one's own position and conviction. Particularly for the theologians and churches in the "North," the urgency of respect for the convictions of churches elsewhere is maintained. The "new churches" should be respected for interpretations maybe even closer to the biblical world than Western academic theology could offer. It is noteworthy how the report gives account of the vulnerability of all partners involved in giving accounts of the use of the Christian tradition.

The Bangalore meeting (1978) tried even more to give account together of the given tradition, the faith in the triune God. The mutual encounter makes the churches mutually accountable for how they have stewarded this treasure. Bangalore also focused on how the giving of accounts implies the willingness to take risks. This type of attitude is an important supplementary aspect of being accountable in a fellowship. It is the risk of dialogue, to encounter one another without a domineering, self-defensive approach.

The debate on methodology unveiled important distinctions in what mutual accountability should imply in the ecumenical fellowship. Accountability to the common treasure in Scripture (and Tradition) cannot be ignored. The open and mutual encounter could, however, be the most privileged place to test whether the churches have been accountable to their common foundation. But the criteria for this mutual testing are seen very differently. Some emphasize the need to lay aside what might be historical and contextually arbitrary. Others ask how the biblical message has become historically and contextually relevant, stressing that the concept of truth is a matter of reliability, not universal statements. The first position is criticized as a Platonic dream, the second as a method making experience a second source of revelation and reducing catholicity to a matter of communication.

This debate shows that the hermeneutic of dialogue is a matter of process as well as of substance. The problems of ecumenical methodology and hermeneutics have to be discussed in respect to ecumenical attitudes. Making one another mutually accountable is a tough, radical critique as well as a more sensitive, accepting approach to contextual diversity. The notion of "mutual accountability" must, therefore, be qualified when it is used to define standards for ecumenical dialogue. The common reports emphasize a willingness to take a radical self-critical approach. The churches should be accountable in the sense of faithfulness to the sources and foundation of the Church. The "Giving Account" study made clear, however, that the problem was how that could be realized in a setting of theologically legitimized diversity.

Generally speaking, the "Giving Account" study continued the line from Montreal. The task to define The Tradition embodied in the many traditions is here discussed not in respect to confessional diversity but contextual differences. The problem is sharpened: the churches are asked to be accountable to one another not only for the inherited interpretations, practice, and confessions, but also for how the Tradition is made relevant as an account of hope *today*. The integration of the agenda for a common expression of Christian hope with the task of being contextually relevant was, however, not solved. Nevertheless, one lasting result of the study could be the recognition of having no alternative to develop mutually accountable practices and attitudes, if the communion of churches is to handle the problems of legitimate diversity.

The Convergence of the Document *Baptism, Eucharist and Ministry* (BEM): A Result of a Mutually Accountable Process

The Success Story of Faith and Order?

The text *Baptism, Eucharist and Ministry* (BEM), approved at the 1982 commission meeting in Lima for official responses in the churches, had the longest maturation time of all Faith and Order texts. It is a "convergence text" on themes of ecumenical ecclesiology that are important not only for unity, but also because of the ecumenical problems of different understandings and practices related to them. The text, the most widely translated and distributed document in the ecumenical movement, has been more frequently discussed and given more official and more authoritative and accountable answers than any other publication from the World Council of Churches.[175] Hence, the potential contributions from this study to a theory of mutual accountability would be particularly significant.

The work on these three issues has been influenced by and has had an impact on the other Faith and Order study processes. The entire BEM process can, therefore, be seen as a weaving together of the most significant threads of the work of Faith and Order. The history of the document presented to the churches in 1982 goes back to the very beginning of the Faith and Order movement.[176] Already in Lausanne (1927) these issues were raised. Studies and reports on these three themes have accompanied the work of Faith and Order more or less continuously. The methodological change of Lund (1952) toward a common christological approach opened the way for a convergence between different languages and thought-forms, expressed in a favorably received report[177] in Montreal in 1963. The understanding of Tradition achieved in Montreal became—at least to a certain degree—operative throughout subsequent studies, searching for convergence of the many traditions. The most intense developing and maturing process was in the years between Louvain (1971) and Lima (1982).[178] The decision of the Accra meeting, confirmed by

---

175. See BEM Report 1990:9f., 14–16. The evaluation group states that "it is by far the most 'successful' publication of the World Council of Churches" (9). In 1990 there were received 186 responses from churches (including the Roman Catholic Church). The publication of the responses (6 vols.) is the largest issuance from Faith and Order ever.

176. The history of this long process is described well, e.g., in BEM 1974:76ff., and in Thurian 1986:2ff.

177. Baptism 1960. Section IV discusses baptism and eucharist, Section II ministry (Montreal 1963:61–69; 72–75).

178. After Montreal new studies were initiated. The commission meeting in Louvain in 1971 received three documents on baptism, eucharist, and ministry. Further work led to the text *One Baptism, One Eucharist and a Mutually Recognized Ministry* (BEM 1974). This text was discussed, revised, and received at the commission meeting in Accra in 1974, before it was recommended that it should be submitted to the member churches "for consideration and comment." This was strongly approved by the Nairobi assembly in 1975.

On the basis of the comments the document *Baptism, Eucharist and Ministry* was revised and presented to the commission meeting in Lima in 1982. After making some amendments, the commission voted on a motion put before the commission that the text had been ". . . brought to such a stage of maturity that it is now ready for transmission to the churches in accordance with the mandate given at the Fifth Assembly of the World Council of Churches, Nairobi 1975." It passed without negative votes or abstentions. This showed the common mutual commitment and accountability to the process given by the main Church traditions represented in the Faith and Order Commission in Lima. At the end of the discussions in Lima, the appointed committee for decisions of amendments argued strongly that the text was acceptable to specialists in liturgy and sacramental theology, accountable to academic standards. It also expected the BEM text as a common standard for other ecumenical dialogues, to which they would have to

the Nairobi assembly (1975), to initiate a comprehensive and authoritative reception process in all *churches*, was a decisive and unprecedented step toward a common authoritative account of the faith of the churches.

It is, therefore, of interest to examine if and, eventually, how recommendations of attitudes resembling my preliminary definition of mutual accountability were significant for this particularly remarkable result of the Faith and Order work. The analysis of the BEM process and the BEM text[179] here is sharpened by three questions: (1) Has a notion of mutual accountability influenced the methodology—in respect to *the proceedings*—of the study and the reception process? (2) Does the hermeneutic of "convergence" used in this text reflect a manifestation of the attitude of mutual accountability? (3) Does the text itself reflect substantially on the relevance of mutual accountability for the solutions to the problems of ecumenical ecclesiology elaborated in this text?

Mutual Accountability in the BEM Process

According to the evaluation given by the Faith and Order Commission when summing up their "gratitude for a unique process," the process leading to Lima as well as the process of reception after Lima can be described from the perspective of "mutual accountability": "The entire process has brought the churches into a new stage of mutual accountability and is in itself an expression of growth towards visible unity."[180] The "entire process" is in this context both the many years of discussion, which "was already a new and major step in the ecumenical pilgrimage of the churches," and "the exchange and reflection on BEM that followed." The number of official responses overwhelmed the commission. In their evaluation of "The BEM Process" the commission members elaborate what they think of when defining the result as a "new stage of mutual accountability."[181] Their comments correspond quite well to my preliminary definition of mutual accountability. This can be seen in four aspects of the process.

First, a strong sense of mutual accountability can be observed in the remarkable *long process of maturity*: listening, reflecting, developing, and formulating a growing consensus, which in the end in Lima was defined as "convergence." The results were dependent on accountability to what had been achieved through the process. The theologians accepted through the process

be accountable. Later the same year, the Central Committee of the World Council of Churches authorized the transmission to the churches, enclosing questions of recognition.

179. I will concentrate on the final BEM text from Lima 1982, but have in some cases a view to the preliminary texts, particularly the version recommended by the Accra meeting in 1974 (BEM 1974).

180. BEM Process and Responses 1990:16.

181. BEM Report 1990:6–16.

their mutual accountability for the same text and its implications. Through the open presentation of their own traditions, mutually challenging one another by listening to the representatives from other traditions (including the Orthodox and the Roman Catholic from Montreal 1963 onward), the theologians involved in the Faith and Order movement had been able to crystallize a presentation of important aspects of the common Tradition in regard to baptism and eucharist.

Accepting the relevance of elements other than each tradition had before was an exercise of the sense of openness to represent and discuss seriously important parts of one's own tradition. The attempt to establish a consensus (which was the original plan) of a common expression of the Christian Tradition required willingness to let one's own tradition be seen in a critical perspective, open to supplement and critique. This was the case, although the result finally was called a *convergence* text, giving a platform for mutual recognition.

The *second* aspect of mutual accountability was the *mutuality* in the procedure between the Faith and Order Commission and the churches. After the recommendation to request responses from the churches on the basis of the text presented and modified in Accra in 1974[182] (approved by the Nairobi assembly in 1975), there was until 1990 a comprehensive exchange. Already this step required a higher level of accountability from the churches in their mutual relations to other churches (through Faith and Order) than had ever happened before. Furthermore, it was a mutual procedure in several respects. By summarizing the findings, sending the results back to the churches, pinpointing the crucial points of agreement and the still challenging difficult points, the Faith and Order Commission involved the churches in a deep kind of mutual process.[183] On this basis the final years of improving the BEM text before Lima—the finishing of the text, the questions to the churches, the gathering of six volumes of answers, and a final evaluation of them—was a second, larger "lap" of the same procedure. This way of relating to one another in a responsible way can, indeed, be described as "mutual accountability."

The *third* aspect of mutual accountability was *to mobilize "the highest appropriate authority" in the churches*. This decision in the Lima Faith and Order meeting reflects the strong will, evident first at Nairobi, to achieve a conciliar fellowship among the churches. To make any step further toward that goal, a common understanding and approach to the sacraments and a mutual recognition of ministry was required. Without getting accountable answers, there could be no estimate of possibilities for achieving such a goal.

---

182. BEM 1974.
183. BEM Response 1977.

The fourth aspect of mutual accountability in this process was a matter of procedure as well as theology. The Faith and Order Commission, through the questions raised in the cover letter to the churches, aimed at a *reception* of the text by *recognizing* the text as an expression of the *faith through the ages (the apostolic faith)*.

The churches were asked to

> prepare an official response to this text at the highest appropriate level of authority, whether it be a council, synod, conference, assembly or other body. In support of this process of reception, the Commission would be pleased to know as precisely as possible
> - the extent to which your church can recognize in this text the faith of the Church through the ages;
> - the consequences your church can draw from this text for its relations and dialogues with other churches, particularly with those churches which also recognize the text as an expression of apostolic faith;
> - the guidance your church can take from this text for its worship, educational, ethical, and spiritual life and witness;
> - the suggestion your church can make for the ongoing work of Faith and Order as it relates the material of this text on Baptism, Eucharist and Ministry to its long-range research project "Towards the Apostolic Faith Today."[184]

There are two sets of problems in the understanding of these questions that can be discussed from the perspective of mutual accountability. The *first* is what kind of *Verbindlichkeit* was asked for through these questions. In other words: What was meant by "recognize" here? There are several signs in the responses that some churches understood it as "reception," to approbate the content of this text as one's own tradition or position. The questions did not aim at reception primarily in a canonical sense. Recognition in the sense of acceptance of something as belonging to the Christian Tradition and as a genuine (or at least an acceptable) element of this Tradition is a presupposition for this kind of "reception."[185]

How does "mutual accountability" correspond to the distinctions made here? "Reception" is (in the qualified sense) indeed an expression of mutual accountability if it leads to binding statements making these results of mutual

---
184. BEM 1982:x (preface).
185. Gerard Kelly has studied the responses from this perspective, and proposes that the blurring of the concepts of "recognition" and "reception" in this part of the BEM process became an important problem (Kelly 1996:157–81). Kelly defines "reception" as a rather binding type of procedure, and follows to a large extent the definition of "recognition" elaborated by Tillard; cf. Tillard 1992b.

dialogue part of one's own tradition. A church that has bound itself to the content of the text in this sense would be mutually accountable to the other partners making the same commitment.

Nevertheless, the level of "recognition" requires elements of mutual accountability, too. It requires an attitude of active listening. But it implies more than that. It means a qualified, participatory approach involving an attitude of openness and self-criticism. To recognize something other than one's own tradition means to accept a potential diversity, at least to some extent: there might be other appropriate ways to form and use the Christian Tradition than we have done. It also means openness to other perspectives and interpretations of the Christian tradition, implying a willingness to scrutinize the other's tradition for the purpose of learning from it.

The strongest element of conciliar fellowship in the meaning of *Verbindlichkeit* is, of course, to be found in the concept of "reception." This could be used to draw the conclusion that there are (at least) two types of mutual accountability that need to be clearly distinguished. It might even be an argument for using the terms *recognition* and *reception* to make these distinctions transparent. However, the perspective launched by exploring the *attitude* of mutual accountability brings in a further dimension besides "recognition" and "reception." This attitude is made operative in the ecumenical fellowship in those dimensions but is not limited to them. Mutual accountability is, therefore, an attitude required in the phase of dialogue as well as in the process of recognition or reception, even in a permanent, well-structured conciliar fellowship.

Some of the critical responses from the churches could be interpreted as reinforcement of a confessional, if not to say a confessionalistic, approach to the ecumenical process.[186] This could be seen as failing accountability to the BEM process. However, these signs of a serious theological discussion of the BEM text could be interpreted, conversely, as a sign of mutual accountability. If the text had been received without taking into account the confessional basis of the churches, and without signs of challenging confessional positions, there would be less reliability and less potential for a significant self-critical reception.[187]

The *second* set of problems involved in the questions following the BEM text is a matter of understanding "catholicity," "conciliarity," and "tradition." The questions show how the project aimed at more than mutual accountability on the synchronic level among the churches involved and responding at the end of the 20th century. It also aimed at accountability to "the faith through the

---

186. According to the profile of some critical responses referred to in BEM Report 1990:29–31.

187. The rather optimistic evaluation of the impact of the churches' responses to BEM, in spite of the fact that several churches were critical to BEM from their confessional positions, could be based on this kind of reflection. It is, however, not explicitly said in the evaluation (BEM Report 1990).

ages," what Montreal called *The Tradition*. But how was the relation between mutual accountability to the contributions, questions and positions from the traditions of today and The One Tradition understood?

The question raised in the Faith and Order Commission's evaluation of the responses was: Were these points of convergence (in the BEM document and in the responses) expressions of The Tradition found only in the many traditions or were they articulations of The Tradition, which had been formulated, for instance, in the early Church and could be formulated as such through the ecumenical dialogue?[188] The discussion raised the question of the significance of the "undivided church,"[189] and it obviously touched on the relevance of the concepts from Montreal and the concept of "reconciled diversity."

The relevance of this discussion for the definition of mutual accountability is this: Were the churches (when they were asked to recognize the BEM text) asked to be mutually accountable to a gathering of elements from the diversity among them; or were the churches asked to confirm their readiness to be mutually accountable to a formulation of The Tradition not identical to one of the traditions maintained by the churches?

The text of BEM was matured through reflecting on contributions from the churches and their confessional traditions. There was also a strong desire to find and formulate the common elements of understanding the BEM issues found in the Scriptures and in the early church. But there were also some new approaches, matured through the ecumenical movement, that made it possible to identify a "new ecumenical theologoumen" or even more.[190] The question at stake might, therefore, be more complicated than an either-or.

The rationale of the BEM process had been to establish a common text, consensus, or convergence, which should challenge all churches by its attempt to formulate the common Tradition. For example, the Lutheran churches were not explicitly asked to recognize the Roman Catholic or the Anglican

---

188. This is the question discussed by Kelly; see Kelly 1996:196–200. He identifies the positions in the discussion by the statements of Mary Tanner in Stavanger (1985) and Günther Gassmann the year after in the Standing Commission meeting in Potsdam. According to Kelly, Tanner understood the BEM endeavour to be a way "to get hold of the common tradition," not to look for how much the text is recognizable for one's own tradition. Gassmann (again according to Kelly) held the position that the "faith through the ages" could not be found in abstraction from the confessional and ecclesial traditions through which this faith comes to expression. This might be an exaggeration of the differences between Tanner and Gassmann.

189. Emphasized by Tanner; see Kelly 1996:196.

190. In his analysis of the "ecumenical ecclesiology" found in the BEM responses, Anton Houtepen describes several "basic ecclesial convergences" in the material received; cf. Houtepen 1989:222–23. He calls the understanding of Church as mystery and sacrament, as sign and instrument of the salvation of humanity "a rather recent ecumenical theologoumen," which seemed to have found a solid place in Faith and Order's constituency (ibid., 228).

understanding of eucharist and ministry, but to recognize a text that had been established by the Faith and Order Commission as a common expression of what was believed to be "the faith through the ages," in which the importance of "*epiklesis*" and "apostolic succession" was argued for. Hence, there was no way to present the text as a gathering of confessional points of view. The proper interrelation between the two alternatives is, therefore, given a form in the BEM text and process.

This solution given in the BEM text might become even clearer when seen from the perspective of mutual accountability. If the attitude required in the BEM process—being open to others, combined with ability to self-critique and to be reliable in a fellowship—is emphasized, the most important question is not whether what is common for the fellowship (The Tradition) exists on its own, separate from the manifold of traditions. What does matter is whether there is willingness to be mutually accountable to *this* expression of The Tradition given in the text.

The main theological significance today of the so-called undivided church is the challenge to remain accountable to the content of the origin of Christian Tradition in the Scriptures, as this has been expressed, for instance, in the studies leading to the BEM text. To deny the potential of somehow finding a common expression of The Tradition is counterproductive, and can be seen as a tendency toward confessional or contextual isolation, avoiding the demand of being held accountable in a wider forum.

If the concept of The Tradition is used very rigidly, however, it might become a matter of domineering power from the mainline traditions. The perspective of mutual accountability emphasizes the need to listen to the other, and not only to the dominant tradition. This theological point is excellently expressed at the very end of the BEM text itself: "Openness to each other holds the possibility that the Spirit may well speak to one church through the insight of another."[191] These issues can be further elaborated through some examples from the BEM text.

The Hermeneutics of the BEM Text as an Example of Mutual Accountability

It is not said explicitly in the BEM text that mutual accountability should be a goal or a guiding principle for the endeavour. According to the profile of the entire process, it is, nevertheless, relevant to ask whether the hermeneutics of "convergence" in the BEM text can be interpreted as an exercise of mutual accountability. This type of accountability between the traditions and the churches cannot be seen apart from the accountability to the origin of the Christian Tradition manifested in the reflections of BEM, particularly the

---

191. BEM 1982:32 (M54).

content of the Bible texts, and the texts and practice from the early Church. This is a (often implicit) platform for the common statements as well as the openness to some diversity. But there is no explicit hermeneutical reflection in the BEM texts on the relation between the New Testament texts, the creeds, and other texts from the early Church, and the later expressions of "the faith through the ages."

Reflections on the interrelations between the text and the context of the problems treated in the text can be traced in the "commentaries" alongside the main text. The first "commentary" is devoted to the division among churches due to "the inability of the churches mutually to recognize their various practices of baptism as sharing in the one baptism." This is identified as one of the most important problems to be solved by the ecumenical endeavour. The commentary ends: "The need to recover baptismal unity is at the heart of the ecumenical task as it is central for the realization of genuine partnership within the Christian communities."[192] The "various practices of baptism" causing and exposing the division between churches that practice infant baptism, thereby emphasizing God's action for salvation in baptism, and churches that baptize only those able to make a confession of faith for themselves, is a major concern in the BEM text.[193]

The first paragraphs of the *Baptism* text (B) present what is supposed to be the common Christian tradition on baptism, basically referring to New Testament aspects of baptism. Arguments for several positions are thereby defined within the one apostolic tradition. It is maintained that "baptism is both God's gift and our human response to that gift," "a washing away from sin" that has "ethical implications."[194] These sentences show clearly the attempt to qualify the concerns of different positions as belonging to genuine Christian Tradition—in this case the emphasis on the unconditional gift of grace in baptism and the emphasis on the life in faith and discipleship according to baptism.[195]

There are other explicit references to different positions:

> Both the baptism of believers and the baptism of infants take place in the church as the community of faith. . . . In both cases, the baptized person will have to grow in the understanding of faith. . . . All baptism is rooted in and declares Christ's faithfulness unto death. . . . At every baptism the whole

---

192. BEM 1982:3 (Commentary to B6).

193. Other differences between the churches concerning baptism are addressed in the BEM text, but this has a central place and can serve as an adequate example of the argument in the text.

194. BEM 1982:2f. (B8, B2, B4).

195. The first sentence (gift and response to the gift) was criticized by several churches, mostly Lutheran—not surprisingly, for blurring the different status of the gift of God and the reception of the gift. See BEM Report 1990:44.

congregation reaffirms its faith in God and pledges itself to provide an environment of witness and service.[196]
The differences between infant and believers' baptism become less sharp when it is recognized that both forms of baptism embody God's own initiative in Christ and express a response of faith made within the believing community. . . . Both forms of baptism require a similar and responsible attitude towards Christian nurture.[197]

These and other examples show that the text is aiming at taking the accounts of the different traditions seriously. This text reflects mutual listening to the accounts. The reasons given for the different positions are presented as parts of a common Christian tradition. Presenting this text to the churches means to require accountability to the different accents in the biblical theology of baptism, each of them emphasized by different church traditions.

These hermeneutics toward convergence through being mutually accountable in the formulation of what is a common Christian tradition of baptism is prolonged into explicit challenges to the churches representing the respective positions. These challenges link the hermeneutics of the previous phases of dialogue and the formulation of The Tradition in the BEM text directly to the process of reception. They are formulated as challenges to the *attitudes* of the churches in their practice of their form of baptism:

> Both forms of baptism require a similar and responsible attitude towards Christian nurture. A rediscovery of the continuing character of Christian nurture may facilitate the mutual acceptance of different initiation practices.[198]

> In order to overcome their differences, believer baptists and those who practice infant baptism should reconsider certain aspects of their practices. The first may seek to express more visibly the fact that children are placed under the protection of God's grace. The latter must guard themselves against the practice of apparently indiscriminate baptism and take more seriously their responsibility for the nurture of baptized children to mature commitment to Christ.[199]

This point is made even more specific, emphasizing the situation of mutual challenge implied in the BEM text: "In many large European and North

---

196. BEM 1982:4 (B12).
197. BEM 1982:5 (Comm. B12).
198. BEM 1982:5 (Comm. B12).
199. BEM 1982:6 (B16).

American majority churches infant baptism is often practiced in an apparently indiscriminate way. This contributes to the reluctance of churches which practice believers' baptism to acknowledge the validity of infant baptism; this fact should lead to more critical reflection on the meaning of baptism within those majority churches themselves."[200]

The attitude required is the responsibility to strengthen the aspects that could be defended as genuine expressions of the common Tradition. In the first passage it implies demonstrating the unbreakable relation between baptism and (nurturing of) Christian faith and life. The two latter passages are some of the most profound examples of how the BEM text requires an attitude of willingness to be self-critical to one's own practice and theology supporting the respective practices. Taking into account the common Tradition (baptism as sign of God's grace and as the start of discipleship and commitment to Christ), the problems of the respective positions are identified rather frankly. Thus, we here find that one important link between the three stages (dialogue, convergence, reception) is the practice of mutual accountability in the entire ecumenical process.

It is significant for our discussion of mutual accountability that these requirements of ecumenical attitudes in the churches are primarily formulated in terms of accountability to the original and common Christian Tradition. Indirectly, it is also a requirement of *mutual* accountability to the aspects of baptism emphasized in other traditions (e.g., the admonition to those who practice infant baptism to reinforce the importance of Christian commitment). These two perspectives of accountability (to the one Tradition and to one another) are not separated in the BEM text. The text is first of all formulated as a definition of the common Tradition, to which the churches are called to be accountable. However, they can only be so in mutual accountability to the others and to the insights of differing traditions: the formulation of BEM is relying on the insights from both multilateral and bilateral dialogues. Accountability to the common Tradition is the premise for the mutual accountability between the churches in the communion of churches.

Finally, it is interesting to see that when it comes to the controversial and challenging points of the argument, the *practice* of baptism is more in focus than is the understanding. The practice of baptism exposes whether and how the churches could be more faithful to the common Christian Tradition and overcome their divisions. The practice can be changed in a way that can be observed and recognized. This focus on practice reinforces the aspect of mutual

---

200. BEM 1982:7 (Comm. B21 [b]).

accountability required as an attitude, which could and should be demonstrated in action more than in intentions and statements.

Some of the same features can be seen in the text on *Eucharist* (E). The text pays much attention to two basic elements of the Christian Tradition on the eucharist: *anamnesis*, defined as the "memorial of the crucified and risen Christ," and *epiklesis*, "the invocation of the Spirit."[201] The biblical origin of the aspect of *anamnesis* is widely demonstrated and discussed as the tradition from Jesus Christ himself. The reflections on *epiklesis* are an application of trinitarian theology to the eucharist. Both aspects are therefore presented as the most central part of the common Tradition of the Church.

In two commentaries, stronger accountability to these aspects of the common Tradition is recommended as a proper way to overcome the divisions and controversies on the meaning of "sacrifice" and the definition of the moment of consecration.

> In the light of the biblical conception of memorial, all churches might want to review the old controversies about "sacrifice" and deepen their understanding of the reasons why other traditions than their own have either used or rejected this term. The invocation of the Spirit was made both on the community and on the elements of bread and wine. Recovery of such an understanding may help us overcome our difficulties concerning a special moment of consecration.[202]

The specific emphasis of different traditions is taken into account concerning the understanding of eucharist as sacrifice.[203] The text also tries to combine the concern for the preaching of God's word as the proper *anamnesis* and the Roman Catholic and Orthodox focus on the eucharist as the real *anamnesis*.[204]

---

201. BEM 1982:11 (E5), 13 (title of part C). BEM 1982:11 (Comm. E8) and 13 (Comm. E14). Already in the previous phases of the formulation of the Eucharist text, the concepts of anamnesis and epiklesis are marked as significant points of convergence; cf. Presentation of BEM 1977.

202. BEM 1982:11 (Comm. E8) and 13 (Comm. E14).

203. The Lutheran tradition is taken into account by the stress of the sacrifice once for all and the statement that it is not only a calling to mind of what is past and of its significance. The Reformed tradition is brought forward through the use of the terminology on the eucharist as "the living and effective sign of his sacrifice." The Roman Catholic tradition is referred to by saying "it is in the light of the significance of the eucharist as intercession that references to the eucharist in Catholic theology as 'propitiatory sacrifice' may be understood. . . . In the memorial of the eucharist, however, the Church offers its intercession in communion with Christ, our great High Priest" (BEM 1982:11 [E5–8.10 and Comm. E8]). (The RCC did not, however, find the perspective of "intercession" satisfying to explain their tradition about eucharist as sacrifice; cf. BEM Report 1990:66f.)

204. "Since the *anamnesis* of Christ is the very content of the preached Word as it is of the

Again, the churches are challenged to confirm their accountability to the basic elements of the common Tradition, through recognition of different positions, practices, and aspects as legitimate expressions of this Tradition. Particular weight is given to understanding the intention behind them. To sum up: the challenges to overcome the old differences are formulated as a call to accountability to the common Tradition, embedded in the many traditions, and to take a critical view of one's own tradition.

The same feature can be seen in the discussion of the *epiklesis*. To confirm the common Christian Tradition means to focus the trinitarian structure of the eucharist, according to the text. That would make a contradiction between the words of Christ and the invocation of the Spirit unnecessary. "The bond between the eucharistic celebration and the mystery of the Triune God reveals the role of the Holy Spirit as the One who makes the historical words of Jesus present and alive."[205]

Whether the *epiklesis* should be over the elements or the community is a matter commented on in the responses to BEM. In the comments to the responses from the commission, the methodology of the BEM text is repeated in another clarification of this point. The comments are taking into account both views, but subsuming them under the impossibility of separating the community and the elements, according to the old Christian Tradition.[206]

The BEM texts on eucharist pose a remarkably clear challenge to the churches to prolong the hermeneutics of the BEM text, adjusting and revising their theology and praxis continuously in the light of their accountability to the common Tradition. "The best way towards unity in eucharistic celebration and communion is the renewal of the eucharist itself in the different churches in regard to teaching and liturgy. The churches should test their liturgies in the light of the eucharistic agreement now in the process of attainment."[207]

Another example of this hermeneutic can be seen in the text on *Ministry* (M). The reflections on *succession in the apostolic tradition* represent a relevant and interesting example, particularly in regard to the later reception of BEM.[208] "Apostolic tradition in the Church means continuity in the permanent characteristics of the Church of the apostles: witness to the apostolic faith, proclamation and fresh interpretation of the Gospel, celebration of baptism and the eucharist, the transmission of ministerial responsibilities, communion in prayer, love, joy and suffering, service to the sick and the needy, unity among

---

eucharistic meal, each reinforces the other. The celebration of the eucharist properly includes the proclamation of the Word" (BEM 1982:12 [E12]).

205. BEM 1982:13 (E14).

206. BEM Report 1990:116.

207. BEM 1982:16 (E28).

208. BEM 1982:28–30 (M34–38 with commentaries).

the local churches and sharing the gifts which the Lord has given to each."[209] This list of "permanent characteristics" can be interpreted as acts which show the accountability to the apostolic tradition: to do what the apostles did, participating in the great mission of God in the world through the Church; in witness, celebration, proclamation, sharing, and service. Doing this, the Church shows its legitimacy through being faithful to the pattern of life, the teaching, and the challenges given in the tradition from the apostles, the "original transmitters of the Gospel, of the tradition of the saving words and acts of Jesus Christ which constitute the life of the Church."[210]

This understanding of the apostolic tradition is a challenge not only to reductionism of the tradition to "the Word," but also to tendencies to identify the criterion of apostolicity as the historic episcopal succession. To the task of ministry belong continuity and renewal, the witness to the apostolic faith as well as the "fresh interpretation of the Gospel." Thus, accountability to the apostolic tradition is seen primarily as a matter for the whole mutual fellowship of faith that lives from the apostolic witness of the gospel. This fellowship should be united in manifestations of attitudes: "prayer, love, joy and suffering, service to the sick and needy."

This framework is important for understanding the solution provided to the problem of *apostolic succession*. The whole Church is, according to this list of characteristics, participating in the accountable care and continuation of the apostolic tradition.[211]

The text describes the succession in terms that all churches could be supposed to accept.[212] Then the language shifts slightly, to talking about the "succession" in terms of the succession of ministry. However, it is still focused on the common mission of the Church.[213] One further attempt is made to qualify the particular *episcopal* succession as an important element of the process of serving the apostolic tradition.[214]

---

209. BEM 1982:28 (M34).

210. BEM 1982:28 (Comm. M34).

211. "Within this apostolic tradition is an apostolic succession of the ministry which serves the continuity of the Church in its life in Christ and its faithfulness to the words and acts of Jesus transmitted by the apostles. . . . A distinction should be made, therefore, between the apostolic tradition of the whole Church and the succession of the apostolic ministry" (BEM 1982:28 [Comm. M34]).

212. "The primary manifestation of the apostolic succession is to be found in the apostolic tradition of the Church as a whole" (BEM 1982:28 [M35]).

213. "The succession is an expression of the orderly transmission of the permanence, and, therefore, of the continuity of Christ's own mission in which the Church participates. The orderly transmission of the ordained ministry is therefore a powerful expression of the continuity of the Church throughout history" (BEM 1982:28f. [M35]).

214. By a reference to the "growing Church in the early centuries" where "the succession of

In the reflections on succession, the BEM text does not go further, saying that historic episcopal succession is absolutely necessary to be accountable to the apostolic tradition or something like that. It presents challenges in both directions, without minimizing the importance of the general principle of "orderly transmission." Whether this means the historical episcopal succession as traditionally defined is not quite clear. The challenge to those "seeing little importance in orderly transmission" is "to change their conception of continuity in the apostolic tradition." To the others, the challenge is to reform the ordained ministry if it does not "serve the proclamation of the apostolic faith."[215]

These challenges are, obviously, formulated to make both positions more accountable to the content of the apostolic tradition and the intention in the tradition of historical succession. This is done through a description of how the two positions could be mutually accountable to one another, each recognizing the good intentions in the other position.

The churches that practice the historical succession through the episcopate should increasingly recognize the apostolicity of other churches in their faith, worship, and mission, as well as their intention to perform ordination in accountability.[216] The text then makes a remarkable logical turn. It says that this recognition of the good intentions of the churches without episcopal succession could "enable churches which have not retained the episcopate to appreciate the episcopal succession as a sign, though not a guarantee, of the continuity and unity of the Church."[217] In other words, the text presumes that when the nonepiscopalian churches experience that the episcopalian are recognizing their intention of being apostolic, the nonepiscopalian will be able to recognize the historical succession as a sign of the continuity of the Church.

It is important to see how the text here describes carefully a *process* of growing together—a process of growing accountability to the common Tradition through mutual recognition of the adequacy of traditions and practices of the other churches. In this process, the text warns against denials of the apostolic authenticity in faith and life of the other part. It is particularly important to avoid any suggestion that "the ministry exercised in their own tradition should

---

bishops became one of the ways . . . in which the apostolic tradition was expressed" (BEM 1982:29 [M36]). This is further elaborated in the Commentary to M36, referring to Clement of Rome for the focus on historical continuity, and to Ignatius of Antioch for the historical succession as manifestation of a spiritual reality.

215. BEM 1982:29 (M35).

216. BEM 1982:29 (M37).

217. BEM 1982:29 (M38).

be invalid until the moment that it enters into an existing line of episcopal succession."[218]

Thus, the *Ministry* text gives an illustration of how the hermeneutics of convergence practiced in BEM combines search for the common, one Tradition with the principles of mutual recognition and a demand for reception. This mutual recognition presupposes an ecumenical attitude of mutual accountability: the recognition of something different implies willingness to be accountable for one's own practice. This accountability to the common Tradition manifested in the many traditions is fulfilled in the various levels and expression of reception, where the new elements are accepted and taken into the life and premises of each church. The adequate attitude is the dynamic of the entire process. This methodology of pursuing a mutually accountable process has become one of the most important results of the BEM text.[219]

Mutual Accountability: An Important Element in the Ecclesiology of BEM

We now turn to the third dimension of the analysis: Is the attitude of mutual accountability significant in the theological elaboration of the themes in BEM? The BEM text is written not to give a complete or comprehensive dogmatic treatment of the issues of baptism, eucharist, and ministry, but what is relevant for the ecumenical problems related to them.[220] Nevertheless, the elaboration of these themes has led to a significant discussion of some of the most substantial elements of ecumenical ecclesiology in a more general sense. These issues are crucial for the understanding of the unity of the Church not only because of their controversial character. These issues deal with theological perspectives of substantial importance for the communion between churches. Because of

---

218. BEM 1982:30 (M38).

219. The Anglican–Lutheran conversations have both contributed to and extensively used the BEM text. The understanding of succession in the Porvoo Common Statement is founded on the BEM text, and prolongs the premises laid in BEM into a recommendation of "mutual acknowledgment" of episcopal ministry in the involved churches, "prior to the use of the sign of laying on of hands in the historic succession." However, this leaves some lack of clarity in respect to principal recognition of *episkopé* without "the use of the sign," e.g., the Church of Norway has interpreted this as *realiter* a mutual recognition of the episcopal ministries—*before* signing the agreement. See Porvoo 1993:28 (§53) and Tveit 1995.

220. Cf. the preface of the BEM text, ix: "Readers should not expect to find a complete theological treatment of baptism, eucharist and ministry. That would be neither appropriate nor desirable here. The agreed text purposely concentrates on those aspects of the theme that have been directly or indirectly related to the problems of mutual recognition leading to unity. The main text demonstrates the major areas of theological convergence; the added commentaries either indicate historical differences that have been overcome or identify disputed issues still in need of further research and reconciliation."

the comprehensive and mature process leading to the launching of the BEM text, it deserves particular attention in respect of what it is really saying about ecclesiology. The terminology of "mutual accountability" is not used in the BEM text itself. However, there are several passages that have much to do with the content of this concept.

Baptism is defined as the gift that makes accountable both the person baptized and the communion into which the person is baptized. "The New Testament underlines the ethical implications of baptism," and the baptized are given "a new ethical orientation under the guidance of the Holy Spirit." "Baptism is both God's gift and our human response to that gift."[221] This implies participation in the life, death, and resurrection of Christ.[222] The BEM text states strongly how baptism implies a *communal* perspective. The gift of baptism is not a private matter between the baptized and God:

> Administered in obedience to our Lord, baptism is a sign and seal of our common discipleship. Through baptism, Christians are brought into union with Christ, with each other and with the Church of every time and place. Our common baptism, which unites us to Christ in faith, is thus a basic bound of unity. . . . When baptismal unity is realized in one holy, catholic, apostolic Church, a genuine Christian witness can be made to the healing and reconciling love of God. Therefore, our common baptism into Christ constitutes a call to the churches to overcome their divisions and visibly manifest their fellowship.[223]

Thus the BEM text is a profound expression of the theology of the Church as a fellowship in which the baptized are accountable to God through the communion of the baptized. The faith of the baptized aims at "responsible membership in the body of Christ."[224] The baptized cannot act or think as if they were not accountable to the others participating in the same baptism into Christ. The responsibility of the baptized to God cannot be isolated from their mutual responsibility to each other within the one Church. Belonging together in a mutual relationship, accountable to one another, is a crucial part of this ecclesiology of baptism. The mutual accountability established through baptism is not only the *platform* for the process toward unity but belongs also to the *definition* of unity in the Church.

---

221. BEM 1982:2 (B4) and 3 (B8).
222. This is elaborated in B3 and B4, BEM 1982:2.
223. BEM 1982:3 (B6).
224. BEM 1982:3 (B8).

The communal aspect of baptism should, according to the BEM text, be clearly expressed in the celebration of baptism as *a public act* in the community of believers.

> In the celebration of baptism the symbolic dimension of water should be taken seriously and not minimized.
>
> Since baptism is intimately connected with the corporate life and worship of the Church, it should normally be administered during public worship, so that the members of the congregation may be reminded of their own baptism and may welcome into their fellowship those who are baptized and whom they are committed to nurture in the Christian faith.[225]

The different acts to signify the gift of the Holy Spirit should be performed vividly to express the reality of baptism.[226] The congregation reaffirms its faith through a baptismal ceremony.

This public performance is an important aspect of the ecclesiological character of baptism. When public in the corporate life of the Church, the celebration of baptism becomes an act through which the newly baptized and the community of the baptized are made mutually accountable to each other. The baptized person becomes a participant in the fellowship; the fellowship becomes responsible for the nurture and support of the Christian faith. Whether it is infant baptism or baptism on the basis of a personal confession, the growth of personal response in faith and Christian nurture is the way to be accountable for the gift of baptism.

The short, definitive statement, "Baptism is an unrepeatable act," is remarkable in this context. The statement is a consequence of defining baptism as the gift of God. In the context of the BEM text, however, it can also be seen as a consequence of the communal aspect of mutual accountability implied in baptism.[227] If every baptism is made in the worldwide fellowship of the churches sharing the same baptism into Christ, the church that does the baptizing is mutually accountable within this fellowship for what it is doing. A demand of repetition of baptism would therefore become an extreme sign of lack of mutual accountability to those in charge of the baptism already conducted, and a sign of neglecting the other as belonging to the body of Christ.

The BEM text on baptism opens the perspective of accountability even *beyond the communion of baptized*. To whom the baptized are mutually accountable is not limited to the members of the churches. Baptism is seen as a sign

---

225. BEM 1982:5–7 (B18 and B23). See also B12 and B17–23.

226. BEM 1982:6 (B19).

227. BEM 1982:4 (B13). This is placed after the paragraph on baptism as an act in and of the community (12).

of the kingdom of God and of the life of the world to come. This has many implications: "Through the gifts of faith, hope and love, baptism has a dynamic which embraces the whole of life, extends to all nations, and anticipates the day when every tongue will confess that Jesus Christ is Lord to the glory of God the Father."[228] This is a rather ambitious language and no less ambitious as a programme for every baptized person. Facing this enormous task, "to reflect the glory of the Lord," it is no exaggeration to say that "the life of the Christian is necessarily one of continuing struggle yet also of continuing experience of grace."[229]

These universal aspects of baptism can be seen as an application to the theology of baptism of the points made in the "Giving Account" study. "They [the baptized believers] have a common responsibility, here and now, to bear witness to the Gospel of Christ, the Liberator of all human beings. The context of this witness is the Church and the world. Within a fellowship of witness and service, Christians discover the full significance of the one baptism as the gift of God to all God's people."[230] The text makes two quite important points here. *First*, there is a principal theological accountability to humanity implied in baptism. This, of course, has very different forms and can be expressed and explained in countless ways. The openness of the BEM text at this point makes this indeed subject to different types of accounts, given "here and now." The accountability of baptism can be realized in any interrelation between human beings, giving account of the new and liberated life in the context where the baptized live. *Second*, the responsibility implied in being baptized is a *common* responsibility, which means a *mutual* responsibility. It is within a "fellowship of witness and service" that the churches can realize the implications of baptism. The full significance of baptism is only experienced when it is seen as a gift to a communion. However, this communion has no meaning if isolated.

The text on eucharist has a section on "The Eucharist as Communion of the Faithful," with important reflections on the implications of eucharist for ecumenical ecclesiology.[231] These reflections can be interpreted as a definition of the Church as a fellowship characterized by mutual accountability.

> The eucharistic communion with Christ who nourishes the life of the Church is at the same time communion within the body of Christ which is the Church. The sharing in one bread and the common cup in a given place demonstrates and effects the oneness of the sharers with Christ and with their

---

228. BEM 1982:3 (B7).
229. BEM 1982:4 (B9).
230. BEM 1982:4 (B10).
231. BEM 1982:14, (E19–21).

fellow sharers in all times and places. It is in the eucharist that the community of God's people is fully manifested, Eucharist celebrations always have to do with the whole church, and the whole church is involved in each local eucharistic celebration. In so far as a church claims to be a manifestation of the whole Church, it will take care to order its own life in ways which take seriously the interests and concerns of other churches.[232]

The main statement of the paragraph is the qualification of the eucharistic communion as the communion of the Church. The image "the body of Christ" is used to emphasize the indisputable belonging together implied in the sharing of the same bread and the same cup. Eucharist is even specified as the real and most substantial ("fully") manifestation of communion. It is of great significance that the text unfolds this ecclesiological qualification of eucharist by maintaining that every eucharistic celebration is done in the forum of "the whole Church." It cannot be an act of isolation or separation. This could, in our terminology, be called the "status of being mutually accountable" inevitably implied in the sharing of the eucharist.

The elaboration of this significant ecclesiological premise is a description of the attitude corresponding to this status. It is the attitude shown in the "will [to] take care to order its own life in ways which take seriously the interests and concerns of other churches." This is a strong and profound description of the Church as a mutually accountable fellowship. It is so integrated in the theology of eucharist that the dogmatic statement and the ethical demand of a proper ecumenical attitude are defined in the same breath.

Hence, without using the term, this paragraph describes the *catholicity* of the Church. It is important to notice how "the whole Church" is identified from the perspective of the eucharistic gift, given in the participation of the gifts of Christ. The manifestation of the catholicity of the Church is the eucharistic communion locally. The ecumenical attitude corresponding to eucharist, according to the text, should not be observed and practiced through declarations of sympathies, but through how the churches "order" their life "in ways which take seriously the interests and concerns of other churches." How to celebrate eucharist in an ecumenically accountable way is one important part of this.[233] But the unclear expression "interests and concerns of other churches" most likely recommends mutual accountability for what is beyond

---

232. BEM 1982:14 (E19).

233. The elements of the eucharist belonging to the common Tradition are explicitly defined and discussed (BEM 1982:15ff. [E27–33]). After a long list of what should be important elements of any eucharistic liturgy, we find the significant conclusion and challenge: "The best way towards unity in eucharistic celebration and communion is the renewal of the eucharist itself in the different churches in regard to teaching and liturgy" (E28).

the framework of the celebration of the eucharistic liturgy. It points to involvement in all kinds of aspects of the life of the other churches, their tasks and problems, resources and strength.

This impression is supported by the theme of the two succeeding paragraphs, which also elaborate the communal dimension of eucharist:

> The eucharist embraces all aspects of life. It is a representative act of thanksgiving and offering on behalf of the whole world. The eucharistic celebration demands reconciliation and sharing among all those regarded as brothers and sisters in the one family of God and is a constant challenge in the search for appropriate relationship in social, economic and political life (Matt. 5: 23f; I Cor. 10: 16f; I Cor. 11: 20-22; Gal. 3: 28). All kinds of injustice, racism, separation and lack of freedom are radically changed when we share in the body and blood of Christ.[234]

The premise here is that participating in eucharist is in itself a challenge for the individual participant; in this context it is primarily a challenge for the churches. Through eucharist they are involved in a mutual relation that makes the participant accountable to all others having a share in the same eucharist. This eucharistic "status of being" corresponds to, even "demands," an attitude of ecumenical accountability. This dimension of catholicity is not even limited to the persons actively participating in the life of the Church. The border between the ecclesial fellowship and the fellowship of humanity is deliberately open: "As participants in the eucharist, therefore, we prove inconsistent if we are not actively participating in this ongoing restoration of the world's situation and the human condition."[235]

This intrinsic accountability of eucharist means, therefore, being accountable for the consequences for those affected directly or indirectly of what a church or community of churches is doing. If the communion celebrating eucharist is not open for anybody regardless of gender, race, social status, and so forth, it is neither accountable to God nor to the world to which it should be a sign. This eucharistic attitude corresponds to the attitude of Christ, expressed through acts of "responsible care" for one another:

> Solidarity in the eucharistic communion of the body of Christ and responsible care of Christians for one another and the world find specific expression in the liturgies: in the mutual forgiveness of sins; the sign of peace; intercession for all; the eating and drinking together; the taking of the elements to the sick and those in prison or the celebration of the eucharist with them. All

---

234. BEM 1982:14 (E20).
235. BEM 1982:14 (E20).

these manifestations of love in the eucharist are directly related to Christ's own testimony as a servant, in whose servanthood Christians themselves participate. As God in Christ has entered into the human situation, so eucharist liturgy is near to the concrete and particular situations of men and women.[236]

When it comes to the understanding of ministry, we find reflections on the basis for ministry and the forms of ministerial service in the Church that indicate an awareness of the importance of mutual accountability for ecumenical ecclesiology. The emphasis on the *wholeness* of the Church is the ecclesiological basis for the attempts toward convergence in the difficult ecumenical issues of ministry. The Church shares in the wholeness of the triune God and in God's purpose for the whole world. The gifts of the Spirit—manifested in certain services and ministries—are given for the common good. To overcome the differences between the churches, "the churches need to work from the perspective of the calling of the whole people of God."[237]

The text describes manifestations of attitudes corresponding to this calling from Christ: "Living in this communion with God, all members of the Church are called to confess their faith and to give account of hope. They are to identify with joys and sufferings of all people as they seek to witness in caring love. The members of Christ's body are to struggle with the oppressed towards that freedom and dignity promised with the coming of the Kingdom."[238]

Under the perspective of the "complementary gifts," the required mutual accountability within the community is vividly described as reciprocal openness to the gifts of others, a demand to use the gifts in an open way for the sake of the community and the willingness to contribute with one's own gifts: "All members are called to discover, with the help of the community, the gifts they have received and to use them for the building up of the Church and for the service of the world to which the Church is sent."[239]

The argument is parallel to the one used in the texts on baptism and eucharist. In terms of my notion of mutual accountability this means: participation in the Church (through baptism and eucharist) brings the participant (individual and group/church) into a status of accountability to God, which can be realized only in a mutual accountability to the whole Church and further to

---

236. BEM 1982:14 (E21).

237. BEM 1982:20f. (M1, 4, 6; quotation M6).

238. BEM 1982:20 (M4). Themes elaborated in the former study on "Giving Account of the Hope That Is Within Us," the later study on "The Apostolic Faith Today" as well as the parallel ongoing study on "The Unity of Humankind and the Unity of the Church" run together in these perspectives of the common accountability to God and to the world.

239. BEM 1982:20 (M5).

the rest of humanity. This is described in more specific terms in respect to the ordained ministry in the Church.

The text emphasizes the diversity of roles so significant for the Christian community from the time of the apostles.[240] Corresponding to this diversity, there is an implied interrelatedness of those participating in the ordained ministry, mutually accountable relations based on the common calling and gifts of the Church. This is particularly emphasized when it comes to the definition of *authority*. The attitude of mutuality is a criterion for all parts. The accountable relationship is not primarily a controlling relation, one part demanding the other to be like them in everything. We find here an important elaboration of the mutuality and accountability of the ministry of the Church:

> In them [ordained ministers] the Church seeks an example of holiness and loving concern. On the other hand, ordained ministers can fulfill their calling only in and for the community. They cannot dispense with the recognition, the support and the encouragement of the community. . . . Authority has the character of responsibility before God and is exercised with the cooperation of the whole community. Therefore, ordained ministers must not be autocrats or impersonal functionaries. Although called to exercise wise and loving leadership on the basis of the Word of God, they are bound to the faithful in interdependence and reciprocity. Only when they seek the response and acknowledgment of the community can their authority be protected from the distortions of isolation and domination. They manifest and exercise the authority of Christ in the way Christ himself revealed God's authority to the world, by committing their life to the community.[241]

The common calling of the Church is taken care of and pursued (not exclusively this way, though) through a special calling and ordination of a few to be accountable for the common tasks of all baptized believers sharing in the eucharist. Through this authorizing there is no complete delegation of responsibility to the ordained. In the calling of the ordained the baptized articulate and are themselves reminded of the calling to them all. In other words: the ordained ministers are made accountable for the calling of the Church, to make the whole Church accountable for this calling to live and act according to the gifts of baptism and eucharist. The ordained cannot fulfill their task in isolation, only in a mutually accountable relation to the community and to other ordained ministers.

This perspective of mutuality is tentatively brought into the question of *the roles of women and men in the Church*. It is done on the basis of a strong

240. BEM 1982:21 (M9).
241. BEM 1982:22f. (M15, 16).

declaration of the "new humanity" where "human barriers are broken down." "There is in Christ no male or female (Gal 3:28)." The text speaks rather strongly about the necessity that "both women and men discover their contributions to the service of Christ in the Church." The genders must be mutually accountable to one another in respect of the gifts and contributions of the other. They are and should show their interdependence.[242]

The BEM text proposes a "guiding principle for the exercise of the ordained ministry in the Church" widely echoed in the succeeding reception of this text. In many regards this remarkable definition can be described as a recommendation for an ordered exercise of mutual accountability. "The ordained ministry should be exercised in a personal, collegial and communal way."[243]

In the BEM text we find reflections on the importance of exercising the ministry in a mutually accountable setting. The last two aspects of ministry point this way especially. To be within a *college* means to share the task of ministry, where mutuality and accountability are presupposed. The reason for the *communal* aspect is even more explicitly related to mutual accountability: ". . . the exercise of the ordained ministry is rooted on the life of the community and requires the community's effective participation in the discovery of God's will and the guidance of the Spirit."[244] If the community should "effectively participate" in the task of the ordained, the minister must listen and learn in an open and receptive way and the community must give account of their experiences, wisdom, and knowledge.

In this perspective, the emphasis on the *personal* element could be understood as a matter of mutual accountability as well. "It should be *personal* because the presence of Christ among his people can most effectively be pointed to by the person ordained to proclaim the Gospel and to call the community to serve the Lord in unity of life and witness."[245]

It is emphasized that this is the most "effective" pointing to the presence of Christ among his people. This can be interpreted as meaning the minister is the personal replacement for Christ in the Church or as a preference for the theology of episcopally ordered churches. But since no minister is representing Christ alone, but only in a community, it can also be interpreted in another direction: the main perspective of the context is that of proper *relations*—not relations between instances or principles, constitutions, or whatever, but between human persons. Only in personal relations can there be faces to whom we are accountable, acts for which we are accountable, relations that can be

---

242. BEM 1982:23f. (M18).
243. BEM 1982:26 (M26).
244. BEM 1982:26 (M26).
245. BEM 1982:26 (M26).

described as mutual, open, and reliable. The life of the Church is a relational life between human persons. It makes sense to emphasize that in these categories Christ can be present in the Church. This corresponds to what the BEM documents say about representation and imitating Christ in the life for each other and the world.

Summary

As we have seen, the Faith and Order commission was right to conclude that the churches through the entire BEM process had achieved a new level of mutual accountability. This conclusion can be further specified, according to the preliminary definition of mutual accountability presented in this study.

First of all, and according to the statement of the commission, *the methodology of the proceedings* in the BEM process led the churches to be more seriously, responsibly involved in the ecumenical endeavour than ever before. The churches became more bound to the process and its results and, therefore, potentially more reliable to one another. Not only the representatives involved in ecumenical dialogue, but also the most authoritative institutions of the churches were involved and made accountable.

The increased mutual accountability was a result of the challenges formulated in the questions posed to the churches. The recognition recommended was more than a weak and polite acceptance of this as a valuable text. It was a testing of the text in accordance with the tradition and faith of each church. The churches were challenged to rethink and revise their liturgical practice and their relation to other confessions in mutual accountability to this common account of the apostolic faith. That this challenge was formed in terms of acts of the churches, not only confessional documents, is important for my interpretation of this process as an improvement of ecumenical *attitudes*.[246]

I have interpreted *the hermeneutic of convergence* used in this project as an example of exercising mutual accountability. In the light of the intentions of the process and the formulation of the questions, this was an effort to grasp The Tradition—or "the faith through the ages." It was indeed a comprehensive procedure before the formulation of the BEM text was finally formulated. Crucial to the results, the dialogue was based upon a comprehensive work on the biblical texts, the origin of all Christian tradition in Scriptures. This structured the formulation of The Tradition as an expression of the common, *apostolic* Tradition. The churches got involved in several stages and in a mutual process with the work of the commission—contributing through their respective traditions to the formulation of The Tradition. Thus, the entire process implied mutual recognition of interpretations of the apostolic tradition from other churches as expressions of The Tradition. The teaching (dogma) and the

---

246. See pp. 10–15.

lived faith of other churches become thereby important elements in the process of convergence. The BEM text, as an attempt to formulate The Tradition, was then presented as a contribution to critical self-reflection for the churches, to renew their faith and practices. The ideas of Montreal twenty years before,[247] establishing expressions of The Tradition through a dialogue between the traditions, had been put into practice in this text.

Hence, the BEM text—without using the term—calls for mutual accountability as *Verbindlichkeit*. This implies binding, reliable, faithful relations. However, the BEM text and process also emphasize other aspects of my preliminary definition of mutual accountability: openness, willingness to be self-critical, and taking contributions from the others into account.

This text does not present one particular tradition or one confessional approach to be accepted by the other churches. But it challenges the churches to recognize that the apostolic tradition has elements to which all churches have not paid sufficient attention, elements of such importance that they should be recognized as "the faith through the ages." In recognizing the BEM text, churches are implicitly and explicitly asked to become mutually accountable for how they manage and care for the common treasure in the calling and gifts of baptism, eucharist, and ministry.

Hence, mutual accountability as an important aspect of the ecclesiology of BEM is expressed in the process, as well as in the hermeneutics of the text and in the recommended reception. But it is *also expressed in the substantial elaboration of the ecclesiological significance of baptism, eucharist, and ministry in the BEM text itself.* To be baptized is to become a member of a mutually accountable fellowship. To celebrate eucharist is to participate in the gift of the triune God, as well as the thanksgiving and the task of the whole Church. Eucharist gives and requires a sense of catholicity. This catholic communion is made accountable for how it contributes to overcoming divisions, conflicts, and discrimination in this world. The ministry of the Church is identified as a mutual responsibility for the common calling of the Church. The mutual accountability between those who are personally given a special task through ordination is described as the principle of "collegiality." The relation of the ordained ministers to the community of the faithful—and the Church as a whole—is described as the principle of "communality." Both principles imply that the ordained ministers are made accountable for the task of the whole Church in a special way to make the whole community accountable for it. This is not a senseless circular argument, but a principle of mutuality required to take the common accountability of the Church seriously.

The personal dimension of the ministry emphasizes further the responsibility and the attitudes required in this service for the Lord and the Church in

---

247. See pp. 49–80.

the world. This is naturally extended to the realm of interchurch fellowship. No church can live alone. The ordained ministry, particularly the ministry of *episkopé*, should serve mutual awareness between the local churches.

Analysis of the BEM process and text supports my thesis of the implicit importance of mutual accountability in the work of Faith and Order. It also emphasizes the relevance of focusing this description of ecumenical attitude for the establishment of *ecumenical ecclesiology*.

The reflections on baptism and eucharist as the basis for mutual accountability in the Church show how the *moral* dimension of unity cannot be isolated from the *dogmatic*. The moral obligation of searching for unity as mutual accountability is not an idea taken from just anywhere, but flows out of the most central elements of Christian theology. This is not to say that dogmatics and ethics are the same, or that the work God has done for us is at the same level as our acts. However, the gift of being baptized and the gift given to those who participate in the eucharist cannot be isolated from the mutually accountable relations established precisely through participation in these sacraments. The ministry of the Church is not a private enterprise, an affair between the ordained and God, but is always a matter of the communion and the accountability to the calling of God to care for the demands of the world. Mutual accountability as the morality of the Christian communion is not a general aspect of responsibility and solidarity in a fellowship. It is rooted directly in the doctrine of the work of the triune God and participation in the community with God.

On the basis of my summary so far, I would also point to how the BEM process and text reveal *the significance of mutual accountability as ecumenical attitude for the correspondence between "faith" and "order."* The process focused on the formulation of The Tradition, as it is found in the sources of Christianity (Scripture and the early Church) and embodied in the many historical traditions. Elaboration of substantial aspects of the *content* of "the faith through the ages" is thoroughly intertwined with a reflection on how this faith finds its expression in the *life* of the Church—in the sacraments, in the life of the faithful in accordance with these sacraments, and in the ministry in and over against the Church. Thus, the visibility of the unity of the Church cannot, on the basis of the insight gained through the BEM process, be separated from the unity in both "faith" and "order."

Besides that, the BEM process and the BEM text display the need for an open, dynamic, reliable, and self-critical relation between the churches for the work toward unity in "faith" and "order." The quality of relation is of great significance for and an important element of both "faith" and "order." Attitudes between the members of the churches and between the churches are not marginal in ecumenical ecclesiology. Thus, the focus on mutual accountability in this analysis of BEM has made us aware of how "faith" as well as "order" must be supplemented by a proper reflection on "relation."

Finally, we can point to how the BEM process and text, partly due to their awareness of the ecumenical importance of mutual accountability, offer insight into *the proper relation between unity and diversity*. The BEM text shows that the visible unity of the Church requires a certain amount of mutual recognition of what is the common apostolic tradition. It also requires a certain degree of mutual recognition of the ministry in the churches as legitimate and in accordance with common calling of the whole Church. This does not presuppose uniformity in formulation of all loci in the Christian's faith, nor a total conformity of the order of the churches. In the BEM text, diversity (to some degree) is qualified as acceptable, even enriching.

Status quo in the relations between the churches and confessional traditions is not accepted, however. The implicit demand of mutual accountability makes the pursuit of unity dynamic. It becomes not a matter of dominance or reunion according to the premises of the strongest parts, but a matter of being open to be enriched and corrected through an encounter with an expression of The Tradition. To remain untouched and unchanged in a defensive position after such an encounter is not an expression of being accountable for The Tradition given to the Church. To be mutually accountable is, therefore, more than a matter of diplomatic politeness. It has to do with the understanding of what it means to be church in a fellowship of churches, or, to have a sense of "the whole Church," the catholicity of the Church. This is necessary for the conciliar fellowship that the BEM process should foster.

Toward a Manifestation of Mutual Accountability to the One, Apostolic Faith

Sharing the One Faith as Condition for Conciliar Fellowship

Throughout the work of Faith and Order, it has always been regarded as a prerequisite for unity among the churches that they somehow manifest that they share the same Christian faith. It has even been an assumption that to some degree the churches do so. There have also been attempts to formulate this common faith.[248] Nevertheless, there has been no conclusion as to *how* this manifestation could be realized in a satisfying way.

248. The attempts made at Faith and Order conferences and WCC assemblies are documented in Apostolic Faith Today 1985:63–144. According to Link 1988a, none of them has been officially accepted as the common expression faith for all churches. In his presentation of the preliminary results of the "Apostolic Faith" study, Hans-Georg Link suggests a brief ecumenical quadrilateral to be officially recognized by the churches as expression of their unity in one

The Faith and Order initiative for a study of the apostolic faith from 1981 to 1990 was taken according to the formulation of the goal of unity as *conciliar fellowship*.[249] The fifth assembly of the World Council of Churches in Nairobi in 1975 made a strong recommendation to the member churches in this respect.

> We ask the churches to undertake a common effort to receive, re-appropriate and confess together, as contemporary occasion requires, the Christian truth and faith, derived through the apostles and handed down through the centuries. Such common action, arising from free and inclusive discussion under the commonly acknowledged authority of God's word, must aim both to clarify and to embody the unity and the diversity which are proper to the Church's life and mission.[250]

As mentioned above, the Faith and Order Commission pointed out three requirements for the unity of the Church as a conciliar fellowship.[251] The first requirement of "consensus in the apostolic faith" was from the very beginning an important aspect of the goal of the study "Giving Account of the Hope That Is Within Us." The difficult work on the report from the "Giving Account" study in Bangalore represented an end to this approach and raised anew the question: "What way of confessing the apostolic faith is required for the Church to live in visible unity?"[252]

Already in Bangalore, a working group attempted to deal with the question by working out a "Common Statement of Faith." According to the minutes, this brought into sharp focus the problems involved in the question, like the role of tradition and the ancient creeds of the Church.[253] It is also noticeable

---

apostolic faith. This is the apostolic faith "as witnessed to in the scriptures of the Old and New Testaments: as summarized in the ancient church creeds, the Nicene-Constantinopolitan Creed of 381 and the Apostles' Creed; as celebrated in the church's liturgy, i.e. in the Eucharist; and as interpreted by the ecumenical councils of the church" (Link 1988a:11).

249. The study process is well described in an appendix to the final document, COF 1990; Limouris 1990.

250. Nairobi 1975:66.

251. This was (a) consensus in the apostolic faith; (b) mutual recognition of baptism, the eucharist, and ministry; (c) structures making possible common teaching and decision making (Bangalore 1978:243; cf. pp. 106–109 above). As we have seen through the analysis above, the second requirement was already pursued through the production of a text of rather high degree of maturity (BEM 1982). The third requirement was discussed, but not solved through the comprehensive deliberations of "conciliar fellowship" and the study on authoritative teaching.

252. Minutes Bangalore 1978:40.

253. Bangalore 1978:243–46.

how much the BEM study, text, and reception process focused on the formulation of the "faith through the ages."

The theme was not totally new. But it was new to *explore and explicate* "The Apostolic Faith" as such, although "faith" is the most basic theme of the Faith and Order endeavours. The project was rather ambitious, attempting to formulate the central issues of the apostolic faith in a way that could clarify the unity as well as the diversity of faith. This implied also clarifying difficult questions in regard to how the issues of faith should be addressed in respect to unity: What degree of consensus is required for conciliar fellowship? and How can we make some progress in respect to documenting or establishing such a consensus? What is needed to manifest the unity in faith—a new creed, a consensus document on Christian faith, or acceptance of old creeds? Behind these questions is a (not always articulated) question about the level at which these questions can be solved: at the level of a (new) theological formulation, at the level of loyalty to a common creed, at the level of common celebration in the liturgy, at the level of specific statements clarifying the common faith encountering particular challenges to the churches?

The study process was conducted through a wide scale of consultations that gathered highly qualified theologians. The result of the study is a comprehensive book, probably the largest and most substantial theological document from Faith and Order ever.[254] It is almost a compendium of the most central issues of faith, their biblical background, and contemporary relevance.[255] This book has not been received in the mutually accountable way BEM has been. There is, therefore, a discrepancy between the declared significance and urgency of the theme, the ambitions and comprehensiveness, and the very modest outcome in terms of clear common manifestations of faith among the churches.

On this background, I find it interesting to analyze this study from the perspective of mutual accountability. Here I will not look so much for explicit reflections of mutual accountability and ecumenical attitude as in the analyses above. I will discuss how this effort could be *interpreted* as an attempt to establish mutual accountability between the churches in respect to their accountability for the given apostolic faith. Thus, I will also analyze the result of the project in regard to the role of ecumenical attitudes for the handling of the task of manifesting unity in faith, including the problems and disagreements unveiled through this effort.

---

254. COF 1991; cf. Appendix IV, listing the participants, 125–39. The list mentions 333 names (some of them are repetitions of participants from the steering committee and the secretariat).

255. Thus, it is understandable that the text can be used as a reading book for introductory courses in dogmatics, e.g., in the curriculum of The Norwegian Lutheran School of Theology, Oslo.

Making the Churches Mutually Accountable for the Common Faith?

Recognition, Explication, and Confession

After Bangalore the need for a confirmation of the unity in faith was discussed as an urgent task of ecumenism. Faith and Order raised the issue within the framework of the Joint Commission for the Roman Catholic Church and the World Council of Churches already in a 1978 consultation in Venice. Quite remarkably, the argument for a concentration on the common faith starts with a strong focus on the attitudes between the churches. The report from Venice deals with the need for repentance and mutual sharing of the gifts between the churches, and of the need for acts of common commitment to be able to confess the common faith.

> Its [each church's] repentance will be genuine only to the extent to which it implies a resolve to what the complete reestablishment of communion demands of it: conversion through a constant return to the source which is Christ, a persevering effort of purification, a desire of authentic change. Such repentance will be truly constructive of unity only if it leads to offer to others its own characteristic goods and to receive from others what it lacks itself. Now, at the heart of such repentance is the need to reach agreement on a common profession of faith, which, after centuries of mutual exclusion, will permit the churches to recognize each other as true brothers, to live in communion, and to commit themselves together to mission without reservations. . . . Just as a theology "in act" normally precedes the enunciation of doctrines, so communion in common commitment in the name of the faith leads to the profession of common faith. It is in doing the truth that we come to the light.[256]

The work for a new common expression of faith is described as necessary to fulfill the task of manifesting unity for the reliability of the mission of the Church. This common basis is necessary to promote the attitudes required for overcoming the divisions: "To get out of the impasse into which confessional divisions have led it, it has need of an expression of faith, which, at this fundamental level, will reestablish mutual confidence between the churches and clear away suspicions or reservations."[257]

The text concentrates deliberately on "what may be called the essential core of the Christian faith."[258] More than vague statements are required; rather, "firm and precise expression of evangelical conviction" is needed if the confession is to have any force against powers "incompatible with the spirit of the

---

256. Towards Confession 1980:1f.
257. Towards Confession 1980:8.
258. Towards Confession 1980:12.

Gospel."²⁵⁹ On the other hand—and this became a methodological problem throughout the entire endeavour—what is required is both a unanimous statement of the central matters of faith and a response to the alternative faiths and hopes of Christian faith today. The project had to face the *double accountability*, to "remain faithful" both to the universal communion of receivers of the good message of faith (described as "the catholicity of the evangelical message") and to the origin of faith ("its authentic content") in the revelation of Jesus in Scriptures.²⁶⁰ To achieve reconciliation necessary for a conciliar fellowship, the churches had to "search for an authentic consensus concerning the faith."²⁶¹ On this basis the commission proceeded into the study.

In the commission plenary in Lima in 1982 a threefold intention of this study, elaborated by a working group, was approved. ²⁶²

> Our hope then is that we can initiate a threefold study project, aiming:
> - to ask the churches to make a common recognition of the apostolic faith as expressed in the Ecumenical Symbol of that faith: The Nicene Creed;
> - to ask the churches how they understand its content today in their own particular situations of worship, fellowship and witness; and
> - to ask the churches "to undertake a common effort to confess together, as contemporary occasion requires, the Christian truth and faith, delivered through the Apostles and handed down through the centuries."²⁶³

Through some elaboration, the aim was coded into three key words: *recognition, explication, confession.*²⁶⁴ In the following I will describe how this threefold goal can be interpreted as an attempt to define how a higher degree of mutual accountability to the common Christian faith can be established.

The first intention, to pursue a "common *recognition* of the apostolic faith expressed in the Nicene Creed," is elaborated as a challenge to the churches, to make them self-critically "reconsider their attitude." It is discussed how

---

259. Towards Confession 1980:9.

260. Towards Confession 1980:8f.

261. Towards Confession 1980:11.

262. The preparation of this presentation in Lima was initiated in the Bangalore meeting in 1978. Besides the work in the framework of the joint working group between the Roman Catholic Church and the World Council of Churches, presented in the report Towards Confession 1980, there had been held two consultations by Faith and Order in 1981 (Chambésy and Odessa).

263. "Report of the working group," Lima II 1982:28–46, at 32.

264. This terminology was used in the elaborations of the three points in the Lima report, and used as headings when the Standing Commission in Crete 1984 described the "content" of the study, and call it "three main emphases"; cf. Apostolic Faith Today 1985:270f.

"recognition" of creeds can bind the whole Church together. Furthermore, it is suggested that this process of recognition of the Nicene Creed should lead to self-critical evaluation, "to reconsider the status of their own teaching in its light."[265] These arguments focused particularly on the potential of a process (in the light of the creed) of transparency and self-examination:

> The Creed provides the churches which use it, in whatever ways, with the opportunity of examining their beliefs and actions today in relation to it, and so to interpret its meaning (theologically, ethically, liturgically, socially . . .) . . . When we study the Creed, we are compelled to compare its language and content with that of Scriptures. When we do this, we not only encounter many issues concerning the Bible, but many issues concerning Christian tradition, theology, worship and mission which are of critical importance within the movement for unity among the churches today. . . . The study of the Creed urges us in all churches to examine the similarities and differences in our creedal statements and doctrinal confessions, and our uses of creeds in liturgy, catechesis and mission; and it compels us to decide whether our creeds, or lack of creeds, are expressive of genuine difference of faith and conviction between the churches, or are merely differences of words and expressions.[266]

The recognition of the Nicene Creed as a genuine expression of the apostolic faith in Scripture could establish a criterion for all ecumenical endeavours. That could have an immense effect on mutual critique and mutual recognition between the churches.

To some extent the documentation from the standing commission, particularly the outline of the project made in Lima, confirmed that the common expression was not something to be made; it was already given in the Nicene Creed (thus called "the Ecumenical Creed"). The primary goal was, accordingly, to achieve a common recognition of this creed.[267] "The unity of the apostolic faith is expressed in the Ecumenical Creed, proclaimed on behalf of the entire Church as a summary of the central teaching of the scripture and therefore serving as a criterion for the unity of other statements of faith with

---

265. Lima II 1982:33, 35. This referred to the arguments for affirming the ecumenical importance of the Nicene Creed articulated in the consultation on Odessa in 1981.

266. From "The Ecumenical Importance of the Nicene-Constantinipolitan Creed. Odessa Report 1981," Apostolic Faith Today 1985:248.

267. "It seems appropriate, therefore, to ask the churches, when they try to express their common understanding of the apostolic faith today, to recognize this Creed from the time of the early Church as the ecumenical expression of the apostolic faith which unites Christians of all ages in all places" (Lima II 1982:32).

the teaching of the Church."[268] The recognition of the creed is later (1984) described by the Faith and Order Commission as a task to "strengthen the links with the faith of the early church and the *oikoumene* throughout the centuries."[269] This motive of unity from the "unidivided church" played a certain role in this project, although not always accepted as a historically valid premise for ecumenical work.

In combination with the third point of "*confession*," the relevance of describing the goal and intention of the study as establishing mutual accountability becomes even more apparent. "Confessing Jesus Christ" is described as a personal, but always "communal event." Confession is here primarily regarded as a matter of the unity of the Church, the common glorification of the triune God in the liturgy as the common expression of the apostolic faith. The common confession is related to the development of ecumenical attitudes, bringing those who confess into a fellowship in which their attitude to one another is challenged in terms of "repentance" and "conversion":

> If confession means participation in the unity of the body of Christ by joining the acclamation of Jesus as Lord, it must overcome the inherited divisions among the faithful. Therefore the element of repentance and conversion in the act of confession also applies to the separation and division of the churches. . . . The very fact that the act of confession is communal, therefore, obliges the churches to overcome their divisions and to seek a common confession of the apostolic faith that would enable them to enter into conciliar fellowship.[270]

Furthermore, the working group saw a potentially common confession of the Creed as an establishment of a *criterion* for the unity of other statements and confessions of faith. This should have a self-critical effect. But it could also, according to these expectations, have the effect of bringing the churches into more mutually open and accountable relations with other churches and traditions, accepting *other* traditions as adequate expressions of the common faith:

---

268. Lima II 1982:42. The recognition of the same "ground of unity" is important for the ecumenical movement: ". . . so that without common recognition of the Nicene Creed as the ecumenical symbol of the apostolic faith, it is difficult if not impossible to understand how we were to advance 'to the goal of visible unity in one faith and in one eucharistic fellowship expressed in worship and in common life in Christ . . . in order that the world may believe'" (WCC Constitution III,1).

269. Apostolic Faith Today 1985:270. The concept of "recognition" was used also in the BEM reception as a description of acceptance and binding loyalty.

270. Lima II 1982:32.

The more they come to evaluate their particular confessional traditions in the light of the Creed, the more they may learn to understand other traditions as expressing the same faith under different circumstances and in different situations. While each church should be ready to interpret its own confessional heritage in the light of the apostolic faith as summarized in the Ecumenical Creed, it might also be able to accept other churches and their confessional heritage on the same basis. In such a process of interpreting the confessional positions of one's own church on this basis, it might become possible to overcome condemnations (anathemas) that have been formulated and understood in the past to exclude the teaching of other churches.[271]

Hence, the argument in this text from Lima is that *Verbindlichkeit* should be established to a common faith, and, as a result of this, a self-critical approach and a sense of more openness to one another. There is no reason to understand these intentions of establishing a binding platform primarily in terms of juridical aspects. The matter is theological questions, discussed and handled in a way that could disclose a meaningful and substantial approval of the common faith. A rigid and unchangeable formulation of responsibility or loyalty was not sought, but something that could serve the purpose of establishing a conciliar fellowship.[272] The binding element on the side of the churches is, therefore, not to be expected at the level of juridical settlements or complete theological agreement. Therefore, I find it most relevant to describe the desired type of binding relation to the same faith as an expression of *attitude*. The concept of mutual accountability, as predefined in my study, seems to be an adequate expression of what was the intention of this endeavour.

There is, however, another focal point in respect to what "confession" should mean in the "Apostolic Faith" study.[273] Besides the confession as a premise and expression of unity through liturgy, the confession of the faith is

---

271. Lima II 1982:43.

272. Hans-Georg Link provides a well-balanced reflection on what level of precision should and could be expected in statements of this kind. According to Link, particular theologians have tended to expect too much stringency and sophistication in texts like this, without understanding this "new form of theological literature" found in ecumenical documents. He lists five guiding principles for a proper interpretation: (1) the texts deal only with essential aspects of faith, not details; (2) they try to formulate common insights acceptable for Christians from different traditions; (3) they are facing current problems, not all theological issues; (4) they are linking doctrinal affirmations with present ethical problems; (5) they intend to make necessary clarifications for the developments of our time, not a complete dogmatic. Cf. Link 1988a:6.

273. This is the primary context formulated in Lima (Lima II 1982:41): "The normal place for the confessing the Creed in the life of the liturgy is its liturgy. . . . Thus they devote themselves to the Lord so that they may share communion with him in the eucharistic meal."

a consequence of the accountability the churches have to give witness to the world.[274] Obviously, this is deliberately played down in the Lima text.

The question remains, then, whether the point of "common explication" could be seen as an intention of establishing mutual accountability between the churches.[275] The study was pursued—in fact—only as a work on a common explication of the Nicene Creed. Thus, this question will be answered in the following analysis of the pursuit of the study.

The Discussion of the Goal and Methodology of the Project as a Quest for Different Standards of Accountability

The discussions of the goal and methodology of this study show how different types of manifestations of sharing the one apostolic faith could represent different approaches to the problem of mutually accountable relationship between the churches. Some major positions, each of them typical for different ways to approach the task of establishing unity in faith, can illuminate this.[276]

The Nicene Creed as the Expression of the Apostolic Faith

For the Orthodox churches, according to Damaskinous Papandreou, the reception process of the Nicene Creed is the important task and possibility of the ecumenical movement. It is a spiritual event, accepting the Council's claim to be the voice of the Spirit. This is so because the ancient creeds ". . . are a guarantee of orthodoxy, an expression of universal validity in the Christian faith, an absolute experience, not just statements of knowledge. . . . The Orthodox Church . . . [does not] see the need for a new creed."[277]

The Nicene Creed is regarded as an expression of the divine life. In its use in the liturgy it expresses the living tradition. Consequently, it transcends any other denominational confession. The apophatic theology implies reluctance to express the incomprehensible and inexpressible mystery of God today. But it is not—in Orthodox theology—an obstacle to concentrate on the formulations

---

274. This was more strongly emphasized in the "Giving Account" study. Even in the "Apostolic Faith" study this played a significant role. The tensions between these two foci led to different opinions of the task of the "Apostolic Faith" study, which will be discussed below.

275. "Such study and reflection [on the apostolic faith] should lead towards a fresh understanding of the apostolic faith and thus towards a common recognition and confession of this faith today" (COF 1991:6).

276. Three members of the steering committee of the "Apostolic Faith" study gave the contributions discussed below: Tillard, Pannenberg, Maraschin. Together with Papandreou and Flesseman-van Leer, they represent classic Orthodoxy, Roman Catholicism, European academic Lutheran and Reformed theology, and Latin American Episcopal liberation theology.

277. Papandreou 1982:85. Metropolitan Damaskinos of Tranoupolis was a representative of the Ecumenical Patriarchate of Constantinople at the preliminary consultation at Chambésy, Switzerland, in July 1981.

of the ancient creeds.[278] Therefore, the basic structure of mutual accountability according to his tradition would be: "Christians and the churches in the west and the east must address themselves to the question: Does our faith in Christ agree with the Niceno-Constantinopolitan confession?"[279]

This absolute reverence for the Nicene Creed does not mean disregarding the diversity of confessions in the local churches and different church traditions. This has been, according to Papandreou, the situation since the time of the formulations of the creed. He claims that the Orthodox tradition is rather open to diversified historical and contextual expressions of the faith. The diversity in unity is a sign of the living church.[280] The incarnation of the truth in every historical period should bear the garb of that particular era.[281] The divided churches in East and West should refrain from rejecting the doctrinal formulas of the other as illegitimate, but understand them as consistent with one and the same truth. Thus, there should be a mutual recognition of the value of other formulations of faith.[282] This mutual openness and acknowledgment between different traditions are important elements of a mutually accountable relation. They are, however, subordinated to a common recognition that the original text of the Nicene Creed is the only possible common reference point of accountability for the one apostolic faith.

This emphatic interest from the Orthodox churches in a project of ecumenical *recognition* of the Nicene Creed was, naturally, of great importance to establish confidence in the ecumenical potential of this approach. There are, however, some problems in this approach. If the definition of the "living tradition" is only the living manifestation of the sense of the liturgy, the concept of "the living tradition" cannot be the horizon for a really *mutually* challenging and accountable *dialogue* between churches. In terms of formulation of the common faith, everything is already given. Thus, the great emphasis on a common *explication* of the creed pursued in the "Apostolic Faith" study seems to be in tension with the Orthodox emphasis on the

---

278. Papandreou 1982:86.

279. Papandreou 1982:89.

280. Papandreou 1982:81–83. "Unity in diversity and diversity in unity characterize any living Church of Christ which is trying to maintain an organic relation to the world and history and to give the truth of the gospel contemporary flesh without affecting its essential continuity. The historical garb assumed by incarnate truth in every period changes nothing of the essence of the truth. The problem of the Church is that some of its members can no longer distinguish between essence and form, with the result that they treat formal aspects as essential (the terror of traditionalsim) or make the central essence relative (the error of misguided reformism)" (Papandreou 1982:87).

281. Papandreou 1982:89.

282. Papandreou 1982:83. The "filioque" clause in the Nicene Creed should (of course) be omitted.

potential of a common *use* of the creed in doxology. The Orthodox representative even stressed the legitimacy of a rather diversified elaboration of the Christian faith, as long as the mystery of the apostolic faith is confirmed in the liturgy.

Wolfhart Pannenberg, too, maintained that the Nicene Creed was the necessary common point of reference for the common faith, seen even from a Lutheran position.[283] He concluded that the Lutheran confession is basically a confirmation of the content and the definitive character of "the Niceno-Constantinopolitan Creed."[284] If other churches, too, could interpret their tradition as an expression of the faith of this creed, this creed could serve as the basis for unity it was meant to be. Pannenberg, therefore, sees a unique potential for an ecumenical dialogue based on the Nicene Creed as a criterion by which the churches must show their accountability to the apostolic faith. "Only in that creed, in its original form, moreover, are the churches of all succeeding ages confronted with a summary of the church's faith which is at the same time an expression of the unity of the Church across all differences of culture and historical period. By this creed, therefore, every church is questioned with particular sharpness as to whether or not its faith is the same as that which was expressed in this ecumenical creed."[285]

---

283. Wolfhart Pannenberg was a member of the working group in Bangalore that attempted to write a new confession of today; cf. Minutes Bangalore 1978:27–28. In his paper presented in Chambésy in July 1981, he had definitely turned his attention to the affirmation of the Nicene Creed as the way forward. In a copy of a letter to Hans Vorster, dated 2 May 1989, sent to the director of Faith and Order, Günther Gassmann, Pannenberg defended the concentration on the Nicene Creed as a genuine Lutheran approach. "Eine Unterordnung der reformatorischen Bekenntnisse unter das altkirchliche Glaubensbekenntnis, das in der form des NC das Ganze des Glaubens der Kirche zusammenfassend und mit die ganze Kirche verpflichtende Autorität auszusagen bemüht war, liegt also im Sinne der reformatorischen Bekenntnisbildung selber." He claimed that his paper in Chambésy together with the Orthodox contribution had lasting influence on the method of the "Apostolic Faith" study: "Dieser Vortrag hatte für die Entscheidung, das Projekt über den Apostolischen Glauben an seiner Auslegung des NC zu orientieren, die auf die Sitzung in Chambésy getroffen und in Lima bestätigt wurde, eine nicht ganz unbedeutende Funktion, zusammen mit den Stellungnahmen von orthodoxer Seite" (Pannenberg 1989b).

284. Pannenberg argues that the real confession of faith in *Confessio Augustana* is the first part of it. Hence, the doctrines of the Lutheran churches are nothing other than an interpretation of the ancient creeds, and in this regard in no real disagreement with the Roman Catholic Church. He emphasizes the complete version of the received and recognized creed from 381, hence his use of the full name "Niceno-Constantinoplitan Creed."

285. Pannenberg 1982:78. The so-called Apostles' Creed carries only the status as one of the local baptismal symbols of early Christianity, according to Pannenberg. Nevertheless, it played an important role in the in the Reformation period, e.g., in the outline of the first part (articles 1–17) of the Augsburg Confession. "On the contrary, the unique importance of the Niceno-Constantinopolitan Creed, even for the western Church—as the only summary of the Christian faith which can claim to be, and was actually produced to be, binding on the whole of

Pannenberg's argument for the uniqueness and ecumenical potentiality of the definite creed is, however, a Lutheran approach to confession and not quite the same as the Orthodox. Pannenberg exposes the eschatological dimension of Christian confession as a background for the Lutheran proclivity to maintain the permanent, unchangeable confession. The role of *confession* is principally the same at the personal as at the common, ecclesial level. What is at stake is the eschatological judgment. The confession must be given openly, "for the whole world." The accountability of confession is a combination of these two, according to Luther's own statements and by reference to Luke 12:8f.: "Everyone who confesses me before men, the Son of Man will confess before the angels of God."[286]

The Lutheran churches are, according to Pannenberg, more inclined to emphasize the faithful adherence to the confession of the Lutheran Reformation than a new formulation of confession. Legitimacy for any Christian and any church is participation in the personal faith expressed (after Easter) in the common confession of the risen Christ. This is not a matter of formality, but of the substance of the confession. "This content is what is fundamental for the whole Christian faith."[287] Pannenberg's argumentation leads, however, toward an emphasis on the formal status of the creed.[288]

Accordingly, it is of enormous significance for the unity of the Church to manifest accountability to the one faith. The first common comprehensive formula of the faith, binding for the whole of Christendom, was made at the Council of Nicea in 325.[289] Pannenberg thereby prescribes this formula of faith, with its completion in Constantinople in 381 and confirmation in Chalcedon in 451, a unique position in the Church for all times.[290] "This unique

---

Christendom—has been increasingly recognized today. A contemporary interpretation of the faith of the ancient Church, with its claim to be binding on the whole Church in all succeeding ages, can take its bearings, therefore, in contrast to the Reformation period, *only* from the Niceno-Constantinopolitan Creed" (Pannenberg 1982:76–78).

286. Pannenberg 1982:72f. Pannenberg uses here the term *accountability*. Pannenberg argues particularly for the accountability to the common fixed text of confession through reference to the new use of the terminology of "confession" (not as the confession of sins) by Luther. The substance of the confession was taken from the eucharistic liturgy (Pannenberg 1982:72–73). He refers here to the treatise on the Lord's Supper of 1528 which Luther called "confession." "Confessio" was, according to Pannenberg, in the medieval Latin Church used primarily for the confession of sins.

287. Pannenberg 1982:74.

288. He argues elsewhere that the role of confessions in the Church has the character of a mutual contract, the same function as "the homology of the ancient jurisprudence" (Pannenberg 1993:113).

289. Pannenberg 1982:75.

290. Pannenberg 1982:75–76.

authority of the Niceno-Constantinopolitan Creed, its claim to be binding on the whole Church, its claim to definitive validity, therefore, reproduces at the level of the representative utterance of the whole Church the dimension of eschatological validity inherent in the Christian act of confession from the beginning."[291]

Hence, the only remaining area for discussion is *the interpretation and explication* of the creed. To make a new creed would be to proclaim a faith *different* from "the faith of Nicea." For Pannenberg, the best way to come to a common ecumenical confession today would be, accordingly, to emphasize the faithfulness to the common Nicene Creed, not through focus on the particular confessional confessions.[292] Thus, the *explication* of the Nicene Creed has, in his eyes, an enormous potential for ecumenical ecclesiology if there is mutual accountability among the churches for their relation to this creed.[293]

Pannenberg's position has much in common with the Orthodox position referred to above. But he is paying remarkably less attention to the question of legitimate diversity among Christian traditions in and after the time of the ancient Church. Pannenberg's focus is on overcoming the divisions by getting beyond them, to establish accountability to the fixed, unalterable expression of faith, not only in its liturgical use, but also as a definition of the whole Christian faith, which every church should accept.[294] The development of the Christian traditions after 381 seems to be seen primarily as a problem, not a source for exposition of the apostolic faith.

To define the whole faith as embedded in the content of the Nicene Creed is more than a question of recognizing the creed. Then, the accountability of the churches is linked very closely to the formulations of the text itself. This easily implies the paradoxical demand of accountability not only to the creed, but also to one particular, commonly accepted explanation of the creed.

The same problem could appear in relation to any explication of it. It would not necessarily mean the same all over the world. Although these problems do not rule out the possibility of having the Nicene Creed as a common reference, ignoring them might make it more difficult to achieve a wide mutual accountability demonstrating unity in faith.

In this approach there is a significant appeal to the ecumenical attitudes of the churches. First of all, Pannenberg appeals to the churches to demonstrate

---

291. Pannenberg 1982:75f.

292. Pannenberg 1982:70–72.

293. Pannenberg 1982:75.

294. In my understanding, Pannenberg goes rather far in identifying one historical contingent expression of faith as the Christian faith itself. This approach could be seen as an example of a modern concept of unity, emphasizing universal validity and inner logic unity, formulating presumptive universal and even timeless truths.

willingness to share the faith of the apostles that is the saving faith in an eschatological perspective. This willingness is a kind of loyalty, being open to look critically at one's own tradition from the perspective of the creed.[295] The accountability required must be openness, transparency. He is not asking for a uniform interpretation in all respects, but an approach of critical and confirming accountability. This is evident in his final appeal to an "unprejudiced eye for the ecumenical breadth contained in embryo in our own traditions."[296]

A New Confession as a Common, Contextual, and Accountable Act

A rather different approach to the definition of the goal of the "Apostolic Faith" study is marked by skepticism toward using the Nicene Creed at all as the dominant common substance in this endeavour. The articulations of this view have in common that they demand a focus on legitimate plurality and more accountability to the actual contextual situation in which the churches are living. Here we find a tendency toward defining unity in faith as mutual accountability among the churches to the confessions formulated when facing contemporary challenges, not as a mutual testing with the Nicene Creed as criterion.

According to the title of the study project defined in Lima, emphasizing "towards," the common expression of faith was not yet formulated, but should be realized. The outline of the project from Lima denies that there should be something replacing the Nicene Creed,[297] but it gives the impression that what is sought could be one common text as well as a diversity of confessions. Both should be built upon the creeds and new material from the ecumenical movement.[298]

---

295. In this approach, the texts of the Bible are linked together by the Nicene Creed as a common reference point of accountability for the Christian faith. Pannenberg regarded the process of developing the common Christian confession as a trinitarian statement of faith, based on the Easter *kerygma*, as not completed before the Niceno-Constantinopolitan Creed was finished. This is a challenge to some types of understanding of the principle "*sola Scriptura*," particularly emphasizing the finality of the biblical texts. Pannenberg thus recognizes the plurality of the New Testament, and finds the Nicene Creed as a better text to formulate the common faith. Pannenberg's position could, however, also be a limitation of the potential richness and comprehensiveness in the biblical texts, e.g., by giving the Nicene Creed not much focus on the teaching and acts of the history of Jesus. Therefore, Pannenberg is challenging some aspects of Lutheran theology here. However, the focus on the thematic center in the Holy Scriptures ("Die Mitte der Schrift") is a central concept in Lutheran theology, and the particular Lutheran confessional documents (like *Confessio Augustana*) are recognizing and paying reverence to the ecumenical creeds from the early Church.

296. Pannenberg 1982:78.

297. Lima II 1982:33.

298. Lima II 1982:44.

Writing a common new creed was tried at the meeting in Bangalore. It seemed to have played a role in the discussions of planning of the project until the standing commission meeting at Crete in 1984.[299] But the confession of the faith "today" would naturally lead to a diversity of confessions in different situations and contexts. Discussing the challenges to this project from those afraid of a uniform expression of the Christian faith bound to ancient Greco-Roman forms of thought, the original outline states that to speak about the common expression of apostolic faith does not necessarily mean a single verbal formulation: "Faith may be common even where wordings differ. The immediate task is to move towards mutually recognizable expressions of faith."[300]

One profound spokesman for aiming at confession, not explication of the confession, was C. S. Song.[301] A parallel project to the "Apostolic Faith" study was going on until 1985, one of gathering confessions from different parts of the world. This was pursued as a prolongation of the "Giving Account" approach, but it was stopped without being completed.[302] There was open controversy within the secretariat and commission because of the choice between different methods. Song, who was in charge of the publications of this serial in the secretariat, emphasized that a confession according to Peter's confession (Matthew 16) should answer the question "Who do *you* say I am?," not the "preconfessional" question of "Who do people say that I am?" According to Song, Faith and Order has been employed with historical preconfessional or explanatory postconfessional studies, not with the necessary confessing approach in the search for unity.[303] In the contextual and actual confessions he find the real confessions. Or, in my terminology, the really accountable confessions are those where people or churches are accountable in a particular situation for their own faith, not the formulations of the faith from the past. In this type of confession he sees the potential for unity, not in general studies of confessions. The Faith and Order Commission should ". . . redirect the ecumenical search for unity to its 'logical' and thus 'primary' place, that is,

---

299. The argument for not designing a new creed was, besides the unique position and significance of the Nicene Creed, that the World Council of Churches did not have the authority of an ecumenical council—which did not yet exist (Lima II 1982:33). The shift of director of Faith and Order from William Lazareth to Günther Gassmann between Lima 1982 and Crete 1984 might have influenced the reduction of this reluctance.

300. Lima II 1982:40.

301. Reformed, Korean, working for the Faith and Order secretariat in this period.

302. Four volumes were published under the title: "Confessing Our Faith Around the World"; cf. the bibliography, below.

303. Cf. foreword by C. S. Song in Confessing I 1980:1–7. Song left the Faith and Order secretariat after the Faith and Order Standing Dommission chose a different direction in this study.

confessions that Christians today are making in various parts of the world at the risk of their safety and their lives."[304]

The problem related to this approach is how a contextual confession can unite the churches all over the world, or how the churches can be mutually accountable to one another on the basis of that kind of confession. However, the potential of unity in a common confession between those churches living in and fighting against the same problem is an important ecumenical experience and treasure (e.g., the 1933 Barmen Declaration in Germany). But at the level of Faith and Order's worldwide approach, the the Faith and Order Commission saw the problems of adopting the contextually oriented confessions in the whole Church as a problem of accountability: these confessions could not be binding for the whole catholic Church. They should be tested, rather, in respect to their accountability to the one faith expressed in the Ecumenical Creed.

> The plurality and variety of documents which occur in the act of confessing in particular situations do not imply that each new creed or symbol binds the whole catholic Church. It is true that Christian witness should always aim to express the whole faith of the one Church; but the whole Church is not thereby bound to each particular act of confessing. These various acts and documents of confession rather apply the one apostolic faith to particular situations, and are to be judged, therefore, by the criterion of their consonance with that apostolic faith as confessed in the Ecumenical Creed of the Church.[305]

Accordingly, here is an important distinction of the nature of accountability; on the one hand, being (locally/contextually) accountable for the whole faith of the Church, and, on the other hand, making the whole Church accountable for each (local/contextual) confession of faith. This distinction is understandable, as it avoids a lot of theological problems. How and why should or could all churches recognize or approve all the local confessions? The distinction also solves an insurmountable problem of handling such procedures.

Nevertheless, logical as this distinction might be, it also conceals a major concern implied in the idea that churches are mutually accountable to one another. If the churches belong to the whole catholic Church, the churches are participating in the life of one another. The quoted distinction can be used to ignore the ecumenical attitude of mutual accountability by making clear the formal limits of the binding status of confessions. If a church finds itself being

---

304. Song, in Confessing I 1980:7.
305. From the report of the working group preparing the "Apostolic Faith" study, approved by the commission in Lima in 1982 (Lima II 1982:33).

in a *status confessionis*, it is not their problem only, it is a matter of the whole Church—if there is a moral request of being mutually accountable.

The potential for unity in mutually sharing contextual confessions was not activated, according to Song. Another, more open argument for the ecumenical potential of being mutually accountable to one another in respect to the local confessions is made by Anton Houtepen. He finds no undermining contradiction between the presented creedal statements and the creed of the Church, but important supplements to the ancient creeds in the field of ethics and the historical ministry of Jesus. What is important for our study are his remarks on the potential of achieving a common expression of faith through a "communication of faith" and through a "mutual exchange of confessions between the churches."[306]

Representing a position of liberation theology, Jaci Maraschin[307] claims forcefully that the confession of faith as a system of formal dogmatic positions tends not to be accountable to the situation in which people live. The problem is not that theologians and churches are insufficiently updated in the actual situations, or have insufficient ability to communicate the reasonability of the Christian faith. The problem, according to Maraschin, is the historic link between this approach and misuse of power. This "formal, dogmatic, authoritarian, infallible and systematic" way of confessing the faith has been the mark of the faith of the colonizers. It has given assurance to those in power and implied disastrous servility by the Church to them, conveying resignation to the poor and oppressed.[308]

Maraschin challenges the understanding of *division* presupposed in this Faith and Order study. In his part of the world, the main division among Christians is not denominational but between oppressors and oppressed. The challenge for the unity of the Church are the powers of death and the ideologies behind the situation of oppression.[309] Consequently, he claims the need

306. Confessing II 1983:viii–ix (foreword): "We hope that the "communication of faith" and the mutual exchange of confessions between churches prepare for the time when the churches can meet together with one heart and one voice. It is not our intention either to replace the Ancient Creeds or the official "Confessions" of the churches. Nor are we wanting to make propaganda for new credal formulations. Our only aim is to enable communication between the churches about confessional articulation which is going on in many parts of the world."

307. Maraschin is a Brazilian Episcopalian. According to Appendix IV in COF 1991:125–39, he was member of the steering committee and participated in all of its meetings, except the last one.

308. Maraschin 1982:24–25.

309. "In Latin American society, churches are divided according to the divisions of society; the main divisions between the churches are not, in this part of the world, the traditional, denominational divisions, but the divisions between oppressors and oppressed, between rich and poor (though not always at the level of conscience)." "The question of the people is not, primarily, a question about the unity of the divided denominational churches, but a question about the

for another understanding of Christian faith and confession, which is not concerned about accountability toward the classic Western academic traditions, but the people who are in need of liberation and new life.[310] Further, Maraschin raises the demand of a new theology. The traditional theology led to a superstitious way of being Christian. His point can be described in our terminology like this: the local accountability to the situation of the people is the best way to be accountable to the origins of the Christian faith.

Maraschin also challenges the traditional understanding of the universality of the Christian faith. Faith is always individual and personal, but not isolated. It is no universal Christian faith if it is not contextual and particular.[311] His major problem with the ideas of the planned Faith and Order study was, therefore, the idea of a "common expression" based on an ancient document accountable to questions of another time in a totally different culture.[312] He thereby challenged the premises for the whole study. A common recognition and confessing of the Nicene Creed would not in itself bring unity in the type of divisions he defines. The explanation of the faith in accountability to Western challenges of secularism would not help in this regard, either.

It can be asked critically to this position: How could there be any mutually accountable manifestation of the unity in faith of the Church, if there is no common expression of faith to which it can be referred? Maraschin does not answer this question directly. But he does so indirectly, by redefining "faith" from a conceptual notion to a notion of life, struggle, and hope. He does not underestimate the communal aspect of faith; rather, to the contrary, he leaves the question of the common formulation of faith open.

This is a problem, even for the approach to Christian faith Maraschin proclaims. We must presume that somehow what is a Christian faith must be defined, particularly if it is a matter of life and death. It might, therefore, be asked if he was, at least implicitly, arguing more for *another and new common understanding* of the Christian faith than against the need for a common confession. Thereby he confirmed the presupposition in the intention of the project, namely: mutual accountability to the common faith is necessary for

---

unity of life" (Maraschin 1982:24, 26).

310. "Christian faith is not a system . . . , [it] is above all a living experience, a mode of being, an atmosphere in which Christians move. . . . Christian faith is a faith, not a philosophy. It does not depend on rational categories but on the gift of God, full of love, of his Son Jesus Christ nurtured by the power of the Holy Spirit" (Maraschin 1982:25).

311. "Christian faith is confessed within the scope of a culture. That is why it is always confessed in a particular way. The confession of the Christian faith which is universal only becomes possible *in my specific place and in my particular time*. It is in this way that the universal gets meaning" (Maraschin 1982:26).

312. Maraschin 1982:27.

the unity of the Church. To bring unity to the Church, according to Maraschin, a new approach of the faith, for instance, in the rich–poor relations, is unavoidable.

The contribution from this position is relevant for a theory of mutual accountability. It should be out of the question to ignore the consequences of a statement or confession of faith. Sharing the faith must imply being mutually accountable for how statements of faith can have consequences in regard to justice, peace, and freedom. There should be particular attention to the accountability over against the nonprivileged parts of humanity if the Church is accountable to the origin of the apostolic faith. This accountability was made explicit in the BEM text at several points.[313] For Maraschin and liberation theology, this is the primary place for any confession of faith. Maraschin raises the question how the confession of faith could be a Christian confession at all if its not accountable in the sense of understandable to and in solidarity with those participating or listening.[314]

This is to some extent the main point in respect to accountability in the position of Ellen Flessemann-van Leer, advising something else than a reconfirmation of the creed or a reformulation of it today.[315] She emphasizes, at least indirectly, the vivid diversity of expressions and images in the biblical material as well as in the experiences with God. She points to *the limits of our accountability* in describing God, reminding a reader of the Third Commandment prohibition of describing God per se. But she is not denying the possibility of saying anything in common. Her main concern is that it must be more directly linked to the manifold biblical material than the creed is, being accountable to the actual questions within and outside the Church today.

According to Flessemann-van Leer, the accountability to Scripture and to the challenges of the Church today have the same focal point: any confession of faith today must be accountable to the soteriological emphasis of Scripture and the soteriological needs and expectations of today's believers.[316]

The Required and Sufficient Essence of the Living Tradition

Another perspective, combining a focus on the Nicene Creed and the need to take diversity seriously in the process of establishing a common confession

---

313. Cf. on BEM above, pp. 156–85.

314. This type of question was not totally ignored in the "Apostolic Faith" study, but served as an argument behind the "explications." On the other hand, the final text has in many regards the character of stating a consensus on general, universal, and systematic concepts on the content of faith. It is, consequently, to some degree still a target of the critique from Maraschin and other theologians sharing his views.

315. Flesseman-van Leer 1982:101–112.

316. Flesseman-van Leer 1982:111.

of faith is articulated by one who became the moderator of the steering committee of the "Apostolic Faith" study, the Roman Catholic Jean M. R. Tillard OP.[317] Of importance for our theme, the starting point of his reflections is the requirement of a mutual *recognition* of sharing the common faith to establish a conciliar fellowship.[318] He thereby settles the dialectic between unity in "faith," "order," and "quality of relation" as a crucial element in this endeavour. The diversity in and between the Christian churches should not be ruled out. Any idea of conciliar fellowship demanding too much perfection or uniformity is unrealistic and not to the point.[319] The demand, therefore, is to develop a methodology to express and establish mutual recognition according to what is required and sufficient to have a common faith, "*quod requiritur et sufficit.*" Anything compatible with this "essence" should be accepted.[320] The ancient creeds from the period of the great councils, as a common basis, can define this.[321]

Like Pannenberg, Tillard stresses the need for a defined common standard of faith to which the churches should be mutually accountable, as well as the central role of the creeds. In 1981 he also confirmed the special role and potentiality of the Nicene Creed. But he prescribes something else than just a scholarly explication of the creed.[322] These common expressions are not

---

317. He gave three lectures to define the goal of the project, in Bangalore 1978, Chambésy 1981, and in Stavanger 1985. They are all papers printed in official Faith and Order reports from those meetings.

318. "Concilar fellowship can only be authentically *Christian communion* if it rests on a measure of agreement sufficient for all to be able to consider themselves in truth as one in faith and mission." "I must be able to recognize authentic Christian faith in the faith of the representative of another church, even if fairly remote from my own, seated beside me at the conciliar table" (See Tillard in *Towards Confession* 1980:224f).

319. "But both the history of the Church and our ecumenical experience show that it is impossible to equate unanimity in faith with uniformity in expressing or even understanding this faith, being transcendent and catholic, this faith remains the same in a variety of embodiments and in different explanations which derive in part from the plurality of cultures and situations." "It should be added that this margin of difference is not simply an *a posteriori* concession, but also corresponds to the other of what is *a priori* desirable." ". . . to start out by seeking to make reconciliation between churches conditional on their meeting the requirements of perfection would be to destroy any hope of seeing conciliar fellowship established one day" (Tillard 1978:224f.).

320. "Everything, then, which does not in itself contradict this essence of the given faith should be recognized as compatible with the degree of communion in the faith *quod requiritur*. In other words, wherever this essence is preserved, even if there is a wide doctrinal diversity, the degree of faith *quod sufficit* also exists" (Tillard 1978:228).

321. ". . . the great formative period . . . must therefore give us our bearings in our search for *quod recuiritur et sufficit*" (Tillard 1978:228).

322. The ancient creeds were fulfilled under the promise of the Spirit. Therefore, they ". . . constitute a rule of faith because of this guarantee of the Spirit" (Tillard 1982:53).

enough to arrive at a consensus on the most central required elements of the faith. The content of the creeds has to be translated into new situations and times. This has been the task of the faithful through the ages. This implies an important variety.[323] Further, the churches have in our time been led to focus on other aspects in the apostolic tradition than those elevated in the ancient creeds, that is, the demand for justice, peace, and nondiscrimination.[324] Besides that, he sees crucial elements of a common faith not mentioned in the Nicene Creed, like eucharist and ministry. The truth of the faith goes beyond verbal confessions into "ecclesial praxis." There must be a distinction between the *res* to which the faith is focused and the *verba*.[325]

To achieve a common understanding and acceptance of this "essence," Tillard recommends a process aiming not only at what I would call accountability to a fixed standard, but to mutual accountability to the diversity between the different church traditions. The churches have a double task, according to Tillard. First, they must, through a mutual listening and common work, decide the content of this "essence." Second, they must, in accountability to this common definition of an essence, critically review their own doctrines, whether consensus on them is required for unity in faith.[326] This is the way toward recognition of the richness of the Christian traditions and to a unity in faith: "The authentic conciliar fellowship requires that, after centuries of isolation and frequent opposition, we should let ourselves be questioned and

---

323. Tillard 1978:228.

324. Tillard 1978:226.

325. "The faith is focused on the res, not on the formulas" (Tillard 1978:227). "Its absolute is the absolute of God, immeasurably transcending all formulations and explaining all commitments without being identified with any of them. This alone is the *res*, the reality of the faith" (Tillard 1982:60).

326. "Without cheating and without lapsing into cheap compromises but rather endeavoring to listen seriously to one another, they must together decide the content of faith *quod requiritur et sufficit*, if they are to share in a council which would be really ecumenical in the sense that the early councils were ecumenical and not just a ramshackle assembly of delegates who are unable to recognize each other as sharing the same faith, the same eucharist, the same ministry." "Each church must apply to its own doctrinal tradition the distinction between essentials and non-essentials so as to be in a position not to require of others more than is really required, while still being convinced that by consenting to the *quod sufficit* it is not selling the faith short. This is something which it can only do for itself, something moreover which could have considerable consequences for its own internal life." Tillard gives some clear and challenging examples: "The Disciples of Christ, for example, have to ask themselves whether their position on the creeds counts among the essentials; the same question arises for the Baptists in respect of their view on baptism. Can the Roman Catholic Church acknowledge that the fundamental articles of faith are fewer in number than the Catholic dogmas, and by not insisting on acceptance of the last two Marian definitions as a condition of entry into a 'communion of faith' with itself, it would not be playing fast and loose with the will of Christ" (Tillard 1978:230).

enriched by each other. It really is not just a matter of gluing broken fragments together."[327] That could imply that some churches either have to go through a conversion. He sees this mutually accountable process as promising for each church and the communion between them.

This approach is, according to Tillard in 1981, the proper Roman Catholic understanding of the "living tradition," what "reception" of "the faith of the fathers" means. Later developments after the fathers should not, according to Tillard, be understood in a "quasi-quantitative" way. It has not the same guaranteed validity by the Spirit as the ecumenical councils; adding new dogmas is not necessary to safeguard the truth formulated in the ancient creeds. But it contributes to the *splendor veritatis*. Holding the received declarations of faith as sacrosanct is to acknowledge the meaning of the creeds, which is not necessarily identical on all points to what has been read into the text in the centuries that followed. The aim of reception is, accordingly, progressively clarifying the meaning and purpose of the propositions of the faith of the fathers. Later research would maybe change past theological positions, but it cannot change the belief that the Spirit guarantees the link between the ancient creeds and the real sense of the revealed datum.[328]

Tillard emphasizes that the task of the Catholic Church today is to recognize "a new stage in the living tradition." Christianity outside the Western countries is developing new translations of the faith of the fathers into their rites, language, and concepts. This embodiment of the faith in other human traditions is necessary. The faith of the fathers, as the faith today, is expressed in a diversity of "registers," not only in the formulated creeds.[329] The only way to handle this situation is a wide mutually accountable dialogue, relating to what is common in the wide perspective of catholicity (not only the one text of the Nicene Creed): "It will of course be necessary to ensure that the essential elements of the tradition are not obscured or distorted by the local values. This can only be done through fraternal dialogue between churches, guided not by a shabby policy of concessions or toleration but by a broad view of the catholicity of the Church."[330]

---

327. Tillard 1978:231.

328. Tillard 1982:54–56.

329. Tillard 1982:57–61. "If the faith of the fathers is to continue to be a saving faith, it will therefore have to be increasingly embodied in human traditions and ways of thought that are very remote from our western ethos" (58). "This is because conceptual thinking has played a key role in the culture of the west. It cannot be the same in all cultures" (59).

330. Tillard 1982:58.

Later, in 1985, Tillard defended the use of the Nicene Creed as the link between today's faith and the faith of the apostolic communities against the accusation that the goal of the "Apostolic Faith" study was an "archaizing option remote from the present situation of the churches." In 1985 he focused on the need for a common explanation of the Nicene Creed, as a tool for the mutually accountable comparison of churches' doctrines with the Nicene Creed as norm.[331]

The hermeneutic problem related to defining one universal expression of faith is relevant even for the position of Tillard: to make one new definition of the meaning of the creed (to which all should subscribe today) means presupposing that new terminology would mean the same to everybody in the whole world. The problem of different conceptualizations between the ancient church and now is not easily removed by making a set of new concepts that every church should accept.

Tillard addressed the problem, however. He said that adherence to the "content of the Nicene-Constantinopolitan faith" is not a premise for unity isolated from the "call to transplant this datum into the immense variety of human soils."[332] Thereby he tried to define the task of establishing unity in faith in relation to the growing understanding of the contextuality of any expression of faith. His terminology for a double accountability is the "twofold fidelity," which cannot be pursued separately. The expected common explanation cannot live its own life as a universal expression of the apostolic faith, but only as a tool for comparison between the church traditions. This modified expectation of the explanation represents an important alternative for a definition of mutual accountability as principle of ecumenical theology, a line that was pursued in the "Apostolic Faith" study.

---

331. "The Nicene-Constantinopolitan Creed links today's faith with that of the apostolic communities. Now, however, it is a matter of first explaining its content as clearly as possible so that all may be able to compare their own faith and that of others with its norm, at a level deeper than that of words and expressions which are perhaps without resonance for us today. This is a vital step if we wish to verify with some degree of certitude the real measure of our 'communion' in the apostolic faith. The purpose of this undertaking, moreover, is primarily the solidity and strength of ecclesial unity." "If we all adhere to the content of the Niceno-Constantinopolitan faith, knowing what we are about, then the certitude that we are all "in communion" in the same, the one faith will not be called into question by a diversity of formulations and translations" (Tillard 1985:113).

332. Tillard 1985:114.

The Methodology of the "Apostolic Faith" Study Exposed in the Final Report

Explication of the Nicene Creed

All of the positions referred to above focus on the need for establishing mutual accountability (without using the terminology) between the churches as regards a manifestation of sharing the same faith. None of them ignores the importance of relating accountably to one another in that respect. But there are remarkable differences when it comes to how the churches should manifest their accountability, what the churches should be accountable for, and to whom they are accountable.

In Lima the Faith and Order Commission realized that authorizing a new creed was beyond its mandate. Such an endeavour of "proposing an ecumenical symbol of the apostolic faith presupposes the authority of an ecumenical council." A prerequisite of such a council would, however, be a common recognition of the Nicene Creed.[333]

There were presented strong arguments for using the Nicene Creed as the common point of reference for a manifestation of sharing the apostolic faith.[334] The final report of the "Apostolic Faith" study (*Confessing our Faith*, or COF) declares that the intention of *explication* of the faith expressed in the Nicene Creed was focused rather exclusively. Only indirectly should the study stimulate reflection that could lead to processes of recognition and confession, and it should not in itself be a consensus document, not even a convergence document.[335]

The COF text can be interpreted as a presentation of how truly far-reaching the agreement is between the churches on central faith issues. This is also

---

333. Lin a 1982:33.

334. These arguments were presented in the introduction to COF (COF 1991:4): its ecumenically wide liturgical use as the most profound expression of the Christian faith; the theological significance of its content; the potential of including the Orthodox churches on their own premises; the potential of uniting Roman Catholic interest for the catholic tradition and the concern for the right apostolic faith in many Protestant churches; the relevance also for "non-creedal" churches, due to the potential of showing the consonance between the creed and the Scriptures; and the possibility of a manifestation of sharing the common faith by having one (and the most) historically and theologically significant text. These arguments had, according to the choice of methodology demonstrated in the final report, the upper hand in the Faith and Order Commission during this study.

335. "*Confessing the One Faith* is not intended to represent a consensus or even convergence document which could as such provide a basis for the common recognition and confession of the apostolic faith as an essential element of visible unity among the churches. Rather, this study document should be seen as an instrument to help the churches to focus on and reflect together upon the apostolic faith. Such study and reflection should lead towards a fresh understanding of the apostolic faith and thus towards a common recognition and confession of this faith today" (COF 1991:5f.).

announced in the text's introduction. However, several signs in the text itself indicate that there also was an intention to make common statements on important issues of Christian faith in the text itself.[336] The text gives, therefore, an impression of being a contemporary confession. The final report of the study shows that the commission emphasized the ecumenical potential of preparing the recognition of the Nicene Creed, through a study that could give account of its biblical basis and provide a contemporary explanation of it. Here we find interesting terminology:

> Churches, which belong to different Christian traditions and live in diverse cultural, social, political and religious contexts, need to *reappropriate* their common basis in the apostolic faith so that they may confess their faith together. In so doing, they will give common witness to the saving purposes of the Triune God for all humanity and all creation. . . . The unity of the churches requires mutual trust. In the full communion which churches are looking for, each church must be able to recognize in the other the fullness of the apostolic faith.[337]

The task of "reappropriation" is significant here. It identifies the premise that the churches already share and have appropriated as the same faith, but it needs to be done again in the present mutual and accountable setting. It corresponds to the terminology of "recognition," as it is used in the introduction of COF. The churches should be stimulated to test whether they share the faith of the Nicene Creed, and eventually revise their tradition and practice according to that.

> Recognition, therefore, has in this study process a very specific meaning. Each church has first of all to become aware of how much in its own life and commitment it is faithful to the apostolic faith and how far it is confessing it in its words and deeds. At the same time every church that is committed to visible unity needs to recognize the fidelity to the apostolic faith in the confessional statements, liturgical life and witness, proclamation and practice of other churches.[338]

---

336. "The explication will seek to respond to the question as to what degree and in which form the fundamentals of the apostolic faith as witnesses to by the Holy Scriptures, proclaimed in the Tradition of the Church, and expressed in the Creed, can be commonly understood and expressed by churches of different confessional traditions, living in different cultural, social, economical, political and religious contexts" (COF 1991:5). This can hardly be very different from what is intended by convergence documents in bilateral or multilateral dialogues.

337. COF 1991:2; italics mine.

338. COF 1991:6. The definition of "recognition" is very close to the elaboration of this concept

Hence, the goal is an affirmation of sharing the same faith, to get the required binding common criterion. This is the type of mutual accountability aimed at, primarily. But the introduction to COF tries, as far as possible, to link it to the other alternative, as the quotation above shows. The reappropriation of the common basis can lead to mutual trust that makes the churches open to recognizing different traditions as expressions of the same faith: "The purpose of this common explication of the Nicene Creed is to increase mutual confidence so that all churches may be helped to recognize the apostolic faith in each other."[339]

Thus, the text brings both dimensions of mutual accountability together under the perspective of "recognition." As the quotation also indicates, the affirmation of the common faith should not be done for the internal relations between churches per se, but to make the churches able to give a common witness. The text harmonizes to some extent the alternatives between focusing on affirmation of one common creed and recognizing contextual creedal confessions, as well as between emphasizing the confession of the one creed and focusing the confession in the world. This can be understood as a typical ecumenical solution, demonstrating the imprecise methodology of ecumenical documents. It can also be interpreted as a confirmation of the adequacy of the different approaches. Hence, the COF text seems to show that there is no absolute alternative between mutual accountability through binding affirmations of one creed and mutual accountability to the contextual and historical creedal statements made in particular situations.

The formulation of a common confession in a particular situation could be a more binding sign of sharing the same apostolic faith of the creed than a general statement of acceptance of the Nicene Creed. If there is presupposed an absolute necessary order of what must come first, a general or a specific statement of confession, it easily becomes a discussion of what came first, the hen or the egg.[340] If there should be any principally given order, the protesting "no" can be articulated more clearly but presuppose the general—and not always articulated—"yes." The definition of "recognition" quoted above shows that

by Tillard.

339. COF 1991:7.

340. The formulation, completion, and confirmation of the Nicene Creed in the ancient Church was in itself a sign that the purpose of uniting the Church and the need for taking a common stand in a particular challenge are two aspects that run together. The history of dogma indicates that the faith is positively formulated and reformulated in regard to particular challenges. General formulations of the faith with no particular address or occasion belong, rather, to handbooks for theological students. Even publications of study books for "dogmatics" is hardly a neutral matter, but shaped by the context and concern of the author. The adoption of the Nicene Creed into the liturgy is a sign of the theological and canonical significance applied to the creed, but does not mean that everything that has to be said for all times about the faith or a general statement of faith.

recognition of the one faith formulated in the Nicene Creed, the recognition of the expressions of faith in other traditions, and the recognition of contextual confessions should not be separated in pursuing unity in the relation between churches.

From Inductive to Deductive Methodology

However, the choice of methodology in the COF document gives priority to the deductive approach, explicating the principle "yes" more than the specific "no" to what is against the Christian faith and hope. Thereby the COF text presupposes that mutual recognition of sharing the one faith implies being open, transparent, and mutually accountable to one another in regard of the expressions of the faith each tradition has in creeds, liturgy, and practice, but these expressions should be evaluated in accountability to the critical light given in the Nicene Creed (interpreted as articulation of the given apostolic faith).

The inductive and contextual methodology of the "Giving Account" study was definitely replaced by a general deduction of the meaning of the creed and its basis in Scripture. The "Apostolic Faith" study was basically done through consultations in different regions of the world, with a wide participation of theologians. The reports from the consultations were revised and abridged by the steering committee, which implied unification, and some variety and diversity of perspectives were left out.[341]

The structure of the final report makes the deductive approach apparent: the treatment of each article of the creed is structured in three "loci" (e.g., for the first article: "The One God," "The Father Almighty," "The Creator and His Creation"). Under each part this scheme is followed: after a short introduction to the theme, a section of the creed and its "biblical witness" is given before the "explication for today" is applied. The explication for today can be an apologetic reflection (such as, under the first article: "Challenges posed by other religions and living faiths, " 26f.), a dogmatic reflection with references to Bible texts (as in "Creation and the Triune God," 39f.), or a more general reflection of theological principles (like "Ethics of creation," 42).

The references to biblical texts are not so much exegesis of texts as references to texts where something is said to the theme.[342] Some details make the text a combination of a confession and an explanation. Here are two of many examples:

---

341. Dietrich Ritschl, the drafter of the report on the consultation on Christology, criticized this structural problem of Faith and Order and the consequences in shift and narrowing of perspectives. Cf. Ritschl 1988, esp. 96–98.

342. E.g.: "The belief in the creative power of God's word (Gen. 1; John 1:1-3; Heb. 11:3) and the confidence that God is able to create 'out of nothing' (Rom 4:17; Heb. 11:3; cf. Mat. 3:9) is characteristic of the Christian belief in God the Creator" (COF 1991:38).

Confession: (§6) Christians *believe* that "the One true God," who made himself known to Israel, has revealed himself supremely in the "one whom he has sent," namely Jesus Christ (John 17:3).

Explanation: §8: Many who agree with Christians in a belief in one God find the Trinitarian affirmation of Christians difficult to understand.[343]

Confession here is, however, more a principle and general statement than the contextual confessions asked for in the "Giving Account" study and published in the other series. The dominant feature of the text is the elaboration of the *themes* raised by the creed, discussed on the basis of the text of the creed, biblical texts, and theological reflection, not particular statements on special occasions.

The text has a rich variety of perspectives and reflections. Some of them have a rather general character, like discussions of the challenge from "atheism," and so forth.[344] The text has many features of what could be expected in an introduction to dogmatics. The particular feature of this text is the richness of perspectives and the attempts to find a convergence or consensus in issues of divergence between church traditions.

Mutual Accountability to the Many Traditions

The COF text has some common features with the hermeneutic we found in the BEM text. The churches were not as much involved in the "Apostolic Faith" study as in the preparation of BEM, but there were more theologians involved in the processes that led to the drafting of texts. There was a hearing before the final version of the document was published, which gave the commission a lot of responses.[345] At some points the different traditions are taken into account, given attention, and set together with other traditions. One significant example is the merger of the Eastern and Western traditions of the Trinity understood respectively as "internal"/"immanent" Trinity and "divine economy": "Economic and eternal trinity is but one reality."[346] This is maybe even more transparent in the section of the third article, where the text deals with baptism.[347] The delineation of the tension between a symbolic and a sacramental view of baptism ends with a mutual challenge to both sides.[348] The

---

343. COF 1991:17.
344. E.g., COF 1991:23f.
345. According to COF 1991:8.
346. COF 1991:20f. The consonance between the two traditions is elaborated further in the text.
347. COF 1991:90–96.
348. COF 1991:94.

same type of challenge to become mutually accountable is found in the short remark on justification.[349]

The similarity to the hermeneutic in BEM is significant. However, the challenges to be mutually accountable in the COF document are somewhat more general and not related to so specific points of interconfessional divergences as they are in BEM. The most distinct point of confessional controversy handled in the COF document is the *filioque* question.

The mutually accountable approach to traditions is not only a matter of acknowledging classical confessional traditions. In some cases, contributions from liberation theology are included in the common explication of the one Tradition or the one faith. One example is the explication of the meaning of the suffering of Christ as compassion with all who suffer: "God enables them to *struggle* against suffering and death in all their manifestations. In the particular case of human oppression, the victim is assured that God is never on the side of the oppressor, the bringer of death, but will, in his justice, protect the rights and lives of the victims."[350]

Hence, we might say that the methodology of the study process was not to gather accounts of faith and hope, but to deduct from the Nicene Creed and Scripture what the common faith is. This was to some extent a hermeneutic of taking different traditions into account in the attempt to explicate the one Tradition. But to a large extent the process was pursued, steered, and dominated by a few theologians, presenting their contribution to the understanding of what the Christian faith means in respect to the themes mentioned in the Nicene Creed. They were, nevertheless, accountable to a wide range of inputs from other theologians highly qualified in knowing the Christian traditions. This characterizes the result, too.

The Result: A Manifestation of Mutual Accountability to the One Apostolic Faith?

The Final Report: "Confessing the One Faith" (COF)

The result of the "Apostolic Faith" study could be evaluated according to the goal of the study within the ecumenical process. Although the terminology of "conciliar fellowship" became less frequently used in the 1980s than in the 1970s, the three recommendations from Bangalore were still the reason behind the entire project. According to the definition of the goal in the final report, the project should have a goal in terms of ecumenical *process*. It was not a study only for the sake of knowledge, information, and agreement.[351] In the termi-

---

349. COF 1991:95. The Western doctrine is questioned as too forensic, the Orthodox as not taking the sinfulness of Christians seriously enough.

350. COF 1991:63.

351. "The present project of Faith and Order is intended to help the churches *move towards* the

nology of my study, the criterion of evaluation would be: Did the final report of the "Apostolic Faith" study establish a basis that could make the churches more mutually accountable for the common faith and to the common faith, and thereby help to manifest visible unity through establishing a conciliar fellowship?

This is not the place to give a comprehensive and substantial evaluation of the content of the final report. I will limit myself to some further comments on the text, from the perspective of the overarching goal of making a platform for visible unity. Thus, it will be discussed as a contribution to mutual recognition and mutual accountability. The *reception* of the text belongs therefore to this evaluation of the results.

The *text* of the final report has *several significant qualities* in respect to the goal:

- The COF text demonstrates how much the churches have in common in respect to apostolic faith if they recognize the Nicene Creed.

- The text exposes how far the common understanding of the apostolic faith reaches in respect to the loci of faith mentioned in the Nicene Creed. Although the churches have not approved the text, theologians from different confessions and traditions have presented the text as a witness of the comprehensive consensus in significant aspects of the faith.

- The text conveys important impulses from other Faith and Order projects, presenting what appear to be common ecumenical points of view in important matters of faith. In this way, the text contributes to a more accountable attitude to the results of the work already done in the ecumenical movement.[352]

- The text elaborates the biblical background for the content and formulations of the creed. Thereby, the text presents a contribution to establishing the Bible as a common point of accountability. The multitude of references to biblical texts as "prooftexts" for the elements of the creed has a function of appeal to a nondisputable common source and authority. This is probably far beyond what has been done in other Faith and

---

common confession of apostolic faith" (COF 1991:1; italics mine).

352. Some examples: The text makes a distinction between [theologically legitimated] "secularization" and ideological "secularism" (23–26) important for the struggle about modernism. The text offers different interpretations of Christ's death (58–64), concluding, "the real concerns implicit in these interpretations are not alternatives" (59). In respect to the *filioque* problem, the text conveys the balanced approach from the study of that particular problem (78f.). The same can be said about the passage on baptism (referring to BEM). The elaboration in the "Giving Account" study of the eschatological hope for today is presented (97–104, esp. 101).

Order studies in that respect. The text thereby gives noncreedal churches a basis for recognition of the content of the creed even if they do not use it liturgically or approve it as a confessional document.

- The text does not address the issue of faith from the angle of controversial issues, but from the creed supposed to express common faith.
- The text elaborates and explicates important matters of faith without focusing or dwelling long on details that have caused or could cause difficulties and divergence.
- The text could serve as a platform for ecumenical theological studies, for the purpose of manifesting what is the common basis—in spite of divisions.[353]
- The text conveys significant theological reflections concerning the implications of the Christian faith encountering other religious beliefs, ideologies, and ethical challenges.

Hence, the COF text has potential to be a resource for a process toward recognition of the Nicene Creed as common faith and recognition of different expressions and traditions as consonant with the common Christian faith. Thus, it could also serve as an instrument toward more mutual accountability between the churches. But the text has not to any significant extent released that process as intended. The COF text so far has not led to what has been declared or understood as a common confession or a mutually declared recognition of the Nicene Creed.

There are some explanations why this methodology has not conveyed the desired degree of mutual accountability in the ecumenical process. The purpose of presenting them here is not to give a critique of the "Apostolic Faith" study as such, but to reflect on what it contributes to mutual accountability between the churches. These explanations relate both to the text and to the reception process of it.

The most prominent theological point relates to *the genre of the text*. The text is not, according to the formulated intentions, a confessional document to which the churches should give their approving voice. However, in the traditions of the churches—and that is the point of reference for a possible accountable recognition of a text like this—it is not that easy to draw sharp lines between a creed, a creedal statement, a confessional document (*Bekenntnisschrift*), a catechism, a confession in a particular situation, and "an explication

---

353. The text has served this purpose in an ecumenical theological forum in Norway. The response from Norsk Teologisk Samtaleforum under Norges Kristne Råd is an example. Cf. the Faith and Order archives (reference not given from the Faith and Order Secretariat).

of the faith today." Therefore, already the fact of publication of what is meant to be *a* common explication of what the apostolic faith is today implies a distinction from *the* common explication of the faith today, even *the* faith today. The explication of the creed in the contemporary context could—in practice—be quite the same as a contemporary expression of the Christian faith, not only an explication. The confessional documents have in several instances been an affirmation of being in consonance with the ancient creeds, of which *Confessio Augustana* is a typical example. This has been done as an explication of what the classical creeds mean in a specific "today."[354]

The explanatory style of the COF text gives, however, a mixed picture, conveying an ambiguity that could be one reason why the text hasn't led to recognition, approval, and reception. The many descriptions of historical circumstances, challenging ideologies, and the like give an impression of a text meant for learning, for instance, in theological schools.[355] On the other hand, the form of several passages and the theological substance and dignity of the scope and themes of the text leads the expectations of a reader from "explication" toward "confession."

The text invites the churches to accept the creed *under this explication* as a common confession of faith. The sense of making a text like this is to say as precisely as possible what *the* content of the faith *is*. Consequently, and naturally, the text has introductory remarks to every part of the creed where the COF text explicitly says "the Church/Christians *confess* that . . ."[356] If the churches should recognize and receive this COF text as a premise for concluding that they share the confession of the apostolic faith, what is then the real theological difference between this text and a confession? The text is not meant to be one arbitrary attempt to formulate what the common apostolic faith *might be*. The theologically most significant passages (like the first introductions to each passage of the creed) are *not* presented as an explication that could be replaced by any other text the next day. That would undermine the rationality of the endeavour.

But that kind of statement cannot be evaluated, discussed, and eventually recognized at the same level as the descriptive passages or those passages attempting to define the content of the Bible. The problem of the use of the text for the process toward a mutually accountable recognition of confessing

---

354. Already the first consultation of the project after Lima (Rome 1983) pointed to the unclear distinction between "explication" and "confession" (Root 1994:18).

355. The publication is presented at the front page as "A Faith and Order Study Document"; the covering letter to the churches also gives this impression of "proposal" as it invites to study and asks for contributions to Faith and Order "as it continues its work on confession of the apostolic faith." Cf. the presentation of the questions below.

356. Italics mine.

the same apostolic faith is, therefore, implicit in the text itself as a theological problem of what common confession means, what kind of theological level is pursued for that task.

Another dimension of this problem is that the COF text *does not present a clear focus* to which the churches could respond; it appears as a multitude of important issues. The confessional statements during the history of the churches have mostly been made as an answer to particular challenges in particular circumstances. The COF text is not conceptualized as a statement of faith addressing one particular challenge, but as an attempt to formulate a common basis somewhat beyond the difficult points of divergence between the churches. Only a few burning and difficult ecumenical diverging points are explicitly mentioned in the text. The comments to such problems that are given in COF are usually formulated in a general and open style.[357] Thus, it is difficult for the churches to see clearly what kind of solution is proposed to a particular problem. The text is not transparent enough in that sense.[358]

The comprehensiveness of the text, commenting on most of the issues of faith that can be related to the formulations in the creed, gives the reader a sense of facing an encyclopedia. At the same time, some crucial ecumenical issues are not handled or only touched (like eucharist, the doctrine of justification, the ordained ministry). The picture of the challenge to the churches lacks a clear focus. What should they respond to, more precisely, in a binding, accountable way? In spite of the good intentions, the many relevant descriptions of the challenges to the faith, as well as the significant answers to those challenges, remain in a sphere of interesting generalities. This probably makes it difficult to find a way to receive this text in an ecumenical procedure.

A significant theological problem in all this is whether the Christian faith can be formulated for a mutual binding statement in a general way like this. On the one hand, statements of faith relating to particular contextual problems cannot be universalized without losing some of their identity. On the other hand, even general statements of faith can only be articulated in a particular historical situation, and will be saying something in that situation according to the hermeneutical framework in which they are received.[359]

---

357. In the response from the Norsk Teologisk Samtaleforum, the COF text is welcomed and appreciated as important for the sake of unity. Still, what the COF text says about the *filioque*, the response critically asks whether the text begs the practical ecumenical problem of sharing one and the same text of the creed or not.

358. The response from the Evangelical Lutheran Church in Finland says that it is difficult to answer something else than "yes" to the question of whether they find something in they text to be given a "positive" evaluation.

359. The COF text was conceptualized in the 1980s, relating to the secularism of some ideologies and the indifference to religion in Western societies. To some extent the political challenges addressed by liberation theology had an impact on the formulations; cf. the commentaries to the

The "Apostolic Faith" study addressed the theme of The Tradition, and tried to give The Tradition a formulation. This approach made the idea of The Tradition more "operable" and limited. However, it also narrowed the perspectives. The richness of the biblical material, particularly the texts of the Gospels, is not exposed; neither is the confessional material describing The Tradition in the many traditions. This version of *"solus Niceanum"* conveys the same problems as the study of "Tradition/traditions" found to be the case with some interpretations of *"sola Scriptura"*: neither the Scripture nor the Nicene Creed is at any stage "alone." The Tradition is not something impossible to formulate, either in the ancient Church or in the 20th or 21st century. But when the impression is given that this is *the* way to formulate it, it easily relies too much on general statements and unnecessary narrowing of perspectives, lacking the catholic multitude of perspectives that the ecumenical movement has made unignorable.

An Accountable Reception Process?

This ambiguity in respect to how much the text is *the* basis for a mutual affirmation of sharing the same faith is reflected in the questions from the Faith and Order Commission to the churches, following the COF text. The questions give the impression that this text has a profound content and conveys the content of the faith through the ages. At the same time, the questions ask for surprisingly weak, open, and general responses, compared to the intended crucial role of the text as a basis for a common platform in respect to nothing less than the apostolic faith. Compared to the questions accompanying the BEM document, the accountability of the church authorities is not mobilized in this case through the questions to the churches. Naturally, it would also be difficult to give a binding commentary to a document of such comprehensiveness as the COF text. This ambiguity can be traced in the questions themselves:

1. Would your Church find the explication of the Nicene Creed contained in Confessing the One Faith in basic agreement with "The faith once for all delivered to the saints" as confessed and lived in your ecclesial community?

2. Do any parts of the text impress you as being particularly positive and helpful? Do any sections cause your Church particular difficulties?

3. Would a positive evaluation of Confessing the One Faith by other ecclesial communities be taken by your Church as a significant step toward the common confession of the apostolic faith required for the visible unity of the churches as the one Church of Christ?

---

second article of faith. The awareness of the challenges from globalization and the power of the free market, dominating in the 1990s, were not within this horizon.

4. Would a positive evaluation of the text by your Church open the possibility for its members to join at appropriate times with those of other churches who affirm the text, in a common proclamation of the Nicene Creed as ecumenical symbol of the Church's one apostolic faith and as a common witness of this faith to our contemporaries as churches and Christians move toward a fuller unity on faith, life and service to the world?

5. What particular recommendations can your Church offer to Faith and Order as it continues its work on the common confession of the apostolic faith today?[360]

The first two questions address the content of the text, the last three questions address the process "toward a fuller unity" based on a common confession. The first question is the most theologically significant question. It can be interpreted as the challenge for the churches to regard this text as an expression of the one Tradition to which they will be accountable in a unity of churches. The logic of the question is that if all churches could find this text in basic agreement with the one Tradition as "confessed and lived" in their own tradition, there would no reason to have another text to affirm that the churches share the same faith to the required degree for visible unity. The first question, therefore, should investigate whether the churches are willing to be mutually accountable to the Nicene Creed on the basis of the theological explications of this document.[361] This was, actually, to ask for quite a lot, much more than comments of positive "impressions" or "particular difficulties" from "parts of the text" asked for in question 2. This question presupposes a study process in the churches.

Questions 3 and 4 are more or less directly addressing the process leading toward a potential affirmation of mutual accountability to one expression of faith. Question 3 directly asks whether the evaluation of the COF text itself would change the status of the relation between the churches in respect of "visible unity." But to ask for a "positive evaluation" is an unclear term in this respect, and conveys the same kind of ambiguity in respect to the genre and status of the COF text, as we find in the text itself. Question 4 asks for the consequences for interchurch relations between those churches that "affirm" the COF text. The questions set this affirmation and its consequences into the framework of the whole ecumenical endeavour. Thus, it is obviously meant to be a crucial matter in that regard. But again, the phrase "positive evaluation"

---

360. From the accompanying letter to the churches from the Faith and Order Secretariat in 1991, signed by its director, Günther Gassmann.

361. The response from the Church of Norway to this question comments on the challenge of accountability in this question, to pursue the proper self-critique of one's own tradition implied in a comparison of this kind; cf. CoN Response 1993, WCC Archives.

gives a picture of ambiguity. It is unclear whether this mutually positive affirmation should lead to binding statements and real change of relations, or should just reflect on potential possibilities.

Because of the openness to different levels of binding responses, this approach could be seen as a request for a reformed ecumenical attitude. However, the feeble tone of the questions does not really stimulate genuine expressions of attitude but, rather, an unclear, distanced role of observance. The same could be said about question 5. Hence, the churches through the COF text and the questions were not asked to give the kind of accountable answers that could be used to establish a new relation between the churches.[362] It is, therefore, not surprising when the Faith and Order Commission changed strategy from asking for responses from the churches to putting their energy into producing a "study guide" to the COF text. Thus, the commission itself regarded the potential effect of the document to be a long-lasting interest and understanding of the common sources and content of the Christian faith. The real accountable response demands, however, more enthusiasm than has been shown so far.

The relatively small response to the questions can be a sign that the COF text approached the ecumenical task from an angle that was not the most burning perspective for most of the churches. The Orthodox churches in Europe, who were expected to have a particular interest in this endeavour, have not responded, maybe due to the understandable shift of attention through the great changes in Europe after 1989. These and other reasons may explain the small response. There are, as discussed above, more reasons in the material itself that could explain why this approach to mutually accountable affirmations of a common faith did not succeed. The problem left over after the project is whether it is possible to find a method to establish a common basis of faith, or whether the churches are really interested in these issues.

Summary

This study process presupposed the importance of unity in faith—for the unity of the Church as conciliar fellowship. The process should unveil and

---

362. The responses given to the Faith and Order Secretariat are (except one explicitly negative, from the Methodist Church in New Zealand) generally positive to the content and the potential effects of COF (e.g., from the Church of Norway, The Evangelical-Lutheran Church of Finland, The Lutheran Church of Canada). But even these generally positive answers—with some constructive, critical remarks, still—could not lead to affirmations that the Faith and Order Secretariat could transform into a platform for a new status between the churches. This is not only because they are so few. They do not have the same status and significance as the responses to BEM, reading COF more like a preliminary study document. The very few responses to the COF text are only available as private copies from the archive files in the Faith and Order Secretariat. They have never been evaluated or commented on publicly by the Faith and Order Commission or Secretariat.

manifest the unity in faith through recognition, explication, and confession of the common faith. This enterprise can be interpreted as an attempt to make the churches mutually accountable to one another for their accountability to the apostolic faith. In comparison to the "Giving Account" study, the goal of giving account of the common faith together was to some extent the same; the method, style, and main actors were different.

According to my analysis of the discussions of the methodology of this endeavour, as well as the results of the process in terms of final report and reception, major questions and problems of this endeavour can be interpreted through the perspective of mutual accountability. The study also contributes to the understanding of the dialectic between focus on "faith" and "relation" (in respect to ecumenical attitudes). To sum up the most interesting points for my study:

- The project addressed the need for mutual confirmations of the reliability of the churches in terms of faithfulness to the apostolic faith, or in other words, the *common accountability* to the apostolic tradition given in Scripture.

- The project was planned under the premise that this attitude of faithfulness to the common faith required a real common manifestation of sharing the common faith, a statement, *a confession*, by which this reliability could be manifested as a firm position. In the pursuit of the "Apostolic Faith" study, there is an explicit and implicit dissatisfaction with the method and outcome of the "Giving Account" study. The unity in faith opens for diversity, according to the apostolic faith, too, but the unity of faith is comprehended as something given in a specific text.

- This study emphasized that the churches cannot be accountable to the given Tradition and at the same time neglect the Nicene Creed. This is due to the unique position this creed has as a common expression of faith used regularly in liturgy in both East and West. Through the explication of the creed, the study should confirm the consistency between the statements of the creed and the biblical texts; thus, it should be theologically significant even for the so-called noncreedal churches.

- The planning of the project addressed that the manifestation of sharing the same faith required more than unilateral declarations or repetitions of former statements; the process required *mutual recognition* based on mutual openness, mutual trust, and willingness to learn and to be self-critical.

- The discussion of methodology of this project showed different—but not absolutely mutually exclusive—conceptions of *for what* the churches should be accountable in respect to faith, and differences in terms of *to whom* the churches are accountable and when their position of faith should be manifested and assessed. It also unveiled how much the actors were coloured by the urgent issues of their context at this time of post-colonialism. The accountability of the use of power was particularly addressed.

- Confession is described as a matter of accountability to God, to the world, and to one another in an ecclesial fellowship. There is an unbreakable connection between these perspectives of accountability; the accountability to God is shown in the account given among fellow human beings. Thus, the accountable statement over against the need of the world should not be something else than the common account of the faith in the triune God.

- This is applied also to interchurch relations; the accountability to the given faith implies accountability to other Christian traditions also in terms of being complemented through their contributions. The apostolic faith as The Tradition is understood as a living tradition with substance and flexibility, not to be understood traditionalistically and rigidly.

- The intention of mutual reappropriation of the given faith corresponds to a process of mutual recognition and mutual trust; it is not something the churches should do in isolation.

- The process of taking into account the concerns of different traditions and checking the results through a hearing drew on experiences from the BEM process. The mutual accountability conveyed through the procedure was important here as well.

- The reception process, however, was not conducted with the same success in terms of establishing new mutual accountability between the churches as in the case of BEM. This can partly be explained by the ambiguity of the genre of the COF document (partly as a confession—proclaiming what the churches confesss—and partly as a comprehensive explication and commentary on the creed). It became difficult to give clear, substantial responses. The attitude of mutual accountability was more difficult to manifest when it became unclear what the churches should be accountable for. The questions distributed probably did not help in that respect, either.

Hence, the "Apostolic Faith" study raised several important aspects of what mutual accountability should be in respect to unity in faith. The concern for the quality of relation between the churches and the groups within the churches was to some extent acknowledged as important in that context. However, it remained unclear how the churches could establish mutual accountability between them in respect to unity in faith, and what kind of common firm position should be defined and maintained.

The final document from this process has not explicitly been received and approved in a way that can be interpreted as a lasting confirmation of mutual accountability for the accountability to the common apostolic faith. It might be that the COF document is too comprehensive and does not have a clear enough profile to become a sufficiently concrete point of reference for the churches to manifest their eventual ecumenical attitude of mutual accountability through that statement. Another interpretation of this picture is that the COF text gives documentation of what the churches more or less have presupposed to be common ground of shared confession in the churches.[363] If so, the COF process explicated the presupposed unity in faith more than had been done before. The churches have not felt obliged or provoked to give responses to this kind of documentation, thereby showing their attitude of mutual accountability to the common faith *indirectly.* A higher degree of clarity and exposure of their position of mutual accountability to the common faith must perhaps be given when and where this presupposed common basis is challenged at a particular point.

Ecumenical Attitudes and the Unity of Church and Humankind

From the first initiatives to establish conciliarity as the paradigm of unity in Uppsala in 1968 to the end of the 1980s, Faith and Order attempted to study the interrelation between the quest for unity in the Church and unity in the world.[364] Conciliarity in the common life in Christ as a sign that "men are one"

---

363. Therefore, the document can be a stimulation to formulate what separate churches share in respect to their Christian faith, without pushing hard on the dividing issues.

364. The Uppsala assembly in 1968 gave Faith and Order the task to make a study on this theme. A working group of Faith and Order made a draft study one year after. Later on it was discussed and shaped into a study in Louvain in 1971. In Lima in 1982 a new study project was launched, which can be perceived as a continuation (at least thematically) of the initiatives from Uppsala. The study document "Church and World" was finished after the Standing Commission meeting in Dunblane in 1990.

began to penetrate reflections on the significance of an ecumenical council.[365] A genuinely ecumenical council presupposes that barriers between human groups defined by sex, race, nation, and so forth are overcome. Conciliar life should foster certain kinds of attitudes, offering those standards to the world.[366]

The theme of this study has to some extent been close to the theme of the "Giving Account" study (in respect to emphasizing the significance of a contextual approach to ecumenism), and has some links to the reflections on the implicit responsibility for the world in the BEM study.[367]

Reports from meetings discussing this study reveal that the theme has stimulated strong involvement as well as tough discussions.[368] The general impression is that the theme of this study has had an existence in between other themes, and has never really "taken off" as a Faith and Order issue. The first part of the study process (until 1978) was not concluded in a final report of convergence like the BEM and the COF reports.[369] The second phase (1982–1990) concluded in the study document *Church and World*, which was never really made an issue of official reception.

In the first period, which began in 1968, from 1971 to 1978 the study carried the name "Unity of the Church—Unity of Mankind." In the second active period from 1982 to 1990 it was relaunched and renamed "The Unity of the Church and the Renewal of Human Community." The shift of name indicates more than awareness of problems with sexist terminology. The focus on "renewal" and "community" rather than "unity" and "mankind" implies also an ambiguity over against secular forces toward great unities and unity, and a growing interest in the quality of life in proper relations in a "new community." Other parallel projects in the WCC structure, for instance, on racism and the relation between women and men in the Church were pursued, influenced by and influencing the approach in Faith and Order.

---

365. This dimension is important in the Uppsala report. It is exactly in the context of promoting conciliar fellowship as the "unity in Christ" that the Uppsala report links the quest for the unity of the Church with the quest for "the unity of mankind": "The Church is bold in speaking of itself as the sign of the coming unity of mankind" (Uppsala 1968:13, 17).

366. "Christians are nevertheless permitted to believe that God desires to use His Church as a sign of the future unity of mankind. They are permitted to hope that the conciliar way of dealing with conflicts—within churches, between churches and in the service to the world—may become an example to help the world to deal with its conflicts" (Conciliarity 1974:22).

367. See pp. 128–56, 156–85.

368. This is well documented in Louvain 1971:171–99, and in Müller-Fahrenholz 1978.

369. There was only a "Summary and Evaluation" presented by Geiko Müller-Fahrenholz, including drafts, study contributions, reports and comments (Church-Mankind 1978).

Signs of the Accountable Church

Unity of Church and Mankind (1968–1978)

The texts from this study do not use the terminology "mutual accountability" but convey several reflections on ecumenical attitudes. There are reflections on the role of the Church in God's purpose for the whole of humanity. We find also reflections on which qualities of the community of the Church are to be offered to the world. There are also specifications of attitudes required to dismantle the barriers between human beings in the Church (as a community in the "world").

The attitude of *solidarity* runs as a thread though most of the material from these studies. This is understood as a consequence of the theology of creation, and a basis for the role of the Church in history: "In support of the statement that mankind is one, we may in the first place appeal to the fact that God created all men. Their solidarity has been given in and with this act; it must be recognized, lived and developed. . . . The task of the Church, then, is not merely to give effect to the solidarity established in creation but to fulfil the role assigned to it in the present interaction of historical relationship."[370]

This demand of solidarity requires a refreshed approach to the understanding of unity and diversity, as the Church quite often has been identified with classes and nations. "Oneness is not simply equality; it is the association of differences in community. Equality as a formal principle can therefore be destructive of community. . . . Today as always, the Church is inclined—in its attitudes and structures if not in its theology—to stress the need for the particular rather than the solidarity of mankind as a community."[371]

The attitudes of the Church should correspond to the solidarity established between "free men" through the liberation of Christ. In a christological perspective, this solidarity is a freedom given by Christ to be an example for the Church; to realize this freedom might even be at the cost of one's own freedom and privileges. The key issue for the relation between Church and "men" is, therefore, the attitude of *responsibility*. This responsibility to "all men" should be realized first of all *within* the Church, as a sign of true community. Hence solidarity and responsibility for one another become the hallmarks of the Church as community. This aspect of proper attitudes is striking in the section titled "Ecclesiological considerations":

> Genuine community is a community of free men. Such community God creates in Christ. By relinquishing his own freedom and allowing men to share in God's life, He makes them capable of community. . . . But freedom is the

---

370. Church-Mankind 1978:38.
371. Church-Mankind 1978:40.

result of the liberation of men. It presupposes the supreme freedom, namely the freedom to relinquish freedom. By making possible the community of free men, Christ imparts the experience of true community. The appointed place for this experience is the church service, above all, the eucharist. . . . Freedom and community come into being as the Church allows itself to be involved in the movement which it sees in Christ, namely, to be released from freedom for the sake of community. The characteristics of the Church are responsibility and service. . . . The Church is a sign that, in all their diversity, men belong together. It must therefore prove itself the Church by its ability to really embrace the diverse forms of human life and to relate them to one another.[372]

This approach to diversity of humanity was identified as an implicit task of the catholicity of the Church, developing a " centered diversity" in the Church. This catholicity, as "the opposite of all kinds of egoism and particularism," caring for the "powerless and marginalized" according to the example of Christ, is defined as "the quality of life of the one Church." These qualities of the community of the Church are essential in the understanding of the Church as a sign of the unity of humanity. Being a sign of the salvation of God means being a sign of God's justice, patience, and love, also of God's judgment over the Church.[373] This corresponds to the idea of mutual accountability, combining the mutual affirmation of one another's gifts while remaining mutually critical.

These demands of proper Church attitudes were presented to the Working Commission of Faith and Order in 1969. This rather demanding picture of the capability of the Church was—not surprisingly—followed by a word of caution from the commission in which they warned against false triumphalism. The Church has rightly been accused of being an instrument of barriers between human beings, even structures of oppression. That comment also made clear that this focus on human diversity and unity is not sufficient for a doctrine of the unity of the Church.[374] However, the commission admits that the "unity of mankind" belongs to the understanding of unity in Christ.[375]

In the just-quoted ecclesiological reflections, the attitudes (a matter of "human unity") are defined explicitly theologically: the Church should, as the body of Christ, make perceivable the attitudes of Christ—attitudes of human solidarity according to the purpose of the Creator. Therefore, I find that the question of ecumenical attitudes here belongs exactly to the intersection

---

372. Church-Mankind 1978:42f. What has been quoted so far is taken from the draft study of a small working group, presented to the Faith and Order Working Commission in 1969.

373. See Church-Mankind 1978:70–74.

374. Church-Mankind 1978:50.

375. Church-Mankind 1978:47–51.

between the unity of the Church as a matter of humanity and the unity given to the Church as the body of Christ.

The commission deals with the dilemma of the double role of the Church embodying both the "priestly mission of reconciliation among men" and the "prophetic mission of rebuking evil," "openness to sinners and the struggle against sin." Thereby the question of defining acceptable and nonacceptable diversity and controversy is pinpointed as maybe the most the important question in the quest for proper relation between unity of the Church and unity of "mankind." In this delicate matter we find sober reflections of attitudes required between, on the one hand, "indifferentism and relativism," and, on the other hand, destructive controversy. The reflections led toward the conclusion that a frank openness belongs to mutual responsibility in the catholic Church:

> To the degree that she [the Church] embraces the diversities of mankind in a Catholic unity, to that degree she must also have the courage to embrace and purify and make fruitful the controversies among men, always with the aim of concentrating the attack upon the real evil. . . . it may mean insisting that those Christians who differ profoundly, particularly on issues of social and political importance, should learn what it means to have vigorous and productive controversy in Christian congregations, how to respect the principles of healthy controversy ("speaking the truth in love," Eph. 4), and to commune with each other responsibility as witnesses and brothers of Christ.[376]

In the report from a working group, discussed by the Faith and Order Commission in Zagorsk in 1973, this double priestly-prophetic role of the Church is elaborated as an important (but not the only) aspect of the Church as *sign*. Thus, this realistic double approach, both accepting/reconciling/liberating and challenging/judging, is regarded as *accountable signs* in the world. It is not to promote a political programme, but to proclaim and demonstrate the attitudes corresponding to the kingdom of God.

> To speak of the Church as sign of God's kingdom emphasizes its identification with the justice of God and the liberating power of his Spirit. Within history the Church is called to live as a sign of that kingdom which transcends and fulfils history. To acknowledge Christ as Lord over the whole universe does not oblige the Church to become the promoter of a universal programme or idea nor the catalyst of a new world. It will have to be a prophetic sign calling

---

376. Church-Mankind 1978:51. This double priestly-prophetic role of the Church was discussed by the Faith and Order Commission in Zagorsk in 1973.

to repentance over against the temptation both of blind enthusiasm and of paralysing despair.[377]

In the same report we find a specific discussion of the distinction between "legitimate and sinful diversity," between diversity to be embraced and division to be overcome. This is a crucial question of any ecumenical discussion. This problem should be handled in the "*koinonia* in Christ." This is defined through qualities of relations implicit in being "in Christ."

This is a "basic *koinonia* in Christ" where formerly divisive issues, for example, in terms of racial, cultural, and sexual differences arising out of "the tendency to absolutize particular expressions of the truth of Jesus Christ," could "change their quality." This is, in my view, an important recognition of the importance of how unity in faith and sacraments could be a basis for the efforts to improve the quality of relations in the Church in a wider sense. On the other hand, that is an unclear statement as long it is not specific about what is acceptable in terms of doctrinal issues "in the *koinonia* of Christ."

This combination of mutual recognition and critical approach in the *koinonia* of Christ is also defined through the terminology of "cheap unity." The unity in faith demands firm attitudes against any "oppression on political, cultural, racial or sexual grounds"; Christ "stands against 'cheap' unity as he opposes 'cheap' grace."[378]

Hence, in the first part of this study (1969–1978) we find that the problems raised are to some extent handled by recommendations of the ecumenical attitude of solidarity, specified as mutual reconciliation, recognition, care, responsibility, and avoiding any kind of false triumphalism. This attitude should be expressed through mutual openness, frankness, and critique.[379] According to the texts from this study, this type of attitude belongs to the core of the ecclesiology demanded for the Church to take upon itself the responsibility to

377. Church-Mankind 1978:82. According to n.1 (p. 219) the document from this working group presented and discussed in Zagorsk has never been published, but its ecclesiological reflections are taken into Church-Mankind 1978:78–88.

378. To focus on the quality of relation through the biblical concept of *koinonia* became the most central issue of the Faith and Order work in the 1990s; cf. pp. 265–89. The specific reference to the firm attitudes avoiding any "cheap" unity (in correspondence to Bonhoeffer's concept of "cheap" grace) became also an important key in the study on ecclesiology and ethics in the 1990s; cf. pp. 251-58 below.

379. The reports show that the discussion of these themes in Louvain in 1971 became also a discussion of which attitudes are destroying the ecumenical fellowship, whether focus on human unity would lead to "utopianism" and "secularized triumphalism," or missing this focus could lead to "sacramental insulation" or "sacramental triumphalism" (Louvain 1971:171–99, and Church-Mankind 1978:65–68). One of the conclusions made from the controversy was that the ecumenical movement lives from this type of open and frank encounter. So did Ernst Lange; cf. Church-Mankind 1978:68, and Lange 1979:37f.

promote unity of humanity. Thus, it belongs to the core of the definition of the Church as sign; it corresponds to the notion of "catholicity" and is realized through the model of conciliar fellowship. But this first phase of the study did not succeed in maturing these reflections into a document useful for a broad reception process.

Church and World (1982–1990)

The Lima 1982 commission meeting decided to make a new start on the study,[380] focusing on Church unity as *sign* and the *renewal* of human community. The basic thoughts from the former period in respect to ecumenical attitudes are carried over into the new study but some new focal points are registered.

Between the two periods, 1978–1982, the WCC pursued a study titled *The Community of Women and Men in the Church*, also called the "community study," which was "located in the Commission of Faith and Order and carried out in cooperation with the Sub-Unit on Women in Church and Society."[381] The quality of relation ("quality of life") in the "new community" was a focal point in the whole endeavour. For Faith and Order it was significant to get not only the interconfessional problems on the agenda, but also to see how the barriers, divisions, and oppression destroying the community between the genders in the world is something to be found *within* the Church as well.

> Agreement reached on doctrine and sacramental expression of baptism, eucharist and ministry is only a part of what a life of unity is about. The unity of the Church has to do profoundly with the quality of our lives together as Christians. Unity must involve breaking down the barriers erected by sexism, classism and racism, realities which are within the Church as well as in the torn and divided world. . . . We can only discover what organic union or conciliar fellowship is as we struggle to live in response to a call for fellowship (*koinonia*) in which women and men, black and white, rich and poor are brought within that fellowship and play their valued parts.[382]

---

380. For a description of the discussion and decision to start a new study, and for an overview of the process, see Church and World 1990:5–7, 91.

381. The study enjoyed, according to the Sheffield Report (Sheffield 1981:ix [preface]), the "most extensive grassroots participation of any such project in the history of the World Council of Churches." It made no comprehensive report, but the report from the conference in Sheffield in 1981 includes a "Letter from Sheffield to the Churches" and a personal reflection by the director of the programme (Parvey 1983). Mary Tanner presented a substantial summary pointing to the significant points for Faith and Order (Tanner 1982).

382. Tanner 1982:159.

This ability to learn from contexts not dominating the classical ecumenical agenda has something do with theological "accountability."[383] The accountability toward not-privileged groups, being aware of the consequences of a theological position for them, can be formulated as a theological criterion according to the gospel. Liberation theology and feminist theology have given substantial contributions in this respect.

Being aware of this raises an important question in my deliberations on mutual accountability: *To whom* are the churches accountable? One of the most important contributions from the studies presented here, and particularly the "community study," in respect to my theme is exactly an awareness of this question. The ecumenical problem of divisions and barriers to be overcome by new qualities of relations cannot be limited to confessional, doctrinal problems. The problems of oppression, division, and the like in the world are also problems *in* the Church.

The quality of life of "the new community" is explored in its different aspects in section reports from Sheffield.[384] Racism and sexism are to be found in "attitude, action or structure," and must be replaced by attitudes qualified by justice and freedom. These attitudes are manifested in institutions; hence, a critical approach to institutions is required to improve the qualities of relations in the Church. However, it is not sufficient to replace the institutions. "The problem is to bring power and leadership under the control of the Spirit of Christ and to order the structures so as to liberate people: for structures are made for people and not people for structures. For Christians the structures of the church should reflect the relational model of the Trinity."[385]

When the conference addressed itself to the churches, it appealed to the attitude of willingness to *listen and see one another*; the struggle of women against violence, poverty, exploitation, and disparagement; the captivity of men in their execution of power.[386]

Another important emphasis in this material is the significance of *mutuality* between the Church and the world when it comes to making real the attitudes which correspond to the "new community." The Church simply has something to learn. The proper attitude of the Church is not only to give account of the solidarity intended by the Creator and demonstrated by Christ, but also to learn from others what it means. The attitude of triumphalism can destroy the account of truth:

---

383. This theme has been discussed in Kostermann 1993.

384. Sheffield 1981:102–154.

385. Sheffield 1981:138; see also 145f.

386. Sheffield 1981:91(–93).

To talk of the relationship between the Church and the world as "sign" can become triumphalisitc and miss the truth that the Church and the world are signs one to another. The Community Study drew upon many insights of those outside the Church who have discovered new ways of understanding the relationship between women and men and created new ways of living lives of equality and partnership. The Church does not have a monopoly of truth and needs to be open to fresh insights and signs in the world in the belief that God is there in the midst ahead of us.[387]

The Church needs this interaction with the world, to be made accountable by the world for the purpose and truth of the Church. This was proposed as a premise for the new initiative to study the relation between Church and world: "The world questions the Church. It challenges the Church's claim to the truth. It tests the Church's faithfulness to Jesus Christ. . . . The world demands that the Church live up to its own message."[388]

This theme was pursued in the second study (1982–1990) and was manifested in the final report (*Church and World*) as a discussion of how the Church is "in" or "of" the world. The Church participates in the brokenness of humanity but is "conformed to this world" if it neglects its nature and calling to be a prophetic sign for the world. Although the Church is the redeemed part of humanity, it is still constituted by the "stuff" of the world. This is of great importance for describing the adequate attitudes of the hope of the Church: "What is gathered, reconciled and renewed in the church is, in fact, 'world' in its estrangement from God and therefore this renewing process continually refers back to the world and forward to its final redemption. . . . As the church witnesses to the final fulfillment, which is also the world's future, it bears the world's problem within itself in solidarity and in hope."[389]

The attitudes of the Church are set in an *eschatological* perspective in this document. The kingdom of God is the reality of "already—but not yet," which

---

387. Tanner 1982:165. This ability to learn from contexts not dominating the ecumenical agenda has something to do with theological accountability. This theme has been discussed in Kostermann 1993. The accountability toward not-privileged groups, being aware of the consequences of a theological position for them, can be formulated as a theological criterion according to the gospel. Liberation theology and feminist theology have given substantial contributions in this respect. Being aware of this emphasizes one important question in my deliberations of mutual accountability: *To whom* are the churches accountable? One of the most important contributions from these studies in regard to my theme is the awareness of this question. The ecumenical problem of divisions and barriers to be overcome by new qualities of relations cannot be limited to confessional, doctrinal problems. The problems of oppression, division, etc. in the world are also problems in the Church.

388. Song 1978:125.

389. Church and World 1990:25; see also 1f.

provides the identity of the Church and the proper relation between Church and world (as the common goal for both).[390] This is significant for the definition of the required attitudes needed in the Church to be a true sign of the kingdom. The text focuses on two themes.

First, the Church is the foretaste of the coming kingdom. The gifts of the kingdom are "justice and peace and joy" (Rom. 14:17).[391] The great theological perspectives such as the solidarity of creation, the image of Christ, and the eschatological reality of the kingdom should be manifested in the qualities of relation in the Church as community:

> As mystery and prophetic sign the church must act on behalf of that justice which is a constitutive aspect of the reign of God. The specific contribution of Christians will be to apply the principles of life and teaching of Christ, who as a just man hung and died on the cross (cf. Luke 23:47), to the concrete situations of injustice in today's world. And the church must express justice within its own life, so as to be a sign and promise of the eschatological kingdom of justice which is yet to be. The church must proclaim in word and in deed the fundamental equality of women and men, created in the image of God and now called to maturity in the image of Christ the first-born of all creation, the first-born of the dead who reconciles all in himself (cf. Col. 1:15-20, 28) The church must be a community in which power is used to serve and not arbitrarily to exclude others, which fosters relationships of mutuality and communion, which promotes the full exercise of the charisms poured out upon the people of God, and which corrects the ways in which the use of language perpetuates prejudice and inequality.[392]

Second, the call of the kingdom is the call to "constant conversion and renewal in the power of the Holy Spirit."[393] This eschatological *judgment* is crucial for the efforts toward manifestation of unity in the Church: "The judgment that the vision of the kingdom of God delivers on the church reveals the truth concerning our disunity. The divisions within and between the churches are demonic forces that diminish the church's effectiveness as sign and instrument."[394]

---

390. "In God's creation all human beings are made in the image of God. In the kingdom of God both the church and the whole of humanity have their goal" (Church and World 1990:22).

391. Church and World 1990:17ff., 38ff.

392. Church and World 1990:74f.

393. Church and World 1990:23f.

394. Church and World 1990:75. Here again there is a tendency to understand the divisions of the Church one-sidedly, in moral (not doctrinal) categories. This is understandable in respect to the focus of this study on the renewal of human community. Although this moral condemnation

Along these two lines (of sign and judgment) the document explores the unity of the Church as an offer to the world through an elaboration of the ecumenical attitudes implied in justice, peace, and joy. This contribution to the renewal of human community in and beyond the Church is to a great extent characterized as improved qualities of relations, attitudes manifesting proper mutuality, equality, care for the other, and humility. Although the terminology of "mutual accountability" is not used, we find a picture of the Church as an accountable sign of the kingdom of God designed by attitudes corresponding to our preliminary definition of mutual accountability.

Summary

The study of the relation between the unity of the Church and the unity, then the renewal, of human community was a difficult one, and did not lead to a formally received convergence or consensus document. However, the complicated two-phase process brought several important insights to the surface, significant for the understanding of attitudes and their role in the ecumenical call and endeavour.

First of all, the study focused on the required solidarity given in creation, broken through human sin, particularism, and egoism. The Church has been called to realize this solidarity as a sign for the world, being the body of Christ and a foretaste of the kingdom of God. The solidarity implies a new approach to diversity, particularly as the Church realizes that it must go beyond the limits of groups, classes, and nations. Therefore, these studies raised clearly one important theme in a theory of mutual accountability: To *whom* are the churches accountable? If the problem of disunity and division in the Church is not only a matter of doctrinal condemnations (but they should not be neglected or underestimated), the mutual accountability of leaders, groups, and churches has to be more than a matter of relating to parallel institutions. The accountability of being one Church is not limited to that.

The dialectic between reconciliation/acceptance and challenge/judgment is at the core of the identity of the Church as sign. This double approach corresponds to the double profile of mutual accountability. Thus, the intersection between the concern for unity of the Church and the unity of humanity is found here. This intersection must be qualified though the *koinonia* in Christ, which means that some differences are to be relativized and some are to be sharpened. The firm attitude required is not promoting a "cheap" unity

---

of the division of the Church corresponds to my interest in a moral dimension of Church community, still, the attitudes of the Church are not sufficient for a proper understanding of the ecumenical problem to present it like that. There can be doctrinal reasons for marking a limit for what can be accepted as "Church." This concern for the limits of the Christian faith was raised through the struggle against apartheid, but cannot be limited to that case.

accepting injustice, discrimination, and oppression. This theme is explored in the study of the community between women and men in the Church, discussing the qualities of life in the "new community."

The study started by noting that the Church has to learn from Christ what the attitudes of the kingdom really are, explicating the freedom of solidarity that also relinquishes its own freedom for the sake of the other. Toward the end the attitudes of the kingdom (justice, peace, joy) are described as given to the Church as the body of Christ, but also as something to be learned from the world. The human dimension of the unity of the Church is not to be seen exclusively in a theological perspective, but is realized even in the human community beyond the Church. The Church and the world have something to learn mutually, being accountable to one another. The solidarity to be developed to break down human barriers is found in the Church as well as in the world.

Without using the terminology "mutual accountability," this complicated and unfulfilled study process raised questions important for the whole endeavour of Faith and Order. The mutually critical solidarity and the focus on the quality of life together give the concept of "mutual accountability" as well as "conciliar fellowship" (as the larger framework of this period) important dimensions.

Conclusion: Mutual Accountability—An Intrinsic Element of Conciliar Fellowship

Without repeating the summaries above, the great contours from the landscape in the period from Uppsala to Canberra can be described briefly in respect to the thesis of my study.

The efforts to lay premises for conciliar fellowship had several references to attitudes that can be subsumed as mutual accountability. That is the case particularly in passages discussing how to overcome the obstacles toward an ecumenical council, and passages reflecting on the interrelations between churches in conciliar fellowship and the authority of councils expressed in reception of councils. In some cases mutuality and accountability (in the sense of binding commitment and relationship) are described as qualities of relations important for any stage or level toward or of conciliar fellowship. However, there seemed to be insurmountable obstacles to gathering the churches in a common understanding of what a conciliar fellowship should mean, particularly in terms of who should be representing the churches there and what kind of authority a council should have.

In spite of great differences and even tensions between the studies and projects analyzed in this chapter, the multitude of efforts to solve specific ecumenical tasks and problems in Faith and Order studies between Uppsala and Canberra can be interpreted as attempts to establish premises for a conciliar fellowship not yet finally defined. In all of these studies there are some implicit recommendations of mutual accountability as ecumenical attitudes. These recommendations are integrated in discussions on methodology, particularly in the "Giving Account" and the "Apostolic Faith" studies. The analysis of the methodology actually used in some of the studies unveiled the significance of practicing mutual accountability to the common Tradition through mutual accountability to the traditions of the churches. This was a controversial point in the "Giving Account" study.

Mutual accountability to the traditions of the churches was an important and more accepted premise of the method that provided huge steps forward toward mutual recognition of *Baptism, Eucharist and Ministry* in the churches. This includes also the comprehensive reception processes pursued in that study. The idea of the "Apostolic Faith" study could to a large extent be described as establishing a criterion for evaluation of mutual accountability between the churches as to whether they share the same faith. The goal seemed to be to establish a manifestation of more mutual accountability in terms of faith, although the proportions between the goal and the reception process so far have left the conclusion open in that respect.

In reflections on issues of ecclesiology there were recommendations of mutual accountability. In the exploration of what authoritative teaching means, there was noticeable emphasis on mutuality, openness, and critique. The coherence between authority, authenticity, and accountability should be noticed. Describing the ecclesiological dimensions and implications of the recommended converged understanding of baptism, eucharist, and ministry, the BEM document conveys significant reflections on the importance of the issues implied in my preliminary definition of mutual accountability. The same can be said about the document *Church and World*, although some of the focal points—but indeed not all of them—were different in those studies.

The partly implicit, partly explicit confirmations of the importance of ecumenical attitudes as mutual accountability in these studies could lead to at least three types of conclusions. First, the fact that mutual accountability is not discussed directly, but is apparently intrinsic to the core of methodology and argument, could be a sign that this is so important and obvious that it is felt almost strange to explicate it.

Second, the Faith and Order projects of this period dealt mostly with concrete ecumenical tasks, giving common accounts of faith, establishing premises for shared authority, exploring and establishing a common Tradition in terms of sacraments and ministry, formulating the common apostolic faith, exploring the relation between unity in the Church and unity in the world. This is different from the more general themes of unity and relations in the succeeding period, when mutual accountability was explicitly recommended rather frequently. In this chapter we have found that what matters in the concept of mutual accountability did play a role in the efforts to solve the more specific ecumenical problems and obstacles.

Third, some of the controversies in this period can be seen as disagreements in respect to what kind of mutual accountability is required for the unity of the Church. In other words, which part of my preliminary definition is more important than others? For example, the fight over the relevance of contributions from contextual theologies for the sake of formulating the common hope and faith unveils disagreement in terms of how the churches should be open to the diversity of accounts to establish a common grasp of The Tradition. There was disagreement in what the churches should be accountable for. On the other hand, the quest for convergence or even consensus in faith could be interpreted as an effort to establish a firm platform for a binding, reliable relationship.

Thus, the studies of this period support the thesis of the significance of mutual accountability for interchurch relationship, although we found mostly implicit recommendations. The quest for unity in issues of "faith" and "order" was indeed in focus in this period. The dimension of "relation" was not elaborated directly to a high degree. Nevertheless, the analyses of the texts showed that this third dimension was an intrinsic element in the pursuit toward unity in Faith and Order. The shift of focus in the succeeding period is striking, though.

CHAPTER 4

Mutual Accountability and the Church as *Koinonia* (until 1998)

The purpose of this chapter is to analyze what role the concept of mutual accountability as ecumenical attitude has played during a period when the reflections and work of Faith and Order have been based on the rich meaning of *koinonia*. This is roughly the last decade (1988–1998) of the period I am analyzing. This theme of the melody was sounded in the contribution from Faith and Order to the Canberra 1991 statement on the understanding of unity: "The Unity We Seek: *Koinonia*—Gift and Calling." The theme was played out in a wide symphony of perspectives in the preparations and pursuit of the fifth World Conference on Faith and Order in Santiago de Compostela in August 1993.

Koinonia as the guiding perspective of Faith and Order implies a more substantial theological approach to the definition of the unity of the Church than "conciliar fellowship." The significance of models of unity seems to have declined toward the end of the 1980s and beginning of the 1990s, revealing a need for a wider perspective—taking into account what has been achieved but avoiding being locked to the terminological and ecclesiological problems of "conciliar fellowship." The great endeavours of preparing the way for conciliar fellowship were now pursued with some important results, and some results not really received. I am thinking of the great efforts analyzed in chapter 3: big steps toward mutual recognition of baptism, common understanding and celebration of the eucharist, mutual recognition of ministry, a manifestation of sharing the same apostolic faith, and a theological basis for common witness and service in the world.

Focus on the unity of the Church as *koinonia* implies a shift of emphasis toward the *relation* between the churches, or, to be more specific, the *quality of the relation*. Thus, the texts of Faith and Order from this period are of special significance for our study, although they mostly are not elaborated to a level of maturity like the BEM and COF texts from the period analyzed in chapter 3.

A remarkable difference in respect to my theme in this period is the fact that the explicit terminology "mutual accountability" occurs frequently in the texts. The term is used quite often in important passages to make clear what is urgent if the goal of *koinonia* in the relations between the churches is to be realized. Thus, in this chapter it is necessary to analyze both the role and the meaning of this terminology in its context, and to analyze what role mutual accountability as ecumenical attitude plays in the general elaboration of the concept of *koinonia*. The shift of focus from specific ecumenical obstacles to the more overreaching perspective of *koinonia* might be illuminated by this shift from a more implicit concern for ecumenical attitudes toward explicit recommendations of mutual accountability.

The concepts of *koinonia* and "mutual accountability" as prisms for the definition of the unity of the Church have had an impact also in some WCC processes and documents that have been influencing, or have been influenced substantially by, the Faith and Order work. Hence, some of them deserve attention in this chapter as well. The quest for a better integration of the tracks of ecumenism is one of them. At that point texts and processes leading toward the themes of the 1990s, but produced already some years before, should be considered.

Mutual Accountability and the Coherence of Ecumenism

The Search for a Vital and Coherent Theology

The sixth assembly of the WCC in Vancouver in 1983 recommended that work be done to bind together the diversity of theology exposed in the programmes, goals, units, and movements involved in the work of the WCC.[1] The

---

1. "The Assembly, through the report of the Program Guidelines Committee, perceived the period before us must be one in which we grow more and more into Christ and therefore towards unity, justice and peace, vital and coherent theology, new dimensions of our self-understanding as churches, and a community of confessing and learning" (Vancouver 1983:Preface). The programme guidelines committee recommended focus on a "coherent" theology to *bring together* what was growing into a problematic diversity of theological approaches within the organization, but not to control them (ibid., 253–54).

Argentinean theologian and well-experienced participant in the work of the WCC and Faith and Order, José Míguez Bonino, was asked by the general secretary of the WCC to lead a study on the internal diversity of theologies among the units and the staff of the WCC. In his concluding reflections he suggests the need for "mutual accountability" as a leading principle for dealing with the constantly growing diversity within the ecumenical movement in order to articulate a common ecumenical theology for the work of the WCC.[2] This seems to be one important entrance for this terminology into the language of the WCC.

The request from the general secretary was a rather ambitious one. The combination of the two keywords *vital* and *coherent* could imply a tension, not to say a contradiction in terms. Bonino was asked to define some ". . . frame of reference for theologies to be recognized as ecumenical . . . indicating some signposts without which there is no way to build upon common acquired convictions." This should be done so as to stimulate the "cross-fertilization among WCC-programs" and provide "enough flexibility and fluidity to allow for a lot of freedom."[3]

Exactly this formulation of the most significant challenge for the WCC initiated reflection on the significance of "accountability" and "mutual accountability." Interpreting the concerns of the programme guidelines committee (PGC) at the assembly in Vancouver, Bonino first mentions what he calls "ecclesial responsibility and accountability."[4] He refers to the interpretation of the Central Committee to support his own interpretation of the concern expressed by the PGC in Vancouver: to study whether theological diversity in the WCC has limits or not. "Accountability" is here parallel to "responsibility,"

---

2. Bonino spent two months at the Ecumenical Center in Geneva for this purpose; cf. Bonino 1989:160. Bonino participated in the conference in Rønde in February 1993 (cf. pp. 251–58), and presented an elaboration of his thoughts of "mutual accountability" as a key to define the role of liberation theology within the ecumenical movement in Oslo in March 1993; cf. the bibliography.

3. Bonino 1989:160.

4. Bonino 1989:163. The expression is not found in the report from the programme guidelines committee, but seems to be Bonino's own way of articulating his interpretation of it. This might reflect a terminology familiar in his own church tradition, used to describe the interrelatedness between different parts of a worldwide structure within The United Methodist Church; cf. The United Methodist Church 1992:111–14: "The connectional principle [that] Methodists everywhere have embraced [is] the idea that as a people of faith we journey together in connection and in covenant with one another. Expressing the high degree of cohesiveness and centralized organization among Methodists, the connectional principle became the distinctive mark. . . . This principle [i.e., community] provides for relationships of Holy Spirit-empowered community wherein support, supervision, healing, accountability, and growth can take place for persons across the denomination. Our life together, with is mutual accountability and relationships, keeps us ever alert to being faithful to the gospel in all our efforts."

reinforcing an attitude of general responsibility, including also the willingness to give account. And in this context, it is the account of how the theologies promoted in the work of the WCC can "place themselves within the broad lines of the church's tradition." Loyalty to the mainline traditions represented in the work of the WCC should be the standard for determining the limit of diversity. Bonino accepts this kind of accountability, and finds it "legitimate." But he warns, with the support of a claimed "majority view" in Vancouver, against an extreme interpretation of this concern, namely, in the direction of establishing a "theological tribunal."

Instead of focusing on the limits, Bonino tries to develop the concept of "coherence," not as a matter of logical coherence in a systematic treatise, but "the coherence for which we may hope and work for in the WCC—as a goal—is that of a living, growing organism."[5] Such "coherence" is not a contradiction to vitality and diversity; on the contrary, according to Bonino, it presupposes these qualities. This understanding of "coherence" is elaborated in terms that can be interpreted as—or corresponding to—certain *attitudes* important for the quality of relation between churches: "The coherence that we can today already create and evidence is that of a purposeful, explicit mutual interaction, accountability, enrichment and correction within our diversity, divergences, even contradictions and conflicts."[6] This understanding is supported by Bonino's working hypothesis of what has become a kind of common heritage of the member churches of the WCC:

> During the four decades of its existence, the WCC has defined certain lines, goals, convictions, which are now, however provisional and incomplete, the patrimony of all. They are the signs of a definite ecumenical attitude and commitment—definite enough to be articulated and formulated as a *specific way* in which churches relate to each other, deal with their differences and conflicts, or define the thrust of their attitude towards the world as they pursue the road towards a realization and fulfillment of their unity.[7]

Although Bonino admits that these attitudes are far from explicit and operative throughout the council, his exposition of this dimension of ecumenical endeavour entails a description of something achieved. It is presented as an important aspect of the pursued goal, giving substance to the more general "visible unity." Bonino names the three most significant common convictions of this patrimony. He finds theological consensus, based on attitudes

---

5. Bonino 1989:163.
6. Bonino 1989:164.
7. Bonino 1989:165.

gained through encounter in the ecumenical movement, in "the rejection of racism," "the rejection of sexism," and the "solidarity of the church with the poor." These three standards have become criteria for accountability between the churches: "But whatever the nuances and differences, no church can today ignore these issues; ecumenically all churches involved in the ecumenical movement—even outside the WCC—recognize themselves as theologically and ethically accountable in this respect. This is an important element of ecumenical coherence."[8]

Besides his conclusions on already achieved accountability to common attitudes and consensus, Bonino raises the difficult question of unavoidable differences that are due to the unquestionable contextuality of theology.[9] In this context he establishes a definition of mutual accountability as a standard to deal properly with this diversity. A mere status quo, not challenging one another, not really bringing the theologies into a real encounter with one another, is not sufficient.

> Unless we want to remain at a superficial level of theological pluralism (a "supermarket of theologies" or "a peaceful coexistence"), we must move from dialogue to mutual accountability. This in turn requires us to explore the conditions of accountability for all our contextual theologies. A framework to discuss this accountability implies, in my view, three areas:
>
> a) we are all accountable to each other for the way we use and interpret the scriptures (for our hermeneutical approach and our understanding of the authority of scripture),
>
> b) we are all accountable to each other for our theology's relation to the manifold tradition of the church ("historical" or "vertical" ecumenicity); and
>
> c) we are all accountable to each other for the interpretation of reality explicit or implicit in our theological formulations (for our relation to the "world" understood not only as an abstract entity or a mere juxtaposition of contexts, but as an economically, socially and politically structured system). [10]

---

8. Bonino 1989:168.

9. Bonino concludes, maybe a little too optimistically, that all agree "in theory" that all theologies are contextual and dependent on certain extra-theological premises. He even gives examples of the contextuality of the dominating confessional theologies, admitting the risk of generalization, such as the dependence of classical philosophy in Orthodox and classical Roman Catholic theology, the link between modern Protestant theology and the Enlightenment, and the use of sociological analysis in liberation theologies (Bonino 1989:169f.). Apparently, it was important for Bonino to establish a common platform between the dominating confessional and academic theology and the challenging contextual theologies, which he represented as a liberation theologian from Latin America.

10. Bonino 1989:169.

This is significant for a theory of "mutual accountability." Bonino's argument is based on the cooperation with the WCC units but has relevance for ecumenical ecclesiology in general. In the analysis of theological diversity in the ecumenical movement he conceives mutual accountability as a criterion based on ecumenical realism combined with ecumenical ambitions. The goal is to relate the mutual differences and divided parts of Christianity to one another. Contextual theologies should be made relevant for a universal context. Dialogue is one tool toward that goal, mutual accountability is a quality that belongs to the goal. The tendency toward status quo or leaving one another in a kind of protected diversity, in respect to theology as well as ecumenical ecclesiology, does not correspond to the ecumenical goal.[11]

We can derive from these quotations some more specifications of what "accountability" means, according to Bonino:

a. It is important to see the parallel terms here: interaction, enrichment, and correction. They are not identical expressions, but supplement one another. One way to interpret their interrelation would be to say that mutual interaction presupposes and nurtures mutual accountability. This is a promising exercise because through this type of deeper mutual involvement, the partners are, coincidentally, mutually enriched and challenged.

b. Accountability means a proper relation to the church traditions, seen in the light of their interrelatedness through the WCC.

c. Diversity is partly acceptable, but to the extent that it is an unqualified pluralism, it is to be overcome because of the need for coherence. Coherence in a situation of legitimate diversity requires *"mutual* accountability." There is no objective, third-party tribunal here. Coherence requires that the partners inform one another and correct each other reciprocally.

d. All parts of Christianity are accountable to something we have together, given to us all: Scripture. This is the basic framework for all churches and Christians. But in Bonino's framework there is no adequate understanding of Scripture that ignores the contextuality of the interpreter—his or her confessional tradition and place in history and society. It is remarkable that the accountability for adequate interpretation of Scripture is not directed

---

11. Bonino suggests supplements to the Toronto statement, to get a "positive reflection on the 'ecclesial' (perhaps in distinction to 'ecclesiastical') meaning of the ecumenical movement and the WCC as its 'priviliged instrument'." He finds no possibility any more to "merely sit down and write a new theological framework for ecumenical theology." The ecclesial status of the present relations of the WCC cannot be ignored, and the framework for ecumenical theology is given (Bonino 1989:166f.).

to a third instance such as the original meaning of the scriptures. The accountability is "to each other." Hence, the norm to which one might appeal to defend an interpretation of Scripture is not oneself, conscience, or any other instance that could be claimed as a direct relation to God. The accountability to God is not mentioned explicitly. If it is implicit, which I presume, the accountability to God is through and in relation to "each other." Hence, the way to find the truth, understood as the adequate understanding of the Scriptures and "reality," does not go outside a common accountable reflection within the living and global community of churches. Consequently, there is no way of claiming Christian truth that does not take into account how the common Tradition has developed in different traditions through the ages. This is a way of affirming implicitly the relevance of all Christian tradition, which, of course, raises the question of theological premises for making such an affirmation.

e. Any theology should give account of the interpretation of and consequences for the "reality" in which it is situated and used. In other words: Bonino postulates that theology is a human activity, which has to be evaluated as such.[12]

Bonino later on develops his ideas of "mutual accountability" in relation to pneumatology, as the premise and inner dynamic of the process. Doing so, he also makes an ecumenical contribution to the understanding of the Spirit in a global *koinonia*. After presupposing that "we all theologize" within the Church universal, being responsible for theological work to all, he describes this pneumatological premise as "the road of mutual accountability in theological work" this way:

> We believe that in our work we are really and truly being led by the Spirit and that we try to place our presuppositions, methodologies and ideologies under its direction. Such a self-understanding has consequences for our responsibility to recognize the same in the intentions and presuppositions of the other. Therefore, we also recognize the presence of the Spirit in the other and in diverse theological formulations and therefore we can in principle accept their claim that they have also tried to put their presuppositions, methodologies and ideologies under the same direction. Thus, we can and should admit the possibility of being enriched, corrected and even convicted by the Spirit through the work of others.[13]

---

12. This corresponds to his concept of "orthopraxis," a criterion for evaluating theology on its fruits and consequences in a sociological and political framework; cf. Bonino 1976.

13. Bonino 1993b:3.

These principles of a mutually accountable hermeneutic are not yet fully realized. Bonino emphasizes, as he did already in 1987, that this is not a general principle of relative pluralism, but a way to take seriously the God-given diversity and manifoldness in the church. It cannot be handled arbitrarily or selectively. The possibilities have to be tested in disciplined, continuous, and committed conversation at every level of the world Christian community.

Summing up, Bonino contributes significantly to launch mutual accountability as an important theme of ecumenical hermeneutics and ecumenical ecclesiology. He tries to develop it as a concept of acting responsibly, adequately, and in accordance with the universal character of the Church, emphasizing:

- Openness in giving account of one's own tradition, principles, and priorities.

- Responsibility to receive account from others in an accountable way—being able to be corrected.

- Acceptance of God-given diversity, as a work of the Holy Spirit, but not as a situation of unqualified pluralism. He understands pneumatology as a principle of plurality *and* mutuality.

Several of these elements of mutual accountability as an ecumenical principle can be entered in the category of "attitudes" required for a coherent and vital theology, as explored in the succeeding study of ecclesiology and ethics, in a context discussing some of the same problems.

The Quest for Integration of Ethics and Ecclesiology

Costly Unity and Mutual Accountability
One prolongation of the discussion of coherence and vitality related to the work of Faith and Order was the joint study of ecclesiology and ethics, pursued by two units within the WCC from 1993 to 1996.[14] The intention of the study was to bridge the regretted, but well-known, gap between two basic concerns in two movements within the ecumenical movement: "Life and Work" and "Faith and Order."[15] It has been a repeated task to bring their endeavours toward visible unity, on the one hand, and common involvement in the urgent ethical issues, on the other hand, into a fruitful cooperation ever since they

---

14. *Costly Unity* was published in 1993, to serve as preparation for the Santiago conference. The two succeeding reports, *Costly Commitment* and *Costly Obedience*, were produced in meetings in Jerusalem (1994) and Johannesburg (1996); all three reports were published together in 1997 (Ecclesiology and Ethics 1997).

15. More precisely, between Faith and Order/Unit I and JPIC/Unit III.

were established and, later on, joined through their merger by the inauguration of the WCC.

To understand the background for the "Ecclesiology and Ethics" study, it is important to mention an attempt to make some progress in ecumenical ecclesiology in respect to handling the urgent and burning ethical issues in the contemporary world. The sixth assembly of the WCC in Vancouver in 1983 decided to initiate and give priority to a "conciliar process of mutual commitment (covenant) to justice, peace and integrity of all creation."[16] Thereby the concept of "conciliar fellowship" and the new formula of the common task of involvement in burning issues of ethical character ("Justice, Peace and Integrity of Creation"—JPIC) were linked. The "slogan" of Vancouver, "the eucharistic vision," corresponded to the integration of eucharist and moral challenge explored in BEM.

Skepticism about institutional solutions to ecumenical challenges can be perceived in the reports from Vancouver. The quality of relations and the attitudes between those involved were explicitly emphasized in the "Priority areas for WCC programme": "Fostering ecumenical relationships with and between churches, communities, groups and ecumenical organizations on all levels should become a priority for the WCC in the coming years. The growth and vitality of the ecumenical movement depend on the encounter and trust between people more than institutional links."[17] This is an important framework for interpretation of the required "conciliar process." The dimension of "relation" opened the perspectives of "conciliarity" but also provided problems due to the lack of structural clarity and ecclesiological accountability in the endeavours. The problems of shifting from "order" to "relation" became perceivable through the most concrete effort to initiate "a conciliar process" along these lines among the churches, the so-called Convocation on Justice, Peace and the Integrity of Creation in Seoul in 1990. This gathering was planned and pursued primarily in order to strengthen the mutual ethical commitment. The plans of starting an ecclesial, covenanting, and conciliar process between the churches from Vancouver was overshadowed by the attempts to define the nature of and reasons behind the JPIC questions; the lack of ecclesiological realities was not sufficiently taken into account.[18] The task of developing an

---

16. Vancouver 1983:255. This programme was defined in terms of Christology according to the theme of Vancouver ("Gathered for Life"): "The foundation of this emphasis should be confessing Christ as the life of the world and Christian resistance to the demonic powers of death in racism, sexism, caste oppression, economic exploitation, militarism, violations of human rights, and the misuse of science and technology" (ibid.).

17. Vancouver 1983:253.

18. According to Aagaard 1993a:19, the executive committee of the WCC made this shift in 1987 and 1988.

ecumenical ecclesiology for this combined task was not really in focus.[19] However, one of the attempts to reflect on the nature of ecclesial community in this convocation raised the theme of accountability in the reflections of conciliar fellowship. Nevertheless, the Seoul convocation is only a matter of background to the more explicit discussion of mutual accountability as a matter of ecumenical ecclesiology within Faith and Order.[20]

The report *Costly Unity* was the outcome of a consultation in Rønde, Denmark, in 1993, gathering persons involved in the WCC work in Units I and III. It was the first of three reports from this joint study of ecclesiology and ethics. In this setting the small consultation in Rønde made some important efforts to face the need for a theological concept of ecclesiology for the problem defined. At the core of their argument to bring the concern for ethics and ecclesiology together, we find the concept of *koinonia*. Something more than a "linkage" was necessary. To make this more specific and relevant, the report presents a repeated and strongly focused recommendation of "structures of

---

19. Cf. the report and the main papers, compiled in Niles 1992, particularly the so-called Commitments. These commitments and affirmations focused on and presupposed ecumenical attitudes such as reliability and ability to self-critique. The outcome of Seoul in regard to the theme in Rønde is evaluated in the papers presented by Anne Marie Aagaard and Anton Houtepen; both are critical to Seoul. Aagaard concluded that neither the final document nor the message uses concepts as conciliarity, conciliar, or conciliar process. This lack of ecclesiological focus was presented as one of the reasons why the Roman Catholic Church was not ready to be co-inviter to the event (Aagaard 1993a:19f.). "Seoul created an ecclesiological deficit and an ethical surplus, and it did not come anywhere near clarifying the models of relationship between ecclesiology and ethics" (Aagarda 1993:20f.). I would be somewhat more positive, and support Houtepen's conclusion that there is an implicit theology involved in the final commitments, which points to the concepts of koinonia and covenant (Houtepen 1993:37–38). However, the total evaluation of Seoul for the common reflection on ecclesiology is that this was meager and insufficient to find a common concept for this urgent task of the ecumenical movement. Houtepen concluded, rather adequately, I think, that the opportunity was not used ". . . to highlight the relevance of the Christian message, and to develop new plausibility-structures for the unity of the church and an applied ecumenical theology of liberation" (Houtepen 1993:8). The latest document in the joint study of ecclesiology and ethics, *Costly Obedience*, more than suggests that the Seoul convocation was driven by individuals without sufficient accountability to their churches and the complexity of problems implied. After admitting that "list of affirmations" could have some relevance as "heuristic power," the *Costly Obedience* text reflects on the Seoul report this way: "But experience in this area has taught us to proceed with caution. Any such list of moral generalizations or affirmations must be guarded against being merely a list, merely a talisman to be repeated by those who pride themselves on being alert to the world's ills and possibilities" (Ecclesiology and Ethics 1997:85f.).

20. "Who are we before God? We cannot find the answers by ourselves. We are accountable to one another and need one another to learn who we are before God. A global communion of mutual solidarity will grow only when we have learned to listen to one another, to see ourselves through the eyes of the other, to share our perplexities and to assess our failures together" (Niles 1992:167).

mutual accountability." Before I present what is explicitly said about this, it is necessary to describe the line of argument in the text.

The report goes frankly and immediately into the heart of ecumenical ecclesiology, as it raises the question of the "being of the church," the "*esse*" of the church. Boldly, and maybe not completely accurately, it proposes that all deliberations on these issues on ecclesiology and ethics have concluded that the church in its nature and vocation is a *moral community*. Hence, "the church not only has, but is, as social ethic, a *koinonia* ethic." "The being (*esse*) is at stake in the justice, peace, and integrity of creation process."[21]

There seem to be four dimensions of the church as moral community claimed in this text. First, the church(es) should respond *commonly* to the moral challenges *in this world*, particularly those defined as JPIC issues. The ecumenical movement has contributed to the recovery of Christian ethics as a matter of the community, not only of personal lifestyle.[22] Second, common struggle in moral issues "generates" *koinonia*.[23] Third, the church is a community for *moral formation*, in faith and discipleship.[24] Fourth, and of particular

---

21. Costly Unity 1993:83–85.

22. Regarding the moral responsibility "outwards" to the human community, the text proclaims: "We believe that the church is now called to respond above all, as JPIC did to threats to life as a moral imperative" (Costly Unity 1993:88). This statement is the main entrance to the whole discussion, and runs through the whole document: "The cleft between ecumenical forces committed to visible church unity and those focused on witness, service, and moral struggle goes deep and exposes a history of differences which runs the length of the modern ecumenical movement" (ibid., 84). To the *community* aspect of the moral demands of human society, cf. the clarification of the task in the second report from this study of ecclesiology and ethics, *Costly Commitment*: "Is it enough to say (as we did in *Church and World* and *Costly Unity*) that ethical engagement is intrinsic to the church *as* church? Is it enough to say that, if a church is not engaging responsibly with the ethical issues of its day, it is not being fully church? Must we not also say: if the churches are not engaging these ethical issues *together*, then *none of them individually is being fully church?*" (Ecclesiology and Ethics 1997:29). The earliest Faith and Order texts, such as Lausanne 1927 and Lund 1952, described the moral problems of society as something outside the church. Particularly the Faith and Order study on "Unity of the Church—Unity of Mankind" in the early 1970s sought to bring the social ethical issues *into* the life of the church itself, looking at the church as a sign of the coming unity of humanity; cf. Aagaard 1993a:12–14.

23. "The experience of JPIC again and again has been that people have been gathered into a fellowship which can be described as *koinonia*" (Costly Unity 1993:86). This was obviously a debated issue at the conference; cf. the reflections later in the report on "Relationships with Movements and Groups" (ibid., 97f.). Many who despair about the commitment to JPIC issues have found more response outside the traditional church communities. The conclusion of this debate is formulated in an open and preliminary way, nevertheless loaded with substantial terminology, challenging traditional ecclesiology: "It is possible in the light of Jesus Christ to look at forms of caring *koinonia* outside the church as movements of the Holy Spirit gathering people to serve God in ways they may not fully understand" (ibid., 98).

24. "At the same time, faith has always claimed the being of the church as itself a "moral" reality. Faith and discipleship are embodied in and as a community way of life" (Costly Unity

interest for our subject, the *internal relations* between the parts of the church should be characterized by *certain moral standards*.²⁵

There is a close connection between the four meanings of the church as moral community. Adequate relationship within the Church is nurtured by concentration on what it means to be followers of Christ. This is made real in the common moral life in this world. The report does not seem to be very interested in drawing the line between moral issues of society and moral issues to be handled within the church fellowship. The text tends to blur this line. On the other hand, the text is concerned about the ecclesiology and the churches as an entity on its own. For a theory of mutual accountability this problem is relevant when discussing, How widely are we accountable? The entire argument of this report is that the Church is accountable to the other whether one is inside or outside the Church; nevertheless, the internal ecclesiological problem was the most highlighted issue.

The fourth aspect of the church as moral community above leads reflection toward the major concern of the report, announced in the title: the unity of the church must be carried by certain moral standards. These standards are here defined close to what I have called attitudes. They are playing on the terminology launched by one of the theologians dominating the German Confessing Church, Dietrich Bonhoeffer. The "cheap" unity is not willing to pay the cost of wrestling for unity against external forces opposing it. The "costly" unity is marked by the willingness to "transcend loyalty to blood and soil, nation and ethnic or class heritage in the name of the God who is one and whose creation is one."²⁶

The second part of the report deals with "*Koinonia* and Its Implications." After a general reflection on *koinonia* and ethics, the *implications* are described rather specifically under the title "*Koinonia* and Other Biblical Images for the Church":

> Are the different communions ready to see that communion between them—*koinonia*—whether in matters of faith or of ethical responsibility, calls for

---

1993:86f.). The "moral formation" is the main theme of the two succeeding reports.

25. The drafters of the document are aware of the problems of talking about the Church as a moral community like this. A moral activity is not the constitution of the Christian Church in itself. There are also difficulties to define what issues might be at stake involving the esse of the Church. It is defined as caring for what ". . . are in contradictions to the nature and purpose of the church and the central teaching of the life." This is not a final solution to this discussion, as Michael Root has shown; cf. Root 1994.

26. The report refers to the Life and Work reflections in the 1930s, facing the threat of nazism. At that time the concept of "responsibility" to one another was high on the agenda. The same aspect has dominated the common analyses of neocolonialism and structures of dependence and injustice (Costly Unity 1993:91).

steps towards structures of mutual accountability? The Fifth World Conference on Faith and Order will ask if the churches can take further steps toward "conciliar communion." At the very last, this phrase means being responsible to one another in witnessing to faith in Jesus Christ, and to the implications of this faith for justice, peace, and the integrity of creation. How long will the communions refuse to be challenged by what unity really requires?[27]

The succeeding paragraphs explore other ecclesiological aspects of *koinonia*: covenant, conciliar fellowship, the local and the global, diversity and unity, relationship with movements and groups. All of them are more or less discussed also from the perspective of mutual accountability. Most significant is this passage:

> As noted earlier, ecumenical accountability among the churches is weak. There need to be structures of accountability even before conciliar communion is achieved. May conciliarity in some form be possible even before full communion is established? The JPIC movement has pressed for this in order that we may give a united witness to justice, peace, and the integrity of creation. We urge the churches to get into a habit of conciliar accountability, even as we are on the way to a fuller relationship. Of course all efforts to develop such conciliar practices must be fully transparent and above board, or they will not earn the churches' cooperation and respect.[28]

How does this document promote mutual accountability as a principle of ecumenical ecclesiology? The terminology in itself, "structures of mutual accountability," combines ecclesiology and ethics; "structures" refers to ecclesiology, "mutual accountability" to the ethical standard of the structures. These structures are needed to make *koinonia* more than a principle. However, the text reflects on *koinonia* as a biblical principle as such. If *koinonia* should be the guiding ecumenical ecclesiological principle both for the local Christian community and for wider relationships (as it seemed to be at that time, some months ahead of the fifth World Conference on Faith and Order), *koinonia* must be carefully considered.[29]

The core of this reflection is relevant for our theme: *koinonia* is more than "sharing," it is participation in something held or known in common. The text refers to the most central biblical themes, like *koinonia* in God, the Holy Spirit, Christ, in the faith, in the body of Christ, in the blood of Christ. There is an important link here, not quite elaborated in this text: if there is a participation

27. Costly Unity 1993:92.
28. Costly Unity 1993:95.
29. Cf. Costly Unity 1993:92f.

in the common, there is no reason to see the particularities or the particular traditions as property of one part of the communion only. Account of the use of the common must be given in mutuality. The text refers to the responsibility for each other among the first Christian communities, demanded by Paul. Furthermore, the text describes these issues as "imperatives of unity and catholicity" and "covenant," understood as a God-given relationship between God and us and between the members of the church universal.[30]

The logic of the text is that to realize all these significant ecclesiological concepts (*koinonia*, the body of Christ, unity, catholicity, and covenant) the "structures of mutual accountability" must be in place. Because there is a moral dimension of being the church and following Christ, there is a moral obligation for the Church to participate in the same moral struggle in the Church and beyond. For this purpose internal structures must have a standard, namely "mutual accountability."

The closest reference for "mutual accountability" to ecclesiological concepts formerly discussed in Faith and Order is the concept of *conciliar communion/fellowship*. The new aspect brought into that concept is that structures of accountability are a common standard *in* a conciliar fellowship as well as *before* it is established. Thus, the report can talk about "[getting] into a habit of conciliar accountability, even as we are on our way to fuller relationship." Referring to debates in 1970s and 1980s, the report states that conciliar fellowship must be more than "reconciled diversity."[31]

The context refers to the relation between *the local and the global*. This is a way to describe the issue of *catholicity* as an aspect of *koinonia*, thus an important framework for the concept of "mutual accountability": catholicity understood as participation in the whole. The report ends with a recommendation for the WCC to provide a forum where local ecumenism can challenge forms of global ecumenism, and thereby nurture mutual accountability between the two.[32]

Further, the question of *diversity and unity* is raised. The most urgent problem is diversity growing into tribalism. Diversity was dealt with in the early church with love and responsibility. But for the concept of "mutual accountability" an important point is made here. Until recently, there has been a sense of a common framework of Christianity, the text says. Although the braking of that might be traced further back in time, the point is the same: "How can one speak of accountability in such situations?"[33]—that is, If there is no sense

---

30. Costly Unity 1993:93.
31. Costly Unity 1993:94.
32. Costly Unity 1993:104.
33. Costly Unity 1993:96f.

of common framework? The attitudes of the Church cannot exist only as proclamations of goodwill, but need a structural component.

The report uses the concept of "accountability" in two additional contexts. The *bureaucracy* of the churches plays an important role for the cooperation between them. However, the text questions whether that part of the Church is accountable enough.[34] The bureaucracy "may not feel the [same] sense of accountability." Further, the text uses the concept of "accountability" to describe the difference between Christian movements and established institutions of the church. Thereby, accountability becomes a matter of giving account for authority delegated to oneself and becomes a general standard of relation between officers, delegates, and constituency.

The terminology "mutual accountability" is introduced and used as if it was well known, thus presupposing generally felt needs.

Ecumenical Attitudes Required: Costly Commitment and Costly Obedience

The lines from *Costly Unity* are prolonged in the succeeding documents on *Costly Commitment* and *Costly Obedience*.[35] Their titles focus directly on attitudes (commitment, obedience) presumed important for the ecumenical fellowship. While neither of these two succeeding reports explicitly mentions "mutual accountability," they are illuminating for my reflections on mutual accountability as ecumenical attitude.

First of all, an important distinction in *Costly Unity* is significant for what it means to define the Church as moral community. The quality of relations in terms of attitudes is not what the church is "resting" on, but belongs to ecclesiology as something corresponding intrinsically to the gift of the Church: "The church is God's gracious gift to us; this grace calls forth and shapes the moral life of disciples. We rely on God's forgiveness and renewing grace in our faithfulness and infidelity, in our virtue and our sin. The church does not rest on moral achievement, but on justification, on God's justice and not our own. It is on this basis we affirm that moral engagement, common action and reflection are intrinsic to the very life and being of the church."[36]

The most significant contribution from these two latter documents to the question of the Church as moral community is the elaboration of the meaning and implications of *moral formation*. This is described in a comprehensive way, in different types of expressions aiming at ecumenical attitudes.

---

34. Costly Unity 1993:95.

35. The two latter documents was produced by smaller groups than *Costly Unity*, and have not by any means got the same attention as *Costly Unity* gained in Santiago (cf. pp. 277–86). As exposed in the following, the two latter documents seem to be less representative for the traditional line of Faith and Order than the first, not neglecting that the first was criticized as one-sided, too.

36. Costly Commitment 1994:30.

> The process of "moral formation" and discernment within the Christian community means an openness to new realties, insofar as they are consistent with the work of God. Here discernment is not always easy. For example, moral assessment is helpful not least in analyzing patterns of power and power relationships. . . . This process will sometimes call the church to *self*-criticism, reminding it how these same worldly forces and structures affect its own life as an historical institution. Sometimes the church will need to confess that, wittingly or unwittingly, it condones attitudes which allow injustice to continue or which obscure the root causes of injustice. . . . The language of moral formation and discernment would ask: what kind of environment nurtures such moral practices? What patterns of behaviour help create and foster them? What virtues, values, obligations and moral vision do each of these marks imply for Christian catechesis and the life of the church as a whole? . . . Thus in speaking of the "*ethos* of the household of faith" we mean the way of life, the distinctive patterns of thinking, feeling and acting, which characterize those who live within that "household." . . . When the church fails to fulfil its responsibility in this regard, it contributes to the creation of a moral vacuum in society—a vacuum soon filled by distorted forms of the *oikos*. This is seen today in the emergence of new and often violent nationalism, religious fundamentalism, and nihilistic forms of secularism.[37]

The document *Costly Obedience* explores further how this formation can take place. It is critical toward large ideas of one global community or general principles of the unity of the Church, emphasizing the potential of the local communities for developing (what I call) ecumenical attitudes.

The *Costly Obedience* text defines the role of ecumenical accountability in contrast to concepts of Church unity as a global affair. The attitude of solidarity and accountability is defined as the bond between the "local embodiments" of the Church:

> The *oikoumene* is best understood not by trying to reach some generalized global vision and by fostering a worldwide communion of particular, local embodiments of acted-out, shared, obedience to the gospel. South Africa has given us hope that such faithfulness can take on meaningful, specific, local forms and lead to results that enrich human life. Yet we know that not every situation will give us such clear lessons or such encouragement. In each situation we need to find our own way, yet always in relationships of ecumenical support and accountability.[38]

---

37. Costly Commitment 1994:41–44.
38. Costly Obedience 1996:66.

Skepticism about a "global vision" is significant and definitely something other than the melody of, for instance, Uppsala 1968. It might also be controversial to those not sharing this communitarian position. The polemic seems to be directed against concepts of universalism found in the ecumenical movement, implying that the great communion should decide the way in difficult issues for the local churches, on the basis of doctrines and principles of church order applied to all. The required "support and accountability" should, according to this concept, be openness toward one another, but not a tough exercise of authority on behalf of the worldwide communion. The *mutuality* is thereby understood empathetically and in terms of solidarity, not emphasizing the critical aspects.

The document draws heavily on the anthropological concept of "thickness" to define the role of the close and local community conveying moral formation. "A focus on formation points us towards emphasis on actual communities with their cultures: towards what anthropologists call the complex "thickness" of lives actually lived."[39] This concern for "thickness" is significant for the theme of my study because of its correspondence to the theme of "attitudes." The attitudes of a fellowship are developed in a multifaceted relation to one another, not primarily from individuals working on ethical principles or focusing introspectively.

The concept of "thickness" also corresponds to the theme of *qualities of relation* in the church. In *Costly Obedience* the qualities of relation that pursue moral formation are defined as the smaller communion, sometimes even in polemic against ideas of global or universal communities. A clear critique is articulated against what might be regarded as traditional goals and methods of Faith and Order. This critique is formulated against what is called "outward signs" of the unity of the Church: "Our problem sometimes is that the articulable signs have taken over as substitutes for the lived realities to which they refer. Yet often we have little to go on but outward signs, expressed as they are in jurisdictional, confessional or doctrinal agreement, or in willingness to

---

39. Costly Obedience 1996:55. The following endnote illuminates the fascination of this concept among the editors of the text: "The term 'thickness', popularized by the anthropologist Clifford Geertz, is now widely used by human scientists to mean the full and multi-layered complexity of cultures. It admirably links up with the concept of 'formation'. We are 'formed' in rich and enveloping environments, not merely by the 'thin' concepts scholars derive from those environments" (see p. 88, ft. 3), This sociological terminology is explicitly used several times, e.g.: ". . . the diversity of particular situations makes it impossible to generalize: as if no concepts of broad application can possibly grasp the many forms of 'thick' particularity that mark the way traditioned, formed people exercise their moral integrity in each particular case." "But, unless filled out in 'thickness' of specific local application, all such general ideas of justice, peace, the integrity of creation and democracy are likely to remain abstract. No matter how compelling their sound" (Costly Obedience 1996:76f.; cf. also 79).

participate in conciliar relationships. Today we need to share more deeply the liturgical and moral substance to which the traditional marks and our practical interpretations of them refer."[40]

According to this text, the "thick" communion aimed at cannot be initiated and perceived through formal doctrines or jurisdiction, but through a fellowship of "resonance" and "mutual recognition." The concept of "resonance" corresponds to the attitude of listening after the "voice" of Christ in this world in the other communions. "Thus the notion of *oikoumene* is not to be understood as a globalizing, even imperial, concept appropriated from the ancient world as an instrument of subjugation by powerful churches of the West. It is rather to be seen as a conscious *mutual* recognition of the resonating patterns and configurations of activity that follow from the Spirit's working."[41]

The focus on *local* and *moral* "thickness" as *the* quality of relation relevant for the unity of the Church is somewhat balanced in the document. The text emphasizes the sacramental dimension of the communion of the Church, linking the dimension of "liturgy" and the moral through focus on the attitudes corresponding to the meaning of liturgy: "To be in communion is precisely to be willing to share the liturgy in both its senses: as worship and as work. Communion is readiness to celebrate the same liturgy, with the same moral implications, together, as we recognize one another in each place through resonance, recognition, and the presumption created by common markings."[42]

According to my analysis above, however, concern for the "relation" is not absent in what might be regarded as typical Faith and Order projects. The moral dimension is not absent in the quest for unity in Faith and Order. The "thickness" of the church fellowship, still, is more than a matter of morality. It seems, therefore, to be a not quite relevant one-sided critical approach to Faith and Order in this document. Even *Costly Obedience* registers the need for criteria of authenticity of being a church, at least the required framework corresponding to the attitude of being mutually accountable through seeking *the recognition* of other churches. The quest for mutual recognition is the underlying theme in all the other efforts to establish a platform for unity in faith, sacraments, and ministry. At least indirectly, the text confirms the criterion of mutual recognition between churches:

---

40. Costly Obedience 1996:80.
41. Costly Obedience 1996:78.
42. Costly Obedience 1996:80.

We share the experience of the larger church, whose "locality" *is* the *oikoumene*, the inhabited earth. This is why the life of the ecclesia as moral community requires an ecumenical dimension. Every local challenge has a global dimension. Every global issue has a local application.[43]

Outside this network of mutual recognition, no particular local expression of church can be authentic. It is of the essence of the church universal to exist in this web of relationships, in which the local is all important but the ecumenical nexus of recognition is equally indispensable.[44]

Thus, even in this line of argument, the "thickness" of the local community must correspond to a thickness at the level of "catholicity" in a global sense. The "thickness" is further used to argue for the potential ecclesial quality of the interrelations between churches in the WCC; the WCC could be a "space where the ecclesio-moral communion of which we have been speaking can come to expression."[45] Although it is a very open ecclesiological formulation used here ("space"), the need for ecclesiological qualities is confirmed.

Summary

To define the relation between ethics and ecclesiology, the *Costly Unity* report elaborates the Church as a moral community; hence, the demand for certain attitudes to dominate the relations and the structures in the Church is particularly emphasized. To say that real unity is "costly" might even mean that there is no unity with the wrong attitudes, caring for not more than "cheap" unity. The required attitude demands willingness to pay the cost of transcending borders and to take a stance in moral problems threatening the whole earth, including the human beings' world (such as the JPIC issues).

Koinonia is presented as the corresponding biblical ecclesiological principle or image, the basis for this ability to pay the cost of unity. That means participation in the common gift and calling, demanding to share the given treasures with the others. To realize this costly sharing, the church needs "structures of mutual accountability." Hence, the report urges that there can be no sufficient quality of unity without structures; principles or loose relations are not sufficient. The *quality* of these structures is defined by mutual accountability.

Exactly *how* this attitude of mutual accountability should be performed is not really elaborated, except in a statement on the urgency of transparency. But it is presented in a way that seems to presuppose that the audience has an

---

43. Costly Obedience 1996:76.
44. Costly Obedience 1996:81.
45. Costly Obedience 1996:82.

immediate understanding of what is required. This can be a sign of the importance hidden in the sense of being self-evidently important.

The concept of "conciliar fellowship" is identified as the structural dimension of *koinonia*, in which mutual accountability should be operative. In fact, qualifying the ecumenical structures through recommendations of "costliness" and "mutual accountability" replaces the more formal category "conciliar fellowship." Mutual accountability is a standard to be pursued before and in a conciliar fellowship. It is further to be seen as a dimension of the *catholicity* of the Church, seeing oneself related and responsible to the other(s) in the Church.

The critical question about this report is, naturally, whether it overemphasizes the morality of the Church; and whether the calling of *koinonia* is more important than the gift of *koinonia*. This impression might be caused by the context of this document: ethics and ecclesiology.[46] Although the "Church as moral community" is defined in *Costly Commitment* as something other than classifying the morality of the members of the Church as the basis of the Church, the emphasis on the moral dimension of the Church dominates the reflections of the unity of the Church in these three documents. It can be justified because handling the problem of ethics and ecclesiology by focusing on the attitudes of the church fellowship is inevitable. The tendency toward overemphasizing the moral dimension of the Church can, however, raise legitimate critique against the last document.

The most significant feature of the dominant tendency in the document *Costly Commitment*, and even more in *Costly Obedience* is, from my point of view, the emphasis on (what I here would call) "relation." This is here more or less explicitly done at the cost of reducing the significance of the dimensions of "faith" and "order" for the unity of the Church, by criticizing the interest in "doctrinal" and "jurisdictional" aspects.[47] This is to some extent understandable when the question at stake is how the Church as communion can convey moral formation. What is rather new here is the attempt to describe and

---

46. Costly Unity 1993:87: "The church, it must be said, is not *constituted* by or dependent for its ongoing existence upon the moral activities of its members." Michael Root has criticized the document from this point of view; cf. Root 1994.

47. Some participants of the group editing this text obviously would like to go much further in redefining the unity of the Church and the way toward that goal in the line pursued in *Costly Obedience*; cf. Rasmussen 1997:107: "The most promising way forward is not that of finding the language of normative common ground as that might be offered by theologians and agreed to by heads of communions. This understanding of ecumenical formation is essentially doctrinal and jurisdictional. The most promising way is arranging a common table, open to participation by the whole people of God, to see what emerges as living church when faith is freely shared on the burning issues we face. Ecumenical formation here is more inductive than deductive, the outcome of a shared experience of engaged church."

conceptualize dimensions of unity in terms of communitarian anthropology and philosophy. Those perspectives naturally colour the reflections on unity in this document. Nevertheless, the *Costly Obedience* document represents a trend of reflections on unity in the ecumenical movement that might be typical for some—but definitely not all—of the actors in the Faith and Order movement in the 1990s. The critique of traditional Faith and Order issues is not completely new, as we saw in the discussion of the 1970s and 1980s.

This concern for the moral and anthropological "substance" of the unity of the Church indeed corresponds to my interest in ecumenical attitudes as qualities of relations. Hence, these reflections are of relevance for a theory of mutual accountability. These texts represent a challenge to any programme for unity that does not take sufficiently into account the required qualities of relations in an ecumenical fellowship—at any stage of the process. The concern for visibility of unity has been given a wider definition, focusing on the need for more "thickness" in the communion of the churches than formal agreements on issues of "faith" and "order."

It might be that the goal of visible unity has falsely fallen into the shadows in this concept. There is no necessary neglect of the significance of the "thickness" of relation and mutual accountability in the traditional issues of "faith" and "order." This is conceived in these texts, too, in the many references to the importance of the sacramental communion.[48]

The *Costly Obedience* text has good reasons to focus on the importance of elaborating "relation" more than has traditionally been done. The moral dimension of the unity of the Church should be described in substantial terms of anthropology when theologians reflect on the unity of the Church. However, the implied reduction of the significance of issues of "faith" or "order" for the unity of the Church is not quite convincing. The attitudes to be developed, the thickness of communion, and the qualities of relations need the thickness of severe theological tradition to be properly materialized as ecclesial qualities. In addition, the mutual accountability required would easily be lacking significance if the relations do not correspond to the development of common firm positions in terms of doctrine as well as order.

---

48. Cf. the references to and elaboration of the BEM text in Costly Obedience 1996:66–71; cf. pp. 156–85 above.

Mutual Accountability and Unity as *Koinonia*

Koinonia: Gift and Calling—Two Documents on the Way toward Santiago

The Canberra 1991 Statement: "The Unity We Seek"

The first really strong, significant focus on *koinonia* as the key to the ecumenical task is the Canberra statement. Faith and Order contributed to it through the draft for the statement on unity to be made at the seventh WCC assembly in Canberra in 1991.[49] Although the Canberra statement did not explicitly address the need for the ecumenical attitude of mutual accountability, it did so indirectly. Compared to the statements on unity from New Delhi (1961) and Nairobi (1975), it is remarkable how much attention is paid to the *process* of developing the *quality of relations* as a significant perspective to understand the unity of the Church. The emphasis on *relations* in the description of the final goal is not quite new, however; such emphasis is also found in the statements of New Delhi ("fully committed fellowship") and Nairobi ("conciliar fellowship"). But it was a new trend to focus on the perspective of relation in terms of *koinonia* as the main aspect of the unity in the triune God and as the unity God *gives*.

This theological emphasis seems to have been an attempt to bring a new perspective that could get the ecumenical processes further along when there was no consensus on what conciliar fellowship means. It was also an ambiguous conclusion in respect to how far the ecumenical movement really had come after BEM, COF, and *Costly Unity*. The focus on relation through *koinonia* implied a shift away from the more specific models of unity, too. In this situation there seems to be a proclivity toward wider and more open categories. This can be observed in the preparation of the Canberra statement.

On the way toward this statement of unity in Canberra, the first drafts talked about "conciliar communion" as the overall concept of unity.[50] In the elaboration of this conciliar communion (in the draft from 1990), there are

---

49. On the request from the Central Committee in 1987, Faith and Order undertook "a fresh consideration of the concepts and forms of the unity we seek." It proposed a draft for discussion, which was presented to and revised during the seventh WCC assembly in Canberra in 1991; cf. Documentary History 1993:2, and Canberra 1991:172. The commission meeting in Budapest in 1989; a consultation in Etchmiadzin, Armenia, in 1990; and the two succeeding meetings of the Standing Commission in Dunblane, Scotland, in 1990, and Rome in 1991, worked on the issue. The concept of *koinonia* (or "communion") was not even mentioned in the paper for preparation or the group report 1989 (Budapest 1989:242f., 247–49), but played an increasingly important role in the 1990 consultation and later in the final drafts for Canberra.

50. Cf. Budapest 1989:242 and the draft printed in Minutes Dunblane 1990:31: "The goal in history of this pilgrimage is conciliar communion fully manifested both on a local and a universal level."

some attempts to explicate conciliar fellowship in more open terms of improved relations and attitudes. One paragraph deals directly with the required ecumenical attitudes for this goal of unity. It even directly addresses the need for mutual accountability: "The unity of the church to which we are called demands mutual sensitivity, caring and accountability. In taking specific steps together we express and encourage the enrichment and renewal of Christian life, as we learn from one another, work together for justice and peace, care together for God's creation, suffer and rejoice in solidarity, and pray with and for one another. Thus the churches will grow together towards that oneness which is given by God."[51]

In this context mutual accountability is described in terms of solidarity and spirituality, using rather open terms referring to dynamic personal relations expressed in significant actions and clear positions (take specific steps together, learn from one another, work together, care together, pray together) that can be applied in any model of unity. The result of these attitudes in action is proposed to be growing together; in other words, changed relations.[52] In the Canberra statement this passage is partly eliminated, partly changed. The references to "conciliar fellowship" are to a large extent replaced by reflections on what *koinonia* means and implies.

The dimension of qualities of relation is in focus in the Canberra statement. The Church is defined primarily in terms of the proper qualities of "communion" as it is given to the Church from the triune God. [53]As far as I understand the Canberra statement, the intention is to define the unity of the Church more in terms of the substance and content of the communion than in one specific model of unity. Consequently, the statement focuses also on the present and urgent challenge of the "calling" of *koinonia* as far as there are obstacles for these qualities of relations of *koinonia*. The other side of that coin is to encourage a more binding and more committed reception of the ecumenical achievements manifested in the great efforts of the preceding decades of Faith and Order. I understand the profile of the statement, therefore, as a platform for demanding more specific demonstration of mutual accountability for the ecumenical gift and calling.

The specific reference to "mutual accountability" and the parallel, rather open references to sensitivity, common suffering, and joy are replaced by

---

51. Minutes Dunblane 1990:31.

52. This combination of qualities of relations—expressed in perceivable positions through actions—corresponds well to Asheim's definition of "attitude; cf. pp. 10–15.

53. "The purpose of the church is to unite people with Christ in the power of the Spirit, to manifest communion in prayer and action and thus to point to the fullness of communion with God, humanity and the whole creation in the glory of the kingdom" (Canberra 1991:172 [§1.1]).

reference to what is done and what is to be done in respect to bilateral and multilateral dialogues. This can be interpreted as a felt need to give the concept of *koinonia* a substance that takes into account what has been the task and the goal of the ecumenical movement. Thus, there is an emphasis on more "hardware" ecumenism, specific results of dialogues, and the like. Some of the signs of attitudes (learning from one another, care, and so forth) are, however, mentioned in the Canberra text, too.[54] Therefore, it does not mean that the perspective of mutual accountability is excluded, but that the focus on concrete results and specific signs of what the unity of the churches means are important to exemplify the open category of *koinonia* in the Canberra statement.

The Canberra statement is much longer than the New Delhi and Nairobi statements. It includes reflections on what has been done, what has been achieved, what has not been achieved and why, and what are the particular challenges ahead in the process toward the goal. There are specific reflections on the impact of ecumenical attitudes. What has been achieved is defined as a "degree of communion," specified to some extent in actions showing attitudes.[55] What has *not* been achieved is a result of the ecumenical attitudes that are missing. The churches have not been sufficiently (in my terminology) accountable to the results of the ecumenical movement, to the calling and gift they already have received: "Churches have failed to draw consequences for their life from the degree of communion they have already experienced and the agreements already achieved. They have remained satisfied to co-exist in division."[56]

The strong emphasis on unity as a process, linked to a concept of degrees of *koinonia*, ("degree of communion," "fullness" of communion, and "full communion") implies a dynamic element important for this concept of unity.[57] The

54. Canberra 1990:173f. (§3.1).

55. The result of the ecumenical movement is supposed to be: "We acknowledge with gratitude to God that in the ecumenical movement churches walk together in mutual understanding, theological convergence, common suffering and common prayer, shared witness and service as they draw close to one another" (Canberra 1991:173).

56. Canberra 1991:173.

57. It might be a theological problem if the "fullness" of koinonia is understood in terms of human achievements or defined as preferred ecclesial structures. In that case, the idea of process, degrees, and fullness can be a tool for some churches (that in their own eyes have achieved more "fullness" than others) to devaluate other churches. It might imply a tremendous power to be able to say what is "full enough." The idea of more or less "full" communion has been criticized from Protestant theologians, particularly when it appears as a Roman Catholic concept defining the difference between the Roman Catholic Church and Protestant churches. From the Protestant side it is often emphasized that the unity and communion is given completely from God through the gospel and the sacraments. One strong exponent of this critique is Herms 1984:passim. The tendency to talk about levels of communion or "greater/deeper *koinonia*" is even more dominant in the texts from Santiago 1993; cf. pp. 271–77.

ultimate goal of the process is defined in terms of how the churches regard one another, the *mutual attitudes expressed in the mutual recognition of one another.* "The goal of the search for full communion is realized when the churches are able to recognize in one another the one, holy, catholic and apostolic church in its fullness."[58] However, the criteria of the ultimate goal of *koinonia* are not open categories such as sensitivity, "thickness," or tolerance, and the like, but specific references to the content of the main Faith and Order projects of the decades before, particularly as we find them in the BEM document, the "Apostolic Faith" study, and the *Church and World* report.[59]

The extensive description of "the challenge at this moment in the ecumenical movement" calls this movement "a reconciling and renewing movement towards full visible unity."[60] The list of steps toward "full communion" mostly repeats the definitions already made in respect to proper reception of the results of former Faith and Order studies (BEM, the "Apostolic Faith" study, *Church and World*). The calling is not related to new ideas or new fields, but more definite and dedicated commitment to the standards already settled. They includes unity in faith, life, and witness, thus pointing to the theme of the Santiago conference in 1993.

The conclusion of the statement can be read as a unique prescription of the ecumenical attitudes responding in a proper way to this challenge.

> The Holy Spirit as promoter of *koinonia* (2 Cor. 13:13) gives to those who are still divided the thirst and hunger for full communion. We remain restless until we grow together according to the wish and prayer of Christ that those who believe in him may be one (John 17:21). In the process of praying, working and struggling for unity, the Holy Spirit comforts us in pain, disturbs us when we are satisfied to remain in our division, leads us to repentance, and grants us joy when our communion flourishes.[61]

---

58. Canberra 1991:173 (§2.1).

59. "The unity to which we are called is a *koinonia* given and expressed in the common confession of the apostolic faith; a common sacramental life entered but the one baptism and celebrated together in one eucharistic fellowship; a common life in which members and ministries are mutually recognized and reconciled; and a common mission witnessing to the gospel of God's grace to all people and serving the whole of creation" (Canberra 1991:173 [§2.1]).

60. Canberra 1991:174 (§3.2).

61. Canberra 1991:174.

Through its focus of *koinonia*—as restlessness and willingness to sacrifice something for the sake of *koinonia*, even repentance—the Canberra statement concludes that attitudes are crucial perspectives for unity. The concept of "repentance" corresponds to the theme of "conversion," which has been repeatedly emphasized, at least since Amsterdam 1948.[62] Only the giver of *koinonia* can provide the ecumenical attitudes required, however, disturbing and strengthening the Church.

The Santiago Discussion Paper

The Canberra statement is included as premise for the "Santiago Discussion Paper on *Koinonia*."[63] The realism of the Canberra statement is elaborated in this document, into even more frank descriptions of lacking or required relations and ecumenical attitudes. Some examples:

> We have experienced the continuing transformation of relationships between many churches from isolation and estrangement to mutual understanding, cooperation and a sense of solidarity and common commitment. . . . As a result of these developments we find today in many Christian communities a deepened awareness of the catholicity of the Church. . . . Among new problems we observe in certain situations a decrease of enthusiasm and commitment to the goal of the visible unity. . . . For a number of years there has been a growing proliferation of narrowly particularistic concerns within churches or regions. This is even more serious when it is linked to a resurgence of exclusivistic and militant nationalism or ethnicity as indeed seems to be the case in some parts of the world.[64]

---

62. Cf. the definition promoted by the French ecumenical working group *Groupe des Dombes*, published nearly at the same time. This definition seems to be absorbed in other ecumenical texts on this concept: "Conversion is an essential constituent of an identity which seeks to remain alive and, quite plainly, faithful to itself." They deal with Christian, ecclesial, and confessional conversion as parts of the same process, although making some distinctions between the individual, the collective intrachurch level, and the interchurch level. "Confessional conversion is first of all conversion to the God of Jesus Christ and consequently a fraternal reconciliation among the churches as they seek full communion and full ecclesial recognition—not to the detriment of confessional identity, but for purification and deepening in line with the gospel" (Groupe des Dombes 1993:17–29, at 19, 29).

63. The document was discussed by the standing commission at its meeting in Dublin in April 1992, distributed for regional consultations as a "working document," revised according to concrete suggestions, and distributed to the churches as preparation for the Santiago Conference, called a "Discussion Paper." Cf. Discussion Paper 1993:264 (Preface); the Canberra statement is quoted at 269–70.

64. Discussion Paper 1993:266–68.

Quite noteworthy for my study are the remarks on failing ecumenical attitudes and the remarks on increasing influence of attitudes incompatible with the ecumenical project. In this passage we also find a remarkable identification of a "sense of solidarity" and the "awareness of the catholicity of the Church."

The discussion paper offers a wider theological elaboration of the concept of *koinonia*,[65] emphasizing the unity of the Church as participation in the *koinonia* of the triune God, which is *personal and relational*. This is used to legitimize diversity as integrated in a proper understanding of unity: "Their shared life, in which unity and diversity are inseparable, is grounded in the Trinitarian life and reflects it."[66] Another dimension emphasizing the same is elaborated through the New Testament concepts of "being in Christ" and the "body of Christ."[67] These aspects were elaborated in the Santiago conference in 1993, to some degree also in terms of "mutual accountability."

The Santiago Conference 1993

Mutual Accountability and the Way toward *Koinonia*

The fifth World Conference on Faith and Order in Santiago de Compostela, Spain, in August 1993 had at least three major tasks. All of them were related to themes discussed above. All three tasks also had an impact on the definition of the role and meaning of the concept of "mutual accountability." The world conference should "take stock" of the results of 30 years of work of Faith and Order in order to pursue the implementation of what has already been achieved on the way toward visible unity in terms of faith, life, and witness.[68] Further, the conference should take into account the "new voices," representing important perspectives for Christian unity beyond the traditional constituency of Faith and Order.[69] The Santiago conference should also lay the foundation for

---

65. Discussion Paper 1993:271–77.
66. Discussion Paper 1993:273.
67. Discussion Paper 1993:273f.
68. Günther Gassmann described the intention of the conference in Santiago 1993: ix (Preface): ". . . to evaluate the achievements of the last decades, discuss the still-existing barriers to the visible unity and full koinonia of the church of Jesus Christ, and indicate directions and themes for the future work of the Commission on Faith and Order within the World Council of Churches and the wider ecumenical movement." The moderator of the Faith and Order Commission, Dr Mary Tanner, focused in her paper *The Tasks of the World Conference in the Perspective of the Future* on harvesting, envisioning, formulating an agenda and challenging the churches (Tanner 1993:19ff.).
69. One typical formulation for paying attention to accounts from different regions and groups: "The ecumenical movement has changed over the past thirty years. The voices of women and of those from beyond Europe and North America have joined the ecumenical conversation in strength, bringing new insights, new experiences, new diversities" (Santiago 1993:226 [Message, §7]).

a better integration of the ethical challenges implied in the ecumenical endeavour, as elaborated in the preparation phase of the conference.[70]

The conference came together under the theme: "Towards *Koinonia* in Faith, Life and Witness." Through papers, section reports, and a common message, *koinonia* was explained from its biblical roots: What does the unity of the Church theologically mean in terms of *relation* given to the Church through the participation in the life of the triune God? The concept of the conference theme was elaborated in terms of solidarity and belonging as basic perspectives on human life "in the Family of God." It was applied as a dynamic answer to the analysis of the present situation, in order to integrate the different tracks and challenges in one ecumenical movement. To put it in a formula from the Santiago texts: the God-given *koinonia* should be realized as "deeper *koinonia*" or a "greater *koinonia*."[71]

Among the inputs at the conference, three of them were particularly influential on the understanding of theological and ecclesiological significance of improved *quality of relations*. The comprehensive study of *koinonia* presented in the paper from the New Testament scholar John Reumann concluded that *koinonia* is a concept used in the New Testament to reflect the "crossing the boundaries" and the relevance of "ecclesial friendship," but offers no particular structure or government principle.[72]

The South African archbishop Desmond Tutu's "apartheid is too strong for a divided church" became a saying of the integration of unity and justice.[73] He also interpreted the concept of *koinonia* in terms of African thinking of interdependence and complementarity: "*ubuntu*." He gave two expressions to translate this concept: "A person is a person through other persons" and "I am because I belong."[74]

---

70. This was the theme of the "Ethics and Ecclesiology" programme of Unit I and Unit III of the WCC. But it was also the major concern of the "Unity and Renewal" study, presented in the final report *Church and World* (1990); cf. pp. 227–29 and 244–332.

71. E.g., in Santiago 1993:226f. (Message): "A deeper *koinonia* will be a sign of hope for all or it will not be a true *koinonia* in the love of God. Only a Church itself being healed can convincingly proclaim healing of the world" (§5). "At Santiago, we have again sensed the urgency of our need for greater *koinonia* in faith, life and witness" (§9).

72. Reumann 1993; cf. esp. 62–64.

73. Tutu 1993:96; Report of Section IV, Santiago 1993:254.

74. Tutu 1993:99–103. The later director of Faith and Order, Alan Falconer, brought this concept of *ubuntu* into his programme of "kenotic ecclesiology": "The vision of *Ubuntu*, on the basis of our being 'in Christ', is an important expression of an ecclesiology appropriate to the third phase of the ecumenical movement." Basic elements in this concept of ecclesiology is interdependence, conversion, the "sense of community and caring, of relationship and friendship," "from conflict to communion," forgiveness and reconciliation, to become a "sign and sacrament." He found this expressed in South African experiences, interpreted by Tutu, as genuine expressions

A third significant contribution to a theology of relation was the paper of Metropolitan John of Pergamon (Zizioulas). He emphasized that the definition of *koinonia* should not be derived from sociological experience, but from theology, "because we believe in a God who is in his very being *koinonia*. . . . God is Trinitarian; he is a relational being by definition." The "right synthesis between Christology and pneumatology becomes extremely important," too, because the image of "the body of Christ" thereby can be seen as a "corporate person." For ecclesiology this means "there is no church which can be conceived in herself," and "that no Christian can exist as an individual in a direct communion with God." This is particularly relevant also for the mutuality between local churches, avoiding a false centralism of the universal Church: "Whenever pneumatology is weak or dependant in relation to Christology (a sort of 'filoquism' in ecclesiology), there is bound to be a submission of the local church to a universal structure."[75] Thus, he found that this dimension of theologically defined relation is adequate and necessary to handle the traditional dichotomies of ecclesiology (institutional/charismatic; local/universal; conciliarity/primacy, etc.). He also concluded that the concept of *koinonia* could make the perspective of the quality of relation an important aspect of ecumenical ecclesiology: "The theme of *koinonia* can add a quality of life and existential relevance to church unity. The church is a relational entity." This means, for example, that the sympathy in sufferings is a genuine aspect of the *koinonia* of the Church.[76]

The model of "conciliar fellowship" or "conciliar communion" is almost absent in the Santiago documents. The introduction of *koinonia* is replacing it but without the same clear structural dimensions. This seems to require saying something about the need for structures in the ecumenical fellowship, without being that specific in terms of models. In the quest for a dynamic bringing more *koinonia*, it is remarkable how the texts focus on the need for further steps—also in terms of structures—that are qualified by improved attitudes. In fact, when the terminology of "accountability" and "mutual accountability" is explicitly used in the texts from Santiago, it is mostly to be found in the recommendations of how the way *toward* more *koinonia* should be realized in respect to structures.[77] One of the most significant examples is the conclusion of the message of the conference: "At Santiago, we have again sensed the urgency of our need for greater *koinonia* in faith, life and witness. The churches have made some progress in implementing the 1952 Lund principle that they should 'act

of the affirmation of the Santiago report; cf. Falconer 1996:50–52.

75. Zizioulas 1993:104–107.

76. Zizioulas 1993:110f.

77. Although I will not limit myself to the passages where this terminology is explicitly used, those passages are at the center of my attention in the interpretation of the Santiago texts.

together in all matters except those in which deep differences of convictions compel them to act separately'. But they must go further. Unity today calls for structures of mutual accountability."[78]

The request for mutual accountability corresponds to the preceding analysis of the ecumenical situation explored through the conference. Thus, the recommendation is definitely given a key role in the message. Therefore, mutual accountability must be understood in respect to how the message concludes its analysis and how it defines "the ecumenical goal." Then we find significant links to ecumenical attitudes and qualities of relation.

The analysis of the ecumenical situation brings a double message: "Great strides forward" and "concern for waning commitments to Christian unity." The message of the conference is an illuminating description of attitude as a firm position: "We say to the churches: *there is no turning back*."[79] This is the melody throughout the message.

The particular focus on *koinonia* provides a description of the "richness of our life together in Christ: community, communion, sharing, fellowship, participation, solidarity. The *koinonia* we seek and which we have experienced is more than words." All these characteristics are closely related to criteria of relations in respect to attitudes, culminating in a description of this *koinonia* as "the reconciling presence of the love of God." This gift demands the attitude of "gratitude," not "passivity."[80]

To realize the purpose of the Church as "sign of hope for all" it must achieve a "deeper *koinonia*," overcoming all human barriers to a just and healed fellowship. The ecumenical movement is evaluated as having contributed to this task through the "achievements over the past thirty years of the Faith and Order movement." The text then refers to the results presented in the BEM, COF, and "Church and World" documents.[81] The task now is to "receive these convergences into their life." The appreciation of the integration of all those bringing "new insights, new experiences, new diversity" and the concern for "ethical commitment and action" opens the perspectives into other and difficult fields of disagreements on the goal and the methods of the ecumenical movement. To handle these challenges, the way forward is defined as "new ventures and insights in the faith that unites us, not by compromises that merely obscure the problems."[82]

---

78. Santiago 1993:227.
79. Santiago 1993:225.
80. Santiago 1993:225f.
81. Cf. pp. 156–85, 186–227, 227–39.
82. Santiago 1993:226.

The horizon for the concluding requirement of "structures of mutual accountability" is the embarrassment of unclear commitment in spite of significant results. What is needed, then, is firm commitment in terms of more convergence and consensus in the important matters, a reliable reception of results of ecumenical dialogues, and real commitment in terms of open, frank, and honest encounters with one another. This is how to get a "greater *koinonia* in faith, life and witness." From this line of argument, the message explicitly makes mutual accountability a high-ranking principle for the entire ecumenical endeavour, including the dialogues and the efforts to establish mutually recognized fellowship in sacraments and ministry.

The request for mutual accountability is succeeded by specific requirements linked at every stage in these processes: "a deeper understanding of the Church," "must dare concrete steps towards fuller *koinonia*"; "doing all that is possible"; "responsible care"; "mutually respectful evangelism"; "the conversion that true *koinonia* in our time demands," and so forth.[83]

One can ask of this message, Is mutual accountability here conceived as an agreed norm of attitudes for binding structures handling the obstacles for unity in faith and sacramental life? Or, is it more a description of commitment to the fellowship and improved relations, but no real dynamic toward convergence and consensus? There were some voices for the latter alternative in the conference.

One outstanding example of this is the contribution from Bishop S. Joshua from the United Church of North India. He used the report *Costly Unity* to emphasize the importance of mutual accountability to accept unity as a reconciled diversity of the Church. He even characterized the definition of "structures of mutual accountability" formulated in *Costly Unity* "a stroke of revelation." It fit completely into his analysis of the failure of defining the goal as "visible unity," as has traditionally been done in the work of Faith and Order. From his experiences in a uniting church in India, he claimed the failure of the uniting processes guided by the goal of visible unity as a common definition of baptism, eucharist, and ministry. That goal was not even important for the realization of *koinonia* in his church. The *koinonia* that "touches the masses and which is relevant to their immediate socio-political-religious context" is the local *koinonia* between persons. The diversity should not be ruled out and the proper framework for the desired unity in diversity. The guardians against inhuman strokes against this biblical *koinonia* are "the structures of mutual accountability."

> If it is perceived that unity is the unity of persons, then we shift our emphasis from seeking visible unity of churches to what the document *Costly Unity*

---

83. Santiago 1993:227 (§10).

calls "structures of mutual accountability." Past and present experiences show that we would like to keep our own way of life, church order, and to some extent our own theological perceptions and doctrinal emphasis. Our attempts to gather should not be more than gathering the fragments into the basket. Any attempt to make a pulp out of the fragments would be contrary to the very essence of our creatively diverse existence. The World Council of Churches for the time being is the basket in which the fragments can be gathered so that nothing is lost. The document *Costly Unity* has, I believe, by a stroke of revelation indicated the future course open to WCC. The concept of 'structures of accountability' provides for diversity in unity, and at the same time, it will act as a mutual safeguard against ecclesiastical, racial and other divisions. The WCC will be the forum for ongoing theological pursuits, not for the goal of seeking visible unity, but as an end in itself, in ever trying to fathom the mysteries of God revealed in his Son Jesus Christ, our Lord. In this ongoing common exercise in faith, there is no question of anyone being "right" or "wrong". . . . In the apostolic days of Peter, James and John, of Martha, Mary and Salome, what was convincing to the people and which acted as an advertisement of the good news were the *koinonia* of the believers, which included the breaking of bread together and the sharing of resources. There can be a return to such a *koinonia*, if we shift our emphasis from visible unity of the church to the unity of persons, with an agenda of mutual accountability. The time is at hand, and the trumpet call is to move fast![84]

The dominant dimension of the recommendation in this message is the need for more responsible, more *binding*, more serious ways to take care of the ecumenical task of unity as a communion of participation. More diversity requires more qualities in relations in terms of attitudes of tolerance, but also of reliability and faithfulness to the communion and to what is common. Even when it calls for reverence for the complexity and theological legitimacy of church diversity and cultural contextuality, the message emphasizes the one uniting faith. The attitudes that should qualify the structures are not only tolerance and openness; they are defined more as firmness, honesty, commitment, and willingness to receive the results of Faith and Order studies. The aspect of *Verpflichtung* dominates, but it is not only linked to consensus in traditional Faith and Order issues. Not least, the ethical challenges should be faced in accountability to one another. This interpretation will in the following be compared to what the section reports provide for the understanding of the way toward *koinonia* in terms of more mutual accountability.

---

84. Joshua 1993:150–52.

Explicit Recommendations of Mutual Accountability in the Section Reports

The section reports use mutual accountability as an important element in their description of the ecclesiology provided to implement *koinonia*, but it is not a theme comprehensively explored. Mutual accountability is explicitly required where suggestions for solutions to the difficult questions are presented. Hence, it became integrated in the core argument of each section report.

Section I explores "the understanding of *koinonia* and its implications." Toward the end, formulating further "steps on the way," this section raises the question of how the "work of Faith and Order and that of Church and Society are inextricably linked as we seek to be faithful to God's grace." The answer given is a reference to *Costly Unity* and ecumenical accountability:

> The work of Faith and Order and that of Church and Society are inextricably linked as we seek to be faithful to God's grace. We have been helped to see the importance of this relationship linking koinonia to justice, peace and the integrity of creation through its report *Costly Unity* (WCC 1993) . . . In particular we have been challenged by paragraphs 31-34 on conciliar fellowship which well expresses our interdependence and calls for the development of ecumenical accountability.[85]

The meaning and content of "mutual accountability" does not seem to be much changed from the passage in *Costly Unity*, except from the context of more comprehensive reflections on *koinonia*. But this is, of course, important in itself. Here *koinonia* is explicated in terms of "interdependence." This is a *gift* of interrelatedness, being together the body of Christ.[86] This image of the body of Christ is significant for the exposure of *koinonia*; being a Christian and being the Church are basically to be "relational" (quoting the ancient saying *Unus Christianus nullus Christianus*—"a single Christian is not a Christian at all"). There is no existence given as Christians where it is possible to say, "I need you not" (referring to 1 Corinthians 12—the Pauline exposition of the body of Christ). This elaboration of the body-of-Christ image is here used to stress the need to accept diversity, even appreciate it, and have an attitude according to the given diversity. *Koinonia*, in the light of the image of the body of Christ, describes not only the reality of diversity, but also the necessity of it.[87]

---

85. Santiago 1983:235.

86. Cf. Santiago 1993:230–32. Here the report is rather close to the formulations of John of Pergamon (Zizioulas).

87. Among the many passages dealing with the significance of diversity and the call to face it with seriousness and reverence, we find, e.g., Section I: "Our shared life, in which unity and diversity are inseparable, is grounded in the economy of the Triune God. . . . These disciples are one while enriched by their differences. Diversity as well as unity is a gift of God" (231). "The

This picture serves very well to describe the close relation between *koinonia* as a gift and as *calling*.[88] This is a moral claim, the calling of the church in the world. But it is also a calling to take care of the other in the ecclesial fellowship. The church fellowship itself has a moral dimension, articulated through the combination of *koinonia*, "the body of Christ," and the recommendation for "ecumenical accountability." In this way *koinonia* is simultaneously the theological basis and the goal of unity.

The text describes *koinonia* as something there could and indeed should be "more" of. There is "a lack of *koinonia*" and "an anticipation of the fullness of *koinonia*."[89] It might be debated whether this quantification of *koinonia* gives a good account of the Pauline concept. Nevertheless, the focus is directed toward what can bring more *koinonia* in all the aspects presented in the report.

According to what I have already found as a proper meaning of "mutual accountability," it is significant how *openness* is emphasized in the elaboration of *koinonia*. This transparency should include being honest about weaknesses and failures.[90]

Hence, in this report of Section I, exploring "The Understanding of *Koinonia* and Its Implications," ecumenical accountability serves as a useful tool to explicate both understanding and implications. It seems to be particularly relevant for the meaning of accountability that *koinonia* is defined as something to be received and to be implemented, a "gift and calling." Ecumenical accountability corresponds to *koinonia* in respect to how the received gift is used for the benefit of the communion as well as in respect to how the calling has been followed. The fellowship in the Church, described as *koinonia*, has a doctrinal

---

dynamic process of koinonia involves the recognition of the complementarity of human beings. As individuals and as communities, the others confront us in their otherness e.g., theologically, ethnically, culturally. *Koinonia* requires respect for the other and a willingness to listen to the other and seek to understand them" (232). This passage shows the effort to combine these demands with the continued commitment to the goal of visible unity: "As we travel the way of pilgrimage, we will need to be able to understand each other's theological language and cultural ethos. We would be assisted in our journeying by intercontextual dialogues appropriately sponsored by regional ecumenical organizations, and in our interconfessional dialogues by a renewed Faith and Order study on hermeneutics, and new ways of doing theology which provide more adequate tools to express community on the way to the goal of visible unity" (234).

88. Cf. the reflection on "*koinonia* as calling": "The Spirit of God leads us to discover the imperfections of our visible *koinonia*. . . . We must work on the issues which divides us, but recognize, too, that perhaps only a penitent broken-ness can help us avoid the triumphalism of the past, and offer in weakness a diakonia to match the world's need. . . . *Koinonia* with humanity and the whole of creation is broken when gifts of the earth are not shared" (Santiago 1993:233).

89. Cf. Santiago 1993:233 (¶¶ 22, 24). The title of the edited report from the conference also takes this point: "On the Way *Towards* Fuller *Koinonia*" (italics mine).

90. Santiago 1993:232–33.

and ecclesiological connotation as well as a moral one. These connotations can be held together by the concept of "mutual accountability."

Section II focuses on *koinonia* in respect to the *apostolic faith*. This is an interesting framework for the recommendation of "ecumenical accountability" as a way to take seriously the problems related to justice, peace, and integrity of creation as matters for the whole Church. This section, too, feels obliged to raise the question of integration of these classical themes of Faith and Order and the issues of JPIC. As with Section I, it refers to *Costly Unity*. But one important step further is taken: defining these issues as "major concerns of Faith and Order." They simply belong to the issues of faith. To make these issues genuinely integrated in the framework of one, apostolic faith, a certain quality of ecclesiology is required, structures of mutual accountability.

> We appreciate the recent emphasis of those concerned with issues of justice, peace and the integrity of creation (JPIC) that the Church's involvement in such areas be carried on within the framework of a common faith and facilitated by structures of mutual accountability. Since these are also major concerns of Faith and Order, we recommend that Faith and Order seriously consider dialogue with those involved in JPIC, concerning the continuing questions as to how the Church's social ministries are rooted in and shaped by the apostolic faith.[91]

At the beginning of the paragraph the dialectic between "faith" and "order" is described: "Discerning our unity in faith requires structures for common decision-making and teaching."[92] These structures of unity in decision making are not only handled as a matter of the classical problems of "order," such as the definition of ordained ministry. They are also discussed in respect to which qualities of relation, which attitudes, should be pursued in these structures. Thus, we do find here a significant example of the correlation of "faith" and "order" to what I have called "relation." Apparently, it is not sufficient to define "unity in faith" only in terms of classical dogmatic issues; there must also be proper "order" (structures), qualified by the required attitude (qualities of relation). This becomes particularly urgent when the concept of "faith" is widened to integrate also the theology of creation.

Section II characterizes accountability as a quality recommended for the manifestation of *the catholicity of the local church*. The local church is a concrete manifestation of the catholic Church, insofar as it is in communion with all other churches. This kind of affirmation raises the question of structures between the churches. After referring to the threefold qualification of teaching

---

91. Santiago 1993:244.
92. Santiago 1993:242.

authority defined in BEM as "the connection of personal, collegial and synodical responsibility,"[93] the report focuses on the universal level. Without answering this question in regard to the papacy, the report emphasizes the qualities to be maintained regardless of the profile of the universal structure. There must be a proper relation between *communion, communication, and accountability*: "By means of mutual communication, a universal participation in the manifold efforts for the inculturation of the Gospel takes place. Without such living communion, the structure of the universal Church would not be credible. Important for such a worldwide communion of churches would also be interchurch communication by exchanging letters, as was a custom among the Ancient Church, as well as by other forms of accountability to each other."[94]

From the context it is obvious that the basic idea of communication according to this standard is *mutuality*. Thus, *mutual* accountability is here maintained as the common standard of a real communication that can foster "deeper" and "greater" *koinonia* of faith. The reference to the letters in the ancient Church—described as a form of accountability to one another—is interesting but not elaborated. For the theological significance of mutual accountability it is important to see how mutual accountability becomes a prerequisite for *catholicity*. This is serving the apostolicity of the Church, whatever form this structure of catholicity might take.

The report of *section III* deals with the common *life* in Christ, particularly the sacraments and the sacramentality of the Church. In other words, the themes of the most widely distributed and commented-on Faith and Order document: *Baptism, Eucharist and Ministry* (BEM), from the period evaluated in Santiago.[95]

This report (from Section III) is introduced by emphasizing "the need to develop a new methodology 'through which to receive and share insights from one another'."[96] This is already an indication that some of the aspects of "mutual accountability" were discussed through the work of this session. The theme of proper *attitudes* required for a "greater *koinonia*" is raised in the introduction of the report, in terms of "repentance" and mutual acceptance of those who are different within the *koinonia*.[97]

---

93. Santiago 1993:243. The threefold characteristic of ministry, particularly *episkopé*, from the BEM document is referred here and explicitly defined in terms of "responsibility." This supports my interpretation of this definition and its relevance for the concept of mutual accountability, cf. pp. 172–81.

94. Santiago 1993:243.

95. Cf. pp. 156–85.

96 Santiago 1993:244.

97. Santiago 1993:245f. The text addresses the tensions between what is still called "younger churches" and the other churches (who are not given any common label), which is one important

As with sections I and II, mutual accountability is recommended toward the end of the report, summing up the current and urgent need to proceed along the lines drawn in the analysis of the section report. The terminology is introduced as if it were a commonly accepted understanding of what this might be.

Mutual accountability is here described as one of several important "issues" of ecclesiology. As a consequence of the section's recommendations of more work on the ecclesiological implications of *koinonia* in respect to the BEM issues, there is more to be explored: "The exercise and achievement of fuller koinonia require that several other issues be addressed: Structures of mutual accountability and, where possible, common decision-making and action need to be discerned (there are biblical models for this which ought to be explored, e.g. John 12:24-26, 13:13-16; Matt. 5:21-26; 18:15-20; Acts 6 and 15.)"[98]

The word *and* might cause a difficulty of interpretation here, regarding the difference between the structures of mutual accountability and the structures of common decision making and action. There is a progress in the meaning of the sentence: the structure of common decision making and action is a natural follow-up to the structures of mutual accountability. Thus, common decision making and common action are something more than structures of mutual accountability. According to this text, the structures of mutual accountability can exist even when there is no conciliar or synodical structure of common decision making in action. On the other hand, the text makes no attempt to differentiate between them; rather, it describes the notion of the latter as a higher degree of fulfillment of the ideas given in the first, a way to realize the principle implied in the first. Consequently, this text classifies mutual accountability as a standard for decision making in the Church.[99]

The biblical references given for further exploration (not done in the report) can indicate what is meant by these "structures of mutual accountability." The most typical common features of the texts are the need for open

---

theme in the discussion of the role of contextual theology in ecumenism. The section report appeals to the proper attitudes, being accountable to the identity and contributions of the others: "The consequence of both older and newer divisions must be acknowledged in a spirit of repentance. *Koinonia* also includes acceptance of the other, whose culture may be different from ours. From their own experience with the Bible and from the praxis in their own context, the younger churches are in a position to rejuvenate the Tradition in worship, theology, spirituality and Christian ways of life." This corresponds very closely to Bonino's arguments for profiting more from mutual accountability in the ecumenical movement; cf. pp. 244–51.

98. Santiago 1993:251.

99. This corresponds to what was said (more indirectly) in the study of authoritative teaching, cf. pp. 109–28.

encounters, the faithfulness to what has been decided together, and the attitude of willingness to share.[100]

The report recommends a broader study on "ministry in general," including: ". . . the accountability of ministers of oversight (*episkopé*) to a particular community, and their relationship to the whole church."[101] The report also has an interesting example of recommended mutual accountability, describing how the churches could proceed in the question of ordination of women; they should focus on the "mutual respect and openness to the guidance of the Holy Spirit" and on inviting one another to share the analyses and reasons behind the particular stances.[102]

---

100. An interesting list of biblical texts is added, providing "biblical models for this." The section report does not explore them, as the report recommended. This is not the place to go into a comprehensive exegesis of them, but only to make a few points in respect to their potential contributions to our understanding of mutual accountability:

- The text closest to represent a model of mutually accountable church structures, is the text referring the council in Jerusalem (Acts 15). In those deliberations, the apostles tried to take into account the concern to be obedient to God's will known through the Thora and to the revelations of the Christian freedom. The congregations represented at the meeting were also asked *realiter* to live in mutual accountability to this understanding.
- The text from Acts 6 has some of the same features. There is a giving of account of the problems and needs in the community in Jerusalem, leading to a common decision and action by establishing some differences in the ministries of the community.
- John 12:24-26 perhaps convey the most radical understanding of giving account of the life in the context of mutuality. Not only an account of life should be given, but life itself has to be given to fulfill its meaning. To give account of life for the benefit of the mutuality means to share life. The text of John 12 stresses that this attitude of sharing is the mystery of the saving event of the Christ, and it is the only real way to win the life ("to keep it for eternal life").
- The aspect of taking example of the Lord is important in both texts mentioned from the Gospel of John. In John 13:13-16 the serving attitude is the condition for *koinonia* with Christ and with one another. The concept of *koinonia* is directly addressed in *practice*: "Unless I wash you, you have no part with me."
- The text of Matt. 5:21-26 describes the unbreakable interrelatedness between the account to God and the account to each other. The offer cannot be given to God before there is reconciliation between those living in confrontation to each other.
- The reference to the text in Matt. 18:15-20 probably points to the accountability for the sinful thoughts and acts, and the potential of the mutual community to release from sin. The aspect of mutuality in this passage is emphasized. A concept of *common* responsibility for sin can be one reason for giving this reference in this context. There is also an aaspect of mutuality in "binding and loosing."

101. Santiago 1993:250. The theme of *episkopé* was discussed also in Section II under the title "Structures serving unity" (242f.). This theme is further elaborated in consultations on *episkopé* and episcopacy after Santiago, cf. pp. 294–97.

102. Santiago 1993:250.

The report of *Section IV* carries the title "Called to Common Witness for a Renewed World," announcing a threefold *responsibility*: to the Lord and giver of *koinonia*, to the *koinonia* which gives witness in "common," and to the *koinonia* of humanity, which the unity of the Church should serve. This section is the one that deals most comprehensively with how to integrate the ecclesiological reflection of Faith and Order with the concern for justice, peace, and integrity of creation—a major theme at the whole conference.[103] This threefold responsibility is the context in which a particular recommendation of "mutual accountability" occurs.

It is important to get hold of the entire argument in the report. The report gives particular emphasis to *koinonia* as *participation* in the trinitarian life of God; to the *diversity* of witnesses due to cultural diversity where the churches live; and to the participation and *solidarity* with the wider human community in respect for all creation. To be more specific on relevant issues for my theme: the three main themes highlighted on mission[104] could all relate to the theme of mutual accountability. The report deals intensively with the matter of non-accountable mission and evangelism that slips into proselytism. Second, on the basis of the principle of religious freedom, the churches should show a mutual responsibility for the right of others to such freedom. Third, the question is raised of legitimate diversity of culture as well in respect to the understanding of the gospel, but it is not answered. There is one exception: the report criticizes Western Christians who have had insufficient awareness of or, we could say, accountability for their cultural heritage in their mission activity.[105]

That part of the report called "Common witness: discipleship as corporate moral commitment"[106] presents an understanding of ecclesiology that to a great extent describes the Church as a community of common moral commitment.[107] The really difficult question dealt with here is this: How can we

---

103. "This integration of ethics and ecclesiology, and this insistence on the interrelation of Christian koinonia and wider human community has marked our discussions in this conference" (Santiago 1993:254, cf. the comprehensive elaboration of these questions at 255f. and 259–62). This report makes an explicit reference to *Costly Unity* in this respect (as do the three other section reports; 260). The ecclesiology elaborated in the Faith and Order document *Church and World* is an important element in the deliberations in the report, particularly the image of the Church as a foretaste and expectation, the Church as prophetic sign of the coming kingdom of God; cf. Santiago 1993:255f.

104. Santiago 1993:256–58.

105. ". . . their cultural values and habits have falsely been claimed as Gospel truth" (Santiago 1993:257).

106. Santiago 1993:259f.

107. "The being and mission of the Church, therefore, are at stake in witness through proclamation and concrete actions for justice, peace and integrity of creation. This is a defining mark of koinonia and central to our understanding of ecclesiology" (Santiago 1993:259).

come to common Christian discipleship in complex ethical questions, where we even disagree? The text gives two types of answer. First, it raises the model of "council" from Acts 15 as the way toward a "corporate stance to preserve its authenticity and credibility." However, the report is not hiding the fact that a council or a conciliar process does not always lead to that result. There might even be "a call" for some Christian groups "to take an alternative position, depending on their interpretation of the Gospel as well as their perception and experience of social, political, cultural and economic reality."[108] Dialogue is highly recommended in these cases, either to settle a consensus, or to define that there are church-dividing issues at stake. The ecumenical task is not to withdraw, but: "The ecumenical task is continually to seek obedience in relation to the great questions of the day. It is essential that the churches commit themselves to stay together within ecumenical structures and to realize mutual accountability within them as they pursue the answers."[109]

This is taking up the theme of proper ecumenical attitudes announced already in the first reflections of this section report: "*Koinonia* will be costly. There is a cheap unity, which avoids contested issues because they disturb the peace of the Church. Costly unity will not be afraid of legitimate conflict." Here the Santiago report goes one step further than *Costly Unity*, as it requires not only the attitude of moral solidarity, but even the attitude to accept costly unity as living with disagreement in moral issues.[110]

According to the report, this attitude corresponds to the costly *koinonia* that includes openness in terms of divergences. One implication of being open in this respect may also be the acceptance of certain limits in finding a united expression of the gospel. The "particularity" of the cultures may also be "bearers and revealers of God's truth."[111] How this question should be handled in concrete cases is not really answered.

The report defines mutual accountability as the way to proceed when there is willingness to stay within the ecumenical structure *in tensions*. In the perspective of the whole section report, tensions do not necessarily disturb or annul the *koinonia*. The obligation to be mutually accountable is, therefore, given a significant theological foundation: it is one important presupposition of belonging to the God-given *koinonia* of diversity. One interpretation of this position would be that mutual accountability is the attitude of staying firm, committed to the communion, despite the tensions. Another, maybe in

---

108. Santiago 1993:260.
109. Santiago 1993:260.
110. Santiago 1993:255.
111. Santiago 1993:257.

combination with the first, would be that this firm position includes a high degree of tolerating plurality.[112]

Mutual accountability is here described as the mutual respect and openness needed to handle diversity appropriately. To be in this God-given *koinonia* means to be accountable to the communion for the way each local or confessional community or church handles the ethical challenges they face. This obligation does not disappear in a situation of diversity. There is, however, a *tension* in the report itself here, almost a contradiction in terms. The text stresses the common moral commitment as a sign of discipleship in *koinonia*; on the other hand, diversity is acknowledged, even in moral issues important for the community. One explanation of this tension could be that a distinction between different types of moral issues could classify them according to their significance for *koinonia*. At least, this tension unveils the great intrinsic problems when the church-dividing moral issues are handled as one bundle. It might also unveil different positions in respect to what kind of diversity can be accepted.

Structures of mutual accountability are launched as the last and strongest bond of unity in the *koinonia*, useful even in moral disagreements. There seems to be no tension about this. Still, there is a tendency in this section report to describe mutual accountability as a matter of mutual tolerance, accepting differences or even divisions, more than emphasizing mutual accountability as the dynamic toward convergence or consensus in central matters of faith and order, or in matters of life and witness. This tendency is more easily perceivable in some input in the succeeding work of Faith and Order.[113] Whether this is what (at least some of) the participants meant by "waning commitments to Christian unity" in the message has to remain an open question.[114]

Summary

The Santiago conference brought the *qualities of relation* into the heart of its reflections on unity when defining unity of the Church as *koinonia*. These qualities of relation are explored in the light of the unity in the triune God, particularly emphasizing the unity in diversity, the given unity, and the "relation-ality" of being a Church and a Christian. The theme of mutual accountability was not really elaborated as a separate theme, but became a significant issue in describing the problems identified and the way forward "towards *koinonia* in faith, life and witness." The fact that "mutual accountability" is used at crucial

---

112. This corresponds to Joshua's description of mutual accountability as a principle of how to structure plurality in theological and moral issues; cf. pp. 271–77.

113. E.g., in the last report from the "Ecclesiology and Ethics" study (*Costly Obedience*) we found this tendency, cf. pp. 258–63. This is also one feature in the study of hermeneutics, cf. pp. 298–308.

114. Santiago 1993:225 (§3).

points in the official reports of this important event in the life of Faith and Order (the first world conference in 30 years), is a clear sign of the importance of this theme in the conceptions of Faith and Order. It is a significant theme when taking stock of what has happened, defining what should be done and how this movement understands the unity of the Church. Since this is the first statement from a wide-scale event where "mutual accountability" explicitly is used, it is interesting to see whether this terminology is used in correspondence to the preliminary definitions I suggested in chapter 1.

Mutual accountability became a key issue for the *integration* of, on the one hand, traditional Faith and Order concerns of unity in respect of apostolic faith, sacraments, and ministry, and, on the other hand, the concern for a common moral commitment, particularly the concern for justice, peace, and integrity of creation (JPIC). This was indeed a major concern in the Santiago conference, taking into account the agendas of the churches in different parts of the world and the inputs from the document *Costly Unity*. The attempt was to see these questions as more than mere ethical matters, but as matters of faith and ecclesiology. These challenges to the Church demanded an accountable Church, accountable to one another for how the Christian faith equips the churches to act in accountability to those living with the problems identified through the JPIC questions.

The message and to some degree also the section reports talk about *structures* of mutual accountability. These structures are described as necessary to realize the identity of unity as gift and calling, or, in other words, to give the unity of the Church its proper doctrinal as well as ethical dimension. The unity in "faith" needs an "order" qualified by certain qualities of "relation." Thus, the Santiago reports confirm this "tria-lectic" I have been suggesting throughout this study.

Mutual accountability belongs to the dynamic required, described either as "towards fuller *koinonia*," "greater" *koinonia*, or the double definition "gift and calling." The message of the conference builds up a double analysis and argument, conceiving what is promising because of committed involvement and proper reception of results, as well as the proclivity toward "waning commitment to unity." Finding the way forward, the message confirms the position (or attitude) of "no turning back," renewed commitment to what has been achieved, and being frank and honest facing the obstacles. This double line of argument culminates in the requirement of what should keep the proper dynamic going: structures of mutual accountability. Hence, I find this message to support my understanding of mutual accountability as a requirement of an ecumenical *attitude*.

The texts from Santiago are somewhat open in respect to exactly *what* structures of mutual accountability are required. There seems to be more focus on *which qualities* the structures of unity should have. The message says nothing more exact about the form of unity than "structures of mutual accountability." There are, however, references to the need for accountability in the exercise of *episkopé* and of conciliar forms of unity in the section reports.

The standards required by "mutual accountability" are, seen in the perspective of the entire reports from Santiago, most of all *reliability* in the *commitment* to the unity of the Church as gift and calling. The focus in the requirements of mutual accountability is the *firmness* required from the participating churches. This reliability and firmness should be shown in the commitment to one another, dedicating oneself to the classical Faith and Order quest toward unity in faith, shared sacraments, and mutually recognized ministry. Mutual accountability, therefore, is not a substitute for convergence and proper structures of unity, but a more fundamental perspective, *qualifying* the relations established through convergence in doctrine and common church order. This can be seen as a consequence of emphasizing *koinonia* and not one particular model of unity.

The Santiago conference dealt extensively with the matter of diversity, particularly cultural diversity and tensions in ethical questions. The first is indirectly related to the theme of "mutual accountability," the latter directly. *Koinonia* is not broken by diversity; it even needs this. The problem is when tensions seem to undermine the *koinonia*. Here one section report (IV) speaks boldly of daring to face tensions and diversity, through being mutually accountable. Hence, there were voices and tendencies in Santiago toward defining the concept of "mutual accountability" as a boundary of tolerance around a communion of great diversity, even tensions in regard to issues in faith, order, and life. This shows an ambiguity in the concept, necessary to be aware of when attempting to establish a theory of mutual accountability as ecumenical attitude.

To some degree the reports from Santiago focused on openness in terms of willingness to give account of one's own culture, tradition, and faith, and not least, to be willing and able to take such accounts from others really into account. It is both giving and taking; it is participation in the gift and the calling, it is *koinonia*. Indirectly this dimension is related to the requirements of mutual accountability.

The Role of Mutual Accountability in the Faith and Order "Ecclesiology" Study (1998)

An Integrated Element of the Ecumenical Tradition

This attempt to present a preliminary convergence text of ecumenical ecclesiology was pursued partly as a prolonging of the Santiago agenda of "taking stock" of the results of the ecumenical movement.[115] The document is shaped according to its scope. The main text presents how far the dialogue on ecclesiology has come; separate supplements (boxes) discuss remaining questions and differences. This study process on ecclesiology, called for and discussed before 1993[116] but launched after the strong recommendations from the Santiago conference, has so far presented a report which elaborates some important features of a common ecumenical tradition of ecclesiology.[117]

According to this perspective on the text, mutual accountability belongs to the common tradition of ecumenical ecclesiology. It is used here to explicate other basic principles of ecclesiology and to suggest solutions to problems still remaining. Hence, it appears as a criterion and a well-known common point of reference. This indicates the significance of this concept and supports exploring it as a matter of ecumenical ecclesiology today.

---

115. "The main purpose of this study is to give expression to what the churches can now say together about the nature and purpose of the Church and within that perspective to state the remaining areas of disagreement. Thus, in the style of *BEM*, this document seeks to evolve into what could be called a convergence text. The present test is a first attempt to state that convergence" (Church 1998:7). Cf. the subtitle of the document: "A stage on the way to a common statement." The document is divided into six chapters, announcing themes resembling crucial themes from the studies analyzed above: "The Church of the Triune God"; "The Church in History"; "The Church as *Koinonia* (Communion)"; "Life in Communion"; "Service in the World: Following our Calling: From Converging Understanding to Mutual Recognition."

116. This was seen as a natural follow-up of the BEM; "Apostolic Faith" and "Unity and Renewal" studies; cf. Budapest 1989:202–219, and Minutes Dunblane 1990:68–71.

117. The idea of a common ecumenical tradition was a theme in the work on "coherent and vital theology"; cf. pp. 244–51. It also appeared in the WCC process on visions and identity, taking stock of the ecumenical movement so far: ". . . an emerging common tradition of shared convictions on faith, life and witness [which] has begun to enrich theological reflection" (CUV 1997:5). The report *The Nature and the Purpose of the Church: A Stage on the Way to a Common Statement* (Church 1998) does not tell who has been working on this study. According to the minutes of the Faith and Order board, e.g., Minutes Abbaye de Fontgombault 1997:72f., there were a group of seven members of the Faith and Order board and two staffpersons in the ecclesiology group. The results have been discussed in the board meetings (Minutes Bangkok 1996:38–48; Minutes Abbaye de Fontgombault 1997:23–28). This procedure can explain that the study report so far does not have the character of a really new dialogue on ecclesiology, but is a reception and an effort to systematize results from former studies.

"Mutual Accountability" in the Definition of Koinonia

In the outline of what *koinonia* means, the text presents a reflection on its etymology, in which "mutual accountability" appears as part of the explanation:

> The basic verbal form from which the noun *koinonia* derives means "to have something in common," "to share," "to participate," "to have part in," "to act together" or "to be in a contractual relationship involving obligations of mutual accountability." The word *koinonia* appears in key situations, for example, the reconciliation of Paul and Peter, James and John (Gal 2:9), the collection for the poor (Rom 15:26; 2 Cor 8:4), the experience and witness of the Church (Acts 2:42-45).[118]

The link to reciprocal contracting between partners is a useful hint of the field from which this terminology can be traced. Mutual accountability is here used to define the moral implication of having something in common. It is called an obligation but is qualified in a way that can be both the status of being accountable and the attitude of being accountable to one another.[119] What is particularly interesting is the context in which this is said, referring to other biblical images of *koinonia*, most of them used in already analyzed documents. *Koinonia* is defined as "the reality to which these images refer."[120] To this is added a reference to the Old Testament term *shalom*. The rich meaning of this word, its connotation of a mature, mutual, stable relation of mutual trust and fidelity is interesting as a framework to understand the moral aspects of "mutual accountability."

The terminological definitions are immediately succeeded, in the same paragraph, by reflections on New Testament examples of *koinonia*. These texts show how the Faith and Order Commission understands the context in which "mutual accountability" is adequate to describe ecclesiological sharing and agreement. Particularly the text from Galatians seems to be the background for the description of "mutual accountability." The encounter between Paul and the other apostles in the meeting in Jerusalem (called the "reconciliation of Paul and Peter, James and John") is an interesting reference in our context. In Galatians 2 Paul emphasizes that he was subsequently accountable in the sense of being faithful to the gospel he was preaching—and thereby to the calling given to him to preach for the uncircumcised. His accountability to the gospel was linked to the accountability to the heathen. This type of accountability was

---

118. Church 1998:25.

119. Cf. the oscillation between these two meanings of "mutual accountability" discussed in the preliminary definition, pp. 22–27.

120. Church 1998:25.

the basis for the "contractual relationship" of *koinonia* established (Gal. 2:9). This agreement was an agreement of mutuality—not of superiority or hierarchy, but of equality (a point Paul stresses in 2:6). To this agreement of *koinonia* all parts were supposed to be mutually accountable, and it served as the basis for Paul's argument in the struggle with his opponents.

The reference to the collection for the poor that Paul recommends in Romans 15 and 2 Corinthians 8 points to the experience and witness of common sharing. This basic sharing of *koinonia* (Acts 2) corresponds to an idea of "mutual accountability" where all have to be accountable to one another, not a situation where one part is an owner and the others are renters or stewards.

The study document continues with a reflection on how the *koinonia* in the Church and between parts of the Church has its goal in the *koinonia* of all people and the whole creation. This is presented as a common legacy of the many struggles about ethics and ecclesiology in the ecumenical movement. Although the term is not used, this description gives a picture of the "accountable Church in the world," accountable to God's work and plan.

A sidebar, dealing with remaining difficulties on issues of "Faith and Ethics," addresses the problem of new, "potentially church-dividing" issues.[121] The growing *koinonia* implies that the churches get closer to one another, but also closer to the difficult moral questions as the churches deal with them differently. This reflection refers to an increasingly hot ecumenical issue (but not yet comprehensively addressed in the ecumenical movement), namely human sexuality. The ecumenical movement is in this respect risking "damaging or destroying the bonds of *koinonia* already existing." The reflection ends with a brief catalogue of tools required to deal with such issues: "The closer churches come to an agreement on ecclesiology, the more they are challenged to address the tolerable limits of moral diversity compatible with *koinonia*. Continual ecumenical dialogue, discernment, accountability and Christian charity are required to that end."[122]

This is a prolongation of problems raised in Santiago. New here are the explicit parallels to accountability in respect to discernment and the diaconical dimension of the Church.[123] This indicates how ecumenical accountability is regarded as something more than a theoretical principle of tolerance; it really affects the decisions and the attitudes of the Church. Particularly, "accountability" and "charity" refer to what must be called ecumenical *attitudes*. Therefore, the report takes for granted that these attitudes are typical for the heritage of the common ecumenical legacy. They should be activated when facing new

---

121. Church 1998:58.
122. Church 1998:58.
123. Cf. the analysis of the report of Section IV, pp. 22–27.

challenges, even in questions that are not traditionally regarded as matters of ecumenical dialogue.

From this it can be concluded that the "Ecclesiology" study regards accountability as an ecumenical attitude implied in the ecumenical ecclesiology of *koinoina*. This attitude is obviously not regarded as hallmark of the provisional and imperfect *koinonia*, the "not realized *koinonia*," as a kind of necessary substitute for the visible unity not achieved. But it is described as a necessary element of a *koinonia* according to the nature and purpose of the Church. It is a sign of the "real" *koinonia* belonging to the dynamic required for the process toward the "not realized *koinonia*."

Mutual Accountability and Wrestling with Diversity

A whole section in the chapter on *koinonia* is devoted to wrestling with the question of what is an "authentic diversity." The text about remaining difficulties is here just as long as the text discussing what is common.[124]

The different gifts of the Spirit are not only accepted but also *desired*. Among the common statements of ecumenical ecclesiological tradition is the emphasis on the difference between unity and "uniformity." The rich diversity of cultural and historical context should not be suppressed.

Nevertheless, the cutting edge is: When is one particular expression dominating or capturing the heart of the gospel? The problem is seen in the relation between gospel and culture and in the discussion on how much emphasis on the specific elements of each church tradition can be designated as legitimate or authentic diversity.

One ecumenical problem is the difference in how much churches can accept diversity.[125] There seems to be potential here for neverending discussion. The only answer this text gives to this particular problem is a reflection on the proper standard of relations between churches as they wrestle with these issues: "One of the pressing ecumenical questions is how churches at this stage of the ecumenical movement can live in mutual accountability so that they can sustain one another in unity and legitimate diversity and prevent new issues from becoming causes of division within and between churches."[126]

Hence, the text accepts to some degree that what the churches can do is to find a *modus vivendi* that avoids "division." But if some of the churches cannot live with a certain amount of diversity at certain points, it may be asked

---

124. Church 1998:28–31.

125. Cf. Church 1998, esp. 31.

126. Church 1998:31.

whether all of them really can accept this conclusion. The text is not very transparent at this point.[127]

While the text is not particularly clear here, it looks as if mutual accountability is thought of as a principle of legitimate diversity mutually accepted. Apparently, there are problems in respect to definitions. That would imply taking a stand in weighting the issues at stake, for instance, the theology of baptism.[128] Seeing it from the perspective of "mutual accountability" applies a framework that allows differences to occur without remaining in broken relations. But even then, the size of this framework is a crucial issue.

Mutually Accountable Structures Serving Unity in Diversity

Dealing with the questions of ministry, the text attempts to establish some general principles. One of them is that "The Church is a communion of co-responsible persons: no function, no gift, no charisma is exercised outside or above this communion. . . . All have received gifts and all are responsible."[129] This is to some degree an application of the need for mutual accountability on every relation in the Church. The text is more specific when it describes certain ministries and structures serving the unity of the church. The ministry of oversight is described this way: "The ministry of *episkope* entails a mutual responsibility between those who are entrusted with oversight and the whole apostolic community of the Church."[130]

The mutual interdependence is here described in terms of responsibility. The same feature is used to describe a common perspective for both conciliar and synodical structures. The concern of the text seems to be to describe the common standards of these structures, whatever they might be:

> Communal life sustains all the baptized in a web of belonging, of mutual accountability and support. It implies unity in diversity and is expressed in one heart and one mind (Phil 2:1-2). It is the way Christians are held in unity and travel together as the one Church and the one Church is manifested in the life of each local church.[131]

---

127. The critical commentary from the Orthodox theologian Apostola (see below) gives a signal of how "mutual accountability" can be understood as a demand to accept more diversity than some churches can do. This is, as the text indicates, a matter also "within" the churches.
128. Cf., e.g., Church 1998:38.
129. Church 1998:41, 47.
130. Church 1998:45.
131. Church 1998:50.

Within this communality there is need for collegiality, particularly among those sharing the ministry of oversight. Collegiality provides for mutual support and mutual accountability.[132]

The required attitudes of structures of episcopacy were illuminated in two separate consultations, a sign of the relative weight applied to that issue as ecumenical problem in the 1990s.

Two Consultations on Episkopé and Episcopacy

Faith and Order convoked two consultations in 1997 on the theme "*Episcopé and Episcopacy and the Quest for Visible Unity*" after recommendations from Santiago. There had also been requests to do so from two other meetings where this theme had gained urgency, encounters between representatives from churches involved in bilateral agreements crossing the classic division between episcopal and nonepiscopal churches.[133] In two cases of the report from these consultations mutual accountability is taken into the reflection on how important and difficult dimensions of episcopacy can be handled. These reflections supply what is said very briefly in the "Ecclesiology" document.

The first is a part of a reflection on the *power* given to those who carry the responsibility of oversight. Power is not the problem, but lack of openness and mutuality in the exercise of power. It is essential that they should "be committed to an open process of teaching and learning by which the conscience of the whole people of God is informed and built up." Through open processes and gatherings they could be challenged for their exercise of power, and thereby contribute to build up "a common mind of the people of God." In this context the principle of accountability is crucial in the deliberations: "'Accountability' in the Christian context includes a prior and proper accountability to God, who is the author and giver of every good gift; accountability to fellow Christians for mutual sharing, admonition, teaching and learning; and the common accountability of each member of the community to the good of the whole, which is shared particularly by those whose ministry entails responsibility for the *koinonia* as a whole."[134]

This accountability is discussed as much more than a matter of procedure. It is a basic feature of the relations within the "Christian context"; particularly significant for any positions and power bestowed, but also for any participation

---

132. Church 1998:51.

133. Episkopé 1997:vii (Preface). The referreed reflections on mutual accountability were made in two meetings, one for "United and Uniting Churches" in Ocho Rios, Jamaica; the other was a meeting of churches involved in the Leuenberg, Meissen, and Porvoo agreements. In the latter, the significance of the failure of historical episcopacy in some of the Reformed and Lutheran churches was debated as a matter of compatibility between these agreements. Cf. Birmelé 1996:70; Hill 1996:113; and Frieling 1996:169–71.

134. Episkopé 1997:38f.

granted in this *koinonia*. The attitude of accountability is described as proper acts of sharing, admonition, and so forth, and in dialectic to the status of being held accountable by God and fellow Christians.

This mutual accountability is significant for the stewardship of the truth or, in other words, to make the governing bodies of the Church able to find a way forward: "There is no absolute precision about which mode of government would protect the church completely from the occurrence of errors. In the present state of ecclesial disunity, strategies and occasions for mutual listening, encouragement and correction are needed. There is a necessary provisionality or tentativeness to decisions even of a legal competent body, affording time for due reflection."[135] Saying that these signs of ecumenical attitude are "needed," this text uses a language that is rather close to the concepts of *notae ecclesiae*. Probably, the need of these qualities of relations is not conditioned by the present state of disunity only. I understand the text to be saying, rather, that what is always important is particularly important now.

The second specific reflection is found in a passage discussing the appropriate way to handle *diversity* in an open but reliable encounter, launched as "ecumenical space."

> "Ecumenical space" is the milieu in which, even in a state of division, we bear witness to our common allegiance to Jesus Christ and cooperate to advance the visible unity of the church. In this space we affirm our common Christian identity. For this reason, we have the possibility of a new discourse: we talk to one another in a new way. In turn, we have a greater opportunity to discern together Christ's will for the church in ways that are not possible in isolation one from another. Space thus understood brings the churches into living encounters with one another. It is helpful to enumerate the presuppositions, characteristics, opportunities and obligations of being together in "ecumenical space".[136]

This somewhat—and apparently deliberately—open concept is used to illuminate what "bonds of communion and mutual accountability" in ecumenical processes mean. In the definition of this dynamic of establishing bounds and room for development, mutual accountability is explicitly mentioned. There are also other descriptions of ecumenical attitudes corresponding to what seems to be a proper definition of mutual accountability, presented as "characteristics" and "obligations" of the "ecumenical space":

---

135. Episkopé 1997:39.

136. Episkopé 1997:43. The description of this "appropriate milieu" resembles what is said about the "real but imperfect *koinonia*" within the process discussing the identity of the WCC in the same period, where mutual accountability should be given a higher status, cf. pp. 308–14.

[Characteristics:]
- frank and serious discussion, including search and discovery, questioning and listening;
- mutual respect, so that no church is required to deny its identity or heritage;
- restraint from judgment, thus excluding a purely negative attitude on the part of one church towards another;

[Obligations:]
- compatibility of attitude and behaviour within and outside this ecumenical space;
- avoidance of actions inconsistent with brotherly/sisterly relationships;
- mutual support, forbearance and accountability.[137]

The reflection concludes with considerations of how churches should actualize their accountability to other churches, for example, in respect to exercise of *episkopé* across the churches:

> It is clear that internal decisions cannot be reached in isolation from partners, and decisions in one region or nation will have an impact on others. For this reason, in any significant decision or agreement concerning church life, compatibility and consistency with partner churches should be tested before finalization. In sum, mutual accountability to partners must be a chief consideration in stage-by-stage unfolding of a process that is under the Spirit and oriented to an ultimate future belonging to the Triune God.[138]

From these passages we see that mutual accountability is a notion used to find what should be characteristic for the ecumenical fellowship, in whatever stage it might be. It is described as both obligation and attitude, necessary for a proper exercise of *episkopé*. To use power properly and to be able to discern the way for the Church, those having the ministry of oversight—whatever form—need mutually accountable relations to benefit from the wisdom of others. Mutual accountability is also recommended as criterion for the procedures in a far more loose ecumenical entity called "ecumenical space." How this type of structure could become mutually accountable can be answered in relation to attitudes but not so easily in respect to interchurch structures. Mutual accountability here becomes a premise for the further development of the unity of the Church, both internal in the churches and in interchurch relations.

---

137. Episkopé 1997:44.
138. Episkopé 1997:44.

Summary

The first report from the study of ecclesiology is to a large extent a re-reception of former studies of Faith and Order, not bringing much substantially new to ecumenical ecclesiology. We find here reflections of the importance of ecumenical attitudes familiar from those we found in earlier stages. However, mutual accountability has explicitly become an important element of ecumenical ecclesiology as presented here. This importance can be derived from two perspectives:

First, the concept seems to fit well into a general understanding of the legacy of the ecumenical tradition. The reader is not granted a particular definition of the concept. There seems to be no urgency to present and explain; it is used parallel to "dialogue," "discernment," "charity," and "support."

Second, the concept of mutual accountability is presented as a required attitude, a prerequisite for the "real, but not realized *koinonia*" as well as a particularly needed quality to handle really difficult ecumenical questions. This attitude belongs to the way toward, as well as to the goal of, *koinonia*. The concept is used to determine specific principles or ministries serving the unity in diversity, particularly the collegiality between those having the service of *episkopé*, and as a principle for conciliar fellowship.

To a large degree the preliminary definition of mutual accountability as ecumenical attitude relevant for ecumenical ecclesiology, as we to a certain degree found implicit in the texts before 1990, is confirmed by the explicit requirements in this text. Particularly when it comes to the elaboration of what personal, collegial, and communal exercise of *episkopé* means, this is the case. The ecclesiology study dwelt upon the handling of diversity in the Church, and recommended, as did Santiago section report IV, mutual accountability for that purpose. Here the ecclesiology study has much in common with the parallel study of hermeneutics.

The Report from the Faith and Order Study on Hermeneutics (1998)

"A New Climate of Mutual Accountability"

The report from the study in ecumenical hermeneutics after Santiago was a final document from this Faith and Order endeavour, not an interim report for further comments. It responds to the requirement identified already in the response to BEM, later on articulated clearly in Santiago, that "Faith and Order could progress fruitfully only with serious exploration of the hermeneutical issues."[139] This document has, therefore, more elaborate reflections and statements than the "Ecclesiology" report discussed above, and contributes probably more to the theme of my study as well.

The report was presented as a contribution for other projects and processes in the ecumenical movement, "an instrument for an ecumenical reflection on hermeneutics."[140] There are several significant thematic links between the reports on the "Ecclesiology" study and that on hermeneutics. The questions of hermeneutics are discussed under the perspective of the *Church* as subject for hermeneutics and for the purpose of establishing an adequate hermeneutic of *unity*. The links between the reports are to some extent related to the meaning of "mutual accountability." Four elements of the introduction of the report can illuminate this:

First, the idea of a "new climate" is typical for the reflections of Faith and Order in this period. The definition is noticeable, as it intends to identify why positive results could have been achieved or are missing. The report concludes: "A new climate of trust and mutual accountability has been nurtured, but at the same time there are hesitations and even retreats because churches are not clear about the meaning of ongoing work toward visible unity."[141]

The combination or parallelism of "mutual accountability" and "trust" in this passage emphasizes mutual accountability as an attitude that signifies *a state of maturity* in the ecumenical movement. Mutual accountability is the positive effect of dialogue as well as the presupposition for further dialogue. In this state of maturity the goal of the ecumenical movement can be further pursued. This is the situation of having "a growing, real though imperfect *koinonia*."[142] Again, we see how mutual accountability is regarded as a premise for ecumenical achievement. It is important, however, to notice that "a climate of mutual accountability" is regarded as *not sufficient*. Perceivable "retreats"—in spite of this new climate—are interpreted as signs churches are not being "clear about the meaning of ongoing work towards visible unity." Mutual accountability cannot serve the purpose of the ecumenical goal, as a climate without more specific agreement and commitment. The focus on qualities of relations cannot totally substitute for traditional results in terms of convergence in faith and growing together in structures ("order").

---

139. Hermeneutics 1998:3. The report presents the process behind it: three consultations and two drafting meetings. There was a rather wide participation from all parts of the world and from a wide range of member churches of the Faith and Order Commission. The process was supported by contributions from scholars in this field.

140. The subtitle of the report is *A Treasure in Earthen Vessels* (Hermeneutics 1998).

141. Hermeneutics 1998:11.

142. Hermeneutics 1998:12. This was a typical statement in Santiago 1993, cf. pp. 271–77 and 277–86.

Second, the introduction presents a definition of the task of "hermeneutics for unity."[143] Ecumenical hermeneutics becomes here a matter of ecclesiology. What is particularly interesting for my theme is the combination of, or *dialectic* between, "hermeneutics of coherence" and "hermeneutics of suspicion." The first implies a reverence and accountability to the common sources of the Christian tradition, "seeking to manifest the integral unity of the Christian faith and community." The second implies accountability in respect to the interpreters, revealing "the timebound character of the traditional forms and formulations as well as any ambiguous or vested interests on the part of the interpreters both past and present."[144] The report gives a brief definition of the double, but integrated, directions of mutual accountability as ecumenical attitude: toward the common heritage, The Tradition, and to one another, the traditions. The uniting qualification of this dialectic is the attitude of accountability (or "responsibility"): "In a constantly ongoing process, a responsible ecumenical hermeneutics will try to serve the truth, alerted by suspicion but always aiming at coherence."[145]

Third, we find an elaboration of the Church as a *hermeneutic community*, a description of ecumenical attitudes close to the preliminary definition of mutual accountability I have pursued through this study. The text talks about "hermeneutics of confidence." Typical for this hermeneutic community is the willingness to understand the other on their own premises, and to be interpreted by the other churches and traditions in an open, respectful encounter. This has been learned through the exercise of ecumenical dialogue, in openness for the Spirit:

> As it engages in ecumenical dialogue each church and tradition opens itself to being interpreted by other churches and traditions. To listen to the other does not necessarily mean to accept what other churches say, but to reckon with the possibility that the Spirit speaks within and through the others. This might be called "*hermeneutics of confidence.*" A hermeneutics for unity should entail an ecumenical method whereby Christians from various cultures and contexts, as well as different confessions, may encounter one another

---

143. "Within theological hermeneutics, *ecumenical* hermeneutics serves the specific task of focusing on how texts, symbols and practices in the various churches may be interpreted, communicated and mutually received as the churches engage in dialogue. . . . A hermeneutics for unity should aim at greater coherence in the interpretation of the faith and in the community of all believers as their voices unite in common praise of God; make possible a mutually recognizable (re)appropriation of the sources of the Christian faith; and prepare ways of common confession and prayer in spirit and truth" (Hermeneutics 1998:9).

144. Hermeneutics 1998:9.

145. Hermeneutics 1998:9.

respectfully, always open to a *metanoia* which is a true "change of mind" and heart.[146]

Later on, the text explicates what this combination of hermeneutics of coherence and suspicion does and does not imply when it comes to mutual challenges of interpreting texts and traditions anew. Again, we find a remarkable focus on the significance of *attitudes*. The hermeneutics of suspicion should unveil the location and hidden choices of interpretation, the structures of power, the prejudices and presuppositions. This should happen in a mutual process, including self-critical approaches, conveying the adequate attitudes of mutuality and accountability: "This does not mean the adoption of an attitude of mistrust but the application to oneself and one's dialogue partners of an approach which perceives how self-interest, power, national or ethnic or class or gender perspectives can affect the reading of texts and the understanding of symbol and practices."[147]

Fourth, the introduction brings the task of ecumenical hermeneutics into the framework of relevant tasks to promote a "growing *koinonia*," as it was defined by the Santiago conference. Three main tasks are pointed out: first, to overcome the criteriological differences in interpreting the gospel, recognizing the multiform richness and diversity in the Christian tradition; second, to handle the questions of gospel and culture; and, finally, "To work toward mutual accountability, discernment and authoritative teaching and towards credibility in common witness before the world, and finally towards the eschatological fullness of the truth in the power of the Holy Spirit."[148]

Again, we find that mutual accountability is required for a growing *koinonia*. The text avoids specific references to models of authoritative teaching, only associating the need for discernment with the more open "mutual accountability," without making efforts to grant further definitions, except the meaning of the context and parallel concepts.[149]

---

146. Hermeneutics 1998:10.

147. Hermeneutics 1998:21f. It is interesting, but not immediately illuminating, that the Catholic–Lutheran dialogue is used as example of this positive effect of "hermeneutic of suspicion." It is easier to see the relevance of the succeeding example: the critique of the theological premises for the apartheid regime (ibid., 22).

148. Hermeneutics 1998:12f. The text refers (in a footnote) to the reports from Santiago section reports III and IV, the same passages as discussed above.

149. The study of authoritative teaching was reluctant to give any clear definition of such structures, too, but studied the theme more explicitly in the framework of "conciliar fellowship"; cf. pp. 94–110.

The Understanding of the One Tradition in the Climate of Mutual Accountability

The new way of handling the question of "Tradition," established after Montreal 1963, is described as a "climate" of mutual listening, understanding, self-critique, and maturity.

In these endeavours of ecumenical hermeneutics, the attitude toward each other is of crucial importance, according to the report. It must transmit the atmosphere of dialogue to the churches, "the sense of mutual confidence." The proper attitude is necessary for churches to know how to relate adequately to other churches. But what is at stake is more than this. It is, according to this report on ecumenical hermeneutics, a matter of finding a way toward insight into the divine mystery. The proper relation to "the other" and the hermeneutic to understand revelation are linked closely to one another. "Since diversity can be an expression of the right gifts of the Holy Spirit, the churches are called to become aware of the possibility of an abiding complimentarity, i.e., of the values inherent in the 'otherness' of one another and even of the right to be different from each other, when such differences are part of the exploration of the divine mystery and the divinely-willed unity."[150]

Here, as in several passages in the document, this sense or climate, in which one learns from the other and the search for common truth, is theologically qualified through statements on the work and guidance of *the Holy Spirit*. Hence, the implicit argument is that mutual accountability as a standard of ecumenical procedures and as a value inherent in the goal of ecumenism, is the result of the work of the Holy Spirit. Mutual accountability becomes a matter of theological methodology for qualifying expressions of the gospel in different contexts. To qualify as an expression corresponding to the will of the Spirit, a contribution must be justified through a legitimate testing procedure of mutual accountability.[151]

Mutual accountability becomes, therefore, a principle of a kind of collective *magisterium*, guided by the Spirit. These questions are closely related to the development of the idea of a common, *living* Christian tradition: "As an hermeneutical community, the Church is called to grow into full *koinonia* by Holy Spirit-guided discernment of the living Tradition."[152] The problem of "How do

---

150. Hermeneutics 1998:22f.

151. Hermeneutics 1998:26. This was also in the argument of Bonino for the legitimacy of the so-called contextual theology of Latin America. cf. above, pp. 244–51. Here this principle appears in an attempt to establish communication between traditional confessional theology and contextual theology.

152. Hermeneutics 1998:67; cf. also 24: "The churches of God as living communities,

you know for sure?" and potential triumphalism and suppression intrinsic in any claim of knowing the truth and will of the Holy Spirit is addressed by the recommendation of real mutuality and critical approach of reception. But it is not solved.[153]

"Mutual Accountability" as a Link between "Contextuality" and "Catholicity"

Bringing confessional diversity into the discussion of the contextuality of the gospel, the text strongly calls for respect and openness, humility, and "willingness to see one's own perspective as well as to listen actively to and communicate with one's own dialogue partner. This call entails an openness to *metanoia*."[154]

The proper attitude of mutual accountability is required to handle the gospel and culture problems as well as the confessional problems:

> Churches are called to grow in God's gift of catholicity by engaging one another in collegial and conciliar structures, by mutual accountability to the Gospel, and by prayer for the eschatological work of the Holy Spirit. As churches look forward to the future of eschatological promise, they also look back to the apostolic community assembled on the morning of Pentecost. This sense of catholicity across the ages, as well as among local Christian communities of diverse contexts in any given age, sustains hope for the full realization of common life in Christ.[155]

Mutual accountability is here used to bring one rather new concept of ecclesiology (but belonging to "the ecumenical tradition")—contextuality—together with a more classic attribute of the Church—catholicity. *Contextuality* is what ". . . appears whenever the gospel works like salt and leaven, not overwhelming a context, but permeating it and enlivening it in distinctive ways. When the church's faith is genuinely contextual, the shame and the stigma

---

constituted by faith in Jesus Christ and empowered by the Holy Spirit, must always re-receive the Gospel in ways that relate to their present experience of life. It is this process of re-reception that the minds of Christian communities are enlightened by the Holy Spirit to discern truth from falsehood and to acknowledge both the richness and the limited-ness of the diverse geographical, historical, religious and social circumstances in which the Gospel is made manifest. Ecumenical hermeneutics is not an unaided human enterprise. It is an ecclesial act led by the Spirit and therefore it should be carried out in a setting of prayer."

153. The relation between mutual accountability, the living Tradition, and the guidance of the Spirit will be discussed further in ch. 5.

154. Hermeneutics 1998:28.

155. Hermeneutics 1998:30f.

imposed on oppressed people begins to be lifted. They find a new dignity as they see not only their own lives but also their culture in God's redeeming light."[156]

This local dimension corresponds to a holistic dimension, *catholicity*, what is according to the whole. But how can we discern what in the local contextual theology belongs to the catholic church? Here the text is not particularly specific. It focuses basically on integration and inclusiveness as explications of catholicity. To achieve the fullness of catholicity, the different parts of the churches must be participating in the gifts of the others.

Nevertheless, the text does comment on this problem by describing the structure to handle this problem and the principles directing these structures. In this context "mutual accountability" can be a principle for dealing appropriately with the relation between contextuality and catholicity.

The report from the study of hermeneutics conveys several important perspectives for a theory of "mutual accountability." According to this rather unusual use of prepositions, there can be mutual accountability not only to a partner but also "*to* the gospel." This implies that that the gospel is, as the context shows, the given common Tradition, a common point of reference.

However, the gospel is also to be found through a "sense of catholicity" looking for it in the many communities in different contexts. To be accountable to the gospel is not only to look backwards, but also to the other contemporaries of the Church, and to look to the future. Consequently, to be accountable to the gospel cannot be separated from being mutually accountable in the catholic Church, understood in this wide sense.[157]

Mutual accountability belongs to the definition of the catholicity of the Church. The different (contextually defined) parts of the Church should be in correspondence to what is according to the whole, The Tradition. To achieve this, procedures characterized by mutual accountability are required. Consequently, no contextual or local interpretation can as such claim to be absolute. It can only be regarded as important and valid for the whole through a confirmation given in a relation of mutual accountability. Thus, diversity could be

---

156. Hermeneutics 1998:30. This is an affirmation of the report of a consultation on intercultural hermeneutics in Jerusalem in 1995, a preparation for the World Conference of Mission in 1998. It had substantial participation from people involved in this study of hermeneutics of Faith and Order. In the report, Jerusalem 1995, the terminology of "mutual accountability" conveys the same concern as we are dealing with here.

157. "Contextual interpretations can contribute to a fuller interpretation of the Gospel and can thereby speak to the Christian community as a whole. When an interpretation of the Gospel in a particular context points to injustice or to liberation, this interpretation is not simply a contextual claim. It may provide an insight to be tested and amended or applied in other contexts. Accordingly, catholicity binds all local communities together, thereby allowing them to contribute to one another's understandings and broaden their horizons" (Hermeneutics 1998:31).

exposed as a result of necessary attempts to discern what the gospel means in different contexts.[158] This pursuit of catholicity through mutual accountability aims at liberation from one-sidedness toward true solidarity, a sign of *koinonia*.

Therefore, the reflection on hermeneutics in ecumenical dialogues and intercultural hermeneutics ends in ecclesiology, the proper meaning of *koinonia* in regard to ethics. The perspective of "mutual accountability" seems to contribute to a dynamic where the different tracks of the ecumenical movement can be integrated.[159]

Structures of Mutual Accountability in the Hermeneutic Community

In its third chapter the report elaborates further the recommendation of structures of mutual accountability from the Santiago message. One section even carries the title "Authority, apostolicity and mutual accountability."[160] The ministry of oversight has a hermeneutical function. In the tedious and still-not-finished quest toward a common understanding of *episkopé*, the text conveys a description of its functions on which there is conceivable agreement.[161]

In spite of disagreement on the form and historicity of this ministry, the text deals with principles that are important for our theme: first, the principle of "co-responsibility" of all persons in the Church, whatsoever the type of ministry one might have. Second, it is presented as an element of ecumenical tradition that no ministry of oversight can be exercised without being transparent, responsible, and in cooperation with the constituency it should serve.[162] Both of these principles could have been described in terms of "accountability." Co-responsibility is particularly manifest in the *collegiality* of those sharing the ministry of oversight. It is a matter of interchurch relationship at any level.[163]

Conveying a wider perspective, the report reflects on all types of structures within the ecumenical movement that nurture the Church worldwide as a hermeneutic community. Common to all of them is that they are "characterized by mutual accountability," including the forms of *episkopé* and collegiality discussed immediately before. For our study, it is noteworthy that the manifold

158. Hermeneutics 1998:31f.

159. Hermeneutics 1998:31f.

160. Hermeneutics 1998:35–38.

161. Hermeneutics 1998:36. The "Hermeneutics" study and the "Ecclesiology" study have much in common at this point.

162. "As the case with all ministries, *episkopé* can only be exercised within and in relation to the whole Church. It needs, as all other ministries, the recognition, collaboration, support and assent of the whole community" (Hermeneutics 1998:35f.).

163. "Any church which is not prepared to listen to the voices of other churches runs the danger of misusing the truth of the Spirit as it operates in the other churches" (Hermeneutics 1998:36f.).

of ecumenical endeavours within the WCC is supposed to be seen as structures of mutual accountability. This confirms the impression found elsewhere, that mutual accountability becomes a criterion to evaluate the entire ecumenical movement and its branches.[164]

Reflecting on more binding, more accountable levels of co-responsibility than already practiced, the concepts of "authoritative teaching" and "common decision making" are launched under the overall perspective of "conciliarity." All achievements mentioned above are seen as preliminary structures, as "a patient preparation for coming together in a genuine ecumenical council able to restore full *koinonia* as God wills." A decisive further step would be mutual knowledge of the criteriological principles guiding one another's authoritative teaching as an important contribution to mutual understanding.[165] In other words, the text demands an extension of mutual accountability into the heart of each tradition and church.

The "hermeneutic community" is not only an ideal for interchurch issues. The report claims there is a remarkable difference between the growing agreements *between* the churches "[which] have improved the climate for mutual consultation, reception and accountability" and the complicated processes of reception *within* the churches.[166]

Summary

This post-Santiago study on hermeneutics confirms the impressions from other documents that "mutual accountability" has gone into the ecumenical legacy and language to describe crucial issues. Here it is used as an overall description of what has led to results in the ecumenical movement, "a climate of mutual accountability." The report uses the hermeneutic insight from Montreal 1963 to define The Tradition as a standard to which the churches are mutually accountable. The Tradition is found (not invented) through an encounter between the many traditions, practicing mutual accountability. Thus, mutual accountability becomes a definition of the "climate" in which the efforts of Faith and Order and related endeavours are realized. Implicitly, this reference to the "climate" unveils how failure to transform ecumenical results into concrete signs of unity contradicts this climate.

---

164. "The various areas of activity within the World Council of Churches provide a wide range of opportunities for common interpretation and praxis of the gospel message. Bilateral relationships concerned with theological dialogue, work for justice, peace and the integrity of creation and collaboration in mission, education and charitable works, offer similar opportunities" (Hermeneutics 1998:37).

165. Hermeneutics 1998:37f.

166. Hermeneutics 1998:39f. The text is here discussing particularly the reception process of the BEM document.

This report deals with the proper attitudes for an ecumenical hermeneutic. Ecumenical hermeneutics cannot be done properly apart from the proper hermeneutic community. The required attitudes can be described by the terminology of "mutual accountability" and its parallels. Without willingness to be open, to understand the other, to be self-critical, and to change in *metanoia*, there are no ways forward for the ecumenical hermeneutic, neither for the reception processes. In structures fostering these attitudes, mutual accountability can be realized and serve the progress of establishing *koinonia*.

The study shows that the questions of contextuality and catholicity are embedded in the problems of traditional ecumenical doctrinal dialogue as well as the problems of intercultural hermeneutics. To handle the question of diversity, contextuality is related to catholicity (understood as "according to the whole"). For discernment in these matters, exercise of mutual accountability is crucial. Consequently, the report defines mutual accountability as the way to allow the legitimate contextuality of the gospel to be realized in the universal Church. The perspective of mutual accountability, therefore, brings the hermeneutic problem of ecumenism and the classical ecclesiological attribute of catholicity together.

The study is interested not only in principles of hermeneutics per se, but elaborates the important correlation between hermeneutics of suspicion and the hermeneutics of coherence. Both are necessary for the ecumenical project. Both are realized through mutual accountability, being transparent and self-critical, and being mutually accountable to what is common for the churches. The report defines all structures where the openness, responsibility, and maturity of the ecumenical movement are exercised as "structures of mutual accountability." Particularly the collegiality of those serving the ministry of oversight and the different forms of conciliarity are characterized as mutual accountable structures.

The WCC can be such a structure, too. This is an important theme in the parallel process of identifying the identity and vision of the WCC, to which the Faith and Order board contributed substantially.

The Common Understanding and Vision of the World Council of Churches

Mutual Accountability in the "Ecumenical Charter for the 21st Century"

The Central Committee of the WCC published a policy statement on the common understanding and vision of the WCC in 1997. It was presented as nothing less than a document "that might serve as an 'ecumenical charter' for the 21st century." Summing up a comprehensive discussion since (at least) 1989, including responses from churches, ecumenical partners, and experts on the ecumenical movement, it was meant to be a document for the eighth assembly in Harare, on the occasion of the WCC's 50th anniversary. It should "articulate the nature and purpose of ecumenical fellowship within the WCC."[167]

The Faith and Order board delivered substantial contributions to the ecclesiologal reflections of the document at the request of the then general secretary of the WCC, Konrad Raiser.[168] He asked Faith and Order to explore the need for revision of the basis and functions of the WCC, the need to update the Toronto 1950 declaration, and the "ecclesial quality" of the WCC. The Faith and Order text answered the last question by referring to and defining "structures of mutual accountability." The *Common Understanding and Vision* (CUV) document uses the terminology "mutual accountability" several times. Hence, both documents deserve attention.

The Faith and Order paper discussed what kind of *koinonia* exists already in the fellowship among the WCC churches, and used the expression "being in council" to apply the qualities of *koinonia* to the WCC. This reference seems to have a deliberate ambiguity, being both descriptive (the churches are de facto members of the WCC) and borrowing ecclesiological significance from the concept of "conciliar fellowship" (which mostly has been defined as something more than membership in the ecumenical councils of the modern ecumenical movement[169]). To clarify the "ecclesial quality" of "being in council," the paper discusses in terms of mutual accountability:

> Being "in council" the churches experience *koinonia* together. The present experience of *koinonia* means a challenge to the churches of the ecumenical movement that they not only give a common account of their hope to the world in word an action, but also establish among themselves structures by which they are held mutually accountable. This would not affect the freedom of each church to maintain the integrity of its own tradition and positions.
>
> In the fellowship of the WCC, member churches are able to explore their relationships with on another and to recognize how they can help one another to fulfil their calling. Each member may freely and voluntarily commit itself to receive the critical evaluations and positive testimonies of other member churches. Such commitment will not, at this stage, limit the autonomy of any

---

167. CUV 1997:3.

168. This text (Towards CUV 1996; cf. the bibliography) was drafted by a small group of members of the Faith and Order board, discussed and revised under the board meeting in 1996, and transmitted to the general secretary of the WCC; cf. Minutes Bangkok 1996:21–23.

169. Cf. the discussions of the definitions of "conciliar fellowship" on pp. 128–56.

member church but it will move gradually towards the mutual accountability for which the Fifth World Conference of Faith and Order called.

Such a mutual accountability will include, for example, that a member church be ready to be challenged by other member churches concerning the consistency of their practice in relation to their declarations, but also in forming new policies the churches will consult each other about the implications of those policies.[170]

Mutual accountability is here defined in regard to two stages of the ecumenical process. The first is the present stage of the WCC with its degree of *koinonia*, where the churches only "freely and voluntarily" listen to the critical comments of other churches, not affecting their "autonomy," keeping their full freedom to not change anything. This first stage of "exploring" their relationship is here presumed to be the forum of maturing, where the ecumenical commitment of the churches will move gradually toward the second stage of mutual accountability.

The second stage is what Santiago recommended. The text seems to perceive the Santiago definition of mutual accountability as more binding, with a higher degree of *Verpflichtung* than the present situation within the WCC. The commitment should be really tested and challenged by the communion.

It is noticeable that this text defines the higher degree of mutual accountability in respect of two criteria. First, the "consistency" between declarations and practice, which could refer to the ecumenical declarations made or received; or it could mean the confessional documents and the like defined by churches individually. Second, the churches should be challenged when "forming new policies." The criterion for this critical approach is the "implications" of new policies. The text does not make explicit whether these implications are the consequences for interchurch relations or the consequences for anybody affected by any "new" church policy.

This shows some important features of how "mutual accountability" is used and defined in the Faith and Order work in the 1990s: the essential meaning of "mutual accountability" is the same, but the degree of accountability is different in the two stages. Hence, the attitude described conveys integrity in the ecumenical efforts to proceed in these stages or levels of ecumenical relations. The ecumenical attitude of mutual accountability is decisive for any effort to realize unity as conciliar fellowship.

This text plays on the terminological link between "give a common *account* of the hope to the world" and the need for "structures of mutual *account*ability" (italics mine). There seems, however, to be more than a matter of terminological association. The task of giving account to others thus characterizes

---

170. Towards CUV 1996:79.

what it means to participate in the *koinonia* of the Church. The link between making common accounts of hope and being mutually accountable within the ecumenical fellowship explored in the analysis of the "Giving Account" study is confirmed. The link between this mutual accountability and accountability for the apostolic tradition of Christ is not reflected explicitly, as it was, for instance, in BEM and in the "Apostolic Faith" study. It is to some degree implicit here; the *koinonia* of the WCC is "a common participation in the reality of the triune God."[171]

Finally, a footnote says that "any agenda concerning mutual accountability" presupposes mutual recognition of baptism. Thereby the text anchors mutual accountability as a theologically significant attitude, more than a matter of polite and proper procedure in an international fellowship. Mutual accountability becomes then the ecumenical attitude corresponding to the communion of the baptized.[172]

The CUV text of 1997 was intended to be a status report of the most prominent institution of the ecumenical movement and its central ideas for the time being. Therefore, it is remarkable how the Central Committee, in the preface of CUV, uses the concept of "mutual accountability" to give a description of how to deal with the existing disagreement on the goal of the ecumenical movement, and the nature of fellowship already existing. The CUV text continues the reflections of Faith and Order (discussed above): "It is of the essence of the churches' fellowship within the ecumenical movement that they continue to wrestle with these differences in a spirit of mutual understanding, commitment and accountability."[173]

According to this passage, not only the common *basis* for the WCC, but also the *way* the churches proceed in their efforts toward unity belongs to the "essence" of the ecumenical movement. This "mode" of ecumenism is described as *attitudes*. Talk about the "spirit of . . ." supports this interpretation (attitudes) of what the churches should have as they pursue their "wrestling." The three characteristics (understanding, commitment, and accountability) are probably best understood as parallel expressions and, therefore, supplementary attitudes. Thus, mutual accountability is flavored by the notion of ability to understand as well as to make oneself understood through transparent information. These are attitudes corresponding to or supplementing the attitude of commitment to remain in communion to pursue the common goals. Adding

---

171. Towards CUV 1996:73; cf. the analysis of the "Giving Account" study, pp. 133–32 and 133–34.

172. Here the text corresponds to the explication of the ecclesiology of baptism in BEM; cf. pp. 172-81.

173. CUV 1997:4.

"accountability" here seems to emphasize the aspects of faithfulness, reliability, and willingness to be challenged in these efforts.

The text reflects further on the contemporary global crisis in which the fellowship of churches exists. One of the noteworthy differences between the political institutions and the "church" is described through the aspect of mutual accountability. Although rather generalized, the formulation is significant. The politicians are losing the confidence of citizens because "their decision-making role is increasingly subordinated to the demands of global business empires whose accountability is measured only in terms of the profits they earn." On the contrary, the churches should be concerned about the accountability to other churches, and to those who need the churches. The churches should ask themselves self-critically whether they are committed to a common vision and mission and not only occupied with "internal and institutional concerns."[174]

In spite of the problems of an increasing gap between rich and poor, the ecological crisis, and the new divisions among Christians, the 50 years of the Council have seen growing participation in the ecumenical fellowship. The declaration from Toronto 1950 in respect to what the WCC should be remains valid in terms of the need for ecumenical accountability: "The churches are . . . willing to consult together to learn of the Lord Jesus Christ what witness he would have them to bear to the world in his name, . . . should recognize their solidarity with each other, render assistance to each other. . . . [and] seek to learn from each other to give help to each other in order that the body of Christ may be built so that that the life of the churches may be renewed."[175]

The CUV document raises the same issues as *Costly Unity*[176] about the internal fragmentation of the ecumenical movement, without taking over all of the arguments from *Costly Unity*. CUV mentions the "eucharistic vision" as a calling to combine the striving for visible unity and the social dimension of ecumenism. The language of "costly" has been integrated in the ecumenical language, too (see quotation below). The solution is not to come to any final definition of "ecumenical," but to take seriously the roots of *koinonia* in the triune God, and to affirm the commitments to unity.

The *catholicity* of the Church is understood as "the essential relatedness of churches and Christian communities locally, nationally, regionally and globally." Thus, the task of the churches is to take seriously the threat from "the growing fragmentation of societies and exclusion for more and more of the human family" in the new kind of global unity. The "integrity of the ecumenical

---

174. CUV 1997:6f.

175. CUV 1997:8. It is noteworthy how the image of the Church as the body of Christ is used in this kind of reflections on the interdependence between churches, since the first years of the WCC.

176. Cf. pp. 251–58.

movement" is based on an alternative to the power of globalization that causes "fragmentation of societies and exclusion for more and more of the human family": ". . . a distinctly different model of relationships, based on solidarity and sharing, mutual accountability and empowerment."[177]

Thereby the CUV report brings the concept of "mutual accountability" into the heart of the problem of ethics and ecclesiology, as *Costly Unity* and the Santiago reports did the ecclesiological alternative to globalization, that is, the standard of ecumenism. Here it is materialized in the concrete forms of ecumenical collaboration. The particular "thickness" of the ecumenical fellowship—in contrast to the secular globalization of profit—should be apparent in mutual accountability and sharing.[178]

It is also noticeable how this is linked to a certain understanding of *catholicity* as "the essential *relatedness* of churches." Hence, mutual accountability is

---

177. CUV 1997:11f.

178. The references to solidarity, sharing, and empowerment in this context could be interpreted as an elaboration of the report from the consultation in El Escorial, Spain, in 1987, *Sharing Life*. The sharing of resources through the comprehensive networks of church agencies for aid was explored throughout this conference. The reports from the working groups and the message from the consultation describe the challenges revealed in terms of developing "mutual accountability." This conference dealt with giving accounts in the original, literal meaning: giving accounts of what the *economical and material resources* are used for. By emphasizing the *mutual* aspect of the accountability in the interchurch fellowship, the usual direction of the demands and offers of accounts was challenged. The giver as well as the receiver should give account of their dispositions. This presupposed an understanding of the resources of the worldwide Church somehow as a common property for which all stewards are accountable. The literal meaning of "accountability" oscillated between the concrete meaning of being held accountable for the use of money, and—on the other hand—the attitude of being mutually account-*able*. The El Escorial report also brings a theological reflection of mutual accountability as a realization of *koinonia*, corresponding to the later explications of *Costly Unity* and the texts from and after the Santiago conference. Particularly interesting is the relation between actual and general aspects of mutual accountability described in the El Escorial text, and the emphasis on the intrinsic connection between being accountable to one another, to God, and to those in particular need of accountable churches: the poor. "Accountability cannot only be reduced to responsible stewardship of the use of resources but demand mutual openness to questions about priorities, use of power, relationships and theological convictions. This spiritual responsibility for one another is also pertinent within local groups and agencies. We are accountable to one another, to the poor and ultimately to God. Maybe the most important question we must ask each other again and again is whether our deepest commitment is to those whom Jesus called the least of his people" (Sharing Life 1997:45). Cf. also the entire chapter, exploring "A Common Discipline of Ecumenical Sharing" in respect to mutuality and accountability (ibid., 36–58). Although the consultation in El Escorial did not solve the problem of imbalance in respect to material resources in the worldwide Church, the consultation obviously raised the awareness within the WCC of the bad effects of the differences, and the theologically important and comprehensive dimensions of "sharing." Some of the same perspectives on "mutual accountability" are elaborated in a consultation convoked by the Lutheran World Federation; cf. Brodd 1994.

Toward a Definition of Mutual Accountability?

When the policy statement attempts to clarify the extent of the fellowship experienced in the WCC, as well as the ecclesiological significance of *koinonia*, six affirmations are made. The churches are related to one another thanks to actions of God in Jesus Christ. The sense of the WCC is the relationship between the churches, not the structure of the WCC. The fellowship is not an end in itself, but a missionary, diaconal, and moral community of churches; the churches are committed to dialogue about the nature of their fellowship and to let it grow. The churches are treated as equally valued participants in the life of the WCC, for what they bring to the fellowship as being in Christ, not for their size or completeness in mutual recognition. On this basis, it is interesting to see how the sixth affirmation concludes and concretizes the other affirmations:

> By their mutual engagement in the Council the churches open themselves to be challenged by one another to deeper, more costly ecumenical commitment. This *mutual accountability* takes many forms; recognizing their solidarity with each other, assisting each other in cases of need, refraining from actions incompatible with brotherly and sisterly relations, entering into spiritual relationships to learn from each other, consulting with each other "to learn of the Lord Jesus Christ what witness he would have them to bear to the world in his name" (Toronto).[179]

This is one of the most comprehensive attempts in the texts analyzed so far to define what mutual accountability is. The lack of explicit definitions in other texts can be interpreted as a presumption that the meaning of "mutual accountability" is so obvious and well known—at least among drafters of ecumenical documents that it does not need any explanation. The fact that it is somewhat elaborated here probably shows the weight of the concept in the argument of the text. It also indicates that this theme at this stage has become more of an object of mature reflection.

The definition includes elements identified in texts already analyzed. To be in the state of mutual accountability is to be aware of the needs of each other and have the readiness to care about them. This implies, of course, mutual information. It also means being constantly aware of being related, in a way that guides what is done or not done, rejecting what is "incompatible with

---

179. CUV 1997:15.

brotherly and sisterly relations." This is to understand mutual accountability as an attitude, demonstrated through actions.

This statement places on the same level, through the aspect of "mutual accountability," the ethical demand of dealing with material needs, the spiritual relationships, and the hermeneutic task to explicate the common faith to be witnessed in the world. It thereby makes mutual accountability an ecclesiological principle of sharing of material resources as well as of theological hermeneutics. This combination of ethics, ecclesiology, and hermeneutics is remarkable. It designates the fellowship of churches as an *accountable hermeneutic community*, in which the common gospel cannot be understood without learning from one another.

These aspects of mutual accountability are elaborated as the text describes what is implied in membership in the body of the WCC: to deal with disagreements on the basis of being related to each other in life, prayer, and dialogue; to help each other "to be faithful to the gospel, questioning one another if any member is perceived to move away from the fundamentals of the faith or obedience to the gospel." Further, it is participation in ministries beyond the single church; to implement the agreements reached (reception); participation in solidarity and sharing; understanding mission as a joint responsibility, avoiding proselytism and competition; a shared worship; and a sharing of financial resources.[180] A rather demanding list, one could say. All these are implications of mutual accountability.

It is important to notice that mutual accountability is more than being reliable to a negotiated contract. It is based upon the given reality of the communion in Christ. Another remarkable aspect here is the description of what might be called a mutual and reciprocal service of oversight, episcopacy, that takes the content of episcopacy into a (pre-)conciliar structure, as a matter of being faithful to the gospel. This is the heart of the argument why mutual accountability is needed: the gospel, the *koinonia* in the triune God, needs appropriate moral standards and appropriate structures. The triangle of faith, order, and relation dominates this attempt to define the ecclesial significance of the WCC.

Summary

The concept of "mutual accountability" has obviously played a significant role in the preparation of this document. The attempts to understand the core of the ecumenical movement in this perspective are remarkable. The directions set already in the report of Bonino in 1987, in the study of ecclesiology and ethics, and in the Santiago reports have been confirmed and pursued.

---

180. CUV 1997:15f.

The new element that has come in at this stage is the context in which it is promoted here. First, it is the alternative to the economical and political globalization of the world, with its implications of marginalization of those not competitive. Second, in a more specific context, it is described as the dynamic to develop the ecclesial character of the WCC. This is the way to be more and more a full conciliar fellowship, full *koinonia*, in full visible unity.

Mutual accountability is the dynamic attitude through which the standards of the full *koinonia* can be realized already in an imperfect *koinonia*. Hence, it is (as intended before, but made clearer here) an attitude that applies both to the present stage of fellowship in the WCC and to the goal of the ecumenical movement itself. This implies that the goal of *koinonia* is also a situation of diversity, in which we can learn and benefit from our diversity, if the churches can be mutually sharing, living in solidarity, and committed to learn from critical encounters with one another.

The definition of mutual accountability as ecumenical attitude explored here deserves attention by those who want to understand the concerns of the WCC today. The description of this attitude is significant for any explication of ecumenical ecclesiology, as it is increasingly given the status of a principle of ecumenical ecclesiology, focusing the reciprocal moral responsibility intrinsic to the participation of interchurch fellowship. The status of this concept is illustrated in a proposal for a liturgical celebration and recommitment to the task of the WCC:

> *Receiving the legacy of those who have gone before us:*
> *[. . .]*
> *We are drawn by the vision of a church*
> *which will express its unity by confessing the apostolic faith,*
> *living in conciliar fellowship,*
> *acting together in mutual accountability.*[181]

Excursus: Two Contributions to a Definition of Mutual Accountability

The June 1998 issue of the *Ecumenical Review* was published under the title "Towards a Common Understanding and Vision of the WCC." In this volume, one article, written by the Romanian Orthodox theologian Nikolas Apostola, deals entirely with the meaning of mutual accountability. An article by the

---

181. "Our Ecumenical Vision," presented by Marlin Van Elderen in an editorial in *Ecumenical Review* 50, no. 3 (July 1998): 266f.

moderator of Faith and Order, Mary Tanner, analyzes the CUV document, discussing explicitly what "mutual accountability" means in the CUV text.[182]

The latter first: Tanner says the issue of mutual accountability is a more difficult question than the other commitments the CUV text recommends. Her attempt to elaborate what it means deserves quotation:

> It is fashionable to talk of mutual accountability. But what sort of accountability does each church owe its partners within the fellowship of the churches of the WCC? Mutual accountability means listening to others, attempting to understand their point of view, recognizing the integrity of those who hold different opinions, even practicing restraint on a matter as the fellowship discerns the mind of Christ for the church today. Mutual accountability means being prepared to issue reports and statements where each member can find its view within the common statement in a way which does not lead to "minority statements" set over against the common mind. It is a sign of mature accountability when this is achieved as a mark of fellowship. This is not a cry for "anything goes": but for recognition of the integrity of those who, in an ongoing process of discernment, do sometimes hold diametrically opposed views. The fellowship of the World Council provides an "ecumenical space" for discernment regarding issues which are hard matters within the churches as well as between churches. This has been from the beginning a special concern for the Orthodox churches. . . .
>
> It is not only the Orthodox who find themselves in this position. Anglican delegates to the Canberra assembly identified with this due to the way the assembly handled the debate and statement of the Gulf war.
>
> The implications of mutual accountability must be addressed if the churches are to stay together in fellowship and face together contemporary dilemmas of faith and moral life. Accountability is a more credible notion for those who are convinced that they share a common purpose and a common goal. The churches will need to accept the costliness of mutual accountability in the years to come. Without this, expressions of our intention to "stay together" will be empty words and some may even leave the fellowship.[183]

This explication of mutual accountability to a large degree confirms what we have found in other documents. Tanner maintains a critical distance from the "fashionable talk of mutual accountability." Nevertheless, she affirms how appropriate this terminology and thinking is for ecumenical ecclesiology. Her premise is that mutual accountability means what she emphasizes as particularly important: the *mature accountability* that restrains from pushing partners

182. Cf. Apostola 1998, and Tanner 1998.
183. Tanner 1998:362f.

into conclusions prematurely or into separating minority statements. Hence, Tanner defines mutual accountability as an ecumenical attitude in a process of *consensus finding*, showing openness, aiming at mutual understanding in patient listening particularly to the minority. That means to reach the level of commitment to the task of unity where the accountability to the other makes it possible to deal with difficult "hard matters," not only matters on the fringe and of less importance for unity. She has the situation of the Orthodox churches in mind (in solidarity with them she mentions the Anglican churches, too) when she calls for this respect for the minorities that are not getting their positions easily into a majority position in the WCC.

Her argument is clearly based on the goal of unity that presupposes a high degree of consensus: "Accountability is a more credible notion for those who are convinced that they share a common purpose and a common goal." This corresponds to what we could call the most demanding definition of "conciliar fellowship." The alternative to this understanding of mutual accountability seems to be the commitment to openness to diversity combined with faithfulness to stay together, accepting diversity, and minority statements of disagreements. Mutual accountability for her is a commitment to strive toward consensus, the moral standard of openness, and the endurance required to avoid the result that some feel they must leave the fellowship. Obviously, it is the threats of and the executed withdrawal of some of the Orthodox from the WCC she has in mind.

Although Tanner defines mutual accountability to a large extent along the lines we find elsewhere, she differs at one important point. She apparently disagrees with definitions of mutual accountability as a way to live together in open, mutual critique, sometimes even in tensions. She certainly does not ignore diversity, but she focuses on the case of those partners that do not want the diversity to be an excuse for changes or mutual radical criticism in traditional churches. Her contribution can be seen as a promotion of maturity as a matter of conservatism and stability in the ecumenical fellowship, urging "younger" partners to be more patient and pay more reverence to "older" positions. Her definition of mutual accountability can, therefore, be interpreted as a defense against new critical approaches to the older, most tradition-oriented churches in the ecumenical movement. This can explain the urgency of establishing a sharp definition of mutual accountability that takes her concerns into account. This is indeed a sign that mutual accountability has become such an integrated and generally accepted principle of ecumenical ecclesiology that it is important to control the definition of it.

The same impression of a struggle to establish a proper meaning of mutual accountability is noticeable in Apostola's article. His principal position is that mutual accountability lies at the heart of Christian revelation. Mutual accountability is the interdependence of all human beings with one another. From a deeper theological perspective one could draw on the concept of *periochoresis* (mutual indwelling) of the persons of the Holy Trinity as a way of understanding the true nature of the Church and, ultimately, human society itself. He is even ready to use to describe the relations between human beings and God through the perspective of mutual accountability. The risk in ". . . creating us in his image was to allow himself to be held accountable for our wellbeing." Incarnation and sacrifice of God's Son were the ultimate consequences of this.[184] Further, mutual accountability can describe the open relationship of love with all human beings, highlighting the "mutuality" of existence so important to Orthodox theology. The Church is not separated from the world in this sense. "There is no communion, no society, no church without mutuality." Hence, the relations of accountability are legion.

From the Orthodox perspective, the difficulty in recommendations of mutual accountability comes when it is viewed, not as an aspect of the relations between persons that bind them to God and to one another in a community of love, but as a philosophy of coexistence involving negotiations among autonomous individuals, a kind of social contract.[185] The proper understanding of unity could, according to him, be threatened by a wrong definition of mutual accountability, if it is a principle of negotiated acceptable diversity. He certainly does not deny the legitimacy of reconciled diversity. But if this means that the goal of full unity in consensus in faith is only an eschatological hope, it is a failure.[186]

Apostola appreciates the CUV document as it describes the *koinonia* of the Church as a dynamic, relational reality; "preserved through the exercise of responsibility for one another in the spirit of common faithfulness to the gospel, rather than by judgment and exclusion." He is principally against what he regards as a juridical connotation of "accountability," as if it was the sense of "mutual accountability that the churches will be holding each other accountable for [in] their actions." This sounds immediately like a contradiction in terms when compared to his elaboration of mutual accountability as a basic structure for all human life, also between churches:

> Accountability involves a response to God's love. . . . Accountability is our obligation to grow into the image of God. One of the consequences of this growth is an openness not only to God, but also to other people and to the whole of the creation. The more aware we are of God's love for us and the

---

184. Apostola 1998:302.
185. Apostola 1998:301.
186. Apostola 1998:302.

more we respond to it, the more responsibility we feel towards other people and towards the whole of creation. We become more sensitive to our own actions and the effects those actions have on others.[187]

The reason for his critical approach to mutual accountability as holding one another accountable for their actions seems to be that he fears a tendency to establish a *basis* for unity that is not really "a common faithfulness to the gospel." He sees a danger that the *partners* to whom the churches are made accountable are not real churches sharing the mutual love in the one Church, but groups that have a basis for their potential "judgment" other than "faith commitment."[188] Thus, one problem of the WCC is not that all human beings are accountable to one another, but that, for example, the Orthodox churches are made accountable by groups within other churches that add social and political issues to the agenda of church unity.[189] Another problem is that the divisions and diversity are handled through democratic negations in a Western pattern.

His remarks raise questions of great importance for the definition of mutual accountability as an issue of ecumenical ecclesiology. First, how important is it to have a common basis of consensus before the principle of accountability is applied to ecclesiology? He is rather clear on this point: "The unity of the church, the only reason why we can hold each other accountable, is founded on a faith commitment." The horizon of mutual accountability as a matter of ecclesial unity must be faced. For me, it seems to beg the question to limit "the social and the political" merely to influence from extra-ecclesial groups.

The mutually accountable relation cannot a priori limit what kind of critical questions can be raised in terms of evaluating what the churches say and do. Rather, the really critical prophetic voices appear from unexpected angles. The churches should ask critically: To whom are the partners in the WCC accountable? Are they accountable to the groups of human beings that are the center of attention in the current debates of the WCC (like women, homosexuals, and others)? His main concern is that mutual accountability primarily must be pursued as the relationship given by being members of the Church as brothers and sisters in Christ, sharing the fellowship with the Holy Trinity. He seems

187. Apostola 1998:302f.

188. "Accountability to considerations that have only the most tenuous foundations in the gospel will not build up the church, but undermine and eventually destroy all attempts at uniting the divided." "The tendency immediately to identify social movements, quasi-Christian organizations or any attempt at spirituality with the church and the Christian faith is a serious misunderstanding of the progression of our growth towards our high calling, towards the salvation that God desires for all people" (Apostola 1998:304–306).

189. Apostola 1998:302. He does not exemplify what kind of issues these groups are promoting besides this wage references to "the social and the political."

to be afraid of too strong a focus on particular groups and their experiences.[190] He thereby limits the possibility for groups of human beings to be partners in mutuality within the Church, challenging and criticizing other parts of the Church.

Thus, we see here two attempts to establish definitions of mutual accountability. Both convey descriptions of mutual accountability as an attitude of openness—even love —to the other, reliability and faithfulness to the communion and what the churches have in common. Through their arguments, both Tanner and Apostola present indirectly other definitions they do not accept. However, those alternatives are not clearly articulated. Tanner argues for recognition of the integrity of those who cannot agree. In this sense her definition of mutual accountability embraces openness to divergence and diversity. But her definition of accountability as the relation between those who share views on purpose and goal can be interpreted as a call to reduce the relative openness in the Santiago message in respect to what kind of structure of mutual accountability is required. She warns against mutual accountability as a standard of communion not clearly aiming at conciliar consensus, not able to wait for the processes to mature long enough to get all churches on board. Thus, her argument leads toward a definition of mutual accountability as an attitude of being faithful to consensus.

Apostola argues that mutual accountability is an explication of the proper attitudes intrinsic to the relations in the Church. His critique against those who call for accountability from unidentified "groups" can be interpreted as an attempt to define the concerns of those groups as not belonging to the agenda of the Church, even though there are churches conveying these concerns in the ecumenical communion. His emphasis on genuine Church criteria for the process of mutual accountability is obviously important for the unity of the Church. Nevertheless, it seems that he wants to reduce the challenges to the churches articulated, for instance, in the WCC. Thus, the consequence of his argument is an attack on the right of the other part to make critical assessments; and the criteria of critique should be defined by the part receiving critique. It is difficult to see how this could be a sufficient definition of mutual accountability as ecumenical attitude, reducing the accountability to what one partner finds relevant to be accountable for.

---

190. Apostola 1998:305f.

Summary: Mutual Accountability as Required Attitude toward Unity as *Koinonia*

In the last decade of the period analyzed in this study some important features of the ecumenical movement illuminate *koinonia* as the key to unity and the corresponding recommendation of *mutual accountability*, particularly *structures* of mutual accountability. The conciliar fellowship as model of unity defined in Nairobi 1975 was not explicitly the theme of studies in the 1980s. The definition of "conciliar fellowship/council/conciliarity" stopped in a blind alley at the end of the 1970s.[191] The presuppositions of a conciliar fellowship, however, in terms of consensus (or at least convergence) in respect to apostolic faith, sacraments, and ministry became the great issues and efforts of Faith and Order in the period after Bangalore until the end of 1980s.[192]

Some of the texts from that period (the end of the 1980s and the beginning of the 1990s) indicate several difficulties and challenges dominating the Faith and Order (and the WCC) agenda: the lack of coherence between Life and Work (or JPIC) and Faith and Order; the inability to realize the concept of conciliar fellowship (e.g., Seoul 1990); the decline of optimistic expectation about achieving conciliar, visible unity, nurtured by the BEM text and the BEM reception, as well as the "Apostolic Faith" study; an apparent "waning commitment" to the unity of the Church; and a growing awareness of the relevance of the challenges from contextual theology, consequently leading to a wider but unavoidable diversity.

There was also a reduced focus on the more or less clear models of unity. However, the way forward required stronger commitment to the ecumenical calling and more efficient reception and recognition. The alternative seems to have been then to launch substantial, but more flexible, principles for the ecumenical ecclesiology.

It is in this setting that the theological definition of unity as *koinonia* should be understood. It focuses on the theologically defined *quality of relations* in the Church, leaving the type of structures open. The *koinonia* of the Church must, however, have a form; the perspective of "order" was not neglected, as we see in the recommendation of the message of the Santiago World Conference in 1993, concluding the analysis of the ecumenical situation and the challenges ahead: "Unity today calls for structures of mutual accountability."

That recommendation had already been launched through studies of how to *integrate* the concern for common witness and service in the world (JPIC) and visible unity. A coherent, vital theology and a costly unity required certain qualities in terms of attitudes. One important intention behind several of the

---

191. Cf. the summary on pp. 106–109.
192. Cf. pp. 156–85 and 186–227.

texts analyzed above has been to integrate the work of Faith and Order and Life and Work, to some extent also the concern for mission. In Santiago the criterion of mutual accountability was applied to any structure of visible unity.

Compared to the most dominating projects of the decade before, the Faith and Order work in the 1990s did not focus much on specific ecumenical knots to be untied or on manifestations of consensus in classical issues of Faith or Order. The work was more involved in taking stock of the ecumenical movement, and laying general premises for the way forward in terms of ecclesiology and hermeneutics. To some extent the question guiding the work is how to establish a common life together while remaining different for historical, contextual, and even theological reasons. When the texts from this period come to potential solutions of problems discussed, in several cases the suggestion (or recommendation) is to strengthen the relations and renew the commitment, to implement *koinonia* as gift and calling, or to mobilize more mutual accountability. This seems to have been a phase when the specific attempts to loosen ecumenical knots were laid aside or handed over to the bilateral dialogues.

Thus, I interpret the focus on *koinonia* and mutual accountability in this period as a sign that Faith and Order emphasized the need to explicate the perspectives of "relation" more than the classical themes of "faith" and "order." The importance of those perspectives for the progress in issues of faith is explored (cf. the study of hermeneutics and several passages in the Santiago reports). The new and more open definitions of the structures of unity in the Church, emphasizing the attitude (mutual accountability) as quality of these structures, is striking. There are some reflections on the form of these structures of mutual accountability, discussing conciliar forms of relations (e.g., "being in council" in the Faith and Order input to the CUV process) and some attempts to explore the personal, collegial, and communal dimensions of common episcopacy as a matter of exercising mutual accountability (cf. the "Ecclesiology" study).

Mutual accountability is described as the *climate* (cf. the "Hermeneutics" study) in which the present stage of the ecumenical movement has achieved its goals. It is a criterion for defining the relations of *koinonia*, the goal of all these efforts. Hence, "mutual accountability" is a standard according to which ecumenical relations should be established and nurtured, at any stage of the process. There are, however, some signals that it becomes important to own the definition of mutual accountability. One important question implied here would be whether the quest for mutual accountability is a way toward living with more diversity, or whether mutual accountability is a standard of relations within a community of consensus, avoiding minority positions (Tanner). Another critical remark is articulated in respect to who should be recognized as partners in the mutually accountable relation, thereby who should have the right to set the criteria for accountability (Apostola).

To a large degree "mutual accountability" is used as an indicator of what has been achieved in terms of a *common ecumenical tradition:* first, mutual accountability presupposes a common understanding that we belong to each other in spite of differences and, therefore, belong to the same Church of Jesus Christ. It is a central aspect of the mutual *recognition* of *koinonia*. It is claimed that a real, but not full communion between churches has been shared in various gifts, differences, in strength or weakness. This exercise of mutual accountability has been proven to be beneficial for the ecumenical process. Second, there has been a growing agreement of accepting a legitimate diversity when it corresponds to the different confessional and historical traditions for the churches, as well as the legitimate cultural diversity among them. This diversity must be cared for and nurtured through a mutual giving of account and a mutual challenging of one-sidedness and prejudices. Third, there has grown a common understanding of being accountable for the situation of the other, particularly the nonprivileged and marginalized ("the option for the poor").

The explicit recommendations of mutual accountability in this period (until 1998), interpreted in their context, to a large extent follow the patterns from the preliminary definition I have been working with throughout the study. The analysis of the passages and contexts in which this terminology is used contributes to *a sharpened picture of this ecumenical attitude*. The attitudes required in the concept of "mutual accountability" can be summed up as follows:

- Reliability in an atmosphere created by and creating mutual trust and confidence.

- Faithfulness to the already real *koinonia* in faith, life, and witness, as it has been unveiled and elaborated through the ecumenical movement as gift and calling.

- Openness and willingness to be transparent, being accountable for the tradition, the priorities, and the goals one has as church, community, or individual.

- Willingness to be accountable to the other also in the sense of taking seriously what they have to bring forward; to care for their concerns and their needs.

- Willingness to regard what one has as something that belongs to the whole catholic Church, whether it is spiritual gifts, theological insight, or material resources.

- Readiness to seek coherence in faithfulness to the common sources of the Church, to be accountable to the Tradition as the apostolic faith and life, particular as it is given to us through Scripture.

- Readiness to be self-critical, and willingness to live in *metanoia* and to share the costliness of unity. This implies the willingness to learn from the other in dialogue, not only to present one's own concerns and points of view.

The concept of "mutual accountability" is related to some *basic theological convictions*, which are presented more or less as common ecumenical tradition:

- The unity of the church is rooted in the *koinonia* of the Trinity. This basic relation makes the churches mutually accountable even before they are concerned about their divisions. In other words, "mutual accountability" presupposes a common understanding of a given unity, belonging to the same body of Christ.

- Belonging to the same body of Christ, the acknowledgment of the diversity through exercise of mutual accountability is absolutely necessary.

- The diversity that we are given access to through a *koinonia* practicing mutual accountability should be celebrated as given by the Holy Spirit. This implies a certain understanding of the church as a hermeneutic community, challenging the different traditions of hierarchical magisterium or individualism.

- It is an underlying premise here that mutual accountability in the *koinonia* with one another is at the same time accountability to the gospel or to God.

- Mutual accountability is a way to understand what the *catholicity* of the Church means when the contextuality of the churches is taken seriously into account.

Note that the *meaning* of the phrase "mutual accountability" is mostly taken for granted. It seems sometimes to be a slip of the tongue or a slogan. On the other hand, this indicates how much it corresponds to a general assessment of the situation and the goal of the ecumenical movement. It conveys aspects nobody really contests as far as they are held in a general sense. When applied more directly to handling ecumenical problems, it becomes more important for some (Tanner, Apostola) to avoid a principle of diversity that doesn't lead to consensus or a too-open list of which issues can be raised in mutual accountability.

Mutual accountability points to one aspect of the ecumenical *koinonia* that the traditional models of unity have not focused on that much: belonging to the *koinonia* of the Church implies a *moral* dimension in the sense of demanding certain *attitudes* between those belonging to this *koinonia*. Without these attitudes, there is no possibility for communion. The repeated recommendations of mutual accountability are requirements of certain attitudes necessary at any stage and in any form of the ecumenical endeavour. A convergence in faith requires, besides clear common structures, a supplement of certain qualities of relations in terms of mutual accountability.

Hence, according to the work of Faith and Order in the 1990s, "relation" supplements the issues of "faith" and "order" as standards of unity of the Church. On the other hand, in my evaluation of the results of the work of Faith and Order in this period, the shift of focus toward "relation" cannot replace the work on specific ecumenical problems. The mutual accountability of *koinonia* must be related to specific issues for which the churches should be mutually accountable, realized in concrete structures materializing that attitude. Probably, the challenge of Faith and Order for the coming years is to make the insights of the focus on "relation" operative in the efforts to handle concrete ecumenical problems. That could mean that the concerns of Faith and Order must be implemented more in dialogues between churches directly, not just at the multilateral level.

CHAPTER 5

A Systematic-Theological Evaluation

A Brief Evaluation of the Outcome of the Analysis

Without repeating the summaries and reflections done of proceeding chapters, I will briefly sum up the findings of this study. I regard the outcome of the analysis to be sufficient to affirm my thesis:

The attitude of mutual accountability is vital to improve and maintain the quality of interchurch relations. It is explicitly and implicitly recommended in Faith and Order texts (and Faith and Order-related WCC texts) from the period from 1948 to 1998. The quality of "relation" is a supplementary perspective to the dimensions of "faith" and "order" in the quest for the unity of the Church. There are significant theological reasons why "mutual accountability" should be an important element in ecumenical ecclesiology.

I am aware of the limitations of the material and the perspectives of this study. It has had a limited scope, searching for implicit and explicit expressions of ecumenical attitudes, particularly those attitudes I have found relevant to subsume under a definition of mutual accountability. That means, of course, that I have been focusing on one particular dimension in the texts and that I have not tried to give a complete, or even a well-balanced, picture of contributions to ecumenical ecclesiology from Faith and Order during this period. Nevertheless, I have perceived a striking coherence between, on the one hand, the major concern in several texts, and, on the other hand, the recommendations of mutual accountability—even attempts to establish mutual accountability between the churches—whether the phrase "mutual accountability" is used or not. Further, it should be admitted that mutual accountability or ecumenical attitudes have not been explicitly defined as a major theme of this study or pursued as a model of unity in the work of Faith and Order, but the recommendations of mutual accountability are implicit in all of these projects.

The theme chosen for this study could have been pursued under other perspectives and with other tools than those I have used.[1] This study is pursued under the conviction that it is sufficiently interesting in this context to explore how the Faith and Order texts argued for the importance of quality of relations and for the role of attitudes, and to explore how these texts have contributed to a theological definition of mutual accountability. The Faith and Order material is the most widely representative contribution to the theological reflections on Church unity from this period of the ecumenical movement in which mutual accountability definitely is directly required. The primary scope of the Faith

---

1. Hence, I have not explored the role of mutual accountability in texts from other ecumenical organizations or from bilateral dialogues. It could also have been of interest to analyze the significance of mutual accountability in the work of other units of the WCC dealing, for instance, with mission and interchurch aid. There are several examples that this terminology is used in such documents; see, e.g., Tveit 1994. Probably, the concern for proper ecumenical attitudes also could be traced in several ecumenical texts. Furthermore, the concept of mutual accountability and the focus on the quality of relation in these Faith and Order texts could have been discussed in the light of theories of dialogue, the free discourse in democracy. Mutual accountability can be seen as a rule of proper conversation or discussed as an expression of the respect for and the need of the perspective of The (unprivileged) Other. Theories on modernity and postmodernity could have illuminated the concept of mutual accountability, too. There are striking similarities between the presentation of responsibility, postmodernity, and theological dialogue in Henriksen 1999:143f., 206–215, and, on the other hand, some of the texts from the 1990s recommending mutual accountability. According to my argument for the importance of "relation," it could be relevant to study ecumenical processes in a sociological or psychological perspective. To expand the study of mutual accountabilty as ecumenical attitude after this study of Faith and Order texts, the theme of mutual accountability could be tested on specific ecumenical problems. It would also be of interest to discuss the understanding of dialogue, cooperation, accountability, and communion in these Faith and Order texts in the light of theories of such themes. Because of the decisions and limitations I have given account of in chapter 1, that has not been my task here. The exploration of ecumenical attitudes and mutual accountability in the Faith and Order texts has been a task to fulfill, important in itself for the theological reflection of the ecumenical movement. Within the framework of this study, it has been important to elaborate the *theological* dimensions implicit in this theme in the text of Faith and Order, confirming Faith and Order as probably the most representative forum for theological ecumenical studies and discussions.

and Order texts has been deliberation toward common theological understanding. Thus, a study from theological perspectives became a first choice also for this study.

With these objections in mind, I still find that my thesis is strongly supported through my analysis. My questions to the texts on the basis of the preliminary definition and Asheim's ethical theory of attitudes have proved to be relevant to find an important feature in the Faith and Order texts dealing with premises for Church unity. It is remarkable how rather different studies and a variety of efforts in the past five decades of Faith and Order have included implicit or explicit reflections on the importance of these attitudes. Such recommendations are quite often given at crucial points in the argument or methodology of a project, discussing proper steps to proceed further.

I have also found such qualities of relations put into practice in the methodology of some projects. Particularly significant is the BEM process and text, in respect to methodology, and hermeneutics providing the convergence text, and in terms of official reception in the churches and later influence in bilateral dialogues ("*Wirkungsgeschichte*").[2] Studies on the Christian Tradition, studies aimed at a common exploration and recognition of the Christian faith, or studies of ecumenical hermeneutics have been carried out in awareness of the need for mutually accountable relations.[3] In studies and statements of the nature of unity, texts dealing with ecumenical ecclesiology, particularly the link between ethics and ecclesiology, we find some more explicit reflections on mutual accountability.[4]

Thus, the perspectives of ecumenical attitudes or quality of relations become a link between rather different projects on unity. The required ecumenical attitudes are not very different in these studies. Hence, there is, through the common (implicit and explicit) recommendations of mutual accountability, coherence in these texts in respect to a common criterion for ecumenical *relations*.

Something remarkably new can be found in the texts from the last part of the period analyzed. It is a noteworthy shift toward emphasis on the rather open, but theologically significant, definition of unity as *koinonia*. This means an unprecedented concentration on *relation* as a theme of Faith and Order. Mutual accountability appears as a definition of quality in *koinonia*, and thus, as a criterion for the goal of unity. This can be perceived as an attempt to find

---

2. See p. 182.

3. See particularly the "Tradition" study (pp. 49–80), the "Giving Account" study (pp. 128-56), the "Apostolic Faith" study (pp. 186–227), and the "Hermeneutics" study (pp. 298–308).

4. This is the case particularly in the analyses of the "Conciliar Fellowship" study (pp. 83–109), the "Authoritative Teaching" study (pp. 109–28), the "Unity and Renewal" study (pp. 227–39), the "Costly Unity" study (pp. 244–332), and the "Ecclesiology" study (pp. 289–98).

a quality of structures realizing *koinonia*, without being locked into former discussions on models and concepts of unity. The concern for such qualities of relations is not new; it is even found in the early days of the WCC, but it has been strengthened and deepened in recent years. Mutual accountability is explicitly recommended as quality of structures—sometimes in terms of conciliarity or a common *episkopé*.

Recent years have shown a tendency to discuss these attitudes independently from surmounting specific ecumenical obstacles. This could imply a separation between the main dimensions of the efforts toward unity. Thus, I have identified a fundamental challenge to the Faith and Order movement: to integrate the quest for unity in faith, for a mutually recognized order, and for appropriate qualities of relations.[5]

Mutual Accountability as Ecumenical Attitude

Some Elements of a Theory

My thesis is supported by the findings of reflections on attitudes like mutual accountability in the Faith and Order texts. It is also supported by my succeeding reflections on these findings in each chapter throughout the study. To make the thesis more specific, and to amplify the arguments for the affirmation of the thesis, I will try to systematize my reflections in some elements of a definition or theory of mutual accountability as ecumenical attitude.

My preliminary definition, used as an analytical tool throughout the previous chapters, has proven to be useful to get hold of important implicit features in texts from the first periods analyzed, and it corresponds to the explicit use of "mutual accountability" in the last period.[6] This definition can be extended by some supplementary reflections.

Ecumenical Attitudes Perceived in Positions, Practice, or Structure

As Asheim emphasized in his theory of attitudes, the attitudes required are intrinsic to the character of the fellowship. Attitudes have an external constitutive element, in terms of positions, actions, or institutions.[7] At the communal level these attitudes are related to structures and institutions, and how the fellowship in and between groups can be built on the basis of trust, respect, predictable actions, and the like, showing firm positions and standards of relations. At this, as well as at the individual, level, personal qualities in terms of

---

5. On the interrelation between faith, order, and relation, see pp. 352–61.
6. See pp. 22–27.
7. See pp. 10–15.

opinions and mentality are not to be regarded as attitudes in a proper sense if they do not have any correspondence to what is done or said in relations.

The attitudes I have found recommended and defined in the Faith and Order texts mostly refer to how the churches and their representatives act in a dialogue with other churches. It is asked whether they present their positions, history, tradition, and purposes; whether they recognize one another through joint statements or agreements; whether they strive to accomplish common goals; and whether they follow up ecumenical dialogues in real and reliable processes of reception.

Already in the Lund statement, the churches were supposed to act together according to their relation in all cases when there were no obstacles to doing so. In the tradition study, the churches were recommended to attain a new phase of dialogue beyond the state of comparison. In the "Giving Account" study, the aspect of practice is prominent, in the sense of giving accounts of hope that provide the attitude of being accountable to the faith with a dimension of reality and reliability.[8] It tried to go beyond the familiar forms of expressing the positions of faith and life (confessional documents and the like) to expressions of what was "really" believed, prayed, and done. When attitudes were included in the standards for conciliar fellowship, the churches were supposed to get into such fellowship by showing their commitment to be adequately represented, to share a common eucharist, and so forth.

In the BEM document I found that mutual accountability was related to the sustainable convergence in specific loci of Christian doctrine.[9] To some extent, recommendations were articulated for a critical revision or even change of practice. This was a dominant dimension in the suggestions for further solutions to ecumenical problems in the BEM text itself, for instance, in respect to a mutual recognition of baptism and eucharist. The eventual convergence in the understanding of baptism and eucharist is supposed to be seen at the level of practice, demonstrating willingness to conduct the administration of sacraments in correspondence to the BEM document, as an expression of the common Tradition. In the ministry section, the attitudes prescribed are seen as changes in mutual recognition of the ordained or consecrated.

In the study of specific ecumenical problems of *order* (such as the "Teaching Authoritatively" study[10]) and issues of *faith* (such as the "Apostolic Faith" study[11]), I found that the attitude of mutual accountability was important in developing a sufficiently clear *common* position. These positions should be

---

8. See pp. 110–32.
9. See pp. 156–85.
10. See pp. 109–28.
11. See pp. 186–227.

manifestations of unity in terms of decision making or common faith. One problem of the "Apostolic Faith" study, though, was exactly the lack of clarity as to what extent the churches are sharing the same faith—which had been so comprehensively explicated in the COF document. The churches were not offered a proper way to show in practice that they share the apostolic faith.

Hence, one important dimension of being mutually accountable is to find relevant criteria to demonstrate that the churches really are accountable to one another. These criteria can be specific positions or structures through which the attitudes can be perceived. To some extent, this is the point of writing reports from ecumenical dialogues and of recommending them for a process of reception in the churches, and the point also of establishing practices of mutual participation in ordinations, common conciliar structures, and so forth.

When the focus of Faith and Order more directly was turned to *relation*, attention to certain attitudes and the number of explicit recommendations of mutual accountability increased. Unity understood as *koinonia* implied a stronger focus on relations as such; the energy was not invested that much in dialogue on specific issues of divergence and establishing accountable reception processes. There is a tendency in the texts from the 1990s to retreat from further concrete ecumenical steps when reflecting on the unavoidable plurality and diversity in and among the churches. In some cases, the attitudes required tend to be more a general sense of mutual acceptance and tolerance than attitudes demonstrated in clear positions in terms of accepting common statements in the realm of faith, or clear actions to take going forward in respect to order.

This is a paradox for Faith and Order; it might even become a problem. In any case, it is important to be aware of. Concentrating on the relations, as such, became important as a supplement to the focus on the traditional issues of Faith and Order. This was particularly relevant to address the new types or, maybe more correctly, the new awareness of contextual diversity and tensions. This perspective of attitudes had been important before, but only more implicitly explored. When the focus shifted, there was an ebbing energy to work on concrete issues of division, to push toward convergence or consensus in positions or in respect to structures.

Consequently, ecumenical attitudes are criteria for the qualities of inter-church relations. They are exposed through results, or pursuit toward results, in terms of specific common positions, common structures, or common actions. Mutual accountability as openness and trust is not sufficiently attained when manifested only in general goodwill and tolerance. Mutual accountability as a quality of ecumenical relations must be shown in firm positions in terms of ability to self-critique, even conversion and change. To perceive this attitude there must be attitudes beyond the level of "climate" or common opinions at a more abstract level.

Mutual Accountability and Common Accountability

There seems to be a rather common understanding of the "faith through the ages" as something given as The Tradition in Scripture, and later formulated and reformulated through the ages. This corresponds to the problem defined in Montreal as the relation between "The Tradition" and "the traditions"—a theme particularly elaborated throughout the BEM process, the "Apostolic Faith" study, and the "Hermeneutics" study.[12] We found a characteristic dialectic between, on the one hand, being accountable to one another as churches with their traditions, and, on the other hand, being accountable to the common, given source in the apostolic witness of Jesus Christ and the formulation of this faith in the creeds.

Faithfulness to the apostolicity of the Church is a recommended attitude in all kinds of Faith and Order studies. The "Apostolic Faith" study intended to explicate not only the faith but also the common accountability to the origins of the apostolic tradition in Scripture—and in the creed of the ancient Church as a crystallization of that tradition.[13]

One crucial point is *how* this faithfulness to the common Tradition should be practiced. In mutual accountability to other traditions, a critical assessment can be combined with respect for the expression of The Tradition found in other traditions. This is a matter of ecumenical procedure. It is more than that, however; it is also a matter of how theological hermeneutics are interwoven in the matters of ecumenical ecclesiology. In other words, it is a question of how and how much the churches *need* to be open toward the substantial elements of other churches. It is a matter of how critical perspectives raised through continuous transparent encounters are a presupposition to carry and maintain the common Tradition properly.

The interdependence between ecumenical hermeneutics and ecumenical ecclesiology becomes evident throughout the material I have analyzed, most clearly in the studies of ecclesiology and hermeneutics in the 1990s. To become accountable to the richness of Tradition, the churches need to be open to the historical and contextual diversity of approaches to maintain the Christian tradition. Mutual accountability as ecumenical attitude is significant to establish the interchurch fellowship as a hermeneutic community in which this type of careful sharing, listening, and learning can be accomplished.[14]

---

12. See pp. 49–71 (Tradition); pp. 158–64 (BEM); pp. 206–10, pp. 215–16 (apostolic faith); and pp. 303–304 (hermeneutics).

13. See pp. 186–227, particularly pp. 186–88.

14. See pp. 298–308.

Because the accountability to the one, apostolic Tradition should be expected from any church as a sign of being a Christian church, the dimension of *mutuality* in this accountability becomes more than a matter of procedure and behavior. The mutual accountability that is required in this context is theologically qualified. It has in some parts of the material a christological direction. This is the internal relationship expressed through the image of the body of Christ. In some texts it is given a pneumatological explication.

The combination of mutual accountability as ecclesiological attitude with the theological dimension of a common accountability can be a challenge in different directions. It challenges the confessionalistic position, presupposing the possibility to relate to God or the word of God directly in isolation from other confessions and positions, without the sense of being accountable for the use and interpretation of the Tradition to those representing other traditions. Here we also find some limits for plurality in the Church: no position can be held in the Church that cannot be given account for in a hermeneutic community of churches, mutually accountable to one another as the body of Christ.

Mutual *commitment* also links *mutual* and *common* accountability. The ecumenical commitment is not only retrospective concerning the *given* Tradition, but also a commitment to the ecumenical *task* now and for the future. Already in the New Delhi statement on unity from 1961,[15] and later at several occasions, the Faith and Order texts repeated the importance of a common commitment to the already established, but not fully realized, communion or unity among the churches. The mutual commitment has to be more than a positive and friendly relation to be a substantial element in an ecumenical *attitude*. Thus, commitment and *reliability* are crucial to establish mutual accountability.

Reliability and Openness

There are, obviously, synonymous meanings or close links to some of the attitudes I have put under the rubric "mutual accountability." Mutual trust, mutual recognition, and mutual commitment belong to the same sphere, and are reciprocally causing or presupposing one another. The same could be said about reliability, firmness, credibility, authenticity, and faithfulness.[16]

The correspondence between reliability and openness is important for the profile of the attitude designated as mutual accountability. There is, however, not always a correspondence between reliability, on the one hand, and, on the other hand, openness to one another, to receive something from others, even critique. Since affinity and faithfulness to something historically given is a

---

15. See pp. 46–49.

16. Cf. the recommended attitudes to realize authentic teaching authority in the Church, pp. 111–24.

dominating premise in the Church, there can be an inclination to define reliability and faithfulness in terms of conservatism, even rigidity. Confessionalism is not a necessary ecclesiological profile of a Church accountable to The Tradition, however. The opposite could also be the case, if the historically given Tradition is respected higher than later confessional documents.[17] In the responses to the BEM document, some churches compared what BEM said with their own documents of confession and other historical pieces in a manner that could be taken as a sign of confessionalism. A different interpretation of these answers could be that bringing the result of ecumenical work in touch with the confessional tradition, the reception process grows as a quality in terms of more accountability. Therefore, confessional awareness can be combined with ecumenical openness.[18]

Reliability is required in respect to representing one's own confession, tradition, or church in a way that is accountable to this background. If participants in dialogue are not really reliable in terms of their own background, they are not really partners in the dialogue. Some of the strength of the BEM project was the multiple checking of the results in the churches, before the final version was made, combined with a genuine sensitivity for what was representative for the respective churches. In the *Costly Unity* report,[19] the problem of insufficient accountability among ecumenical delegates and officers to their respective churches is addressed as a real problem for the ecumenical movement. On the other hand, it is definitely an important ecumenical attitude to be reliable with respect to remaining observant, faithful, and committed to what has been accomplished and decided in ecumenical processes.

To build up a mutual trust of mutual reliability, however, openness is required. This means transparency to the positions (and background for the positions) of each part. This means, also, openness in terms of being able to learn, to receive, to absorb new elements, and to be self-critical. This openness is not being unanchored, floating on every trend, or even easy to put under pressure. A closed reliability easily could become a matter of self-defense. The balanced, trustful, and trustable reliability implies being able and willing to be examined. The self-confidence of openness should be combined with a decisive reliability, not least in interchurch relations. If diversity represents a multitude of "gifts," the fellowship of churches needs reliability in terms of care for these gifts, as well as openness to share the gifts and to recognize the gifts of others.

The specific character of mutual accountability as an *attitude* can be conceived as distinct from an *obligation or duty* to give account to one another.

---

17. Cf., e.g., Wolfhart Pannenberg's premises for the "Apostolic Faith" study, pp. 195–200.

18. That is a important premise for several actors in the "Apostolic Faith" study; see, e.g., pp. 188–210.

19. See pp. 251–58.

But the attitude of being (mutually) accountable in the sense of *being willing to and able to* be account-*able* cannot be isolated from the perspective of *being held* accountable by others.[20] There should be correspondence between duty and attitude. The attitude of mutual accountability is nourished through the status of being held accountable by somebody, for instance, on the basis of a mutual agreement. But in respect to being faithful to The Tradition or to the relationship to others, duties are not sufficient to conceive the dynamic of proper faithfulness.

The demand of mutual accountability as ecumenical attitude is a challenge to any inclination to understand the accountability to The Tradition primarily in terms of confessionalism or individual conscience. Reliability in faithfulness to The Tradition should be tested in mutual openness.[21] Mutual *admonition* could combine reliability and openness, as an expression of mutual accountability. The mutual trust required for the conduct of mutual admonition presupposes a confirmed willingness to participate in an ecumenical process implying changes, even conversion.

Self-criticism, Humility, and Conversion

Self-criticism is a consequence of openness, *conversion* (sometimes it is explicated by the New Testament term *metanoia*), of reliable self-criticism.[22] Recommendations of conversion can sound as pessimism born in desperation because of failing receptions of ecumenical results. Ability for self-criticism belongs to the reliability of churches as partners in dialogues. Therefore, a self-critical approach should not be a kind of destructive denial of the positions of the churches. There is a fine balance to be pursued between willingness to be challenged and not giving in to conformity, between independence

---

20. This distinction can be conceived in German and Norwegian through the pair of terms "*Verpflichtet sein/Pflicht*" and "å være forpliktet/plikt." The former could be an attitude ("*Verpflichtung/forpliktelse*"); the latter means "duty."

21. In these reflections I draw upon my analysis of the intention and problems raised particularly in the "Giving Account" study, the "Authoritative Teaching" study, and the "Apostolic Faith" study; see pp. 109–28, 128–56, and 251–58. In all of these studies the given standards making the churches accountable (the calling to promote hope and faith, the calling to find ways of common decisions, the creed) are related to the corresponding proper attitude of mutual accountability to the communion of faith.

22. Cf. the melody already given in Amsterdam in 1948 (pp. 29–35), the critical evaluation of the ecumenical movement in Lund (pp. 41–44); texts on Tradition challenging the "partisan attitude" with a call for conversation (pp. 52–57, 89–92), conciliarity (pp. 89–92), and the premises for the "Giving Account" study (pp. 135–37); several passages of the document *Church and World* (pp. 227–39); and the quest for integration of ethics and ecclesiology (pp. 210–22).

and interdependence. This balance should be maintained through the mutual giving of real accounts of the insight and position of the churches.[23] This is something different from producing a superficial kind of pleasing ecumenical jargon.

Humility is an important dimension of self-criticism that also corresponds to the standard of reliability. Proper humility can represent a firm position that combines openness and reliability. Humility is an open position. In the perspective of mutuality, humility is not legitimating submissiveness, but ability to stand firm as well as to learn from others.

"Mutual accountability," could, because of the combination of "mutual" and "accountability," convey a balanced dimension of self-criticism. "Accountability" as a principle can be a standard for control and criticism, which very easily leads to a relation of superiority and dominion. In combination with "mutuality," any relevant critique can at any time be a matter of reciprocity. In fact, the appeal to a church or some churches to change something could only be real if the critique is received in a way that it is transformed through reception into self-critique.

The fellowship of the Church needs frank, open, and direct critique. The relation between churches could, however, be hindered by defense and isolationism if the critique is not presented in a form and with an attitude of respect that leaves it to the respective church to convert critical points into a mode of self-criticism. The churches have no real mandate to change one another, but the churches can be encouraged to prepare themselves for a mutually accountable relation by qualifying the attitude of ability to real self-criticism.

Mutual accountability as ecumenical attitude corresponds to the understanding of the Church as a fellowship of *sinful* human beings. Nobody in the Church is right or infallible because of their position, ministry, or church belonging. This might seem to be a self-evident statement supported by all churches. Nevertheless, when it comes to the shape of ecclesiology, it is important to maintain that stance.

The concept of "conversion" corresponds to the understanding of the identity of the Church as a collective of Christians having an identity as forgiven sinners. As conceived, for example, in the BEM document, Christian existence as baptized is a life that should undergo a continual conversion within the relations to other baptized people.[24] "Conversion" should not be understood merely as a denial of everything venerated hitherto and jumping over to something totally new; it is a way of continuous accountable life.

---

23. See, e.g., the efforts to establish this balance in the "Giving Account" study, e.g., the Bangalore report and a text reflecting on "Discipline of Fellowship" (pp. 135–37; 137–42).

24. See pp. 170–81.

The (sometimes) unqualified talk about "sin" to define the reasons for church divisions can obscure realities, blurring the ecumenical task. It can be a superficial verdict of history or a cheap way to create distance from confessional ancestors who took steps that led to petrification of confessional splits. Thus, it might imply an ignorance of real doctrinal differences. Even worse, it might serve as an added *moral* condemnation of the other part today, most often the part that formulated the critique that led to church-dividing processes in the past. Hence, general references to "sin," as the problem that the ecumenical movement should overcome, can become an obstacle to a mutually accountable church fellowship.

Better, and more productive for the *task* of ecumenism, is the profiled and continuous call to conversion in humility, openness, and reliability. Conversion in the interrelations between churches is a fruit of an open and realistic encounter, not a fruit of accusations. Conversion as a matter of continuity and change implies commitment and accountability to the common goal integrated in the self-critical approach.

Mutual Accountability and Solidarity

To be accountable implies being able and willing to take responsibility for the *consequences* of what is said and done. Conducted in a *mutual* relationship, it becomes something other than a matter of *unilateral* control and accounting. Mutual accountability as ecumenical attitude should not be conceived in neutral or general perspectives, but according to particular problems and specific theological questions of interchurch relationship. Hence, being accountable in an ecumenical fellowship implies a continuous awareness of *to whom* the churches are accountable. In the Faith and Order studies the horizon most often is the other churches.

In a mutual fellowship, there are important choices to be made in regard to defining to *whom* one should be accountable, and, if the situation calls for it, to whom one is *primarily* accountable. Theologically speaking, it is a question of what it means to be accountable to God in the encounter with other people.

Within the ecumenical movement there are certain challenges articulated in this respect. There are several Faith and Order texts dealing with the question of how the churches are accountable to the nonprivileged in church and society.[25] When taking stock of the coherence in ecumenical theology,

---

25. Particularly the Faith and Order studies "Giving Account" (pp. 128–56) and "Unity and Renewal" (pp. 227–39) have raised the question of accountability as awareness of consequences of the practice and positions of the ecumenical community for those in more desperate need of hope and the solidarity of others. This was also an important matter in the discussion of methodology in the "Apostolic Faith" study (pp. 186–227), and plays a significant role in the elaboration of eucharist in BEM; see pp. 127–81.

particularly within the WCC, some points were designated as matters of a common "ecumenical tradition." One of them was the so-called option for the poor, to deliberately see a problem from the perspective of the underprivileged in a fellowship. This principle of "the option for the poor" will not be amplified here. This is mentioned here only to point to an important criterion for the definition of mutual accountability as an *ecclesial*, ecumenical attitude.

The question of dominating and dominated partners cannot be removed from the ecumenical fellowship through the quest for mutual accountability as ecumenical attitude. Mutual accountability should be promoted as an ecumenical attitude to take this problem into profound consideration. Mutual accountability in a church fellowship must imply solidarity with those who do not have the strongest voice, the most prominent tradition, or the most dominating position within the fellowship.

Mutual Accountability in Diversity?

In several cases we have found careful considerations on how the ecumenical fellowship should handle diversity among the churches. This theme is quite often discussed in rather general terms in the Faith and Order texts, though. The mutual "recognition" between the *different* churches is at the core of the ecumenical endeavours.[26]

Nevertheless, a more specific discussion of diversity is most often helpful to make distinctions between differences of historical, cultural, and other contextual reasons. It might be disagreements on doctrine, ethics, or ecclesiology where some positions are irreconcilable, or that at least demand serious dialogue to explore whether they are so. Without going deep into these kinds of definitions on a general level, I will explicate two features which I find particularly relevant to focus on in this quest for a theory of mutual accountability.

First, there are arguments for diversity as a gift from God. The *richness* of gifts, abilities, knowledge, experiences, traditions, human races, gender, ages, and the like definitely can be an important *quality of relation* in itself. To benefit from diversity, the partners must be open and willing to share the gifts with one another. To achieve more than a mere superficial contact, watching and enjoying the gifts and specialties of others, there must be some kind of involvement in the life and tradition of one another, which also implies critical perspectives, discussion, and dialogue. Presented gifts must somehow become common property for which the communion—not only one single church or group—is accountable. Such use of contributions from many traditions, bringing them into a common expression of The Tradition, is characteristic for the

---

26. See, e.g., the reflection on the reception processes of BEM, pp. 158–64; and the premises for the "Apostolic Faith" study, pp. 188–94.

methodology behind the valued and ecumenically consequential BEM text.[27] Thus, to benefit from diversity, as a quality of relation, there must be a correspondence between offering diversity and a mutually accountable reception of contributions from the whole communion.

Second, a profound understanding of the distinction between enriching diversity and dividing differences is required. Paradoxically, the definition of this distinction in itself could be a matter of ecumenical division. Such distinctions are not available only through definitions of doctrine or ecclesiology ("faith" or "order")—although they mostly have a lot to do with those fields. On the basis of my analysis of Faith and Order texts, I find that the distinction between what is tolerable and intolerable for the Church as *koinonia* is a complicated question where also ecumenical attitudes are involved.

One important result of the work of Faith and Order has been to raise these issues from several angles and to establish a wider common ground. In this perspective I also understand the explicit and implicit recommendations of mutual accountability. To focus on this attitude could avoid unlimited pluralism as well as rigid confessionalism. Mutual accountability is, however, more than a golden middle way. It means presuming the other as an accountable part, accepting that other churches have respectable and accountable reasons for their positions. It should also mean being accountable *to the relation* to one another, a relation given through the common share in the *koinonia* of the triune God, manifested through the common baptism and the same gospel. In other words, relations between the churches should be tested on the criteria whether there is mutual accountability between the churches to the same given Tradition. Even the good and serious intentions to be accountable to The Tradition should be recognized as far as possible. This is a criterion of testing openness but also a criterion defining reliability within certain limits.

Another dimension relevant for defining criteria for nontolerable diversity is accountability to those influenced or affected by the positions and practice of the churches. The particular accountability to the nonprivileged is emphasized in several cases in the texts analyzed.[28] To claim mutual accountability as criterion implies a focus on significant theological, ecclesiological, and ethical perspectives of a common ecumenical Tradition in the quest for distinctions between the principal "yes" and the necessary "no"—derived from the "yes."

Focus on mutual accountability contributes to the realization of two important elements from the legacy of the modern ecumenical movements. This is the legacy from the common fight against nazism and apartheid in

---

27. See pp. 158–64 and pp. 182–85.

28. E.g., the "Giving Account" study (pp. 109–29), the BEM and the COF texts (pp. 156–85; pp. 186–227), the "Unity and Renewal" study (pp. 227–39), and through the attempts to integrate the strains of the ecumenical movement; see pp. 244–332.

which the communion of churches learned the importance of a clear "yes" to one another as well as a clear "no" when the accountability to the nonprivileged is threatened.[29]

Mutual Accountability: One Attitude or Many?

In the preliminary definition, as well as in the elaboration and extension of it here, there are several elements. Each of them could be defined as an attitude. There are not sharp lines between them, however. This is not very particular in respect to this attitude. In Asheim's study of attitudes, he quite often mentions a whole range of attitudes when describing the required attitudes within different types of fellowships or relations. Attitudes such as respect, trust, and love are interrelated; they can be distinguished from one another but should also be seen together in a rich definition. To define an attitude as a combination of attitudes is, therefore, more a matter of what is appropriate and useful than a matter of exactness. To describe or define attitudes is a task of proper ethical reflection more than a procedure of making terminological distinctions. The task must be to give a relevant and profiled definition; it should be sufficiently precise for the task and, at the same time, wide enough to take into account how qualities of human interrelations must be described with different, but matching and corresponding, colours. The combinations of attitudes are just as important as the distinctions between them.

Hence, it is reasonable to establish a profile of mutual accountability as a crucial attitude to maintain and improve ecumenical relations, including several aspects. The particular combination of attitudes described above is what I found to be the most adequate way to proceed toward a theory of mutual accountability as ecumenical attitude.

Mutual Accountability and Some Theological Premises of Ecumenical Ecclesiology

In the following I will discuss how my understanding of mutual accountability presented so far could throw light on selected classical themes of ecumenical ecclesiology.

Mutual Accountability in the Body of Christ

The image of the Church as the body of Christ has been used nearly in all phases of the Faith and Order work I have analyzed. The so-called christological approach to ecumenism and ecclesiology in the first part of the period is to a large extent an application and elaboration of the image Paul uses for

---

29. See, e.g., the deliberations in the quest for a "coherent and vital theology" (pp. 244–51), the reflections on "Costly Unity" (pp. 210–22), and the study of hermeneutics (pp. 298–308).

interchurch relationship.[30] References to this image can be found in most of the texts, but there has been no comprehensive study of this theme.[31] The intensive use of this image in the first decades of the period analyzed might reflect a need to present arguments for not limiting the body of Christ to one church composed of many churches.

In the Faith and Order texts this image is mostly used to define the *relations* between parts of the Church, between churches, and between groups and individuals. Consequently, I have found reflections on attitudes corresponding to the status of being parts of the body of Christ. These attitudes are mostly described according to Paul's argument in 1 Cor. 12:12ff. regarding the *interdependence* within the one body of Christ: mutual acceptance, appreciation, recognition, solidarity, and empathy. This type of attitude explicates mutual belonging as a hallmark of Christian existence. This mutual belonging implies, naturally, a demand of being mutually accountable to one another. What belongs to one part belongs in reality to the whole body.

Therefore, I find the attitudes in the description of being the body of Christ to be very close to the prelimary definition of "mutual accountability."[32] This was what I found in the significant ecclesiological elaborations of baptism and eucharist in the BEM text as well.[33] To be baptized and to share eucharist means to belong to a body of the baptized, called to share in solidarity and responsibility with those participating in the gifts of God. To some extent the attitudes are described as the characteristics of Christ: love, humility, endurance, commitment.

An undercurrent in several studies of Faith and Order is the concern for those parts of the body that need more attention from the others, because of their vulnerability, or because they have being neglected, even oppressed. The "Giving Account" study intended to raise or amplify voices not always heard in the ecumenical conversation.[34] Some stages of the "Unity and Renewal" study focused on how the unity of the Church should imply a just and inclusive fellowship of different groups of human beings corresponding to being the body of Christ implementing the attitudes of Christ.[35] It is also important in the

---

30. See pp. 29–46. The theme of the christological debates of the ancient Church was not a focus here; the wide ecumenical reception of that tradition seems to have been taken for granted.

31. The use of this image in Roman Catholic ecclesiology, culminating in the Vatican II documents, probably has contributed to the significance of this image in Faith and Order texts as well. The ecumenical potential of this image increases when it became a premise (in the Roman Catholic Church) to recognize other churches as parts of the same body of Christ.

32. See pp. 22–27.

33. See pp. 172–81.

34. See pp. 121–42.

35. See pp. 228–33.

reflection on *koinonia* from Santiago, describing the reality and necessity of diversity.[36]

The image of being together one body could be used to force some to accept their position or status within the common body. The promotion of "mutual accountability" as a principle for ecumenical ecclesiology can serve as an excuse for playing down legitimate freedom and emancipation from dominating parts of the fellowship. Thus, in the quest for mutual accountability as ecumenical attitude, any inclination toward subtle oppression in a body of consensus should be warned against.[37]

Mutual Accountability and the Work of the Holy Spirit

The mutual respect for one another's gifts and tasks is a premise for the common life in the Church that corresponds to the reverence for the work of the Holy Spirit. In the analyzed texts we find references to the work of the Holy Spirit in connection to recommendations of mutual accountability. In some cases, there are clear indications that this is deliberately formulated as significant theological statements, and not only ecumenical jargon. This can be seen in Bonino's reflections, where he claims that through practices of mutual accountability the churches could have a wider and deeper share in how the Holy Spirit has been working in different churches under different circumstances.

References to the Holy Spirit could be used as attempts to guarantee the quality of a statement. They can be interpreted—more or less adequately—as a pretension of some divine insight. They can be expressions of gratitude or hope, but they can indeed be an obstacle to further dialogue on a specific point: Who will argue against the Holy Spirit? The question to be raised at this point is, therefore, the following: Could mutual accountability, as an ecumenical attitude, be qualified as a result of the work of the Holy Spirit or as a premise for an adequate procedure for identifying the work of the Holy Spirit in ecumenical relations?

To some extent, the references to the work of the Holy Spirit can be interpreted as a matter of genre in some confessional traditions or theological schools. For some it is natural to say that what seems to be right or an expression of truth—whether it is the insight of one church or what the ecumenical communion has been "guided" to—is a result of the work of the Holy Spirit. Churches have different theological understandings of how such guidance occurs or could be discerned (e.g., through a magisterium, councils, prophetic witness). Others are usually more skeptical about that kind of theological qualification of what church leaders or institutions claim as true and

---

36. See pp. 277–86.

37. See my reflections on the definition of mutual accountability presented by Nicholas Apostola and Mary Tanner, pp. 317–22.

right. Emphasizing mutual accountability could be a *challenge* to both tendencies—both those who tend to qualify their tradition or positions as result of the work of the Holy Spirit, and those who hesitate to verbalize that kind of qualification.

When a church understands itself as a witness for the gospel, and conveys the faith in formulated doctrines or in an oral tradition, somehow it presumes that it is serving and maintaining the truth. The basis and primary norm of any Christian proclamation of truth is the apostolic tradition of Jesus Christ as it is given in Scripture. Nevertheless, in any preaching, teaching, and decision making, even the structuring of the regular life of the churches from Sunday to Sunday, facing the changing challenges of the faithful, those serving the church through their ministries are developing and maintaining interpretations of that given basis. These interpretations are somehow directly or indirectly qualified as adequate and relevant expressions of the living word of the Lord. Therefore, even churches reluctant to talk about the work of the Holy Spirit in this regard, afraid of blurring the distinction between revelation in Scripture and interpretations, do live and work under the expectance of divine guidance. Anything done in the name of the triune God pretends to be said or done in the guidance of the Holy Spirit.

Hence, I cannot see that sharing—in mutual accountability—what the churches believe to be the guidance of the Holy Spirit in particular cases *has to* be a problem in respect to preserving the reverence for Scripture as norm. The belief in the work of the Holy Spirit cannot be limited to the revelation and inspiration of Scripture, although that revelation has a unique character due to its witness to God's self-revelation in Christ.

Rather, the mutual challenge implied in a mutually accountable relation is a constant warning against any triumphalism, taking for granted that everything that one's own church claims could be qualified as non-negotiable truth. The mutual accountability between the churches is a prerequisite to remaining in a proper humility, being affirmed or criticized, recognized or challenged by other churches that also preach, act, believe, and pray in the name of the triune God.

Thus, the churches claiming to be guided by the Holy Spirit need the mutually accountable attitude just as much as any other. It should be a legitimate claim, at least a hope, of the guidance of the Holy Spirit that there are no reasons not to want the critical discernment of others, the wider perspective conveyed through a mutual exchange. This should be done in *the combination of a hermeneutic of suspicion and a hermeneutic of trust*. There is no absolute tribunal in the Church when it comes to the interpretation of Scripture, but there are better or worse premises for a transparent and faithful definition and use of the common apostolic Tradition. The mutually accountable procedure of such a mutual admonition presupposes that all parts are willing to give account and receive accounts, to give and receive critique.

Thus, any claim of having the assistance of the Holy Spirit should be made only under the premise of established mutual accountability. And, even then, such statements are no guarantees, only expressions of hope and prayer. So, maybe such terminology should be reserved for the liturgy more than for doctrinal and ecclesiological statements.

Another way to formulate this point would be that mutual accountability corresponds to the correlation between "the catholic substance" of the Church and "the Protestant principle."[38] The churches have something to give account of, something given through the presence and work of the Holy Spirit. The churches have a continuous temptation to make absolute their own positions, practice, and doctrines. Therefore, according to the nature of the Church, there is need for legitimate criticism. No person or institution is absolutely right in any spiritual issues due to its own ministry or position. The only way to maintain the catholic substance of the Church is, on the one hand, to remain firm, faithful, and reliable, and, on the other hand, to be open and transparent, able to convert and change. Mutual accountability is required for initiating and performing the dialectic described here. This leads to a reflection on mutual accountability in respect to the definition of "catholicity" as an attribute of the one Church.

---

38. Paul Tillich defined this terminology in his application of the principle of correlation on ecclesiology, explicating the concept of "evangelical catholicity"; cf. Tillich 1963 (STh3): 122 et passim; and the analysis of Tillich's approach in Brodd 1982:266–76. Tillich defined the catholic substance as "spiritual presence," which is the sacramental basis of the Church through the work of the Holy Spirit. This dialectic is a premise for the life of the Church. Significant for my concept, Tillich found that the inclination to demonic absolutism in any claim of "catholic substance" should be met by the Protestant principle of *sola gratia*, judging all human efforts. Tillich even criticized the Lutheran tradition for being demonizing through the absolute claim on dogma. The problem of Protestantism is that its task is to protest against "every religious or cultural realization which seeks to be intrinsically valid," and at the same time "needs realizations if it is to be able to make its protest in any meaningful way" (quoted from Brodd 1982:275). The ecumenical problem is that some churches have maintained only one side of the dialectic. That problem could only be overcome through realization of "evangelical catholicity" according to this dialectic. In regard to the definiton of mutual accountability I am working on here, accountability corresponds to both "catholic substance" and "Protestant principle." Claiming "catholic substance" means having something to give account for in a wider audience; maintaining the "Protestant principle" means that everybody has to be accountable. This, done in mutuality, corresponds to "evangelical catholicity"; the gifts received (in the gospel) are those gifts that belong to the whole Church. Their substance is the gospel (*euangellion*) for the whole world.

Mutual Accountability and the Catholicity of the Church

To one definition of "catholicity" belong *four dimensions* of catholicity: the height, depth, breadth, and length.[39] Probably the two most common perspectives in definitions of "catholicity" in Faith and Order texts are the perspective of universality, being for all (breadth); and the dimension of history of dogma, to be Church according to the Tradition, preserving the classical faith and order of the old Church (depth and length).

The understanding of the catholicity of the Church has been a matter of ecumenical debate the last five decades, and we find signs of this in the Faith and Order texts. The Amsterdam assembly in 1948 used the term *catholic* to classify one type of churches. Particularly in the Uppsala assembly in 1968 and the study processes initiated after that, "catholicity" is seen as the wholeness and unity, something intrinsic with all aspects of the life of the Church. It is explicitly defined in respect to attitudes, as a christological quality of the Church.[40] The catholicity of the Church is both a gift and a calling. Thus, the catholicity of the Church is realized through certain attitudes of church relations. In the years after Uppsala, these perspectives were pursued in the Faith and Order studies under the perspective of "conciliarity."

Several Faith and Order texts promote what I have called "a sense of catholicity"; the attitude of being aware of *belonging* to a wider fellowship, to "the whole"; to live, speak, and think according to the whole Church (Greek: *kat'holon*). The theory developed in this study of mutual accountability amplifies the most common and dominating points of traditional definitions of "catholicity." To belong to the Church means belonging to a fellowship where one part belongs to all, and where Christian existence implies to share what is given as the faith through the ages. Neither an individual Christian nor a church can claim being so without the others, without the Tradition, without being mutually accountable to other parts of the Church. Thus, "mutual accountability" should be integrated in the definition of the catholicity of the Church.

Mutual Accountability and the Church as Moral Community

The catholic Church as a conciliar fellowship demands qualities in terms of attitudes.[41] Does this imply a definition of the Church as a "moral community"? The double identity of the qualities of the Church as gift *and* calling is significant for ecumenical ecclesiology. It is explicated in the Faith and Order

---

39. Cf. Dulles 1985:30ff.

40. Cf. pp. 83–109, above. "Since Christ lived, died and rose again for all mankind, catholicity is the opposite of all kinds of egoism and particularism. It is the quality by which the Church expresses the fullness, the integrity and the totality of the life in Christ" (Uppsala 1968:13).

41. See pp. 87–94.

material, particularly through the concepts of "catholicity" and *koinonia*.[42] The focus on the *costly* unity in the attempts to overcome the dichotomy between Faith and Order and ecumenical programmes based on ethical challenges (such as JPIC) leads to conclusions that the Church not only *has* a moral dimension but also *is* a moral community.[43] The effort of this study to make the aspect of attitudes a crucial dimension of ecclesiology can be understood as one contribution along the same lines. Consequently, I would try to make some distinctions to avoid a theory of mutual accountability sliding into a moralistic understanding of the Church incompatible with the gospel as the gift of grace.

The Church as *communio sanctorum* can be understood as "communion of the holy" or "communion around the holy things" (i.e., the sacraments). In any case, according to Scripture and the ecumenical Nicene Creed, it is a participation in the *forgiveness of sins*. It is nothing other than the unconditional grace of God that causes the participation in the *koinonia* of the Church. The moral qualities are not constitutive for the fellowship of the Church. Therefore, the attitude of mutual accountability cannot be defined as *necessary*—that is, a prerequisite—for the participation in the communion of the Church. However, the Church as a communion of human beings or as a communion of groups of churches cannot be a fellowship pursuing its *task* without certain attitudes qualifying the relations within this communion. To some degree, its task is even to establish certain qualities of relations between human beings.

The dialectic between gift and calling is intrinsically one of belonging to the *koinonia* of the one Church. This is the case in respect to "faith," "order," as well as "relation." The faith is a given entity (*fides quae*). It is established through the triune God's self-revelation as the God who justifies sinners in Jesus Christ. At the same time, faith is a response, a reaction to the gospel; it implies the believing subject and fellowship of believers and the act of their faith (*fides qua*). The same is the case in respect to "relation": the *koinonia* given is the relation to God and to one another. The relations are, at the same time, a constant calling in terms of maintaining qualities as certain attitudes.

Exactly the core of the gospel makes the attitude of communion, defined as mutual accountability, to be something other than a virtue of personal excellence making the member of communion justified. It is the *given* new relation to God that brings forth the fruit of new qualities of relations between human beings in the communion of participants in God's grace, the *koinonia* of the Church. This understanding of the dynamic between doctrine, ecclesiology,

---

42. See pp. 271–89.
43. See pp. 251–58.

and morality is a crucial point in the elaboration of the ecclesiology of baptism and eucharist in BEM.[44]

Because of the concern for the given gospel, the Church should be a communion making one another constantly mutually accountable for how the servants of the Church are stewards of this Tradition. This attitude is examplified in the New Testament. Paul most vividly describes this in the two first chapters of his letter to the Galatians. After the attempt to be accountable himself, letting his calling and message be examined by the leaders of the church in Jerusalem, including Peter (Gal. 1:18; 2:1f.), Paul had to make Peter accountable for his cowardice and inconsequence, face to face (Gal. 2:11-14). This struggle for *mutual* accountability—against unacceptable attitudes—was necessary to preserve the church as a communion based on justification by faith (Gal. 2:15-21), a communion that opposes the accusations of being a servant of sin (Gal. 2:17f.). This mutual accountability is described as the inner dynamic of being "in Christ," or living "in the faith in the Son of God," corresponding to the image used elsewhere in the Pauline letters of the Church as the body of Christ (Rom. 12:5ff.; 1 Cor. 12:12ff.).

To be mutually accountable in the *koinonia* of the Church implies participating in the gift of God. Receiving this gift makes the receiver accountable to God, to others who have received the same gift, and to all those with whom this gift should be shared. The faithfulness to the Tradition as well as the openness to one another are attitudes intrinsic to a community defined through what it has received.

"Relation" as Supplement to "Faith" and "Order"

The Significance of the Quality of Relations in Any Stage of the Ecumenical Process

In the following, I will extend the preceding deliberations by discussing mutual accountability as a criterion for "qualities of relation" in the quest for unity. The question is whether "relation" should be a supplement to the classical perspectives of "faith" and "order."

At several points in my analysis of the texts, I found that the desired mutual accountability was described as a requirement before and during the ecumenical dialogues and processes. It represented standards that belonged to a description of the goal of the ecumenical movement, hence it links the unity and faith and order with the processes aiming at that. Among the common

---

44. See pp. 182–85.

features of the way and the goal are the standards of what is a proper quality of interchurch relations—at any stage of the process.[45]

I found that mutual accountability was described as premises *before a dialogue*, for entering into a real ecumenical dialogue at all. This was an important perspective in the study of "tradition" before Montreal. This can be seen already in the premises laid out in Lund 1952.[46] According to the analysis of the BEM process and text, as well as in the "Apostolic Faith" study, when *participating in a continuous dialogue* in order to proceed deeper into one another's traditions to find what could be the common Tradition, the combination of reliability and openness was particularly important.[47]

Comparing the BEM *reception process* with the reception process of the "Apostolic Faith" study, it became clear how significant the accountability of the responses were for the whole endeavour. The accountability within the respective churches, as well as the accountability to the sense and goal of the process, was decisive for the entire effort.

In the efforts to establish a common understanding of the unity of the church as *conciliar fellowship,* I found reflections on the need for mutual accountability as a criterion of the inner dynamic of conciliarity—at whatever stage of that it might be. In regard to the threefold prerequisite for conciliar fellowship defined in Bangalore in 1978,[48] mutual accountability could and should be applied to all three: common basis of faith, mutual recognition of sacraments and ministry, and a structure for common decision making.

The shift from speaking of "unity" toward focusing on *koinonia* as the goal particularly represented an emphasis on "relation" that brings the descriptions of the goal and the process closer to one another. The *koinonia* of the triune God, the *koinonia* already given to the Church, the *koinonia* experienced, and the *koinonia* not yet realized or manifested are not totally different types of *koinonia*. The particular quality of relation of participation in one another's life can have several dimensions and levels, but the same basis and goal.

Thus, implicitly and explicitly, the significance of the quality of relation (according to what I have tried to subsume under the title "mutual accountability") is a stream through this material. It represents a standard for any level of church fellowship, derived from the *koinonia* of the triune God as the basis and image of the unity of the Church. This is one reason why I suggest that "relation" could be a third pillar in the quest for the manifestation of the unity of the Church, besides "faith" and "order."

---

45. See, e.g., pp. 35–40 (The Toronto statement); pp. 46–49 (New Delhi);

46. See pp. 41–44.

47. See pp. 140–72 (BEM) and the discussions on methodology in pp. 186–88 and 188–210 (apostolic faith)

48. See pp. 106–109 and 109–111.

One might ask at this point whether this focus on "relation" implies that the *process* of ecumenism somehow becomes the *purpose and goal* of ecumenism. According to the understanding of mutual accountability as ecumenical attitude established above, the answer must be both "yes" and "no."

The affirmation has at least three elements: first of all, the purpose of the ecumenical movement cannot be to achieve consensus or a unified structure for its own sake. The obstacles to unity in terms of "faith" and "order" are problems to be encountered and overcome because they hinder a realization of the fellowship already given in Christ. They also hinder the Church from being a sign, witness, and servant for the world according to the calling of the Church. Any manifestation of the given fellowship in Christ that is, according to the quality of relation for which the endeavour has been aiming, is a realization of the purpose of the ecumenical movement.

Second, in this perspective, it particularly makes sense to call these efforts "the ecumenical *movement*." Even when and if the churches can agree that they to some extent have reached the goal of consensus and mutual recognition of order, the importance of the dynamic between continuity and change should not be neglected. The world in which the Church should serve with its unity changes all the time. The more closely people, groups, and churches live together, the more they get involved in each other's life: the good as well as the difficult aspects of life, the smoothness as well as the friction of life according to the given diversity of humanity. Therefore, diversity and tensions would at no point disappear as potential challenges for the unity of the Church. The need for certain qualities of relation will not decline with achieved goals in terms of manifestations of unity. Rather, it will appear as a requirement of any type of church relation, and always belong to the purpose of ecumenical efforts.

Third, signs of the required quality of relations should be regarded as signs of the *goal* of the ecumenical movement. Manifestations of the double status "already, but not yet" will remain a hallmark of Christian existence in an eschatological perspective—until the end of time. Qualities of relation are manifestations of unity already received as well as a sign of what is coming. It is not in the hands of any church or any theologian to limit these potential signs to one particular type of ecumenical model or strategy.

On the other hand, the requested qualities of relation correspond to firm positions transformed into practice, realizing the commitment to the *koinonia* of the Church. This commitment must imply openness for change in terms of improving the relations by overcoming contradictions, whether they are reciprocal condemnations upheld by confessionalistic attitudes, or they are results of pluralistic tolerance causing indifference or even distance. In other words, the quality of relations aimed at cannot be a general acceptance of the status quo in respect to the obstacles to ecumenical fellowship. The quality of relation is not a goal of the ecumenical efforts that replaces the quest for convergence (or consensus). Ecumenical attitudes are not a substitute for the quest toward mutual recognition of what the churches are doing when they celebrate sacraments and worship, nor are they a substitute for structures that can be a platform for common decisions.

"Relation" and "Faith"

In several stages, and from somewhat different angles, Faith and Order has addressed the issue of "faith." It was not easy to define briefly and exactly what has been the goal in respect to the efforts toward "unity in faith." It can be defined as "consensus" or "agreement in faith" or "convergence"; it can be seen as "mutual recognition" of a common statement of faith, creed, or of the respective traditions.

The potential convergence or consensus in "faith" is a matter of dialogue on the content of the biblical witness and on doctrinal issues. It is, however, entirely also a matter of ecclesial *relations* in a *hermeneutic community*. It could be a matter of developing a common platform, to overcome misunderstanding, to declare doctrinal condemnations no longer applicable, to recognize a consensus statement, or to recognize the legitimacy of a certain diversity. It is more than questions of epistemology and exegesis. Attitudes toward one another cannot replace the role of substantial dialogue to develop common understanding of important issues of faith. But to accept what has been achieved through an accountable process, and to remain in a fellowship sharing the same faith, there must continuously be demonstrated an attitude of mutual accountability to the common Tradition and to the traditions of one another's churches.

This is what I can read out of the Faith and Order texts dealing with issues of "faith" through five decades. One of the important results of the study of "tradition" was the understanding of The Tradition as something given in prophetic and apostolic witness of Scripture. To get hold of this Tradition, recognition of accounts from historical traditions and contextual expressions embodying The Tradition was required.[49] In the premises for the "Giving Account" study, it was supposed that a greater consensus could be found if the ecumenical dialogue could be accountable for more than formal positions of faith.[50]

The BEM process and text made it clear that the issues of faith are exposed and, to some extent, explicated through the significant elements of ecclesiology implied in the sacraments and in the ordained ministry. The convergence in understanding and practice of the sacraments was in the reception

---

49. Cf. pp. 49–80.
50. Cf. pp. 128–56.

process defined as a "convergence in faith." The required successful approach implied accountability in the exploration of the potential convergence as well as accountability to the BEM process in terms of willingness to listen and even to change the practice of the Church.[51]

The "Apostolic Faith" study was aiming for the manifestation of sharing the same faith in the triune God. The study exposed the far-reaching common understanding of the apostolic faith among theologians affiliated to the work of Faith and Order. This was shown through the explication of the Nicene Creed as an expression of the apostolic tradition found in Scripture. However, this project also exposed that achieving a manifestation of a consensus in faith should include an accountable process, implying that the churches confirm their positions and committed participation in the endeavour and the results.[52]

"Faith" is not a matter separable from ecclesiology, nor from proper relations in the Church. Hence, there are strong reasons to maintain the links between "faith," "order," and "relation." The *sharing* of one faith as a platform for unity in the Church is always a matter of the quality of relation between those churches who should share the faith. There should be coherence between "faith" as formulated common doctrine and "relation" between those who share the faith, corresponding to the distinction and inseparability between the classical *fides qua* and *fides quae*. The commonality of the faith is a matter both of substance (what is common in what is believed) and of relation (what is common between those who believe).

Attitudes are intrinsic aspects of "faith" in terms of trust, faithfulness, and openness to God. To share the faith in God is to be accountable for the faith through the ages and to be mutually accountable to the traditions carrying the faith through the ages and today. *How* the believers *share* the faith is a matter of how much it is a *common* faith. As faith in the triune God is not a matter finished once and for all in the life of a believer, the common faith of the churches is not a matter settled and finished once and for all. The content of the faith is given historically through the apostolic witness of Scripture. The faith in God is the faith of those who believe.

To establish and to preserve that kind of fellowship requires profound theological elaborations of the important and the controversial substantial issues of faith.[53] At the same time, careful attention must be paid to how this faith is materialized in different situations of life.[54] The hermeneutical approaches must

---

51. Cf. pp. 156–85.
52. Cf. pp. 186–227.
53. Cf. the goal of the "Apostolic Faith" study, pp. 186–227.
54. Cf. the goal of the "Giving Account" study, pp. 128–56.

be cleared in openness and transparency, and the procedures should be pursued in attitudes corresponding to the task.[55] These latter concerns are important supplements but not replacements of the former, more classical ecumenical approach in dialogues dealing with issues of doctrine.

Therefore, in the perspective of mutual accountability, there must be a correspondence between the quest for a common apostolic Tradition and a continuously mutual giving and sharing, receiving, criticizing, and recognizing of accounts of faith. In other words, there is a deep and wide connection between "faith" and "relation." This connection should be materialized in some kind of "order" of the Church as hermeneutic community.

"Relation" and "Order"

If there is interdependence between "relation" and "faith," there is no less correspondence between "relation" and "order." In the examined texts from Faith and Order, we find a continuous awareness of the qualities of relations to manifest unity as "order." These qualities are in many cases described in terms of attitudes that can be subsumed under the concept of "mutual accountability."

When the image of the Church as the body of Christ is used to explicate how the Church is one structure or organism, the point of comparison to a large extent is the *qualities of relation* between the parts of the body. Another typical element in Faith and Order discussions of proper elements of "order," particularly when there is no consensus attainable, some reflections are added, describing attitudes required for the effort toward unity—any way. These combinations of a theological qualification of the Church (e.g., as the body of Christ) and the focus on relations in terms of attitudes support my thesis that there should be a dialectic between the quest for common "order" and the improvement of "relation."

Although the Toronto declaration (1950) of the ecclesiality of the new ecumenical construction was clear about what the WCC should *not* be, the *positive* affirmations of "order" have significant reflections on how to proceed—describing required qualities of relations.[56] This declaration became an important premise for the new approach to ecumenical dialogue and the growing interest in the theology of *councils* in the 1960s, and it was revitalized through the CUV process in the 1990s.[57]

Conciliar fellowship is the most dominant perspective on "order" in the material analyzed. One of the results of my analysis is the significance of attitudes in the definitions of conciliarity. The concept of "conciliarity" belongs to

---

55. Cf. the "Hermeneutics" study, pp. 298–308.

56. See pp. 35–40.

57. See pp. 83–109 (councils) and pp. 308–22 (CUV).

the common tradition of the ecumenical movement. The ecumenical movement took a step toward more accountability through the establishment of the World Council of Churches. The ecumenical council was called for in 1968, and became a background for the studies of the 1970s and 1980s. Although the interest for the exact definition of conciliar fellowship somehow ebbed at the end of the 1970s, partly due to insurmountable problems in pursuing a common definition of "council," the three main criteria for conciliar fellowship became guiding principles of lasting influence on the Faith and Order work.[58] The goal of conciliar fellowship was, therefore, the framework for the pursuit toward a common account of hope, common structures of decision making, common understanding and practice of baptism and eucharist, a mutual recognition of ministries, and a common explication of the faith.[59]

In all these projects we find many examples of the importance of qualities of relations—defined as ecumenical attitudes. These attitudes become links between the different projects and the principal goal of a visible unity in conciliarity. There was a strong interest in the 1970s and 1980s to address specific obstacles for a conciliar fellowship. In that sense, those projects were accountable to the specific problems of the ecumenical movement. A somewhat different climate can be perceived in the deliberations of the 1990s, with a not-so-ambitious reference to "being in council" on the way toward *koinonia*. The significance of ecumenical attitude is not less than before, but it is not so explicitly linked to premises of an ecumenical council as earlier.[60]

On the basis of the results of my analysis, I would argue that ecumenical attitudes are links for the different stages toward establishment of a conciliar fellowship together. These links are qualities of relations, recommended at any stage of the process toward unity in respect to conciliarity. This means that there is a *moral* aspect of conciliarity to be maintained, somewhat distinguished (but not totally separated) from the more formal criteria of a "council." The way and the goal have the same standards. In any phase toward a council, openness, ability to give and receive contributions, as well as critique, firmness, and reliability are all important aspects of the mutual accountability of conciliarity.

This proposal could be elaborated more in the description of a council. Someone that is really accountable to the constituency to be represented should represent the churches in a council. The council itself should be accountable to the wide fellowship of churches, in some cases even those not represented at the council itself, to act as a real gathering of the Church. The churches should be mutually accountable in the preparation during and, not least, in

---

58. I.e., structures of common decision making, mutual recognition of baptism, eucharist, and ministry, and a common confession of the apostolic faith. See pp. 106–109.

59. See pp. 106–109.

60. See the summaries on pp. 239–41 and pp. 322–27.

the reception of a council. The reception process is a test of the accountability of the council and a test of the mutual accountability of the churches. The studies of the councils of the ancient Church showed how the reception and re-reception of councils are integrated elements in conciliarity and, in principle, a process without a final end.

The dialectic between "relation" and "order" is perceivable in the threefold definition of the ordained ministry of oversight in BEM. It should be fulfilled in a "personal, collegial, and communal" way.[61] This is a significant example of how the definition of "order" (here in terms of *episkopé*) cannot be made without a profound element of "relation." It also a profound example of how the dimension of "relation" is qualified through attitudes. Attitudes belong to, but are going beyond, definitions of institutions; they are personal but not individual. Ordained ministry as a matter of "order" is qualified through the accountability of the persons given the ministry, which is to be manifested in relations to colleges and the communion to be served. The potential for achieving mutual recognition of "order" depends also on the attitudes of the churches. It is necessary that they all admit in humility that no one has a theology or practice of ministry without "defect."[62]

The concentration on *koinonia* as the main concept for unity and for ecumenical ecclesiology means that the dimensions of "relation" I am looking for here are ranked high among dimensions of unity in "order." The ecumenical theological reflection seems to be stimulated by this approach, taken from the common sources in the New Testament, conveying the dimensions of *participation*. Participation is a crucial aspect of the Trinity in God being used as a model for describing relations in the Church. Participation in Christ is a

---

61. See pp. 172–81.

62. G. R. Evans presents an interesting conclusion in respect to the status of the efforts toward a united "order" within the frame of her study on "ecumenical ecclesiology." She emphasizes the significance of "order" for unity and the task of aiming for a reconciled ministry. She sees these possibilities only on the basis of changed relations, certain qualities, firm positions, or attitudes, resembling what I have here defined as mutual accountability: "On a basis which seems quite new in the history of ecclesiology, it is now possible for uniting churches to think not in terms of one returning to the other's fold, but of each coming to the others as an ecclesial body in which there has been a mixture of wheat and tares at the human level and consequently perhaps defect and certainly need for repentance. The churches admit that they may not have been open to guidance of the Spirit, that we do not know what may be acceptable to God, that it cannot be certain that the ministry of either church is agreeable to him exactly as it is. Uniting communions can then agree in humility that there may have been defects on all sides in the theology and practicing of ministers" (Evans 1994a:248f.). She argues for a combination of changeability and firmness (corresponding to mutual accountability) with regard to "order" when she urges the importance of "the acceptance that some of what we have ecclesially . . . is provisional" and reminds of "historically well-founded fears of attempts by powerful ecclesial interests to get others to do all the changing" (ibid., 317f.).

fundamental image of the New Testament to describe the implication of baptism and eucharist. This participation in Christ is a mutual participation in the life of one another as Christians and Church. Participation in the one *koinonia* given by God is both a gift and a calling. The calling is very much related to the call to maintain the proper attitudes toward one another. To participate in the life of one another implies being made accountable to one another and for what we have in common. All attitudes related to the participation in the body of Christ must, as it is often said in the texts, be in correspondence to, or an expression of, the attitudes of Christ.

In the texts we find many connections between hermeneutics and ecclesiology. Maybe the most apparent need for such connections is seen in the studies of hermeneutics and ecclesiology after Santiago.[63] These studies illuminate how hermeneutics for the search of the truth of Christianity should be pursued in the Church as a hermeneutic community. The interrelation between theologians and churches are important for the maturity of the expressions of what Christian faith is. These interrelations need certain qualities realized in "order." The hermeneutics of the Church must be a combination of a mutual, critical approach ("hermeneutic of suspicion") and a mutual, open, and recognizing approach ("hermeneutic of trust").[64]

Therefore, "relation" should supplement "faith" and "order" as main themes in the quest for unity in the Church. None of the three can be missing to get a sustainable process toward unity. All three of them are important to a theological platform for unity among separated churches. If "relation" is the only pillar, unity can be reduced to open and peaceful co-existence, without a common basis in faith or a common order within which to be mutually accountable. The proper relation between churches requires the constant challenge to manifest the unity of the Church in faith, life, and witness.

Churches representing all kinds of structures should aim for the qualities of relation described as mutual accountability. The implication of the many aspects of being mutually accountable is not realized simply by having either a hierarchical, episcopal, synodical, or congregational structure—or not having one of these types of structures. The criterion of mutual accountability means several criteria of relationship that might be easier and better realized in some of these structures. The sense of belonging to the *catholic* Church contradicts any tendency to neglect the dimension of relation.

---

63. See pp. 289–98 and 298–308.
64. See pp. 298–302.

A Definition of Mutual Accountability as Ecumenical Attitude

With this background, I would conclude that mutual accountability belongs to any explication of ecumenical ecclesiology. I have concentrated on ecclesiological premises for interchurch relations. The applicability of mutual accountability as a premise of ecclesiology could be extended far beyond that, because any fellowship—in or between churches—requires qualities of relation. "Relation" supplements other aspects of "faith" or "order," but it cannot work as an ecclesiological premise in isolation from the other two. To be more specific about what mutual accountability means as quality of relation, it must be realized *in practice* and examined in reflections on practical ecumenical problems.

The preliminary definition in chapter 1 has been affirmed and amplified through this study. To sum up and conclude: mutual accountability comprehends reliability, faithfulness, trustfulness, solidarity, openness, ability to give and take constructive critique, and receptivity. These elements are interrelated and to some extent integrated. This combination of attitudes should be explicated and applied in the framework of *ecumenical ecclesiology*.

Mutual accountability to others can have different characteristics and degrees, but is always to be examined by what is said or done. Reliability in interchurch relations is only established through practice. Reliability in an interchurch relationship presupposes faithfulness to one's own church tradition but also to what the churches have in common.

Faithfulness does not exclude ability to change. Mutual accountability presupposes willingness to be transparent, to be examined, even criticized. In an interchurch relation, this implies faithfulness to the catholicity of the Church, being aware of belonging to a body in which no part can neglect the others. This sense of catholicity does not mean servility to one another or a right to dominate.

Accountability in a church fellowship implies reliability and faithfulness in the sense of preserving, using, and transmitting the common, apostolic Tradition given in Scripture, according to one's own tradition embodied in the many traditions of the Church. This theological aspect of what reliability means is crucial for any church fellowship. To develop mutual accountability presupposes, but also provides, this type of mutual recognition.

In any phase of developing mutual understanding, transparency is essential. That would be the case in a dialogue situation, which requires growing mutual trust and faithfulness. In receiving results from dialogues, churches need to be open, able to receive and give critical appraisals. Being mutually accountable according to specific agreements or joint declarations implies a higher degree of reliability and, still, openness and willingness to practice continuously mutual admonition. A crucial element of mutual accountability is the mutual openness of churches in respect to one's own history, theology, structures, priorities, decisions, and intentions.

The willingness to give account must, in a mutual relationship, be combined with the openness to receive the accounts of others. What other churches maintain should primarily be regarded as intentions to practice the common Tradition, their contributions as belonging to the whole communion. Mutual accountability within the one, catholic Church means the ability to go through changes on the basis of matured convictions adopted through real dialogue. This ability to give and receive critique corresponds to a moral dimension of interchurch relations, implied in the gift of belonging together in the body of Christ.

Mutual accountability implies mutual solidarity with other churches, sharing one's own resources as well as needs. This requires a particular sensitivity to the nonprivileged parts of the body of Christ. It might even be necessary to make priorities among the partners, according to the criteria of the gospel.

To be open to one another within the communion of churches implies being receptive to the gifts of the Holy Spirit in other churches. That might mean sensitivity to a variety of gifts, including critical and unusual perspectives based on other experiences from other contexts. In a mutually accountable relation this openness is not naïveté, accepting any claim of inspiration, but mutual recognition based on transparency and critical discernment in reverence for The Tradition.

To be mutually accountable in an ecumenical relation is to be accountable to God, sharing and exchanging *in practice* the gifts of God—to the honour of God and for the benefit of the other. Therefore, in mutual accountability the churches can go together toward *koinonia* in ortho-*doxy and* ortho-*praxis*.

BIBLIOGRAPHY

The literature used in this study is presented and referred to in the so-called author-date system of parenthetical references and reference lists found in Kate L. Turabian, *A Manual for Writers of Term Papers, Theses, and Dissertations*, 6th ed., rev. John Grossmann and Alice Bennett (Chicago: The University of Chicago Press, 1996), with the following modifications:

1. The references in the text are not given parenthetically, but in footnotes.

2. The Faith and Order publications and other publications from ecumenical organizations (in the list below) are given a short reference in parentheses before the other information, and listed in chronological order. These short references provide the site and the year of a conference/meeting; in cases of study reports, minutes, and the like, they provide a key term from the title and the year of publishing.

3. The year of publishing of an ecumenical report is presented immediately after the short reference in parentheses. In some cases the year given in the short reference differs from the year of publishing, because the year of a conference/meeting is used in the short reference (to avoid confusion in respect to the history of Faith and Order).

4. The literature is here presented in three parts. The primary sources for the analysis of this study, with a few exceptions, are presented in part 1.

Abbreviations of Periodical Titles

ER	*The Ecumenical Review*
IRM	*International Review of Mission*
JES	*Journal of Ecumenical Studies*
NTT	*Norsk Teologisk Tidsskrift*
OiC	*One in Christ*
ÖR	*Ökumenische Rundschau*
SE	*Study Encounter*

TTK   *Tidsskrift for Teologi og Kirke*
UT   *Ung Teologi*

1. Faith and Order Publications

(Edinburgh 1937) 1938. Hodgson, L., ed. *The Second World Conference on Faith and Order held at Edinburgh, August 3–18, 1937.* London: SCM Press.
(Nature of the Church 1952) 1952. Newton Flew, R., ed. *The Nature of the Church.* Papers presented to the Theological Commission appointed by the Continuation Committee of the World Council of Churches of the World Conference on Faith and Order.
(Lund 1952) 1963. "The Report of the Third World Conference at Lund, Sweden. August 15–28, 1952." In Documentary History 1963:85–130.
(Baptism 1960) 1960. *One Lord, One Baptism.* London: SCM Press.
(Old and New 1961) 1961. *The Old and the New in the Church: Report on Tradition and Traditions; Report on Institutionalism and Unity.* Faith and Order Paper no. 34. London: SCM Press.
(TCTT 1963) 1963. *The Report of the Theological Commission on Tradition and Traditions: Fourth World Conference on Faith and Order, Montreal, Canada, 12–26 July 1963.* Faith and Order Paper no. 40. Geneva: World Council of Churches.
(Christ and the Church 1963) 1963. *Report of the Theological Commission on Christ and the Church.* Faith and Order Paper no. 38. Geneva: World Council of Churches.
(Institutionalism 1963) 1963. *The Report of the Study Commission on Institutionalism.* Faith and Order Paper no. 37. Geneva: World Council of Churches.
(Documentary History 1963) 1963. Vischer, Lukas, ed. *A Documentary History of the Faith and Order Movement 1927–1963.* St. Louis: Bethany Press.
(Montreal 1963) 1964. Rodger, P. C., and Lukas Vischer, eds. *The Fourth World Conference on Faith and Order: The Report from Montreal 1963.* Faith and Order Paper no. 42. London: SCM Press.
(New Directions 1967) 1968. *New Directions in Faith and Order. Bristol 1967. Reports—Minutes Documents.* Faith and Order Paper no. 50. Geneva: World Council of Churches.
(Ancient Church 1968) 1968. "The Importance of the Conciliar Process in the Ancient Church for the Ecumenical Movement." In New Directions 1967: 49–59.
(Eucharist 1968) 1968. "The Holy Eucharist." In New Directions 1967:60–68.
(Councils 1968) 1968. *Councils and the Ecumenical Movement.* World Council Studies no. 5. Geneva: World Council of Churches.
(Louvain 1971) 1971. *Faith and Order, Louvain 1971: Study Reports and Documents.* Faith and Order Paper no. 59. Geneva: World Council of Churches.
(Chalcedon 1971) 1971. "The Council of Chalcedon and its importance for the ecumenical movement." In Louvain 1971:22–34.
(Minutes Utrecht 1972) 1972. *Minutes of the Meeting of the Working Committee 1972 Utrecht.* Faith and Order Paper no. 65. Geneva: World Council of Churches.
(Invitation 1972) 1972. "An Invitation to Study: Giving Account of the Hope That Is in Us." *SE* 8, no. 4 (1972): 4 cover pages (unpaginated).
(Giving Account 1972) 1972. "Giving Account of the Hope That Is in Us: An Invitation to Study." *SE* 8, no. 4 (1972), cover pages 2–4.

(Zagorsk 1973) 1973. *Minutes of the Meeting of the Standing Commission of Faith and Order in Zagorsk, USSR, August 1973.* Faith and Order Paper no. 66. Geneva: World Council of Churches.
(Salamanca 1973) 1973. *What Kind of Unity?* Faith and Order Paper no. 69. Geneva: World Council of Churches.
(Giving Account 1973) 1973. "Giving Account of the Hope That Is in Us: From an Exploratory Conversation." *SE* 9, no. 3 (1973): 1–16.
(Conciliarity 1974) 1974. "Councils, Conciliarity and a Genuine Universal Council." *Study Encounter* 10, no. 2 (1974): 1–24. Published as Faith and Order Paper no. 70. (A contribution from the West German Ecumenical Study Committee.)
(Minutes Accra 1974) 1974. *Minutes of the Meeting of the Standing Commission of Faith and Order Accra, Ghana, July 23—August 4, 1974.* Faith and Order Paper no. 71. Geneva: World Council of Churches.
(Method Accra 1974) 1974. "Reflections on the Methods of Faith and Order Study." In Minutes Accra 1974:66–82.
(Accra 1974) 1975. *Uniting in Hope: Reports and Documents from the Meeting of the Faith and Order Commission.* Faith and Order Paper no. 72. Geneva: World Council of Churches.
(BEM 1974) 1974. "One Baptism, One Eucharist and a Mutually Recognized Ministry: Three Agreed Statements." In Song 1978:37–80.
(Giving Account 1975) 1976. *Giving Account of Hope and Salvation. SE* 11, no. 2.
(Giving Account 1976a) 1976. *Giving Account in These Testing Times. SE* 12, nos. 1–2.
(Giving Account 1976b) 1976. *Giving Account of the Hope Today.* Faith and Order Paper no. 81. Geneva: World Council of Churches.
(Giving Account 1976c) 1976. "Giving Account of the Hope Within Us." Statement by the Faith and Order Standing Committee, April 1976. In *Giving Account of the Hope That Is in Us Newsletter* 3, Appendix II (October 1976). WCC Archives, Faith and Order Box 356. Unpaginated.
(Teach Authoritatively 1976) 1976. "How Does the Church Teach Authoritatively Today? Presentation of the Issues." *One in Christ* 12, no. 3 (1976): 216–39. (A working paper for a study process, made at a preparatory consultation in Geneva in 1976.)
(Lausanne 1977) 1977. *Lausanne 77: Fifty Years of Faith and Order.* Faith and Order Paper no. 82. Geneva: World Council of Churches.
(Presentation of BEM 1977). 1978. Vischer, Lukas: "Presentation of the Response." In Conciliar Fellowship 1978:100–110. (A presentation of the churches' response to the documents on *Baptism, Eucharist and Ministry* [BEM 1974])
(BEM Response 1977) 1978. "Towards an Ecumenical Consensus: Baptism, Eucharist, Ministry. A Response to the Churches." In Conciliar Fellowship 1978:80–100. (With a "Covering letter to the churches," 110–12).
(Odessa 1977) 1979. *How Does the Church Teach Authoritatively Today?* Faith and Order Paper no. 91. Geneva: World Council of Churches. Reprinted from *ER* 31 (January 1979). (Report from a consultation in Odessa, USSR, 11–16 October 1977.)
(Giving Account 1978) 1978. *Giving Account of the Hope Together.* Faith and Order Paper no. 86. Geneva: World Council of Churches.
(Conciliar Fellowship 1978) 1978. In Song 1978.
(Church-Mankind 1978) 1978. Müller-Fahrenholz, Geiko, ed. *Unity in Today's World: The Faith and Order Studies on "Unity of the Church—Unity of Mankind."* Faith and Order Paper no. 88. Geneva: World Council of Churches.

(Bangalore 1978) 1978. *Bangalore 1978. Sharing in One Hope: Reports and Documents from the Meeting of the Faith and Order Commission.* Faith and Order Paper no. 92. Geneva: World Council of Churches.

(Minutes Bangalore 1978) 1979. *Minutes and Supplementary Documents from the Meeting of the Commission on Faith and Order Held at the Ecumenical Christian Centre, Whitefield, Bangalore, India 16–30 August 1978.* Faith and Order Paper no. 93. Geneva: World Council of Churches.

(Towards Confession 1980) 1980. *Towards a Confession of the Common Faith.* Faith and Order Paper no. 100. Geneva: World Council of Churches.

(Confessing I 1980) 1980. *Confessing Our Faith around the World.* Foreword by Choan-Seng Song. Faith and Order Paper no. 104. Geneva: World Council of Churches.

(Klingenthal 1981) 1981. Vischer, Lukas, ed. *Spirit of God—Spirit of Christ.* Faith and Order Paper no. 103. Geneva: World Council of Churches.

(BEM 1982) 1982. *Baptism, Eucharist and Ministry.* Faith and Order Paper no. 111. Geneva: World Council of Churches.

(Lima I 1982) 1982. Kinnamon, Michael, ed. *Towards Visible Unity: Commission on Faith and Order Lima 1982. Volume I: Minutes and Addresses.* Faith and Order Paper no. 112. Geneva: World Council of Churches.

(Lima II 1982) 1982. Kinnamon, Michael, ed. *Towards Visible Unity: Commission on Faith and Order Lima 1982. Volume II: Study Papers and Reports.* Faith and Order Paper no. 113. Geneva: World Council of Churches.

(Confessing II 1983) 1983. Link, Hans-Georg, ed. *Confessing Our Faith around the World II.* With an introduction by Anton Houtepen. Faith and Order Paper, no. 120. Geneva: World Council of Churches.

(Perspectives on BEM 1983) 1983. Thurian, M., ed. *Ecumenical Perspectives on Baptism, Eucharist and Ministry.* Faith and Order Paper, no. 116. Geneva: World Council of Churches.

(Confessing III 1984) 1984. Link, Hans-Georg, ed. *Confessing the Faith around the World III: The Caribbean and Central America.* With an introduction by Elsa Tamez. Faith and Order Paper no. 123. Geneva: World Council of Churches.

(Roots 1984) 1984. Link, Hans-Georg, ed. *The Roots of Our Common Faith: Faith in the Scriptures and the Early Church.* Faith and Order Paper no. 119. Geneva: World Council of Churches.

(Apostolic Faith Today 1985) 1985. Link, Hans-Georg, ed. *Apostolic Faith Today: A Handbook for Study.* Faith and Order Paper no. 124. Geneva: World Council of Churches.

(Confessing IV 1985) 1985. Link, Hans-Georg, ed. *Confessing the Faith around the World IV: South America.* With an introduction by Emilio Castro. Faith and Order Paper no. 126. Geneva: World Council of Churches.

(Stavanger 1985) 1986. Best, T. F., ed. *Faith and Renewal: Reports and Documents of the Commission on Faith and Order Stavanger 1985, Norway.* Faith and Order Paper, no. 131. Geneva: World Council of Churches.

(BEM Response 1986–1988) 1986–1988. Thurian, M., ed. *Churches Respond to BEM: Official Responses to the "Baptism, Eucharist and Ministry" Text.* Vols. I–VI. Faith and Order Papers nos. 1 9, 132, 135, 137, 143, 144. Geneva: World Council of Churches.

(Church—Kingdom—World 1986) 1986. Limouris, G., ed. *Church—Kingdom—World: The Church as Mystery and Prophetic Sign.* Faith and Order Paper no. 130. Geneva: World Council of Churches.

(One God 1988) 1988. Link, Hans-Georg, ed. *One God—One Lord—One Spirit: On the Explication of the Apostolic Faith Today.* Faith and Order Paper no. 139. Geneva: World Council of Churches.
(COF Study 1987) 1987. *Confessing One Faith: Towards an Ecumenical Explication of the Apostolic Faith as Expressed in The Nicene-Constantinopolitan Creed (381).* A Faith and Order Study Document. Faith and Order Paper no. 140. Geneva: World Council of Churches.
(Budapest 1989) 1990. Best, T. F., ed. *Faith and Order 1985–1989: The Commission Meeting at Budapest 1989.* Faith and Order Paper, no. 148. Geneva: World Council of Churches.
(BEM Report 1990) 1990. *Baptism, Eucharist & Ministry 1982–1990: Report on the Process and the Responses.* Faith and Order Paper no. 149. Geneva: World Council of Churches.
(Church and World 1990) 1990. *Church and World: The Unity of the Church and the Renewal of Human Community.* A Faith and Order Study Document. Faith and Order Paper no. 151. Geneva: World Council of Churches.
(Minutes Dunblane 1990) 1990. *Minutes of the Meeting of the Standing Commission 1990 Dunblane, Scotland.* Faith and Order Paper no. 152. Geneva: World Council of Churches.
(COF 1991) 1991. *Confessing the One Faith: An Ecumenical Explication of the Apostolic Faith as It Is Confessed in the Nicene-Constantinopolitan Creed (381).* Faith and Order Paper no. 153. Geneva: World Council of Churches.
(Costly Unity 1993) 1993. Best, T. F., and Wesley Granberg-Michaelson, eds. *Koinonia and Justice, Peace and Creation: Costly Unity. Presentations and Reports from the World Council of Churches' Consultation in Rønde, Denmark, February 1993.* Geneva: World Council of Churches.
(Documentary History 1993) 1993. Gassmann, Günther, ed. *Documentary History of Faith and Order 1963–1993.* Faith and Order Paper no. 159. Geneva: World Council of Churches.
(Lausanne-Santiago 1993) 1993. Crow, P. A., and Günther Gassmann. *Lausanne 1927 to Santiago de Compostela 1993: The Faith and Order World Conferences, and Issues and Results of the Working Period 1963–1993.* Faith and Order Paper no. 160. Geneva: World Council of Churches.
(Discussion Paper 1993) 1993. "Towards *Koinonia* in Faith, Life and Witness: A Discussion Paper." In Santiago 1993:263–95.
(Santiago 1993) 1993. Best, T. F., and Günther Gassmann, eds. *On the Way to Fuller Koinonia: Official Report of the Fifth World Conference of Faith and Order.* Faith and Order Paper no. 166. Geneva: World Council of Churches.
(Minutes Bangkok 1996) 1996. *Minutes of the Meeting of the Faith and Order Board, 7–14 January 1996, Bangkok, Thailand.* Faith and Order Paper no. 172. Geneva: World Council of Churches.
(Towards CUV 1996) 1996. "Towards a Common Understanding and Vision of the WCC." In Minutes Bangkok 1996:62–93.
(Ecumenical Study 1996) 1996. "The Church as *Koinonia*—An Ecumenical Study." In Minutes Bangkok 1996:106–118.
(Study Guide 1996) 1996. *Towards Sharing the One Faith: A Study Guide for Discussion Groups.* Faith and Order Paper no. 173. Geneva: World Council of Churches.
(Moshi 1996) 1998. Falconer, A., ed. *Faith and Order in Moshi: The 1996 Commission Meeting.* Faith and Order Paper no. 177. Geneva: World Council of Churches.
(Lyon Paper 1996) 1997. "Towards a Hermeneutics for a Growing *Koinonia.*" In Minutes Abbaye de Fontgombault 1997:77–95.

(Minutes Abbaye de Fontgombault 1997) 1997. *Minutes of the Meeting of the Faith and Order Board, 8–15 January 1997, Abbaye de Fontgombault, France.* Faith and Order Paper no. 178. Geneva: World Council of Churches.

(Episkopé 1997). 1999. Bouteneff, P. C., and A. D. Falconer, eds. *Episkopé and Episcopacy and the Quest for Visible Unity: Two Consultations.* Faith and Order Paper no. 183. Geneva: World Council of Churches.

(Church 1998) 1998. *The Nature and Purpose of the Church: A Stage on the Way to a Common Statement.* Faith and Order Paper no. 181. Geneva: World Council of Churches.

(Hermeneutics 1998) 1998. *A Treasure in Earthen Vessels: An Instrument for an Ecumenical Reflection on Hermeneutics.* Faith and Order Paper no. 182. Geneva: World Council of Churches.

2. Other Ecumenical Texts

(Amsterdam 1948) 1948. Visser 't Hooft, W. A., ed. *The First Assembly of the World Council of Churches Held at Amsterdam August 22nd to September 4th, 1948: The Official Report.* London: SCM Press.

(Toronto 1950) 1963. "The Church, the Churches and The World Council of Churches: The Ecclesiological Significance of the World Council of Churches." In Documentary History 1963:167–76.

(New Dehli 1961) 1963. "Report of the Section on Unity." In Documentary History 1963:144–63.

(Uppsala 1968) 1968. Goodall, N., ed. "A Message from the Fourth Assembly of the World Council of Churches" and "Reports of the Sections." In *The Uppsala 68 Report: Official Report of the Fourth Assembly of the World Council of Churches, Uppsala, July 4–20, 1968*, 5–97. Geneva: World Council of Churches.

(Nairobi 1975) 1976. Paton, D. M., ed. *Breaking Barriers: Nairobi 1975: The Official Report of the Fifth Assembly of the World Council of Churches, Nairobi, 23 November—10 December 1975.* London: SPCK/Grand Rapids: Eerdmans.

(Ecumenical Methodology 1976) 1976. "The Theology Committee of the Church of Norway. "Ecumenical Methodology." *SE* 12, nos. 1–2 (1976): 26–40.

(DÖSTA 1978) 1978. "Verbindliches Zeugnis der Kirche als ökumenisches Aufgabe. Arbeidtbericht einer Studiengruppe des Deutschen Ökumenischen Studienauschusses." In Verbindliches Lehren 1978:7–29.

(Verbindliches Lehren 1978) 1978. Deutschen Ökumenischen Studienasuschuss, ed. *Verbindliches Lehren die Kirchen heute. Arbeitsbericht aus dem DeutschenÖkumenischen Studienasuschuss und Texte der Faith and Order-Konsultation Odessa 1977.* Frankfurt am Main: Verlag Otto Lembeck.

(Sheffield 1981) 1983. Parvey, Constance F., ed. *The Community of Women and Men in the Church: The Sheffield Report: A Report of the World Council of Churches' Conference, Sheffield, England, 1981.* Geneva: World Council of Churches.

(Vancouver 1983) 1983. Gill, D., ed. *Gathered for Life: Official Report VI Assembly World Council of Churches, Vancouver, Canada, 24 July—10 August 1983.* Geneva: WCC Publications/Grand Rapids: Eerdmans.

(Facing Unity 1985) 1985. Roman Catholic/Lutheran Joint Commision. *Facing Unity: Models, Forms and Phases of Catholic–Lutheran Church Fellowship.* Geneva: Lutheran World Federation.

(Sharing Life 1987) 1989. van Beck, H., ed. 1989. *Sharing Life: Official Report of the World Council of Churches World Consultation on Koinonia: Sharing Life in a World Community. El Escorial, Spain, October 1987.* Geneva: WCC Publications.

(Canberra 1991) 1991. Kinnamon, Michael, ed. *Signs of the Spirit: Official Report Seventh Assembly. Canberra, Australia, 7–20 February 1991.* Geneva: WCC Publications/Grand Rapids: Eerdmans.

(Niles 1992) 1992. Preman, N. D., ed. *Between the Flood and the Rainbow: Interpreting the Conciliar Process of Mutual Commitment (Covenant) to Justice, Peace, and the Integrity of Creation.* Geneva: WCC Publications.

(Porvoo 1993) 1993. Conversations between The British and Irish Anglican Churches and The Nordic and Baltic Lutheran Churches. *Together in Mission and Ministry. The Porvoo Common Statement with Essays on Church and Ministry in Northern Europe.* London: Church House Publishing.

(Groupe des Dombes 1993) 1993. *For the Conversion of the Churches.* Trans. James Greig. Geneva: WCC Publications. French original: *Pour la conversion des Eglises* (Paris: Editions du Centurion).

(Strasbourg 1993) 1994. Birmelé, A., F. Fleinert-Jensen, H. Meyer, E. Parmentier, M. Root, and Y. Tesfai. *Crisis and Challenge of the Ecumenical Movment: Integrity and Indivisibility.* A Statement of the Institute for Ecumenical Research Strasbourg. Geneva: WCC Publications.

(Costly Commitment 1994) 1997. "Costly Commitment. Tantur Ecumenical Institute, Israel, November 1994." In Ecclesiology and Ethics 1997:24–49.

(Jerusalem 1995) 1996. "On Intercultural Hermeneutics: Report of a World Council of Churches Consultation, Jerusalem, 5–12 December 1995." *IRM* 85, no. 337 (1996): 241–52.

(Liebfrauenberg 1995) 1996. Hüffmeier, W., and C. Podmore, eds. *Leuenberg, Meissen and Porvoo: Consultation between the Churches of the Leuenberg Church Fellowship and the Churches involved in the Meissen Agreement and the Porvoo Agreement.* Liebfrauenberg, Elsass, 6–10 September 1995. Leuenberg Texte Heft 4. Frankfurt am Main: Verlag Otto Lembeck.

(Moral Issues 1996) 1996. *The Ecumenical Dialogue on Moral Issues: Potential Sources of Common Witness or of Divisions. A Study Document of the Joint Working Group between the Roman Catholic Church and the World Council of Churches.* Geneva: WCC Publications.

(Costly Obedience 1996) 1997. "Costly Obedience: Johannesburg, South Africa, June 1996." In Ecclesiology and Ethics 1997:50–90.

(Ecclesiology and Ethics 1997) 1997. Best, T. F., and M. Robra, eds. *Ecclesiology and Ethics: Ecumenical Ethical Engagement, Moral Formation and the Nature of the Church.* Geneva: WCC Publications.

(CUV 1997) 1997. The World Council of Churches Central Committee. *Towards a Common Understanding and Vision of The World Council of Churches: A Policy Statement.* Geneva: WCC Publications.

(NTSF 2001) 2001. Norsk Teologisk Samtaleforum. *Trosbekjennelsen i vår tid. En økumenisk kommentar til den nikenske trosbekjennelse.* Oslo: Norges Kristne Råd.

WCC Constitution, 1948. World Council of Churches Constitution and Rules. www.oikoumene.org.

3. Selected Bibliography

This list includes texts consulted in the process of this study. A few of these texts are analyzed as sources besides the Faith and Order material.

Aagaard, Anna Marie. 1993a. "Churches Committed to Justice, Peace and the Intergity of Creation." In Costly Unity 1993:9–21.
———. 1993b. "Realities, Possibilities—and the Will." In Santiago 1993:130–34.
———. 1995. "Pluralism, Ambiguity and Dialogue." In Houtepen 1995a:171–88.
Amaladoss, Michael. 1995. "Gospel and Culture in Cross-Cultural Mission." In Houtepen 1995b:101–116.
Apostola, Nicholas K. 1998. "Mutual Accountability and the Quest for Unity." *ER* 50, no. 3 (July 1998): 301–306.
Asheim, Ivar. 1980. *Embetsplikt og lojalitet. Betenkning avgitt til Bispemøtet våren 1980 og Bispemøtets vedtak.* Oslo: Land og Kirke/Gyldendal Norsk Forlag.
———. 1991. *Øyet og horisonten. Grunnproblemer i aktuell etikkdebatt.* Oslo: Universitetsforlaget.
———. 1994a. "Kirke, menighet og fromhetsliv." In Svein Olaf Thorbjørnsen, ed., *Utfordring og ansvar. Områdeetikk*, 273–99. Oslo: Universitetsforlaget.
———. 1994b. *Mer enn normer. Grunnlagsetikk.* Oslo: Universitetsforlaget.
———. 1997. *Hva betyr holdninger? Studier i dydsetikk.* Oslo: Tano Aschehoug.
———. 1998. "Lutherische Tugendethik?" *Neue Zeitschrift für Systematische Theologie und Religionsphilosophie* 40, no. 3 (1998): 239–60.
Austad, Torleiv. 1974. *Kirkens Grunn. Analyse av en kirkelig bekjennelse fra okkupasjonstiden 1940–45.* Oslo: Luther Forlag.
Barth, Hans-Martin. 1990. *Einander Priester sein. Allgemeines Priestertum in ökumenischer Perspektive.* Göttingen: Vandenhoeck&Ruprecht.
Beinert, Wolfgang. 1987. "Ökumenische Leitbilder und Alternativen." In Hans Jörg Urban and Harald Wagner, eds., *Handbuch der Ökumenik*. Band III/1, 126–78. Im Auftrag des J.-A.-Möhler-Instituts. Paderborn: Verlag Bonifatius-Druckerei.
Békés, Gerard J., and Harding Meyer, eds. 1982. *Confession Fidei. International Ecumenical Colloqium Rome, 3–8 November 1980.* Sacramentum 7; Studia Anselmiana 81. Rome: 1982.
Bergmann, Sigurd. 1993. "Administration in the Communion of Saints: Can the Church as *Gemeinschaft* and as *Gesellschaft* Become One, Holy, Catholic and Apostolic?" In Brodd 1993a:193–212.
———, Per Frostin, Christopher Meakin, and Per Erik Persson, eds. 1992. *Ekumeniken och forskningen. Föreäsningar vid den nordiska forskarkursen "Teorier och metoder inom forskning om ekumenik" i Lund 1991.* Uppsala: Nordiska Ekumeniska Rådet.
Berkhof, Hendrik. 1964. *Die Katholisität der Kirche.* Trans. Marcel Pfändler. Zürich: EVZ-Verlag. (Dutch original: *De Katholociteit der Kerk*. Nijkerk: Verlag G.F. Callenbach, 1962.)
Best, Thomas F. 1991. "Councils of Churches: Local, National, Regional." In Nicholas Lossky, et al., eds., *Dictionary of the Ecumenical Movement*, 231–38. Geneva: WCC Publications/ Grand Rapids: Eerdmans.
———. 1992. "From Seoul to Santiago: The Unity of the Church and JPIC." In Niles 1992:128–51.
Birmelé, André. 1996. "Leuenberg—Meissen—Porvoo. On the Fellowship of the Anglican, Lutheran and United Churches of Europe." In Liebfrauenberg 1996:56–78.

Boeckler, R., ed. 1974. *Interkommunion—Konziliarität.* Zwei Studien im Auftrag des Deutschen Ökumenischen Studienauschusses. Beiheft zur Ökumenischen Rundschau, 25. Korntal bei Stuttgart: Evang. Missionsverlag GMBH.

Bonino, José Míguez. 1976. *Christians and Marxists.* Grand Rapids, Mich.: Eerdmans.

———. 1982. "A 'Third World' Perspective on the Ecumenical Movement." In Lima I 1982:58–67.

———. 1989. "The Concern for a Vital and Coherent Theology." *ER* 41, no. 2 (1989): 160–76.

———. 1993a. "How Ecclesiological Is Our Problem?" In Costly Unity 1993:59–62.

———. 1993b. "Contextuality in Theology: Epistemological and Methodological Questions." Unpublished paper presented in Oslo, 5 March 1993, in a consultation for Norwegian theologians arranged by the Church of Norway Council on Ecumenical and International Relations.

———. 1998. "Autonomy and Connectionality: Methodist Churches in Latin America." In *The Ecumenical Implications of the Discussion of the "Global Nature of the UMC."* New York: The United Methodist Church.

Bouwen, Frans. 1991. " Ecumenical Councils." In Nicholas Lossky, et al., eds., *Dictionary of the Ecumenical Movement,* 336–39. Geneva: WCC Publications/Grand Rapids: Eerdmans.

Bovens, Mark. 1998. *The Quest for Responsibility: Accountability and Citizenship in Complex Organisations.* Cambridge: Cambridge University Press.

Brandt, Hermann, ed. 1986. *Kirchliches Lehren in ökumenischer Verpflichtung.* Stuttgart: Calwer Verlag.

Brinkman, Martien E. 1995. *Progress in Unity? Fifty Years of Theology Within the World Council of Churches: 1945–1995, A Study Guide.* Louvain Theological & Pastoral Monographs no. 18. Louvain: Peeters/Grand Rapids: Eerdmans.

Brodd, Sven-Erik. 1982. *Evangelisk Katolisitet. Ett studium av innehåll och function under 1800- och 1900-talen.* Uppsala: CWK Gleerup.

———, ed. 1993a. *Stewardship: Management, Ethics and Ecclesiology.* Uppsala: Church of Sweden Research Department.

———. 1993b. "A Practical Theology for Church Administration: Reflections and Proposals." In Brodd 1993a:175–92.

———. 1994. "Stewardship and Ecclesiology." In *Stewardship—Our Accountability to God.* LWF Documentation no. 34 (April 1994): 19–29.

Brosseder, Johannes, and Evah Ignestam, eds. 1999. *The Ambivalence of Modernity.* Uppsala: Svenska kyrkans forskningsråd.

Bulhof, Ilse. 1995. "The Postmodern Challenge of the Ecumenical Movement." In Houtepen 1995b: 31–50.

Burgess, Joseph A. 1994. "Montreal (1963): A Case Study." In Hagen 1994:270–86.

Burrows, Mark S. 1992. "Globalization, Pluralism, and Ecumenics: The Old Question of Catholicity in a New Cultural Horizon." *JES* 29 (1992): 3–4, 346–67.

Campbell, Richard. 1976. "Contextual Theology and Its Problems." *SE* 12, nos. 1–2 (1976): 11–25.

Clapsis, Emmanuel. 1995. "Tradition: An Orthodox-Ecumenical View." In Houtepen 1995b:51–84.

Congar, Yves, O.P. 1966. *Tradition and Traditions: An Historical and a Theological Essay.* Trans. M. Naseby and T. Rainborough. London: Burns & Oates. French original: *La Tradition et les Traditions* (Paris: Librairie Arthème Fayard 1960, 1963).

———. 1972. "Reception as an Ecclesiological Reality." *Consilium* 77 (1972): 43–68.

———. 1984. *Diversity and Communion.* Trans. John Bowden. London: SCM Press. French original: *Diversités et Communion. Dossier historique et conclusion théologieque* (Paris: Les Editions du Cerf, 1982).
Congregation for the Doctrine of the Faith. 1992. "The Church as Communion." *Catholic International* 3, no. 16 (1992): 761–67.
Conway, Martin. 1998. "A Common Understanding and Vision—but Precisely on What?" *ER* 50, no. 3 (1998): 367–74.
Crow, Paul A., Jr. 1993. "The Legacy of Four World Conferences on Faith and Order." In Lausanne-Santiago 1993:1–14.
Cullmann, Oscar. 1986. *Einheit durch Vielvalt. Grundlegung und Beitrag zur Diskussion über die Möglichkeiten ihrer Verwirklichung.* Tübingen: J. C. B. Mohr.
Darling-Hammond, Linda, and Jon Snyder. 1992. "Framing Accountability: Creating Learner-Centered Schools." In Ann Lieberman, ed., *The Changing Contexts of Teaching: The Ninety-first Yearbook of the National Society for the Study of Education, Part I,* 11–36. Chicago: University of Chicago Press.
Deschner, John. 1990. "The Changing Shape of the Church Unity Question." In Budapest 1989:44–54.
de Schrijver, George. 1982. "Hermeneutics and Tradition: A Critique of Authority in Contemporary Catholisiscm." *JES* 19, no. 2 (Spring 1982): 32–47.
Deutsche Ökumenische Studienausschuss (DÖSTA), ed. 1978. *Verbindliches Lehren der Kirche heute.* Arbeitsbericht der Deutschen Ökumenischen Studienausschuss und Texte der Faith and Order-Konsultation Odessa 1977. Beiheft zur Ökumenischen Rundschau, Nr. 33. Frankfurt am Main: Verlag Otto Lembeck.
Dulles, Avery, S.J. 1977. *The Resilient Church: The Necessity and Limits of Adaption.* Garden City, NY: Doubleday.
———. 1985. *The Catholicity of the Church.* Oxford: Clarendon Press.
———. 1994. "Tradition and Creativity: A Theological Approach." In Hagen 1994:312–27.
Duprey, Pierre. 1978. "The Unity We Seek." In Song 1978:127–38.
Dwane, Sigqido. 1982. "In Search for an African Contribution to a Meaningful Contemporary Confession of the Christian Faith." In Lima II 1982:62–69.
Earley, James N., II. 1996. *Using a Small Group as a Means of Revitalization in a Small Membership Church.* Unpublished Doctor of Ministry thesis. Washington, DC: Wesley Theological Seminary.
Evans, G. R. 1994a. *The Church and the Churches.* Cambridge: Cambridge University Press.
———. 1994b. "Taking in Santiago: Problems of Reception." *Mid-Stream* 33, no. 3 (July 1994): 253–63.
———. 1996. *Methods in Ecumenical Theology.* Cambridge: Cambridge University Press.
———. 1997. *The Reception of the Faith: Reinterpreting the Gospel for Today.* London: SPCK.
Falconer, Alan D. 1996. "Beyond the Limits of the Familiar Landscape." In Moshi 1996:29–39.
Fischer, Lukas. 1969. "A Genuinely Universal Council." WCC Central Committee Minutes. Geneva: World Council of Churches: 182-89.
Flesseman-van Leer, Ellen. 1982. "The Transition of the Christian Faith from the New Testament-Jewixh Context to the Nicene-Hellenistic Context." In Lima II 1982:101–112.
———, ed. 1983. *The Bible: Its Authority and Interpretation in the Ecumenical Movement.* Faith and Order Paper no. 99. Geneva: World Council of Churches.
Forrester, Duncan. 1997a. *The True Church and Morality: Reflections on Ecclesiology and Ethics.* Risk Book Series. Geneva: WCC Publications.

_____. 1997b. "Living in Truth and Unity: The Church as a Hermeneutic of Law and Gospel." In Ecclesiology and Ethics 1997:92–104.
Fransen, Piet F. 1982. "Criticism of Some Basic Theological Notions in Matters of Church Authority." *JES* 2, no. 19 (1982): 48–74.
Frieling, Reinhard. 1970. *Die Bewegung für Glauben und Kirchenverfassung 1910–1937*. Göttingen: Vandenhoeck & Ruprecht.
_____. 1992. *Der Weg des ökumenischen Gedankens. Eine Ökuemenekunde*. Göttingen: Vandenhoeck & Ruprecht.
_____. 1996. "Kritische Anfragen an Porvoo aus der Sicht der Leuenberger Konkordie." In Liebfrauenberg 1996:163–71.
Gaillardetz, Richard. D. 1997. *Teaching with Authority: A Theology of the Magisterium in the Church*. Collegeville, MN: Liturgical Press (A Michael Glazier Book).
Gassmann, Günther. 1979. *Konzeptionen der Einheit in der Bewegung für Glauben und Kirchenverfassung 1910–1937*. Göttingen: Vandenhoeck & Ruprecht.
_____. 1986. "Nature and Function of Bilateral and Multilateral Dialogues." *Mid-Stream* 25 (1986): 299–308.
_____. 1991. "Scripture, Tradition, and the Church: The Ecumenical Nexus in Faith and Order Work." *JES* 28, no. 3 (1991): 435–54.
_____. 1997. "Confession and Communion: Ecclesiological Implications of the LWF's 1977 *status confessionis* Statement." In Holze 1997, 185-205.
Gaybba, B. 1971. *The Tradition: An Ecumenical Breakthrough? (A Study of a Faith and Order Study)*. Rome: Herder.
Gill, Robert. 1997. *Moral Leadership in a Postmodern Age*. Edinburgh: T&T Clark.
Goodall, N. 1972. *Ecumenical Progress: A Decade of Change in the Ecumenical Movement 1961–1971*. London: Oxford University Press.
Greive, Wolfgang, ed. 1998. *Communion, Community, Society: The Relevance of the Church*. Geneva: The Lutheran World Federation, Department for Theology and Studies.
Grillmeier, Alois, S.J. 1970. "Konzil und Rezeption. Methodische Bemerkungen zu einem Thema der Ökumenischen Diskussion der Gegenwart." *Theologie und Philosophie* 45 (1970): 320–53.
Gross, Jeffrey. 1991. "Response to Günther Gassmann." *JES* 28, no. 3 (1991): 448–54.
Hagen, Kenneth, ed. 1994. *The Quadrilog: Tradition and the Future of Ecumenism: Essays in Honor of George H. Tavard*. Collegeville, MN: Liturgical Press (A Michael Glazier Book).
Halliburton, John. 1987. *The Authority of a Bishop*. London: SPCK.
Handspicker, Meredith H. 1970. "Faith and Order 1948-1968." In Harold E. Fey, ed., *The Ecumenical Advance: A History of the Ecumenical Movement, vol. 2, 1948–1968*, 143–70. London: SPCK.
Heim, S. Mark, ed. 1991. *Faith to Creed: Ecumenical Perspectives on the Affirmation of the Apostolic Faith in the Fourth Century: Papers of the Faith to Creed Consultation Commission on Faith and Order NCCCUSA October 25–27, 1989—Waltham, Massachusetts*. Grand Rapids: Eerdmans.
Henn, William, OFM Cap. 1995. *One Faith: Biblical and Patristical Contributions toward Understanding Unity in Faith*. New York: Paulist Press.
Henriksen, Jan-Olav. 1999. *På grensen til Den andre. Om teologi og postmodernitet*. Oslo: Ad Notam Gyldendal.
Herms, Eilert. 1984. *Einheit der Christen in der Gemeinschaft der Kirchen. Die ökumenische Bewegung der römischen Kirche im Lichte der reformatorischen Theologie. Antwort auf den Rahner-Plan*. Göttingen: Vandenhoeck & Ruprecht.

———. 1990. *Erfahrbare Kirche. Beiträge zur Ekklesiologie.* Tübingen: J. C. B. Mohr (Paul Siebeck).
Hill, Christopher. 1996. "Leuenberg: Critical Questions from an Anglican Perspective." In Liebfrauenberg 1996:108–113.
Holze, Heinrich. 1997a. "Communion, an Ethical Challenge? A Few Historical Remarks on the Discussion in the LWF since 1977." In Holze 1997:207–226.
———, ed. 1997b. *The Church as Communion: Lutheran Contributions to Ecclesiology.* LWF Documentation no. 42. Geneva: The Lutheran World Federation, Department for Theology and Studies.
Houtepen, Anton. 1973. *Onfeilbaarheid en hermeneutiek. De betekenis van het infallibilitas-concept op Vaticanum I.* Brugge: Uitgeverij Emmaüs. (With a summary in German, 367ff.).
———. 1977. *"Teaching Authority" in the Ecumenical Discussion: A Contribution to the Faith and Order Study: "How Does the Church Teach Authoritatively Today?"* FO/77:11, August 1977. (Unprinted document of Faith and Order, a survey presented to the Faith and Order consultation in Odessa, USSR, in 1977.) German text: "'Lehrautorität" in der Ökumenischen Diskussion. Ein Beitrag für die Studie con Glauben und Kirchenverfassung 'Wie lehrt die Kirche verbindlich?'" In Verbindliches Lehren 1978:120–208.
———. 1983. "Reception, Tradition, Communion." In BEM 1983:140–60.
———. 1985. "Bekenntnisse der Kirchen—Bekenntnis der Ökumene. Einheit und Vielfalt, Tradition und Erneuerung im christlichen 'Bekennen.'" *Una Sancta* 40. Jahrgang (1985): 562–81.
———. 1989. "Towards an Ecumenical Vision of the Church." *OiC* 15, no. 3 (1989): 217–37.
———. 1990. " Key Issues in Some JPIC-Texts—A Theological Evaluation." *Exchange* 19, no. 3 (1990): 236–51.
———. 1991. "Die Verbindliche Lehre und das verbindende Leben der Kirche." In Meyer 1991:168–84.
———. 1993. "Discerning the Signs of the Times: Some Reflections on Justice, Peace and Integrity of *the Church* (JPIC)." In Costly Unity 1993:22–43.
———. 1994. "Wachsende Gemeinscahft, abwartende Kirchen?" ÖR 43, no. 1 (January 1994): 2–16.
———, ed. 1995a. *The Living Tradition: Towards an Ecumenical Hermeneutics of the Christian Tradition.* IIMO Research Publication 41. Utrecht: Interuniversitair Instituut voor Missiologie en Oecumencia.
———, ed. 1995b. *Ecumenism and Hermeneutics: Findings of the VIIIth Consultation of Societas Oecumenica. Association of Ecumenical Institutes in Europe.* Driebergen 25–31. August 1995. IIMO Research Publication 43. Utrecht: Interuniversitair Instituut voor Missiologie en Oecumenica.
———. 1995c. "The Faith of the Church through the Ages: Christian Tradition and Postmodernist Challenges." In Houtepen 1995a:35–70.
———. 1995d. "Ecumenism and Hermeneutics." In Houtepen 1995b:3–20.
Huber, Wolfgang. 1979. *Kirche.* Stuttgart-Berlin: Kreuz Verlag.
Hunsberger, George R. 1997. "The Hidden Element of Kairos." *IRM* 86, nos. 340/341 (January-February 1997): 57–59.
Ignatius IV, Patriarch of Antioch and All East. 1990. "Unity as Growing Together in Love." *Mid-Stream* 29 (1990): 33–43.
Joshua, S. B. 1993. "The Future of the Ecumenical Movement: From the Perspective of a Member of a United Church." In Santiago 1993:146–52.

Karrer, Andreas. 1994. *Auf dem Weg zur Gemeinschaft in Bekenntnis. Ein Untersuchung über die Auseinanderstezungen der Ôkumenischen Bewegung mit dem Bekenntnis in ihrer Anfangsphase.* Unpublished diss., Der Evangelisch-theologischen Fakultät der Universität Bern. Tutzing.

Kässmann, Margot. 1992. *Die Eucharistische Vision: Armut und Reichtum als Anfrage an die Einheit der Kirche in der Diskussion des Ökumenischen Rates.* München: Chr. Kaiser Verlag/ Mainz: Matthias-Grünewald-Verlag.

Kelly, Gerard. 1996. *Recognition: Advancing Ecumenical Thinking.* American University Studies, series VII: Theology and Religion, vol. 186. New York: Peter Lang.

Keshishian, A. 1992. *A Conciliar Fellowship: A Common Goal.* Geneva: World Council of Churches.

Khademian, Anne M. 1996. *Checking on Banks: Autonomy and Accountability in Three Federal Agencies.* Washington, DC: Brookings Institution Press.

Kostermann, Anja. 1993. "Accountability as Criterion for Theological Constructions." *Nederlands Theologisch Tijdschrift* 47 (1993): 201–214.

Kühn, Ulrich. 1980. *Kirche.* Gütersloh: Gütersloh Verlagshaus Gerd Mohn.

⸺⸺⸺. 1982. "Towards the Common Expression of the Apostolic Faith Today." In Lima II 1982:13–23.

Küng, Hans. 1982. *The Structures of the Church. With a Preface to the New Paperback Edition "Twenty Years Later."* 2d ed. Trans. Salvator Attansio. New York: Crossroad. (1st Eng. ed.: New York: Thomas Nelson, 1964.) German original: *Strukturen der Kirche* (Freiburg: Herder, 1962).

Küppers, W., ed. 1974. "Councils, Conciliarity and a Genuinely Universal Council: Report of the West German Ecumenical Study Committee." *SE* 10, no. 2 (1974): 1–24.

Lange, Ernst. 1979. *And Yet It Moves . . . Dream and Reality of the Ecumenical Movement.* Trans. Edwin Robertson, abr. Konrad Raiser and Lukas Vischer. Belfast, Dublin, Ottawa/Geneva: Christian Journals Ltd./World Council of Churches. German original: *Die Ökumenische Utopie oder Was bewegt die ökumenische Bewegung?* Stuttgart: Kreuz Verlag, n.d.

Lanne, Emmanuel, O.S.B. 1969. "Unity and Catholicity: Uppsala 1968." *OiC* 10 (1969): 124–50.

⸺⸺⸺. 1982. "The Problem of 'Reception'." In Lima I 1982:44–52.

Lawson, Matthew P. 1994. "Accountability and Fellowship in an Assemblies of God Cell Group." In Robert Wuthnow, ed., *"I Come Away Stronger": How Small Groups Are Shaping American Religion,* 77–96. Grand Rapids: Eerdmans.

Limouris, Gennadios. 1991. "Historical Background of the Apostolic Faith Today." In COF 1991:105–111.

Lindbeck, George A. 1984. *The Nature of Doctrine: Religion and Theology in a Postliberal Age.* Philadelphia: Westminster.

Link, Hans-Georg. 1988a. "Fullness of Faith: The Process of an Ecumenical Explication of the Apostolic Faith. " In One God 1988:2–16.

⸺⸺⸺. 1988b. "The Prophetic Spirit, the Church as Communion and Living Our Hope: Ecumenical Aspects of the Third Article of the Creed." In One God 1988:115–32.

Maraschin, Jaci. 1982. "Listening to Some Contemporary Statements of Faith from Latin America." In Lima II 1982:24–27.

Marzheuser, Richard. 1995. "Globalization and Catholicity: Two Expressions of One Ecclesiology?" *JES* 32, no. 2 (1995): 179–93.

Massachusetts Council of Churches. 1991. "Ecumenical Accountability: What Are Our Responsibilities To and For Each Other?" *Mid-Stream* 30, no. 4 (October 1991): 379–90.

_____. 1996. "Constructive Conflict in Ecumenical Contexts: A Document for Dialogue; Guidelines for Good Practice." *Mid-Stream* 35, no. 2 (1996): 216–29.
May, Melanie A. 1989. "Response to Wolfhart Pannenberg's 'The Future of Faith and Order.'" In Budapest 1989:231–36.
_____. 1998. "Ecumenical Hermeneutics: Working Principles Pondered." In Moshi 1996:132–35.
Meyendorff, John. 1991. "The Nicene Creed: Uniting or Dividing Confession?" In Heim 1991:1–19.
Meyer, Harding. 1986. "Fundamental Difference—Fundamental Consensus." *Mid-Stream* 25 (1986): 247–59.
_____, ed. 1991. *Gemeinsamer Glaube und Strukturen der Gemeinschaft. Erfahrungen—Überlegungen—Perspektiven.* Festschrift: Günther Gassmann zum 60. Geburtstag. Frankfurt am Main: Verlag Otto Lembeck.
_____. 1992. "'Unity in Diversity'—A Concept in Crisis." In Bergmann, et al. 1992:43–56.
_____. 1996. Ökumenische Zielvorstellungen. Bensheimer Hefte 78/Ökumenische Studienhefte 4. Göttingen: Vandenhoeck & Ruprecht.
_____. 1999. "'Suprema auctoritas ideo ab omne errore immunis': The Lutheran Approach to Primacy." In Puglisi 1999:15–34.
Moltmann, Jürgen. 1977. "What Kind of Unity? The Dialogue between the Traditions of East and West." In Lausanne 1977:38–47.
Mondale, Walter F. 1975. *The Accountability of Power: Toward a Responsible Presidency.* New York: David McKay Co.
Mudge, Lewis S. 1992. *The Sense of a People: Toward a Church for the Human Future.* Philadelphia: Trinity Press International.
_____. 1998. *The Church as Moral Community: Ecclesiology and Ethics in Ecumenical Debate.* NewYork: Continuum/Geneva: WCC Publications.
Müller-Fahrenholz, Geiko. 1978. "True Ecumenism and False." In Church-Mankind 1978:190–205.
Nelson, Robert J. 1973. "Einheit muss Ganzheit bedeuten." In Nelson/Pannenberg 1973:249–67.
_____, and Wolfhart Pannenberg, eds. 1973. *Um Einheit und Heil der Menscheit.* Frankfurt am Main: Verlag Otto Lembeck.
Neuner, Peter. 1997. Ökumenische Theologie. Die Suche nach der Einheit der christlichen Kirche. Darmstadt: Wissenschaftliche Buchgesellschaft.
Nichols, Terence L. 1997. *That All May Be One: Hierarchy and Participation in the Church.* Collegeville, MN: Liturgical Press (A Michael Glazier Book).
Nørgaard-Højen, Peder, ed. 1978. *Oekumenische Methodologie. Dokumentation und Bericht.* Geneva: Lutheran World Federation.
_____. 1992a. "Language, Dialogue and Truth. Reflections on the Possibility of Ecumenical Effort." *Exchange* 21, no. 2 (September 1992): 160–71.
_____. 1992b. "Sannhet og metode som økumenisk problem." In Bergmann, et al. 1992:217–36.
_____. 1998. Ökumenisches Engagement und theologisches Erkennen. Beiträge zur ökumenischen Methodologie. Herausgegeben von Theodor Jørgensen, Bente Lybecker und Kirsten Busch Nielsen anlässlich des 60. Geburtstag des Vervassers. Frankfurt am Main: Peter Lang.
O'Brien, John. 1992. *Theology and the Option for the Poor.* Collegeville, MN: Liturgical Press (A Michael Glazier Book).

O'Gara, Margaret. 1995. "A Roman Catholic perspective on the Content and Authority of the Councils of the Church." *OiC* 31 (1995): 433–48.
_____. 1998. *The Ecumenical Gift Exchange*. Collegeville, MN: Liturgical Press (A Michael Glazier Book).
Pannenberg, Wolfhart. 1982. "The Confessing of the Faith in the Lutheran Tradition." In Lima II 1982:70–79.
_____. 1983. *The Church*. Trans. Keith Crim. Philadelphia: Westminster. German original: *Ethik und Ekklesiologie* (Göttingen: Vandenhoeck & Ruprecht, 1977).
_____. 1989a. "The Future Role of Faith and Order." In Budapest 1989:220–30.
_____. 1989b. Letter to H. Vorster 2.5.89. Faith and Order Box 477. World Council of Churches Archives, Geneva.
_____. 1993. "Communion in Faith." In Santiago 1993:112–16.
_____. 1998. *Systematic Theology, Vol. 3*. Trans. Geoffrey W. Bromiley. Grand Rapids: Eerdmans/Edinburgh: T&T Clark. German original: *Systematische Theologie, Band 3*. (Göttingen: Vandenhoeck und Ruprecht, 1993).
Papandreou, Damaskinos. 1982. "One Confession—Many Confessions: Reflections on the Second Ecumenical Council of Constantinople (381)." In Lima II 1982:80–92.
Parvey, Constance F. 1983. "The Community of Women and Men in the Ecumencial Movement. Held Together in Hope and Sustained by God's Promise. A Personal Reflection." In Sheffield 1981:156–83.
Paton, David M. 1964. "A Montreal Diary." In Montreal 1963:9–38.
Pelikan, Jaroslav. 1964. *Obedient Rebels: Catholic Substance and Protestant Principle in Luther's Reformation*. London: SCM Press.
Phelps, Joseph. 1998. *More Light, Less Heat: How Dialogue Can Transform Christian Conflicts Into Growth*. San Fransisco: Jossey-Bass.
Planer-Friedrich, Götz. 1987. "Fredskonsilium och konciliär process." In *En röst för fred—om kyrkorna och den konciliära fredsprocessen*, 40–66. Trans. Birgitta Brodd. KISA-Rapport no. 3. Uppsala: KISA.
Puglisi, James F., ed. 1999. *Petrine Ministry and the Unity of the Church: "Toward a Patient and Fraternal Dialogue." A Symposium Celebrating the 100th Anniversary of the Foundation of the Society of the Atonement. Rome, December 4–6, 1997*. Collegeville, MN: Liturgical Press (A Michael Glazier Book).
Raiser, Konrad. 1971. "Universal Council, Goal of the Ecumenical Movement?" Working Papers for the Lutheran/Reformed Joint Committee, Geneva, February 3–5, 1971, 202–210.
_____. 1972. "Konziliarität. Die Diziplin der Gemeinschaft." *Zeitschrift für Evangelische Ethik* 16 (1972): 371–76.
_____. 1989. "Towards a Sharing Community." In Sharing Life 1987:13–24.
_____. 1991. *Ecumenism in Transition: A Paradigm Shift in the Ecumenical Movement?* Geneva: WCC Publications. German original: Ökumene im Übergang. (München: Chr. Kaiser Verlag, 1989).
_____. 1997. "A Hermeneutics of Unity." In Moshi 1996:115–26. Also in *Mid-Stream* 36, no.1 (January 1997): 65–78.
_____. 1998. "Überholt die Globalisierung die Ökumenische Entwicklung?" *Evangelische Theologie* 58 Jahrgang (1998): 92–100.
Rasmussen, Larry. 1997. "The Right Direction, but a Longer Journey." In Ecclesiology and Ethics 1997:105–111.
Reumann, John. 1994. "*Koinonia* in Scripture: Survey of Biblical Texts." In Santiago 1993:37–69.

Rikhof, Herwi. 1982. "Of Shadows and Substance: Analysis and Evaluation of the Documents in the Schillebeeckx Case." *JES* 2, no. 19 (1982): 244–67.
Rissmann, Frank. "Stewardship and Mutual Accountability." In *Stewardship—Our Accountability to God*. Geneva. LWF Documentation, no.34 (April 1994): 74–86.
Ritschl, Dietrich. 1986. "Wege Ökumenische Entscheidungsfindung." In Wolfgang Huber, Dietrich Ritschl, and Theo Sundermeier, Ökumenische Existenz heute, Bd.1, 11–48. München: Chr. Kaiser Verlag.
_____. 1987. *The Logic of Theology: A Brief Account of the Relationship between Basic Concepts in Theology*. Trans. John Bowden. Philadelphia: Fortress Press. German original: *Zur Logik der Theologie, Kurze Darstellung der Zusammenhänge theologischer Grundgedanken* (Munchen: Chr Kaiser Verlag, 1984).
_____. 1988. "We Believe in One Lord Jesus Christ: Interpretation of the Second Article of the Creed: The Way from Kottayam to Potsdam." In One God 1988:86–98.
_____. 1999. "Ökumenische Forschung im Kontext von Moderne und Postmoderne. Plädoyer für eine Hermeneutik des Vertrauens." In Johannes Brosseder and Evah Ignestam, eds., *The Ambivalence of Modernity*, 42–59. Uppsala: Svenska kyrkans forskningsråd.
_____. 2000. "Konsens ist nicht das höchste Ziel. Gründe für eine Hermeneutik des Vertaruens in den Christus preasens." In Konrad Raiser and Dorothea Sattler, eds., Ökumene vor neuen Zeiten. Für Theodor Schneider, 531–48. Freiburg-Basel-Wien: Herder.
Robbins, Bruce W., ed. 1999. "Exploring the Connection: To God, Other United Methodists, and the World Beyond." In Bruce W. Robbins ed., *The Ecumenical Implications of the Discussion of the "Global Nature of the UMC,"* 132–47. New York: The United Methodist Church.
_____. "Exploring the Connection: To God, Other United Methodists, and the World Beyond." In Robbins 1999:132–47.
Root, Michael. 1994. "The Unity of the Church as a Moral Community. Some Commments on 'Costly Unity.'" *ER* 46, no. 2 (1994): 194–203.
Rusch, William. G. 1988. *Reception: An Ecumenical Opportunity.* Geneva: Lutheran World Federation/Philadelphia: Fortress Press.
Sauca, Ioan. 1993. "Growing Together into Full *Koinonia*—Orthodox Considerations." In Costly Unity 1993:63–69.
Scheele, Paul-Werner. 1991. "Sanctotum Communio. Impulse aus der Dissertation von Dietrich Boenhoeffer für aktuelle Faith and Order-Aufgaben." In Meyer 1991:122–33.
Schellmann, Jutta. 1986. *Das Bekenntnis von 381 (Nicaeno-Constantinoplitanum) in der ökumenischen Debatte der 1980er Jahre*. Bern: Akzessarbeit der Evangelisch-Theologischen Fakultät Bern.
Schlink, Edmund. 1983. Ökumenische Dogmatik: Grundzüge. Göttingen: Vandenhoeck und Ruprecht.
Schori, Kurt. 1992. *Das Problem der Tradition. Eine fundamentaltheologische Untersuchung*. Stuttgart-Berlin-Köln: Verlag W. Kohlhammer.
Schreiter, Robert J., C.P.P.S. 1997. *The New Catholicity: Theology Between the Global and the Local*. Maryknoll, NY: Orbis.
Schwöbel, Christoph. 1997. "The Quest for Communion: Reasons, Reflections and Recommendations." In Holze 1997:227–86.
Sheeran, Michael J., S.J. 1983. *Beyond Majority Rule: Voteless Decisions in the Religious Society of Friends*. Philadelphia: Philadelphia Yearly Meeting.
Skydsgaard, K. E. 1955. "Schrift und Tradition. Bemerkungen zum Traditionsproblem in der neueren Theologie." *Kerygma und Dogma* 1 (1955): 161–79.

Song, Choan-Seng, ed. 1978. *Growing Together into Unity: Texts of the Faith and Order Commission on Conciliar Fellowship*. Madras: The Christian Litterature Society/Geneva: WCC Publications.
Staats, Reinhart. 1996. *Das Glaubensbekenntnis von Nizäa-Konstantinopel. Historische und theologische Grundlagen*. Darmstadt: Wissenschaftliche Buchgesellschaft.
Stobbe, Heinz Günther. 1981. *Hermeneutik—ein ökumenisches Problem. Eine Kritik der katholischen Gadamer-Rezeption*. Gütersloh/Zürich-Köln: Gütersloher Verlagshaus Gerd Mohn/ Benziger Verlag.
Sullivan, Francis A., S.J. 1997. "Authority in an Ecclesiology of Communion." *New Theological Review* 10, no. 3 (1997): 18–30.
Tanner, Mary. 1982. " The Community Study and the Unity of the Church and Renewal of Human Community." In Lima II 1982:153–65.
———. 1990. "Eight Peter Ainslie Lectures on Christian Unity: Ecumenical Attitudes at the End of the Ecumenical Century." *Mid-Stream* 29, no. 2 (1990): 109–119.
———. 1993. "The Tasks of the World Conference in the Perspective of the Future." In Santiago 1993:19–28.
———. 1998. "Towards a Common Understanding and Vision: A Faith and Order Perspective." *ER* 50, no. 3 (July 1998): 357–66.
Tavard, Georg H. 1992. *The Church, Community of Salvation. An Ecumenical Ecclesiology*. New Theological Studies, vol. 1. Collegeville, MN: Liturgical Press (A Michael Glazier Book).
———. 1993. "The Ecumenical Search for Tradition: Thirty Years after the Montreal Statement." *JES* 30, nos. 3–4 (1993): 315–30.
———. 1995. "Considerations on an Ecclesiology of *Koinonia*." *OiC* 31 (1995): 42–51.
Tesfai, Yacob. 1994. "Ecumenism and 'The South': The Irruption of the 'Third World' and Its Impact on the Ecumenical Movement." *JES* 31, nos. 3–4 (1994): 332–44.
Thangaraj, M. Thomas. 1992. "Is Full Church Unity Possible or Desirable?" *ER* 44, no. 1 (1992): 91–99.
Thurian, Max. 1986. "The Lima Document on "Baptism, Eucharist and Ministry," the event and its consequences." In Max Thurian, ed., *Churches Respond to BEM*, vol. 1, 1–27. Faith and Order Paper, no. 129. Geneva: World Council of Churches.
Tillard, Jean-Marie R., O.P. 1982. "The Roman-Catholic Church's Fidelity to the "Faith of the Fathers"." In Lima II 1982:51–61.
———. 1985. "Two Programmes—a Single Task." In Stavanger 1985:107–114.
———. 1989. "Confessing the Apostolic Faith Together." In Budapest 1989:104–113.
———. 1990. "Church and Apostolic Tradition." *Mid-Stream* 29, no. 3 (1990): 247–56.
———. 1992a. *The Church and the Churches: The Ecclesiology of Communion*. Trans. R. C. De Peaux. Collegeville, MN: Liturgical Press (A Michael Glazier Book). French original: Église d'Églises (Paris: Les Editions du Cerf, 1987).
———. 1992b. "Reception—Communion." *OiC* 28, no. 4 (1992): 307–322.
———. 1994. "Tradition, Reception." In Hagen 1994:328–43.
———. 1996. "From BEM to *Koinonia*." In Moshi 1996:182–86.
———. 1998. "The World Council of Churches in Quest of Its Identity." *ER* 50 (1998): 390–98.
———. 1999. "The Ecumenical *Kairos* and Primacy." In Puglisi 1999:185–96.
Tillich, Paul. 1963. *Systematic Theology* Chicago: University of Chicago Press.
Tjørhom, Ola. 1991. "Modeller for kirkelig enhet—noen teser om deres anvendbarhet og begrensninger." *Norsk Teologisk Tidsskrift* 92 (1991): 227ff.

———. 1999. *Kirken—troens mor. Et økumenisk bidrag til en luthersk ekklesiologi.* Oslo: Verbum Forlag.
Tutu, Desmond. 1993. "Towards *Koinonia* in Faith, Life and Witness." In Santiago 1993:93–102.
Tveit, Olav Fykse. 1992. "Church and World. Ein presentasjon av eit økumenisk studieprosjekt." *UT* 3 (1992): 19–29.
———. 1994. "Mutual Accountability—eit nytt økumenisk slagord?" *NTT* 95 (1994): 173–84.
———. 1995. "Den offisielle handsaminga av Porvoo-dokumentet i den norske kyrkja. Presentasjon og kommentar." *TTK* 2 (1995): 129–46.
The United Methodist Church. 1992. *The Book of Discipline of the United Methodist Church—1992.* Nashville: United Methodist Publishing House.
Uzukwu, Elochukwu E. 1996. *A Listening Church: Autonomy and Communion in African Churches.* Maryknoll, NY: Orbis.
Vandervelde, George. 1997. "*Koinonia* Between Church and World." *Exchange* 26, no. 1 (1997): 2–39.
Van Elderen, Marlin. 1991. "Towards a Common Understanding and Vision." *ER* 43, no.1 (January 1991):138-45.
———. 1998. "Our Ecumenical Vision." *ER* 50, no. 3 (July 1998): 266f.
Van Huyssteen, J. Wentzel. 1997. *Essays in Postfoundational Theology.* Grand Rapids: Eerdmans.
Vischer, Lukas. 1970. "'A Genuinely Universal Council . . .' ." *ER* 22, no. 2 (April 1970): 97–106.
———. 1971. "Report of the Secretariat to the Commission on Faith and Order." In *Faith and Order, Louvain 1971: Study Reports and Documents,* 200–211. Faith and Order Paper, no. 59. Geneva: World Council of Churches.
———. 1972a. Ökumenische Skizzen. Beitäge und Aufsätze. Frankfurt am Main: Verlag Otto Lembeck.
———. 1972b. *Accounting for the Hope That Is in Us.* FO 72, no. 4 (June 1972). Archives of the World Council of Churches, Geneva, Faith and Order Box 357. A nearly identical version with the same title was printed in a limited quantity after his 1972 Hoover Lecture on Christian Unity (Chicago: Disciples Divinity House of The University of Chicago).
———. 1973. "Die Kirche als konziliare Bewegung." In Nelson/Pannenberg 1973:235–48.
———. 1974. "Drawn and Held Together by the Reconciling Power of Christ." In Salamanca 1973:7–31.
———. 1976. *Veränderung der Welt—Bekehrung der Kirchen. Denkanstösse der Fünften Vollversamlung des Ökumenischen Rates des Kirchen in Nairobi.* Frankfurt am Main: Verlag Otto Lembeck.
———. 1978. "The Unity We Seek: Origin and Meaning of the Concept 'Conciliar Fellowship'." In Song 1978:182–94.
———. 1992. "Is This Really 'the Unity We Seek'? Comments on the Statement "The Unity of the Church as *Koinonia*: Gift and Calling'." Adopted by the WCC Assembly in Canberra." *ER* 44 (1992): 467–78.
———. 1999. "The Ministry of Unity and the Common Witness of the Churches Today." In Puglisi 1999:137–52.
Visser 't Hooft, W. A. 1968. "The Mandate of the Ecumenical Movement." In Uppsala 1968:313–23.
———. 1970. " The General Ecumenical Development since 1948." In Harold E. Fey, ed, *The Ecumenical Advance: A History of the Ecumenical Movement, vol. 2, 1948–1968,* 1–26. London: SPCK.

Volf, Miroslav. 1998. *After Our Likeness: The Church as the Image of the Trinity.* Grand Rapids: Eerdmans.

Wagner, Harald. 1989. " Conciliarity and Continuity." *OiC* 25 (1989): 255–72.

Wainright, Geoffrey. 1983. *The Ecumenical Movement: Crisis and Opportunity for the Church.* Grand Rapids: Eerdmans.

———. 1984. "Reception of "Baptism, Eucharist, and Ministry" and the Apostolic Faith Study." *JES* 21 (1984): 71–82.

———. 1999. "'The Gift Which He on One Bestows, We All Delight to Prove': A Possible Methodist Approach to a Ministry of Primacy in the Circulation of Love and Truth." In Puglisi 1999:59–82.

Watson, David Lowes. 1985. *The Early Class Meeting: Its Origins and Significance.* Nashville: Discipleship Resources.

———. 1991. *Covenant Discipleship: Christian Formation through Mutual Accountability.* Nashville: Discipleship Resources.

Weinrich, Michael. 1995. *Ökumene am Ende? Plädoyer für einen neuen Realismus.* Neukirchen-Vluyn: Neukirchener Verlag.

———. 1998. *Kirche Glauben. Evangelische Annäherungen an einen ökumenischen Ekklesiologie.* Wuppertal: Foedus Verlag.

West, Gerald. 1995. *Biblical Hermeneutics of Liberation: Modes of Reading the Bible in the South African Context.* 2d rev. ed. Pietermaritzburg: Cluster Publications/Maryknoll, NY: Orbis.

Whitehead, Evelyn Eaton. 1992. "Accountability in Priesthood: Telling the Story of Emerging Ministry." In Donald J. Goergen, O.P., ed., *Being a Priest Today*, 33–49. Collegeville, MN: Liturgical Press (A Michael Glazier Book).

Wood, Susan, 1993. "Ecclesial *Koinonia* in Ecumenical Dialogues." *OiC* 29 (1993): 124–45.

Zizioulas, John D. 1985. "The Theological Problem of Reception." *OiC* 21 (1985): 187–93.

——— (John of Pergamon). 1989. "Suggestions for a Plan of Study of the Church." In Budapest 1989:209–215.

———. 1993. *Being as Communion: Studies in Personhood and the Church.* Crestwood, NY: St. Vladimir's Seminary Press.

——— (Metropolitan John of Pergamon). 1994. "The Church as Communion: A Presentation on the World Conference Theme." In Santiago 1993:103–111.